A SLICE OF APPLE PIE

Your One-Stop Guide to Living in America

JULIE MUSK

Roving Press

Published by Roving Press Ltd
4 Southover Cottages, Frampton, Dorset, DT2 9NQ, UK
Tel: +44 (0)1300 321531
www.rovingpress.co.uk

First Published 2008 by Roving Press Ltd

ISBN: 978-1-906651-00-8

A catalogue record for this book is available from the British Library

Cover illustrations by Merrily Harpur
Text illustrations by Christian Vázquez of Better Half Designs

Set in Minion by Julie Martin
Printed and bound in England by TJ International Ltd.

For photo snapshots of life in America, taken by the author, visit the Roving Press website (www.rovingpress.co.uk). Further *Useful Websites* are also listed there.

Contents

Preface

Why should this book float on top of a sea already awash with publications on the subject of America and Americans? There are plenty of good books out there about life in the USA, most written in a straightforward, serious kind of way. *A Slice of Apple Pie* is a personal and honest look at America by one family (mum, dad, two small children and dog) who spent almost two years living in the Midwest. In writing nearly every day, I have tried to capture the main elements of American life – the fun stuff and the not-so-fun – to provide insight (and indeed foresight) to anyone contemplating a similar move to the States. The book doesn't pretend to cover everything you'll come across, yet should provide a balanced view by drawing on other people's experiences as well as my own, by using quotes, facts and figures, and by including anecdotes from Jim Phillips, a fellow Brit living near us in Ohio.

How do you get to America and back with your sense of humour intact? Moving overseas is both exhilarating and downright nerve-racking. This invaluable book will significantly reduce the administrative burden you'll face in moving to America (and possibly back again), to help you adjust and get on with enjoying life in 'the great US of A'. It gives useful and interesting facts, as well as providing entertainment and some laughs along the way. It will also save you a great deal of trouble, time and money.

So who needs this book?

- anyone considering a move to the US or already living there (for example, military and government personnel, those on work contracts, students and teachers, business people, retirees, expatriates, temporary workers, etc.);
- businesses and organisations that work with Americans, send staff or are relocating to America;
- twinning associations or sister cities;
- travel operators and long-stay tourists;
- relocation agencies selling homes in the US and holiday homeowners;
- travellers/vacationers who want more than just a travel guide;
- anyone who is curious to know what life in America is really like.

The book takes you through preparing for the move, initial feelings on coming to America, how to integrate into your new situation and, most importantly, how to enjoy and make the most of your time there. Based largely on life in Ohio, a state known for its middle-American values and as a barometer of the nation (demographers class it as *the* most American state), the book gives an insight into how America and Americans tick, and the differences between British and American cultures. Finally, it offers some personal thoughts on adjusting back after living the life of Riley.

Acknowledgements

I wish to thank fellow writers Alison, Beth, Amy and Dave, and friend Betty for reading the many drafts of the text and for their valued comments. Also thanks to Jim Phillips for his contributions and often similarly incredulous look at life in America; his comments appear throughout the text in tinted boxes. Finally, thanks to my family for putting up with me being glued to the computer all hours of the day, busy writing, walking around with a pencil and paper or dictaphone, taking notes at inopportune moments, and dragging them to places 'just for the experience'.

Caveats

All reasonable effort has been made to ensure that the information is accurate and up to date at time of printing. This book is sold with the understanding that neither the author nor the publisher is engaged in rendering professional services. If professional advice or other expert assistance is required, the services of a competent professional should be sought. The material contained in this book is given in good faith for general guidance. No liability can be accepted for loss or expense incurred as a result of relying in particular circumstances on statements made in this publication.

Laws, regulations and websites mentioned in the text may go out of date. Readers should check the current position with the relevant authorities. If you discover any error, please kindly inform the publisher so that corrections in subsequent editions may be made.

Where the colloquial terms of *America* and *Americans* are used, the author is referring to the country of the United States of America and its inhabitants, not Canada, or South or Latin America. Where the terms *Britain* or *British* are used, this refers to the countries of England, Scotland, Wales and Northern Ireland and their inhabitants. It is not meant to delineate in any way.

Brand names mentioned in the text are the proprietary property of the applicable firm and their mention does not constitute an endorsement by the publisher.

All ranking estimates are derived from official samples (e.g. the US Census Bureau), but the reader should bear in mind that they are subject to standard error and care should be taken when making inferences. The census is conducted every 10 years, and at the time of writing, 2000 was the last year the census was conducted. Thus the figures can only provide a snapshot of that moment.

Unless otherwise stated, all recommendations and opinions are the author's own, and the contents are bound to contain generalisations and/or specifics to the area discussed. Where some readers will have similar experiences and impressions and be able to say, 'I know just what she's talking about', others may have a different experience altogether. This book is a personal observation of life in America, and as such cannot describe what will be found by all readers, in all parts of the USA.

One's destination is never a place, but a new way of seeing things.

Henry Miller
(Esteemed American writer,
author of *Tropic of Cancer*,
1891–1980)

1 · So, You're Off to America?

Are we *really* going? How do we tell the kids? What do I say to my mother? How do we even begin to get ready? Oh no, is it only *x* weeks away? Yeah hah!

My husband Tim and I had been waiting to hear about our impending move to America for some time. Now that the RAF had confirmed the date, I couldn't quite believe it. There were so many questions. Could we take our dog Jester (life wouldn't be the same without him)? Would William, our 4-year-old, be eligible for school? He'd just started at our local school and he and I were loving it. Could I keep working? Presumably my freelance editing and writing career would be able to adapt to life across the Atlantic. How easy was it going to be to get home? Could we find some trusty tenants for our home? Would Rosie, our 3-year-old, understand or even care?

We were used to moving, having done it many times before with the military, so the move itself was not expected to be too much of an ordeal. In fact, moving always felt uplifting, a chance to clear out and scale down. So we were quite looking forward to it, though this time, as we were going overseas, it would entail more tricky decisions. To take or not to take? To put in storage or leave with the family? Would the copies of *Just William* I had been saving for the children come into play while we were in America, or was it sensible to leave them behind? I began looking round the house, making mental notes of what we might be able to do without, what we should leave out for use on the odd trip back, and must-have's. It was a strange and unclear thought process. How many books did I think I would read in 2 years? How many pants and socks did my husband really need to take with him? Could we cancel our subscription to *BBC Wildlife* part way through the year and get a refund?

While we waited to receive the pack-up of information relating to our move to America, our first action was to put the family out of their misery. Most of them had known it was on the cards and had braced themselves anyway. The three closest family members whom we hadn't spilled the beans to were going to be tricky – our two children, William and Rosie, and my father, who was in the early stages of Alzheimer's. We 'gripped the table' and prepared ourselves.

First, my father. If anyone was going to be affected by our move, it was him. Because I was an only child and Dad was living alone, it was going to be hardest on him. Ascertaining the in's and out's of getting back to the UK for visits and possibly flying him out to America to see us was a priority, so that I could assure him we were not disappearing off the face of the earth. I would have to put some systems in place while I was away. We were doing our best to keep him independent for as long as possible, but there's no saying how quickly Alzheimer's can worsen. We just hoped our move would not be too much of a strain on him.

The children were a different kind of challenge. How do you explain to little people who haven't known anything different since they were born that someone else would be living in their house (could *The Three Bears* help here, I wondered); that they would not be able to go to their favourite local play park for a long time; that their friends would all grow up and be different when they came back; that the world is a huge place with other countries besides England; and, perhaps more pressing than all, that they may not be able to take all their cuddlies with them? It was going to be a tough one. At least school could help us out a little as the topic this term was geography – how perfect. We asked the teacher to stick a flag in America for us.

What Do You Want Out of the Experience?

People choose to move overseas for many reasons. It is a good idea to examine your family's thoughts and ideas, as well as your personal hopes and wishes, to be sure that everyone is a willing participant. At first you might be thinking about the reasons for not going: there may be difficulties in leaving your family (an elderly parent you feel responsible for, for instance, or grandchildren), perhaps close friends you will miss, or a home you are sorry to leave. The stress of physically uprooting yourself can overshadow the positive reasons for such a move and the new opportunities it presents.

Personally, I was hoping to get the following out of the experience:

- to better my understanding of America and Americans;
- to visit some of the major sites and see America's marvellous natural wonders;
- to have some real adventures, such as hiking and camping in the national parks, rafting on the rivers, skiing, ranching and whatever else might come our way;
- to break from the cosy, easy existence we had slipped into, happily knowing that we could come back to it;
- to give ourselves some great family memories and tales to tell.

Your initial thoughts may be a little apprehensive. If you have visited America before, you will have an inkling of what to expect. We had been to the East Coast on holidays, yet I didn't feel I really knew much about America, or even where Ohio was (our new home-to-be). I was pretty ignorant of America's geography. I had heard it was in the

Midwest, rather flat and a bit like East Anglia, which did not inspire me much (apologies to East Anglians). However, at the same time I felt positive and excited because of the opportunities presented to travel, explore and try different things. On the downside, both I and Tim had visions of returning a couple of sizes larger. We were going to the land of plenty and both loved our food and drink. Having experienced a couple of holidays State-side, where we had enjoyed as-much-as-you-can-eat buffets, steak extravaganzas and seafood blow-outs, and returned several pounds heavier, lord knew how our bodies would cope with living there.

You probably have some preconceptions of America and Americans (and may recognise some of these in Chapter 4). I am sorry to say before we left we viewed Americans somewhat disdainfully – as rather arrogant, stove-piped and insular – yet, on the plus side, easy going, enthusiastic and friendly. The image of a skinny young thing, overly conscious of her glossy image and confidently spouting words such as 'Whatever' lay alongside the rather unattractive picture of a rippling man (and I don't mean in the sense of muscles), badly dressed in long shorts and socks, ignorantly and loudly asking stupid questions. Tim was also more than a little anxious about working with American military colleagues and not upsetting them. He did not think his rather tongue-in-cheek sense of humour and honest, purposeful way of doing things would lie particularly well with their laidback and in some instances plain inefficient work ethos. (It turned out he was right, though he just about kept them onside with his British charm.)

Another concern might be where you are going to live. We were exchanging our cosy, rural existence for a modern home based in the suburbs far away. It was with sadness that we envisaged the dismantling of our old home and a complete change of lifestyle. How would we feel after living in such a different world? We were probably going to enjoy the extra space. Would we come back and find our old home too small? The American houses we were looking at on the internet all had double garages, large open-plan rooms, huge front and back yards; some even had swimming pools and basements that doubled as children's play areas, fitness rooms or dens. Would we return to our old home as content with it as we were now?

Schooling may be another issue you need to consider. In the States, children do not start school until age six, which means British children going to school in America will be at least a year ahead, and hence possibly a year behind when they return to England (see Chapter 8 on education). It may not be as big a deal for young children as it is for older kids.

However, the more you think about it, the more you should realise an overseas move is just too good to pass up. There will always be something to hold you back, no matter what time of life the opportunity for change comes along. But friends will still be there when you come home, your house and personal possessions should still be in intact, your family should be able to weather your absence (and indeed can look forward to enjoying some great American holidays with you). So my advice is to grab the bull by the horns, look him in the eye and go for the ride. You may kick yourself if you don't.

Preparing for the Move

During the run-up to the move you will probably experience a mixture of feelings. People kept saying to us, 'I bet you're excited, aren't you?', but in truth we were so involved in preparing for the move, so knee-deep in the mountain of administration, in sorting and deciding what to do with the minutiae of our possessions, that we simply felt drained. We had an administrative burden that at times threatened to engulf us and severely taxed my mental powers. If I didn't add it to my 'To do' list it was in danger of being forgotten. I was waiting for the excitement to kick in, but all I felt was tired and overwhelmed.

Moving house can be liberating, as you consider all the things you have accumulated over the years and decide whether you really need them in the next stage of your life. Moving overseas adds another dimension. Yes, I thought, things were going to be different. Doing up the house had been a tie and we needed a new focus. The simplicity of renting a home in America began to appeal, as I envisaged having more time with the children and being more outward-looking.

As forewarned is forearmed, you might like to take a look at the *Suggested Reading and Viewing* list of selected books, films and documentaries concerning life in America. If you are taking over from a work colleague, your predecessor and his or her family should be a good source of local information and help, especially if they had to go through the same rigmarole you are now experiencing.

Valuing Possessions

You will need to value all your possessions (no mean task) for insurance purposes. The removal company will probably ask you to complete a valuation form, detailing a breakdown of all your possessions, so you could use their inventory to prepare your insurance list (far easier than trying to think of everything yourself).

Moving overseas is often a great opportunity to focus on efficient living – making use of what you've got, and realising in the process how unnecessary much of it is. If you are like me, you hate throwing anything away and so are forced to think up ingenious recipes with all those bottles and jars of things you have had knocking around the kitchen for ages, or at least give generously to your neighbours and friends. Use it, sell it, give it away or chuck it – it's a satisfying mantra. No more hoarding or saving something for a rainy day; enjoy it in the present. I thought I was fairly efficient at making use of things, but was still surprised to find how many 'extras' I'd accumulated. How many different shampoos does a girl need? Just what was I thinking with all those candles and joss-sticks?

As you begin to sift through each and every item in the house, you will probably be amazed at the amount of things you have and the needlessness of many items. As George Carlin (American comedian) said, 'A house is just a pile of stuff with a cover on it'. We live in a consumer world but are not necessarily good consumers, and so much goes to waste because we simply have too much. William Morris, reputed to be the greatest English designer of the nineteenth century (among other attributes), is often quoted as saying

> 'Have nothing in your house that you do not know to be useful, or believe to be beautiful'.

I had tried to follow his doctrine and was an enthusiastic car-booter, regularly offloading things we had outgrown or outlived. When forced to move, you realise how much simpler it would be if you had alleviated yourself of all that so-called precious clutter you felt necessary to have around. The concept of minimalism was beginning to make sense. Decluttering is good for the soul; I was beginning to feel quite religious about it. I was also looking forward to living in a rented home with minimal maintenance required and just the basic household items to sustain us. Perhaps I would turn Amish (see Chapter 15 on religion)?

Can You Take It With You?

Because America uses a 110-volt electricity supply, it is probably best to leave behind small, movable appliances that require high voltage, such as toasters, food mixers, vacuum cleaners and hair driers. You can buy voltage transformers for these, but they are bulky and heavy, and the cost of the transformer is another consideration. Moreover, because American power outlets are a different physical design to British sockets, you will need adapters for any UK plugs. If you do decide to take your appliances, a good tip is to buy a couple of adapters in the UK so you can convert the plugs on your essential electrical appliances as soon as you arrive in America. It avoids some aggravation in those first days of moving in.

Analogue and possibly digital TVs and VCRs are incompatible owing to the different voltage, frequency, number of lines and the way signals are encoded. America uses the NTSC (National TV Standards Committee) system whereas Britain uses PAL (Phase, Active Line). For more about this, see Chapter 9. Steve Kropla's website *Help for World Travellers* may also have some helpful advice (www.kropla.com).

Some items you are prohibited from putting into store or transporting overseas, as follows (contact the removals company to obtain a complete list of prohibited items):

- foodstuffs, cigarettes and alcoholic drinks (so you need to drink all those bottles in the cabinet as you can't take them with you – oh dear);

- batteries – remove batteries from domestic equipment, toys, etc.;
- compressed gas and aerosol containers, e.g. hairspray, deodorant, gas bottles;
- flammable materials such as matches, paints, thinners, dyes and nail varnish remover. Many items in the garden shed and garage are prohibited;
- bleach and disinfectant;
- most other liquids;
- currency.

Storage

If you have to pay for storage of personal possessions in the UK, think carefully about the cost involved. Is the cost of storage greater than the replacement value of the items? If it is, then it may not be worth the expense, unless there is some sentimental value attached. Storage in America is possible while you look for a new home, self-storage lock-ups being easy to find.

Wet items, such as dishwashers, freezers, fridges and washing machines, must be dried out days in advance so that they are perfectly clean, dry and ready for long-term storage. Otherwise they will suffer from mould growth and deterioration. It is recommended that freezers are defrosted and left unplugged and that washing machines and dishwashers are not used 7 days prior to collection. Ideally take them outside to air.

Likewise, bedding such as mattresses, duvets and pillows should be aired and not used the night or two before so that they have a good chance of surviving the storage period unscathed. Recently washed and dry-cleaned clothes should be aired for several days before packing. In fact, it is not advisable to wash, dry clean or polish any items immediately prior to collection as the residual moisture can cause condensation and spread to other items in storage.

Removals

To find a removals company experienced in handling overseas moves, check your local *Yellow Pages* and/or go online to view the *Yellow Pages* that cover the major UK airports (Gatwick, Heathrow, Aberdeen, etc.). The London Baggage Company and Excess Baggage Company are two such operators. We used M&S Shipping.

Any items you want to take to America, for instance gardening equipment, bicycles, shoes and boots, should be thoroughly cleaned as there are strict health regulations concerning dirt. The shipper will probably require you to remove or reverse bicycle pedals and turn handlebars through 90 degrees to minimise volume and prevent damage to other items. Any item containing fuel, e.g. heaters, lamps and lawnmowers, should be drained and left uncapped in an inverted position for at least 3 days prior to removal.

If you pack anything yourself, note the contents. List all the main items you pack and give a copy to the removals company. This is to ensure that all goes smoothly at Customs. It also helps in case a box goes missing and you have to account for the contents.

Ask the airline about weight, size and number of packing cases you are allowed to personally bring with you on board the aircraft so that you aren't left with excess baggage to transport yourself.

What to Do With the House

One of the main decisions for most people on moving overseas is what to do with their house. If you are only going to America for a short or uncertain period of time, you may prefer to leave your house empty. If this is the case, it is a good idea to:

- have burglar alarms, sensor lights, bolts and heavy locks fitted;
- inform the police and any local neighbourhood watch organisation;
- ask a neighbour to check the property periodically;
- arrange for the exterior to be kept clean and tidy;
- take out adequate insurance cover, e.g. the AA provides specific cover for absentee house owners.

An alternative may be to house swap with an American, and there are commercial house-swap companies who can arrange this for you. Selling up is of course another option, or you may prefer to let.

At the time of our move, we were living in a listed cottage in rural Dorset, which we had gradually been doing up. We had extended it, updated the plumbing and electrics, redecorated and refurbished, 'done' the garden and generally devoted our lives and DIY skills to it. It was our treasure. Not able to bear the thought of selling up, we contacted some local letting agents with a view to renting. The rental market was lucrative and buoyant. A couple of agents gave us quotations, and we decided on one who was rather more attuned to us and as it happened less expensive. We felt happy to place the house, our most valuable possession, in their (hopefully) professional hands. The full management charge of 12% of the monthly rent seemed reasonable for the peace of mind and service they were offering – they would oversee all aspects of the tenancy and upkeep of the property, notify the utility companies, organise the statutory annual gas check, and so on. They also proved to be accommodating of the idiosyncrasies of our old house: such as appreciating the necessity of sweeping the chimney regularly; finding tenants who would keep the garden up; using our friendly local jack-of-all tradesman as first port of call if and when work needed doing; and generally managing our home sympathetically.

There were still some snagging jobs that needed doing around the house, things we had lived with but which needed tidying up if we were to let our home in a finished state. So we set to and marveled at how quickly you can do things if you have a deadline to meet. Also it makes sense to ensure that everything is in good working order and recently serviced, to avoid problems and disagreements once tenants take over. We worked on leaving the house clear and in the best possible state for handing over. Not only does this create a good impression initially and help you win a suitable tenant, it also acts as an assurance that your property will be similarly maintained, as specified in the wording of the lease. This is one value of employing an agent – they should monitor the place regularly and at the end of the tenancy ensure the house is handed back in the same state it was in to start with. If not, the deposit monies are used to pay for the necessary work to be done.

Thus we were ready to show our first prospective tenants around. We were fortunate in finding an ideal couple very soon – both in paid employment, with no children or pets, keen gardeners, used to country living and who appeared to appreciate the qualities of an old house. We put together a tenants' file of useful information – contact names and addresses of local suppliers of services, instructions on how things worked, peculiarities of the house and any areas that might need special care. We were leaving enough furnishings in the house to claim the statutory 10% wear and tear deduction against tax for partly furnished properties. Check with your agent, as it is surprising how little you need to leave in a house for it to be considered 'partly furnished'.

If you want to handle the letting yourself, consider using an Assured Short-hold Tenancy agreement – generally for a minimum of 6 months, renewable after that, as you wish. Legal stationers, such as Oyez, have blank forms available online (just do a search by typing in 'assured short-hold tenancy' and see what comes up).
Prior to letting, you may need to undertake the following:

- Find all the keys to the house and get the required number of spare sets cut.
- Have a gas safety check carried out and obtain a landlord's certificate.
- Fill up the oil and/or gas tanks.
- Organise final readings and bills with utility providers (gas, electricity, water, sewerage). (Your letting agent may arrange this for you.)
- Contact British Telecom about the possibility of retaining your existing telephone number on your return.
- Contact the local authority concerning payment of council tax.
- Notify your mortgage company that you will be letting – this normally results in a fee plus an increase in the interest rate. There is a special dispensation for MoD personnel who are forced to move (i.e. who are posted), whereby mortgage lenders are expected to waive any fees or changes to the interest rate, and not penalise you for the forced letting of your home.
- Notify your building insurer that the property is going to be let.

Passports, Visas and Other Matters

It is best to check with the US Embassy and UK Passport Office for the latest rulings on passports and visas, as things do change and everyone's circumstances are different.

A new requirement was introduced in 26 October 2004 specifying that travellers should have a machine-readable passport. A machine-readable passport should have two lines of text (letters, numbers and chevrons, >>>) at the bottom of the personal information page at the back of the passport. If your British passport needs renewing while you are living in America, apply to the British Embassy in Washington, DC.

To stay in the US any longer than 90 days you need to have a visa. There is a long list of different types of visa depending on your situation. Some require an interview at the US Embassy in London, some don't. If you are in a hurry, you could speed things up by using a visa handling agency, e.g. the Visa Service, Trailfinders Visa Service or Worldwide Visas. They charge a fee but offer a reliable, prompt service.

After applying for a visa, your name will be checked by the inter-agency database to ensure you are not a security concern. Non-immigrant visas are issued to people with a permanent residence outside America who are staying temporarily, e.g. students, trainees, intra-company transfers, tourists and military personnel. Immigrant visas are for those who intend to live in America permanently. You can apply for a Permanent Resident Card (or Green Card), allowing you to reside and work in the States. See Chapter 19 for more about this. For entry into America, you have to complete form I-94, which details your visa type and maximum stay allowed.

You are going to need a lot of I.D. in your first months in America. You will be asked to provide endless copies of your passport, visa and UK driving licence, as well as a plethora of passport-sized mug shots, so go prepared. You will also need a big wad of cash as, without a US credit history, you will be asked to pay large deposits before you can sign up with utility providers and such like.

Becoming a US Citizen

If you wish to apply for US citizenship, you are required to undertake a naturalisation test or citizenship exam. You must answer six out of ten questions correctly, taken from a list of 96. The questions are designed to demonstrate knowledge of US history and government. Applicants must pass a written and oral test, and also have a working knowledge of the English language. Illegal aliens who have been in the country for at least 4 years may also apply for naturalisation.

You then attend a naturalisation ceremony at which you affirm your allegiance to the USA. The oath reads as follows:

> 'I hereby declare, on oath, that I absolutely and entirely renounce and abjure all allegiance and

> fidelity to any foreign prince, potentate, state, or sovereignty of whom or which I have heretofore been a subject or citizen; that I will support and defend the Constitution and laws of the United States of America against all enemies, foreign and domestic; that I will bear true faith and allegiance to the same; that I will bear arms on behalf of the United States when required by law; that I will perform noncombatant service in the armed forces of the United States when required by the law; that I will perform work of national importance under civilian direction when required by the law; and that I take this obligation freely without any mental reservation or purpose of evasion; so help me God.'

In some cases, the oath is taken without the clause relating to bearing arms and performing non-combatant service if you can prove that this goes against your religion. It is interesting to compare this wording with the Oath of Citizenship taken by immigrants in order to become British citizens:

> 'I, (name), (swear by Almighty God) do solemnly, sincerely and truly affirm and declare that, on becoming a British citizen, I will be faithful and bear true allegiance to Her Majesty Queen Elizabeth II, her heirs, and successors, according to law.'
>
> 'I will give my loyalty to the United Kingdom and respect its rights and freedoms. I will uphold its democratic values. I will observe its laws faithfully and fulfil my duties and obligations as a British citizen.'

The American oath appears to be calling for a much more active, and indeed aggressive, stance by its new citizens.

Checklist of What's Involved in Moving Overseas

There are many different elements involved in a move overseas. Below is a brief checklist of some of them (other chapters in this book go into much more detail).

- **Health**: arrange medical and dentistry check-ups for all the family; make sure everyone in the family has the necessary immunisations, as the rules vary according to which state you are going to. See Chapter 18, *Health Matters.*
- **Finance**: link and simplify bank and building society accounts; work out how they can be operated from overseas, in particular electronically, ensuring that you have an international phone number for the times you may need to phone from America; some accounts cannot be operated by 'non-residents' (for tax purposes); decide how much ready cash you will need initially for buying cars, equipment, renting, school enrollment, etc. (always more than you think); increase the credit limit on your credit card to cover extra expenses while you are in transit and setting up your new home in America; open a US bank account as soon as possible and transfer money out there in readiness. See Chapter 9, *Systems and Services.*
- **Work**: investigate your tax position; determine how best to split earnings, i.e. how

much money you think you will need to live on overseas and to cover expenses back home – sometimes the exchange rate can be in your favour. See Chapter 19, *The Economy, Work and Retirement.*

- **Children**: contact local American schools and daycare agencies as appropriate; ascertain how your children will fit into their system and what the options are; contact HM Revenue & Customs regarding Child Benefit. See Chapter 8, *Education.*
- **Pets**: microchipping, vaccinations, blood tests and other veterinary formalities; travel arrangements, including purchasing a crate. See Chapter 2, *Flying Cats and Dogs.*
- **Insurance**: for personal possessions going with you; house contents in transit (including marine insurance cover if going by sea); house contents in storage; tenant's liability; travel insurance; military kit/uniform; personal liability; health and medical insurance; renters' insurance. See Chapter 9, *Systems and Services.*
- **Communications**: will your existing mobile phone work in America? Investigate providers of cheap telephone calls to and from the US; ensure your email address will work State-side; add to your address book all the contact details of anyone you might need to contact while you are living out of suitcases initially; ask for international telephone numbers (UK 0845 and 0870 prefixed numbers don't always work in America); set up mail redirection; notify whoever you need to that you are moving and give them a temporary address to use in the short-term if you don't know your permanent US address (if you are in the military you could use your BFPO address). See Chapter 9, *Systems and Services.*
- **Transportation**: timing the selling or disposing of your British car(s) and any other vehicles is a tricky one (as is buying vehicles State-side); cancel insurance; organise a vehicle to use in your final weeks in the UK; research makes and models of cars to buy in America. See Chapter 11, *On the Roads.*
- **Cancellations**: subscriptions; memberships; catalogue shopping; store cards; any other mailing lists you might be on that will no longer be relevant. Now is the time to get your name taken off all those superfluous lists.
- **Maps**: there are plenty of free mapping sources such as Google Maps and Rand McNally. Maps are much cheaper to buy once you arrive in America, and even free from state tourism offices or the AAA if you join.

Being in Transit

The length of time you are in transit may turn out to be longer than expected. If your belongings are being shipped, this can take 6 weeks or more. Plan for delays – an all-too-often occurrence. Even with the greatest of organisation on your part, others in the chain can botch it up. Keep this in mind as you decide what to take with you for your initial weeks in limbo.

You will probably need a briefcase full of paperwork in order to set yourself up on arrival. Such things as proving your identity, registering with the authorities, applying for finance and buying a car all require a frightening amount of official paperwork to back up your circumstances. So if in doubt, take it with you. Simply carrying a little excess paperwork could get you out of a tricky situation.

America, Here We Come

Once we had left our home and familiar surroundings behind, it felt as if we had reached another stage. Our possessions had gone over the horizon, the house was no longer our responsibility and we had entered into a strange state of limbo. A large weight – both physically and mentally – had been lifted; we were in transit, with just our basic personal possessions to hand. It was rather like being on holiday. As we drove away, leaving behind our old life and looking at things for the last time in a rather sad, nostalgic sort of way, it felt as if our adventure had finally begun.

We felt detached and at a loose end during our last days in England. After all the rushing about and mental exercise, it felt strange to just sit around, our bags packed and ready to go, nothing much else left to do. Tim and I felt weird and slightly anxious, like when you set off on holiday and start to worry that you've forgotten something. The children, on the other hand, were excited and constantly asking, 'How much longer till we go to the airport?', as little people do.

There are a few important things to remember before you leave:

- Make sure your footwear is dirt free (so that you are safe to 'import' under American health and safety regulations).
- Go online to check-in 24 hours before your flight. You can check your seats and confirm meals. The children almost missed out on their choices as we discovered we should have booked them 72 hours ahead of departure – but the airline managed to rustle up a couple of late kids meals, which got us off the hook.
- Confirm check-in time: usually around 2 hours before scheduled departure.
- Confirm your US hotel and accommodation details and ensure you have the full addresses handy for the immigration forms.
- Ensure you have plenty of cash with you.
- Check the baggage allowance carefully with your respective airline. You don't want to fall foul of the rules and be embarrassed at the check-in desk, having to raid your bags and hold everyone up. Children are usually classed as passengers and thus have the same allowance as adults – a real boon if you have to carry 6 weeks' worth of stuff with you.

All checked baggage is inspected by X-ray and some bags are opened and physically inspected. Therefore don't lock your bags or you may get them back with the locks broken.

The next morning we set off for Heathrow Airport, the car groaning with bags. Having safely negotiated check-in and ridded ourselves of our hefty baggage (children not included), we heaved a sigh and went through to the departure lounge. The children were each given a snazzy Virgin Atlantic rucksack complete with goodies, which provided a welcome focus for them and us (thank you, Virgin), and there were more freebies on board the aircraft. Soon the kids were ensconced in their seats with their luminous socks, eye masks, headphones and baseball hats – quite happy.

As we took off, it felt as if we were leaving part of ourselves behind – both physically and mentally. I felt a surge of exhilaration *at last* (and I don't think it was just the G force). America, here we come.

First Stop, Washington Dulles Airport

The next day we arrived in Washington, DC, having put 3665 miles between us and London. It was the 1st of July (or should I say July 1, as we are now in America), ironically 3 days before Americans celebrate their independence from us with a long weekend of picnics, parades, and yes, even generous portions of good old apple pie. Stepping off the plane, the summer heat hit us and we instantly knew we were a long way from home.

As we went through the necessary arrivals routine at Dulles Airport, some first impressions struck us:

- There seemed to be many more staff at Dulles compared to Heathrow Airport, often in gaggles, usually working at a slow, easy rate; in fact so slow some appeared to be not working at all. There were floor sweepers (or should I say brush movers as there didn't appear to be anything to sweep up), bin inspectors and trolley pushers. Conversely, other employees were ushering us into queues, moving the flexible lanes to accommodate people as the queues formed, all very efficient.

- The queues were noticeably orderly and no-one appeared to be in a rush.
- Pleasant and smiling visa and passport controllers welcomed us to the United States. Compare this with the usually scary prospect of passing through British immigration control and you will appreciate how refreshing this is.
- That said, despite the impression of being welcomed to America, security is hot and heavy. Immigration staff are very smartly dressed, alert and directing, which has the effect of making you feel uneasy. On arrival you may be photographed, fingerprinted and patted down.
- The children asked what the smell was – popcorn, that all-American staple snack food, a smell we were soon going to be very familiar with.
- Everything is polished and in its place; nothing looks grubby or old.
- We were rather awestruck by the size of the people – so many overweight. Even our 4-year-old couldn't keep his eyes from popping out of his head and had to be reminded not to stare. According to the National Health and Nutrition Examination Survey 2001–2004, two thirds of adults in the US are overweight and almost one third are obese. America: land of plenty.

You can't do much else other than people-watch while you are stuck in a queue. Our fellow travellers were casually, strangely and, on the whole, not very interestingly dressed. Most people were wearing trainers or flip-flops and fairly plain, run-of-the-mill clothes. They appeared not to care much about their dress sense. However, despite being jostled and stared at by our young children, as youngsters do when waiting in a line, the Americans were courteous and friendly towards us – no British grumpiness or tutting here. (This pleasant attitude was something we would find across most of America.)

Arriving in Washington, DC

Once outside the airport we hailed a taxi. On the way into the city, we were struck by the smooth and constant 55 mph speed everyone seemed to be doing on the huge, open roads (not the usual manic driving you get on British motorways). Verges in between the motorways comprised wide tracts of grass, in places even woodland, the equivalent width of about five lanes of traffic. The highway had four lanes or so, with cars unnervingly overtaking on both sides of us, though perhaps this was partly due to the number of filtering off-ramps. We sedately bounced along in our soft-suspensioned, air-conditioned, roomy vehicle, gazing at our new country. The houses were attractive, tidy and open, often of varicoloured clapboard – model homes set on huge grassy plots of land. The office blocks we passed had imaginative and pleasant modern architecture, interesting to look at, and more often than not proudly sporting the stars and stripes banner, just to remind you that you were in America.

During the first 24 hours we still had that feeling of being on an over-planned holiday with too much baggage. We felt laden down with our physical accoutrements and it was a relief to get to our hotel room and 'debus'. We had changed our watches to US time (5 hours behind) straight after take-off from England and had all adjusted well to the time difference. No-one was feeling jetlagged, so, after briefly unpacking, we headed out into the city to explore.

Washington was purposely built to be the political capital of America, and is a magnificent city to visit. The Metrorail system is a good place to start and proved to be a mini adventure for the children. We descended into the darkness on what seemed an eerily long and quiet escalator. There were few people about and those we did see were not rushing; I couldn't help comparing this with London, where everyone seems to be in a hurry. It felt as if we were entering another world (indeed, we had). Our kids found a great viewpoint, peering over the walls above the tunnels. However, to our dismay they took on the appearance of chimney sweeps, having coated themselves in soot. Where are the wet-wipes when you need them?

The ticket machines do not give change so go prepared. If you want to buy a single ticket to a destination for two or more people, look up the price on the machine. Then select Multiple Farecards from the menu. Press the minus button until the correct dollar amount shows, and then insert your money. Children less than 5 years old travel free. For a map of the Metrorail system, see *Useful Websites* at the end of this chapter.

On leaving the train, people mysteriously start forming orderly snaking lines (a world of difference to the jostling you experience on London's Underground), so you simply relax and join the queue. Most of the platforms and trains of Washington's Metro are indistinct from each other and lack adornment, unlike the London Underground with its often individually decorated platforms, advertisement billboards and even poetry to read on the trains. So riding the Metro is a pretty functional and boring experience. However, Grand Union Station deserves a mention as it is worth a visit in itself. It is architecturally and aesthetically monumental, as well as having a great food market downstairs where you can eat cheaply at any number of ethnic outlets.

Of course, it's up to you where you go in Washington. The National Mall area is a focus for tourists as it has so many landmarks and museums in and around it. Below are just some of the highlights:

- The Washington Monument is an unadorned, white marble, hollow shaft, dedicated to America's first president, George Washington, its appearance in keeping with his precise, honest character and lofty stature. If you use the stairway (898 steps) to ascend the Monument you can view the memorial stones set in the interior walls, presented by 200-odd individuals and organisations, each inscribed personally with special words. From eight small windows at the top you can enjoy a view of the city in all directions.

- The famous cherry blossoms near the Monument were gifted by Tokyo in 1912 as a token of friendship and attract many visitors.
- Opposite the Washington Memorial, with the reflecting pool in between, stands the white marble Lincoln Memorial. It was dedicated in 1922 to the Civil War President Abraham Lincoln, who was assassinated in 1865 after striving for equal opportunities and freedom for all. As President he saved the Union, freed the Negro slave, and was the greatest democrat of all time and a continuing inspiration. He is consistently named one of America's best-loved presidents.
- The Capitol is the legislative centre of the government and a national shrine. It houses the Senate and House of Representatives, and is one of the most visited buildings in America, with its impressive statues and pictures of distinguished Americans and dramatic events. The building contains 540 rooms, including restaurants, post offices, travel offices and shops. A magnificent bronze lady – the Statue of Freedom – stands atop the great dome, holding a sword and wreath in the attitude of one having won a battle.
- South of the Mall, in West Potomac Park, is the Jefferson Memorial. Jefferson lived between 1743 and 1826 and was the third US President. He was also the author of the Declaration of Independence and one of the first Americans to argue that slavery was inconsistent in a democratic state. He opposed all forms of tyranny, believing in a simple democratic form of government, freedom of the press and education of the masses. He fought for principles that Americans today still hold as their chief doctrines.
- The Vietnam Memorial commemorates the names of dead soldiers carved into its black granite walls. One wall points towards the Lincoln Memorial, the other towards the Washington Memorial. Every day, Americans visiting the Wall leave behind personal artefacts in remembrance of their lost friends and family; it is a very moving place.

Flying on to Ohio – the Birthplace of Aviation

The departure terminal at Dulles Airport is not user-friendly. It comprises one long concourse with people queuing all along it at different gates. The restrooms are centred, so if you happen to be at one end of the concourse you have to work your way through myriad lines of people to get to them. Better still, go out of one door, walk the length outside, and then nip back in.

On our internal flight to Ohio, almost a year after 9/11, the security checks involved two stages. First, baggage ticketing and weighing. Unluckily we were the 1-in-10 to have our bags scanned, opened and physically checked (and they don't bother refolding your clothes). Second, as we went through security ourselves, Rosie's flashing shoes received close inspection but were judged safe to continue. Two of us were singled out for further scrutiny – myself and Rosie again (I guess we must have looked nervous and shifty). We were treated to a flashing, bleeping rod passing over our legs and feet as we sat on chairs, and then front and back as we stood like scare-crows, trying to look unconcerned. Our hand baggage received similar treatment.

Having been pronounced fit to proceed, our next adventure was the flight from Washington to Dayton, in a tiny 30-seater aircraft, with propellers. We took off and spent the next 2 hours bumping through the clouds on what felt like a mini roller-coaster, lurching up and down (funfair rides aren't one of my favourite things). I adopted a brave face when the children asked what the dips and bumps were. It was a relief when we landed intact, save for upset nerves. The air temperature was noticeably cooler than it had been in the city, and the little airport was friendly after the impersonal feel of Dulles.

So it was with smiles of deliverance on our faces that we arrived at our final destination – Dayton, Ohio.

First Impressions

In the Midwest, outside of the cities, the economy is based on manufacturing and farming. Perhaps this is why most Americans, I noticed, tend to dress casually, plainly and often – quite frankly – unflatteringly. Shorts, t-shirts, trainers and white socks are the norm, no matter what age or size you are. This sporty dress-sense can look rather quizzical on older people and those packing too much weight. It is quite usual to see 'big' families unashamedly exposing unsightly legs and arms in shorts and t-shirts, and rare to see women dressed femininely; even wearing a skirt to a restaurant puts you in a minority and can make you feel overdressed. In fact, I soon noticed a distinct absence of feminine attire. Elegance and modesty are not words I'd use to describe the dress sense.

Even at work, people who are not in public view dress very casually. However, when they have to be formal, Americans tend to be rather stiff and old-fashioned about it, presenting a very clean-cut image; but their suits don't suit. Jim also remarked on this:

> Clothing in America is on the whole good quality and very reasonably priced. Comfortable and casual are bywords and hardly a jacket and tie are seen. This style is, in the main, very welcome and allows more money to be allocated to everyday clothes, rather than to the occasional 'Sunday best'. Therefore, seeing people in formal dress can draw some attention. Given the affordability of everyday clothing, you might be forgiven for expecting that when called upon to dress formally the average American would be resplendent in Armani or Gucci. The truth is less impressive; most Americans in suits look as matched as Paul McCartney and Heather Mills. Stripes, checks and outrageous colours swirl in an ensemble of droopy cuffs and trousers that are too short in the leg. Not all these apparitions are used-car salesmen, so it can only be assumed that the infrequent exposure to well-cut clothing explains the poor choices and fits. Fashion wisdom would therefore suggest buying most clothing styles from the US, except formal.

Despite the preference for casual attire, Americans love uniforms and wearing the proper gear for the job or occasion. Socially and publicly they wear what they are supposed to in any given circumstance. As my stepfather put it, 'It's as if they're hiding behind an image they are expected to portray'. For church, they dress up as we would if going out to dinner. For a cycle ride, they don 'the gear' – they wear the whole kit and caboodle. It's very important to look the part.

What other first impressions did I have? Well, Americans are notoriously overfamiliar, or at least seem so next to our British reserve. In restaurants, you are welcomed chattily by your server (waiter or waitress), who greets you with a long-winded tirade along the lines of, 'Hi, my name's Cindy and I'll be your server today. How you'all? Are you having a good day? If there is anything I can do for you, be sure to let me know. So, what can I get you folks to drink?' (even before you've sat down and looked at the menu). On the telephone, by the time the customer service representative has finished the initial pleasantries, you may have forgotten why you phoned. At the end of the conversation, you are usually treated to that classic Americanism, 'Have a nice day', which I found rather pleasant and not as annoying as we cynical Brits usually make out. Several days later you may receive a follow-up call, to check that you were satisfied with everything. They seem to place very high regard on customer service.

In America you are expected to tip service providers. As servers in restaurants are usually paid a pittance, tips make up their income. Indeed, many are taxed on expected tips, whether earned or not (see Chapter 19). According to servers, religious people and Europeans are notoriously poor tippers; this is probably because we don't appreciate the poor pay American workers receive. A tip of 15–20% is usual for good service (and you rarely receive bad service). Porters expect $1 for each bag carried. Hairdressers, food delivery guys, cabbies and tour guides also expect to be tipped.

The scale of things is definitely bigger in the States. Where we have simple one-lane roads, they have two or three lanes; where we pop into town, park and walk to the shops, they drive to the next parking lot; where we go to a café and order a simple cup of tea, they go for an impressively huge 'choca, mocca, frappa, light toasted, decaf coffee, medium large to go'. While sipping your tea (or coffee if you have gone American), you may also notice there is little formality left in American society. Basic social courtesies such as holding the door for someone are often forgotten or ignored, and you are unlikely to be thanked for doing so yourself.

Sometimes, Americans can be so laid back they don't appear to use their brains. They can be very slow in manner and movement, especially when you are in a rush. This lack of urgency and the blank looks you get when you ask a question can be frustrating. Just remember that you are strange to them and they may simply be overawed by your English accent. Americans rarely respond to pressure by rushing around, being rude or disgruntled with the customer. Their generally cheery (if rather vacant) attitude usually sees them through.

The large amount of administration you have to deal with on first arriving in America can send you into overload. American bureaucracy is very frustrating, for instance when trying to register your vehicle, get the phone connected, or sign up with a doctor. Military bureaucracy is frighteningly complicated and slow. If you do not fit the American norm, you are an anomaly, and often people do not know how to deal with you. My advice here is to keep pestering but stay cool. Be politely British, apologise for being different and charm your way along the chain of command until you get a result. This worked for us. Most Americans are fairly conservative and do not like criticism, so keep things civil.

People in America are generally law abiding. They actually come to a halt at stop signs and proceed correctly at four-way stops. I used to curse the driver in front for stopping at a sign when it was clearly obvious no one else was at the junction until I realised there is a hefty fine if the police catch you not stopping. Indeed, rules and regulations feature heavily in all areas of American life – which you will quickly discern for yourself as you go through the process of arriving and establishing yourself in America. In the work environment, often the front-line staff are young, appear inexperienced, are unable to digress from normal procedures and may be ignorant of what alternative action to take. If you do not fit the usual criteria, this results in a lot of blank looks and calls to supervisors. They either have no initiative or else are unable to make decisions or offer advice on their own. People dealing with you as a newly arrived foreign national rely on a system of computerised support. Also there is a hierarchical decision tree, with expected behaviour depending on the level of work you do. Workers are often told to shut up, not act on their own initiative. This non-egalitarian aspect of everyone having a place in the system is at odds with the classless society America is known for. Appreciate this, and bring with you plenty of relevant paperwork, forms of identification and patience; you will need it.

Missing the Little Things

We had come a long way from home and America is very different to England. Some things we missed straight away, such as:

- quality British newspapers and reporting (you might like to subscribe to the *Weekly Telegraph* to keep up with news back home);
- uninterrupted television – not being able to watch the TV without incessant commercials and previews butting in;
- high streets – walking up and down a high street, nipping in and out of places, being close to all the small shops and other town amenities you need;
- good bread and butter – most American bread is light and sweet and most butter is made with sweet cream and tastes quite different; you have to hunt out basic salted or unsalted butter;
- strong tea.

However, this is all part of the experience of visiting or living in a different country, and you shouldn't let things you miss get you down. Try new products and keep an open mind (see also Chapters 16 and 17 on shopping and food).

Useful Websites

www.britainusa.com – Public Affairs Team of the British Embassy in Washington, DC. Information on current issues in the UK, passport and visa services.
www.fco.gov.uk – the Foreign and Commonwealth Office.
www.firstgov.gov – the US government's official web portal.
www.money.com – CNN website, with a wide range of topics pertaining to America.
www.seeamerica.org – the Travel Industry Association of America's online portal to US travel websites, arranged according to region, with links to individual state and territorial offices of tourism.
www.telegraph.co.uk/global – information on expatriate issues; also where you can subscribe to the *Weekly Telegraph.*
www.travel.state.gov – the US Department of State Bureau of Consulate Affairs. Information on US passports, visas and travel.
www.unitedstatesvisas.gov – Department of State visa information.

www.uscis.gov – US Citizenship and Immigration Services.
www.usembassy.org.uk – to apply for a visa.
http://www.usembassy.org.uk/rctour.html – lists UK telephone numbers of some US destinations represented in Britain.
www.usimmigrationsupport.org – information regarding immigration, visas, green cards, social security numbers, citizen applications and passport applications.
www.wmata.com – the Washington Metrorail system.

2 · Flying Dogs and Cats

Jester was looking concerned. We had been discussing whether or not to take him to America, and whenever the word 'leave' was mentioned he flattened his ears and dropped his head. It didn't take us long to realise that going to America without him was not really an option; he had been our first 'baby', before the children, and was an important member of our pack. Of course, it would entail several jabs from that nasty vet and then sitting in a crate in a scary aircraft for nine hours, but hopefully nothing that would turn his hair for long. We gave him a cuddle and stopped talking about 'leaving'.

Information on exporting pets to America is freely available, but it can be a monumental task to sift through it all. This chapter provides a précis of what is involved and, in particular, discusses the requirements for bringing a dog into the USA. The rules are similar for cats and ferrets. There appear to be scant regulations and restrictions regarding importing fish, reptiles, amphibians, guinea pigs, hamsters, gerbils, rabbits, rats, mice and other small mammals. Rules are constantly changing, so check with the current edition of the International Air Transport Association (IATA) Live Animal Regulations and other veterinary organisations.

Arranging to take the family pet to America involves a lot of research and more expense than you might realise. You probably should not tot up the veterinary, paperwork, shipping and airport costs and charges unless you want a shock. Regardless, if going abroad for a reasonable length of time, most people will, despite the cost, want to take their furry loved ones with them.

Preliminaries

To start with it is necessary to investigate the requirements for animal entry into the US. Keep in mind that every state has its own rules and regulations. Our first port of call was DEFRA's Pet Travel Scheme helpline (PETS for short). We also spoke to our UK vet and a vet in Ohio near to where we would be living, and checked the websites of the airline, the Center for Disease Control (CDC) and the US Department of Agriculture (USDA).

The first practical requirement is to get your pet microchipped with a unique identification number. Your local vet can do this. Check that the chip used will meet ISO specifications so that it can be read by any standard microchip reader. Your pet will be issued with a metal tag that attaches to his collar which reads rather endearingly 'Please scan me'.

Health Issues

Bringing an animal into America does not involve as many health issues as taking one back to Britain (the UK has more stringent laws). With the exception of Hawaii, Alaska and Guam, there is no need for your animal to be detained in quarantine on entering the United States. Moreover, since December 2002, PETS has allowed dogs and cats to return to Britain from America without enforced isolation so long as they meet *all* the requirements of the scheme. Thus long-term quarantining is no longer an issue. However, your animal will still have to spend two to three hours in short-term quarantine while the authorities confirm that you have met the requirements of PETS.

Rabies

Rabies is a viral disease that affects mammals. Principal hosts are wild carnivores (such as raccoons, skunks, coyotes and foxes in the US) and bats. Domestic animals account for less than 10% of reported cases, and only one or two people a year die from rabies, owing to modern-day prophylaxis.

The CDC requires dogs to be vaccinated against rabies at least 30 days prior to entry to the United States. For cats imported into the US there is *usually* no vaccination requirement; however, some states require it, so check with the local health authority at your final destination. Thirty days after the jab, your dog should be blood tested to check that the vaccine has taken effect. Some dogs fail the initial blood test and will need to be revaccinated and retested. Therefore to ensure your animal is covered, start the rabies preventative programme well in advance of travel.

Your pet will then be given his own pet passport and is on the way to becoming a bona fide traveller.

Heartworm

Heartworm is a nasty parasite that affects dogs and cats, and is transmitted by mosquitoes. It is not customary to treat for it in the UK, but throughout the States it is a serious problem and dogs are routinely protected (monthly).

You can start heartworm treatment before you leave the UK (to ensure your animal is immune before he arrives in America). This involves giving him a vial of liquid or a nugget of meat-flavoured medicine each month. After a couple of months, you can get him blood tested by your local UK vet or wait until he arrives in America. In the US you cannot purchase more supplies of preventive heartworm treatment until your dog has the all-clear on the blood test. US vets recommend continuing monthly treatment all year round, not just during the mosquito season. Thereafter, your dog should be annually tested for heartworm.

Other Worms, Fleas and Ticks

It is not necessary to give worm, flea or tick preventative treatment prior to leaving the UK; it is not a requirement for entry into the US. However, it is a requirement for re-entry to Britain. That said, to be on the safe side, check with officials at the time you are arranging travel, as things do change.

Arranging Shipment

It is obviously best for your pet to arrange a non-stop flight, but not always possible or cost-effective. You can either book direct with the airline or make your pet's travel arrangements through a freight shipping company such as PBS International or Air Pets Oceanic. We opted for a flight and crate package through PBS and Delta, flying direct from Gatwick to Cincinnati after the summer embargo. The airline freight charge was a hefty £785 and the crate (which we were allowed to keep for the return leg) cost £145; by the time the shipper had added on handling and 'exceptional security' charges, fuel surcharges, costs for documentation, customs export declaration and attendance, we had totted the bill up to a rather staggering £1089. We were also stung for an extra 3% on top of this because we didn't read the small print carefully enough (stating that payment by credit card incurs additional cost).

Some airlines allow two animals of comparable size to be shipped in one container. You might ask whether the shipper has a used crate, to save what little you can on the cost of buying a new crate. There is not much you can do about the other costs besides shopping around. If you want to buy a crate yourself, be sure that it is a shipping kennel approved by the USDA and/or IATA. I did a search on the internet for 'used pet crates travel UK' and came up with some sites.

To determine the correct size crate for your dog first check his vital statistics:

- Length: with the subject standing, hold his head in an upright, alert position and measure from the nose to the root of the tail (the tail is excluded).
- Height: measure from the top of the head or ear tips (whichever is highest) to the floor.
- Width: measure at the widest point, usually the shoulders.

Do be sure to get your measurements right; otherwise the airline could legally stop your pet from flying if they consider he is oversized. You must allow at least three inches more on each of the above dimensions in order for your pet to be able to stand up, turn around and lie down in a natural manner inside the crate. Then weigh him and record this.

If you are using a shipping company give these measurements to them and they will determine the best size of crate. Even though Jester was only a border collie mutt it was deemed necessary to put him in a giant crate; I baulked at this as of course it cost more, but you have to go by what those 'in the know' decide. Anyhow, the extra roominess probably wasn't a bad thing for such a long flight.

They advise you to collect the crate in advance of the flight, so that you can get your animal used to it before the trauma of flying. We weren't able to, but in the end it didn't matter. Jester took a couple of sniffs, meekly went in and settled down. The shipper supplied him with a wee bit of comfort in the form of shredded paper as bedding and we provided an old familiar soft bed and towel. However, no toys were allowed (because of the possibility of choking). Other basic necessities are allowed in the form of two dishes (one for food, one for water) attached to the inside of the door, both accessible from the outside for easy filling. These should come with a new crate in any case.

Cats usually get away with one standard-sized crate, unless your moggie is unusually large. Some airlines allow small animals to travel with you in the cabin (so long as the crate is small enough to fit under the seat in front of you). Soft-sided carriers may also be permitted. Other airlines require you to check them in as 'excess baggage' and they travel in the cargo hold. 'Air cargo' is used when the pet is not being accompanied by a passenger and is checked in through the cargo terminal.

Flying with your pet on a domestic flight (within the US) may set you back an extra $50 or $75 each way (on top of your ticket). You might see pets rolling through the airport in small wheeled carriers. Disposable diapers (nappies) are another novel sight, though you can appreciate the sense in them. Before flying, you must obtain a health certificate and check whether the state you are going to requires a rabies shot. Travel with your pet's vaccination and registration records. Lastly, be prepared to put on your most apologetic face when your moggie starts 'crying' on the airplane.

Summer and Winter Flying Restrictions

Airlines are used to transporting animals and they have to meet welfare conditions laid down by IATA. This means providing travel in a heated, ventilated and pressurised compartment, with food and water given as appropriate.

If you are flying out to America during the summer or winter, when temperatures can be extreme, you may find you cannot bring your pet with you straight away. Some airlines have an embargo on accepting pets for travel during the hot summer months (Delta's embargo lasts from 15 May to 15 September) owing to the danger of heat stress. Once the temperature falls below 85°F (29°C), it is considered safe for dogs and cats to travel. There is an option for summer flying if you are prepared to pay around double the usual price – you can use a commercial animal shipper. These shippers have the means to keep animals comfortable in extreme heat and can be more flexible over flight schedules. Contact British Airways or Continental Airlines and ask about their Quick Pack Service.

Likewise, if at any point during the trip the temperature is likely to be below 45°F (7°C), an Acclimation Certificate signed by a veterinarian is required before some airlines will accept your animal for flying.

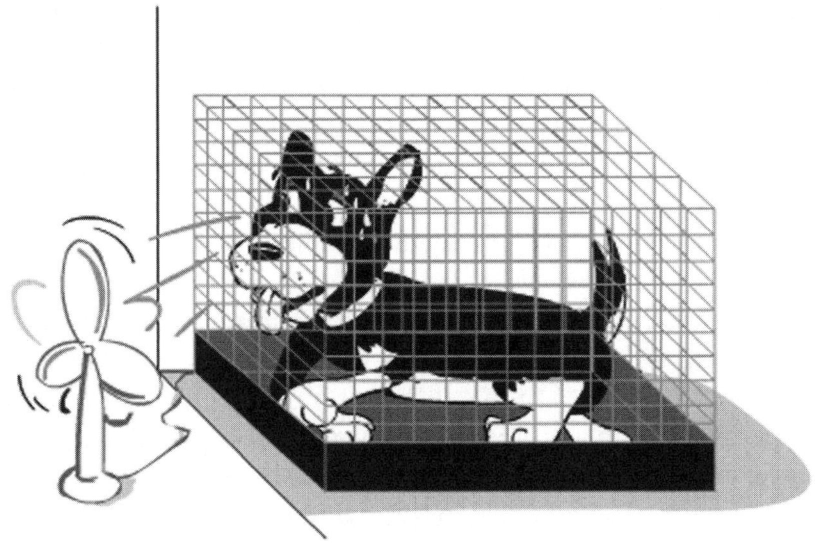

Last Minute Arrangements

Within 10 days of travelling to America, take your pet to the vet to confirm his fitness to travel and obtain a health certificate. This certificate is not generally needed by the federal government, but may be required by the state you are going to or the airline transporting your pet. Contact USDA's Veterinary Services or your shipping company for details. The Acclimation Certificate (if applicable) should also be issued no more than 10 days before departure. Airlines like to see original paperwork, not copies, so ensure you keep all these handy.

A day ahead, you or the shipper should check that it is not too hot to fly your pet out. If it is, you will have to reschedule the travel arrangements.

Prior to check-in, you will be asked to complete a Live Animal Checklist. One of the points asks you to confirm that your pet has been offered food and water within four hours of check-in. The airline may prefer him not to be fed *just* before the flight, for obvious reasons. Your pet should also be given the opportunity to empty himself pre-flight. If in-transit feeding is necessary, provide some food; they do not offer in-flight meal trays and you don't want your poor animal arriving both tired *and* hungry.

You may be wondering whether your precious cargo might benefit from being out of it for the duration of the journey. However, it is not usual to sedate pets for travelling, as pet tranquillisers at high altitudes can be unpredictable. If you wish to drug your pet, you must obtain and provide written proof of consent from your veterinarian. This information should be attached to the crate. Apparently, most animals just go to sleep in flight.

At the Airport (Operation Jester Commences)

Jester arrived at Gatwick and was met at the cargo area by PBS. They handled the paperwork and checking-in. He was scanned and his microchip record was verified. The rabies jab certificate and health certificate were also asked for. All was in order and he was pronounced good to go.

His collar was removed and placed inside a plastic bag, along with other personal effects (leads, bowls and whistle). We crated him up outside. The forklift driver, as he disappeared airside with our nervous-looking pooch, promised he would tape this personal baggage to the top of the crate. To his credit, everything arrived safely; as did Jester. Despite the long journey, he did not suffer any ill effects and was happy to see us. He was a little dopey and subdued for the first couple of days, but soon regained his old playful character and was chewing the kids' balls and digging up the garden as usual.

For the return leg back to England and what that involved, see Chapter 22.

Recap of Time Schedule

- *About 2 months prior to travel (if you have this amount of time)*
  Get your animal microchipped and vaccinated against rabies. This will allow for a blood test 30 days later, at which point you can revaccinate if the first dose did not take effect.
- *At least 30 days prior to travel*
  Ensure the initial or second rabies jab has been given. Thirty days later, blood test to confirm. At the same time, you might ask your vet for a heartworm tablet to start the course of heartworm prevention off. Collect the crate if possible, in order to familiarise your animal with it.
- *Within 10 days of departure*
  Get your vet to issue the health certificate and acclimation certificate (if applicable).

Information Taken from PETS (Abridged Version)

(For the latest information, visit DEFRA's website.)

The PETS helpline is (0044) (0) 870 241 1710 (open between 0830 and 1700) and website http://www.defra.gov.uk/animalh/quarantine/index.htm.

For advice on permanently taking your animal out of the UK contact your local Animal Health Divisional Office. A list of these offices can be found at http://www.defra.gov.uk/corporate/contacts/ahdo.htm.

For information on quarantine or early release from quarantine contact the Quarantine Section on (0044) (0) 1245 358383 or email quarantine@defra.gsi.gov.uk. Information on quarantine procedures can be found at http://www.defra.gov.uk/animalh/quarantine/quarantine/qindex.htm.

Fact sheets on travelling with pets from European Union countries and Non-European Union countries can be found at http://www.defra.gov.uk/animalh/quarantine/factsheet/factsheet.htm.

EU Recognised Blood Testing Laboratories (those approved to do the blood testing for the Scheme) can be found at http://www.defra.gov.uk/animalh/quarantine/pets/procedures/support-info/labs.htm.

Approved routes and carriers which can be used when travelling to the UK from qualifying countries can be found at http://www.defra.gov.uk/animalh/quarantine/pets/procedures/support-info/routes.htm.

Tick and tapeworm treatment is required before pets enter the UK under PETS. See http://www.defra.gov.uk/animalh/quarantine/pets/procedures/support-info/parasites.htm.

Useful Websites

www.airpets.co.uk – pet relocation specialists, based at Heathrow; fly with British Airways.
www.azfreight.com – lists airports, agents, airlines and suppliers for pet transport.
www.cdc.gov – Centers for Disease Control and Prevention; search for 'importation of pets'.
www.continental.com – under 'Travel Information', click on 'Travelling with Animals'.
www.defra.gov.uk/animalh/quarantine/pets – DEFRA's PETS scheme.
www.maff.gov.uk – MAFF Export Section (Dogs and Cats), advice on current documentation and vaccination requirements for your destination.
www.pbs-int.com – PBS International Freight Ltd, animal shippers.

3 · Where Exactly Are We?

America – Big Country

As *Let's Go USA* rightly points out, the North American continent stretches from above the Arctic Circle to below the Tropic of Cancer. The United States of America comprises 50 states and one district (the District of Columbia) spread over a total 3,537,438 sq miles, excluding the Great Lakes area (see Fig. 3.1). On a worldwide scale, only Canada, China and Russia have larger land areas. The East Coast is 5 hours behind GMT and this extends to minus 8 by the time you get to the West Coast. Table 3.1 gives some comparisons between the UK and the US. America is nearly 40 times larger than Britain, 14.3 times larger than France and 2.5 times the size of the European Union, which puts things into perspective. England is similar in size to the state of New York (which is ranked 27th in terms of size within the US); the UK as a whole is slightly smaller than the state of Oregon. For every UK citizen there are 4.5 Americans. As a country, the US has the fourth largest population in the world (behind China, India and Russia). New Jersey is the most populous state, followed by New York and Texas. In 1920, half of all Americans lived in towns and cities; now the figure is 3 in 4.

The largest state, Alaska, is more than twice the size of the next largest state (Texas). It encompasses 656,400 sq miles and has more than 6000 miles of coastline, which is longer than the rest of the states combined. It also has more national parks and preserves than all the other states put together. Most of Alaska is fairly inhospitable and most villages can only be reached by air or water transport. Texas is the second largest state in terms of both area and population (268,581 sq miles and 22 million people, respectively). This one state alone is almost three times the area of the UK. The smallest state, Rhode Island, is about 20% larger in area than the Isle of Wight. It is not actually an island, as most of its land is part of the mainland. It stretches 48 miles north to south and 37 miles east to west.

Figure 3.1 US states (taken from Digital Vector Maps).

Table 3.1 Some comparisons between the US and the UK.

Criteria	US	UK
Largest lake (sq miles)	Lake Michigan (22,500)	Lough Neagh (153)
Highest mountain (m)	Mount McKinley (6194)	Ben Nevis (1343)
Lowest point (m)	Death Valley (– 86)	The Fens (– 4)
Longest river (miles)	Mississippi (2340)	Severn (220)
Total population	303,234,965 (14 January 2008)[1]	60,587,300 (22 August 2007)[2]
Land area (sq miles)	3,537,438	94,251
Distance north to south (miles)	1598	600
Distance east to west (miles)	2807	298
Most populated city ('000 people)	New York City (8085)	London (7285)

[1] From the US Population Clock (http://www.census.gov/main/www/popclock.html), which is continually clicking on.

[2] This was the most up-to-date figure available from the Office of National Statistics (http://www.statistics.gov.uk/cci/nugget.asp?id=6, accessed on 14 January 2008). Interestingly, this figure is less than the estimated figure in mid 2005 (60,609,153), showing that the population of the UK has decreased.

Natural Topography and Vegetation

North America has one of the most varied landscapes in the world, with deserts, rainforests, arctic mountains and tropical shores. Approximately 38% of the land is wilderness and 32% is forested, making the US a leading producer of wood; around 23% is under permanent pasture and meadows. The main topographical features are the Appalachian Mountains in the east, the Rocky Mountains in the west, and the Great Plains in between. The East has hills and low mountains, Alaska has mountains and broad river valleys, while Hawaii is rugged and volcanic.

The Mississippi–Missouri River is the fourth longest river in the world (after the Nile, Amazon and Yangtze). Its name comes from the Indian word meaning 'father of all waters'. The five freshwater lakes in the north that make up the Great Lakes are all shared with Canada except for Lake Michigan, which lies wholly within the US. They are more like seas than lakes, with nothing on the horizon. Lake Superior is the deepest and largest (larger even than Scotland).

As you travel east to west across the continent, deciduous temperate vegetation and grassland give way to prairie lands and boreal forests, and deserts in the south-west. The south-east has subtropical forests and mangroves. The Great Plains stretching between the eastern Appalachians and western Rocky Mountains are prime farming country. Between the Rockies and Pacific Coast lie deserts and valleys, volcanic mountains and the Sierra Nevada. The Pacific Coast Ranges make the western seaboard a hilly one, compared to the fairly flat, low-lying eastern coast, and there are some first-class skiing areas. The West Coast is also great for surfing.

Particularly spectacular natural wonders are the ten-storey-high Ponderosa pines and Douglas firs in coastal western states, and the titanic redwoods of California, with trunks the size of a car. Some trees are around 4000 years old, giving them the distinction of being the world's oldest living things, while others grow to over 370 ft tall, making them the tallest trees in the world. Places such as Death Valley in California and the Grand Canyon in Arizona, one of the seven natural wonders of the world, are truly awesome.

Weather

Whereas Britain enjoys a relatively stable temperate climate, North America – though mostly temperate – swings from tropical Florida and Hawaii to arctic Alaska, from the semi-arid Great Plains west of the Mississippi River to the arid Great South West Basin and Mediterranean California. America really has it all. Despite being on a more southerly latitude than much of the Mediterranean, east and mid-western parts of America experience a humid continental climate owing to prevailing winds bringing cool air down from Canada. The 49th parallel north marks the border between the United States and Canada, and this line of latitude passes through France and Germany. When comparing the latitude of Britain with North America, only Alaska appears on the same line. Cape Sable in Florida is the southernmost point in the continental USA, on the 24th degree of latitude, the same line as Egypt.

However, bear in mind that these lines of latitude are not good indicators of what seasonal temperatures to expect. The North American continent experiences a much wider temperature range than we Europeans are used to. It can reach 135°F (57°C) in Death Valley and a cool –11°F (–24°C) in Fairbanks, Alaska. Death Valley receives a mere 2 inches of rainfall a year, while tropical Hawaii is one of the wettest regions, with 460 inches a year. Chinook winds affect parts of the Great Plains, especially Minnesota and Montana, which makes for big temperature swings.

The Pacific North West has rain year round. The western mountain ranges receive most of the moisture brought down by the polar jet stream, leaving scant supply for the deserts in their rain shadow. The interior of the continent experiences violent storms where contrasting air masses collide over the flat plains, with dramatic swings in temperature and extreme winds. The most severe storms occur in the southern half of America, and Florida is the stormiest state. California, Oregon and Washington are the most storm-free. The Mid-Atlantic and North-East states receive heavy snowfall, partly due to the 'lake effect' of the Great Lakes. Natural hazards include:

- tsunamis – these affect Hawaii every year, with a damaging tsunami happening every 7 years or so; also at high risk are Alaska, California, Oregon and Washington;
- volcanoes and earthquakes around the Pacific Basin;
- hurricanes along the Gulf and Atlantic coasts. 1 June to the end of November is considered to be hurricane season, with peak timing in mid-August to early October;
- mud slides in California;
- flooding and flash floods;
- permafrost in northern Alaska;
- forest fires;
- tornadoes.

Weather warnings for your local area periodically scroll across the television screen, interrupting viewing with a harsh alarm signal that is unignorable. In Ohio, we had a lot of heavy snow, flash flood and tornado warnings.

Tornadoes (or twisters) wreak havoc in the south-east and central states, especially in lowland areas of the Mississippi, Ohio and Missouri River valleys. In 2006 there were 157 tornadoes, with 63 fatalities. Statistically, most tornadoes occur in Texas. In Tornado Alley (an area spanning from northern Texas to Kansas and east to Tennessee), building regulations are stricter than in other parts of America. Most tornadoes originate on the southwest side of a thunderstorm and travel to the northeast. Within a tornado, winds range from 72 up to 300 mph (so if you see one approaching, don't hang about) and the widest funnel observed was 1 mile across.

They last anything from 5 minutes to several hours, and can hop, skip and jump along the ground and turn at any time.

Many towns have tornado sirens and shelters. At the sound of the siren, people run for their nearest shelter or, failing that, their basements. In weather speak, a tornado *watch* means there are favourable conditions for a tornado, a *warning* means one has been sighted. If there is a tornado warning, the advice is to go to a shelter or to the lowest level or innermost part of a building, but don't shelter in a mobile home – like Dorothy in *The Wizard of Oz*, you could end up somewhere else. Failing that, the advice is to lie face down in the nearest ground depression with your arms over your head.

Earthquakes are another natural hazard Americans have to contend with. The Ring of Fire which encircles the basin of the Pacific is a zone of frequent quakes and eruptions and accounts for 90% of the world's earthquakes. Famous hotspots are the San Andreas Fault in California, Mount St Helen's, Washington (which last erupted in 1980), Alaska's Aleutian Islands and Hawaii. Yellowstone National Park in Wyoming is another geologically restless area, attracting thousands of visitors with its famous geysers like Old Faithful, boiling mud pools, springs and calderas.

On newspaper pages showing current and predicted weather conditions for the country, the air quality index (AQI) forecasts ozone or fine-particle pollution. During summer months, more states have an AQI that is 'unhealthy' or 'poor' than 'moderate' or 'good'.

Time Zones

There seems to be some confusion as to how many time zones cross the North American continent. Most Americans work with just four zones:

- Eastern Time – 5 hours behind Greenwich Mean Time (GMT); also known as Washington Time;

- Central Time – 6 hours behind GMT;
- Mountain Time – 7 hours behind GMT; and
- Pacific Time – 8 hours behind GMT.

Hawaii Time and Alaska Time are separate time zones. Just remember that you gain time as you travel westwards and lose time going eastwards.

As in Britain, most states change their clocks in winter and spring, though some choose not to, e.g. Arizona, Hawaii and parts of Indiana. Clocks 'spring forward' to Daylight Saving Time (DST) on or around the first Sunday in April, and 'fall back' to Standard Time (ST) around the last Sunday in October (depending on the year), at 2 a.m. Thus names in each time zone change accordingly, e.g. Eastern Standard Time (EST) becomes Eastern Daylight Time (EDT), and so on.

Travel timetables do not use the 24-hour clock, as we do in Britain. So it can be a bit disconcerting trying to work out what time your train/bus/plane is arriving or leaving, especially when flying across different time zones. Some timetables print afternoon times in bold, which is some help, or add a 'P' for p.m. Moreover, as Americans cite dates with the month first, followed by the day of the month – the opposite way round to us – working out the day let alone the time of your journey can be tricky. For instance, 12/01 is 1 December *not* 12 January. So beware of getting your dates wrong.

Dividing Up the Regions

The United States Department of State divides the US into six geographical regions:

- New England or North-East (NE)
- Mid-Atlantic (MA)
- South (S)
- Midwest (MW)
- Southwest (SW)
- West (W)

However, because 'the West' covers such a large and diverse area, it is often split further into:

- Rocky Mountain (RM)
- Pacific Coast (PC)

The states within these regions are similar historically, topographically and industrially, yet each state retains its individuality and is proud of it. The population is split 36% in the South, 23% in the West, 22% in the Midwest and 18% in the North-East (US Census Bureau 2004). Montana, Wyoming and Vermont have the least number of people per square mile; the heaviest densities of population occur in the North-East, Midwest, California and Florida.

There is an east–west divide, similar to our north–south differences; people from the east are thought of as more cultured, better educated and snobby, while those from the west are viewed as bohemian, environmentally concerned liberals. In fact, both the East and West Coasts, with their trading ports and influx of immigrants, are both considered as liberal and open to new ideas, while the heart of America is more traditional and conservative, owing to its strong farming and rural basis, and more steady population. It was here that the Republican Party was formed and the Progressive Movement started.

New England

(Maine, New Hampshire, Vermont, Massachusetts, Rhode Island and Connecticut)

This area was so named by the English explorer John Smith in 1614. It was originally the cultural and economic centre of the New World and it serves as the cornerstone of American history. The original English Protestants who settled in New England had regular town meetings to allow citizens to participate in state affairs, and this rather unique way of governing still exists today. New Englanders are said to be a thrifty, hard-working lot, and trade and fishing were and still are important industries. Approximately half the people in New England live in Massachusetts. The state capital, Boston, is one of America's most historic and financially important cities. Most of the top colleges and universities (or Ivies) are found in this region.

The Mid-Atlantic

(New York, New Jersey and Pennsylvania)

A wider range of nationalities settled in the Mid-Atlantic region. Pennsylvania has a strong Dutch influence and is both prime farming country and commercially and industrially important. New Jersey is known as the Garden State because it is the richest agricultural state of the east. New York is divided into New York City and Upstate (the remainder), including Niagara Falls and the Hudson River. The latter is a major shipping route.

New York City

New York claims many firsts in the nation and indeed the world – in fact, it calls itself rather grandly 'The Capital of the World'. When listing its notoriety, you can appreciate it is one hell of a city and worthy of the 39 million tourists who visit each year. New York City has five boroughs: Manhattan, the Bronx, Brooklyn, Queens and Staten Island. Only the Bronx is part of the mainland; the rest of the city is built on islands. The city was named New Amsterdam for the first Dutch settlers, and then became known as New York (after the English Duke of York – King James II of England and James VII of Scotland).

- With around 22 million people living within the NY metropolitan area, it is one of the largest urban areas in the world. It overtook London in 1925 as the most populous city in the world.

- The city alone has the seventeenth highest GDP in the world, exceeding Switzerland, and the second highest per capita GDP after Luxembourg.
- It has the highest public transportation use in the nation, including the largest clean-air bus fleet (using hybrid and natural gas buses) and some of the first hybrid taxis. It has the longest subway system in the world; it also has the largest and most-used commuter rail network and busiest airports in America.
- It was the last port evacuated by British ships in 1783 after the War of Independence, and today is the largest shipping port on the East Coast.
- The United Nations' headquarters is in New York City.
- Wall Street is one of the three command centres for the world's economy. The NY Stock Exchange is the largest in the world by volume of dollars, and NASDAQ is the largest by number of listings.
- It has the unenviable reputation for having the dirtiest air, with rates of lung cancer in Manhattan three times the national average.
- It is the most important centre for publishing, journalism and mass media in the States. It also has the second largest American TV and film industry, after Hollywood.
- The extremely high number of foreign immigrants makes NY an archetypal city in this nation of immigrants. Almost 36% of New Yorkers are foreign born, with no particular ethnic group dominating. Of the population, 45% are white, 27% Hispanic, 27% black and 10% Asian.
- A very high number of foreign corporations are based here.
- NY has the largest community of American Jews in the US.
- It is the cultural hub of the nation in terms of the arts, fashion, entertainment, museums, galleries, television, etc. (e.g., it is the HQ of TV networks ABC, NBC and CBS, and three of the four major record labels are based here).

The South

(Alabama, Kentucky, Mississippi and Tennessee, Arkansas, Louisiana, Oklahoma and Texas, Delaware, Florida, Georgia, Maryland, North and South Carolina, Virginia and West Virginia including the District of Columbia)

The 16 states that comprise the South – colloquially known as Dixie – have unique music, literature, customs and cuisine that are quite different from the rest of the country. The South is well known for its Smoky Mountains, 70 miles of unspoilt beaches along the coast of North Carolina, and the Sunshine State of Florida. South Florida only really appeared on the map after the railroads arrived in the 1880s, bringing holiday-makers from the North-East, and is now a mecca for older people and the rich. The place is inundated with second homes, empty for half the year. A friend of mine described it as 'having no culture, just retirees with blue hair, driving around in Cadillacs, and playing golf'.

The Deep South is a region of the Mississippi delta, comprising six of the seven original states that split from the Union (Texas being the seventh). The main industries are cotton, tobacco, soybeans, manufacturing, and coal mining in West Virginia and Kentucky. The climate is hot and sticky, and the mosquitoes can be huge and bothersome. Apart from the resorts, much of the region is still relatively poor following devastation by the Civil War, when Yankee Union troops raided and plundered. Many of the southern states still feel resentment towards the North and antagonism towards federal politics. Racism is still apparent in America, and especially so in the South.

The Midwest

(Illinois, Indiana, Ohio, Iowa, Minnesota, Wisconsin, North and South Dakota, Nebraska, Kentucky)

This is America's 'bread basket' – more grain and corn are grown in this region of the States than in any other agricultural area in the world. It is mostly flat, with the Mississippi River an important feature and inspiration to native writer Mark Twain. Michigan is important for its automobile manufacturing, northern Indiana for its steel factories. Many people visit South Dakota to see Presidents Washington, Jefferson, Lincoln and Theodora Roosevelt immortalised on the hill of Mount Rushmore. Mammoth Cave in Kentucky is the world's largest cave system, with more than 365 miles of explored subterranean labyrinth. Chicago in Illinois is the third largest city in the nation and home of America's tallest building, the Sears Tower. Midwesterners are generally straightforward, open and friendly, with a relaxed attitude, and enjoying a slow pace of life.

Southwest

(Oklahoma, Texas, New Mexico, Arizona)

Along with the Mountain states, the Southwest is the home of the cowboy, where farming and cattle ranching take centre stage, as does the oil industry. It is a land of open space and deserts, interspersed with cities such as Phoenix and Santa Fe. It is ethnically diverse, with a strong Spanish, Mexican and Native American influence. The largest tribe of American Indians lives in the Navajo Reservation, an area covering 16 million acres and spanning north-eastern Arizona, New Mexico and Utah. The Alamo in San Antonio, Texas, was made famous in 1836 when independent Texans, including Davy Crockett, made a brave stand against the Mexican army. The Grand Canyon in northern Arizona is one of the country's most impressive natural features, together with Monument Valley. Arizona, like Florida, is popular with retirees; if places like Paradise Valley, Carefree, Green Valley and Sun City live up to their names, you can guess why.

The Mountain States

(Colorado, Idaho, Montana, Nevada, Utah, Wyoming)

The Rocky Mountains are the dominant feature of this region, with great natural areas and open ranges on which cattle and sheep roam. This is 'Marlboro country', reminiscent of the Wild West. The folks here are liberal and individualistic, with legalised prostitution, gambling, medicinal marijuana and tolerance of same-sex marriages. There are few large cities. Salt Lake City in northern Utah is the home of the Mormons. Yellowstone National Park is America's oldest park, famed for its hot springs and geysers. Arizona and New Mexico can also fall under the heading of the Mountain states.

The Pacific Coast

(California, Oregon, Washington, Alaska, Hawaii)

The Pacific Coastal region of America is scenically stunning, with mountains and deserts and contrasting wet and dry regions. California is America's most populated state, and largely Mexican. There is also a strong Asian culture here. The region elsewhere is underdeveloped and sparsely populated, offering great recreational opportunities. Oregon's coastline is lined by more than 50 state parks and is a beautiful natural area. Famous national parks include Mount Rainier (standing at 4389 m above sea level) in Washington, Yosemite in Sierra Nevada and Crater Lake in Oregon.

The highways in the West are engineering marvels, many boring through giant mountains and passes – amazing structures. Visiting Los Angeles, San Diego and Las Vegas is a real experience for many people, 'to see where US culture has gone crazy', commented one friend. People on the West Coast are known for their laid-back attitude and tolerance.

Los Angeles is the second largest city in America and very densely populated, with 7876 people/sq mile living in some areas of the metropolis. It is the most ethnically diverse city in the world. People flock here to enjoy the year-round warm, dry climate, with an estimated 325 days of sunshine a year. They are also attracted to the vibrant lifestyle and chance to live the American Dream. L.A. is the home of Hollywood and famous for its television and recorded music industries. Many internationally renowned cultural and scientific institutions, company headquarters and higher education establishments are located here. However, there is a price to pay for the city's success, in the form of urban sprawl and air and groundwater pollution; according to the American Lung Association (2004), L.A. is the most polluted city in America.

In contrast, the Pacific Coast region also includes Alaska – an underpopulated and unspoilt wildlife haven. Alaska is about 20% as large as all the contiguous states combined and a vast wilderness. It has dramatic scenery, with flat tundra plains bordered by tall mountain ranges, and volcanic islands.

Hawaii is situated 2300 miles off the Californian west coast. There are more people of Asian origin than European living here. The Polynesian culture predominates, with ancient ceremonies and traditions. Hawaiian Pidgin is the unofficial language, having its origins in the old sugarcane and pineapple plantations. Hawaii had the highest state tax per capita in 2002 and 2003; the general excise tax and hotel room tax imposed on tourists contributes to some of this.

Ohio

The following section on Ohio may or may not be relevant or of interest to you. Ohio is home to the largest air force base in America – Wright Patterson Air Force Base (WPAFB) – with about 23,000 personnel, including many foreigners who work in temporary posts or on contract. There is a high turnover of British personnel posted to WPAFB, and you (like us) may be one of them. Hence the reason for including a section on Ohio.

The state is part of the Midwest, although it is really more north-east, just below the Great Lakes. Louis Bromfield (Pulitzer Prize winner and famous native Ohioan) stated, 'Ohio is the farthest west of the East and the farthest north of the South'. It is the 34th largest state (out of 52) and the seventh most populous.

- Capital city: Columbus, home to Ohio State University, one of the largest and best-known universities in America.
- Principal cities: Cleveland, Cincinnati and Toledo.
- Bordering states: West Virginia, Kentucky, Pennsylvania, Michigan and Indiana.
- Population: above-average number of whites; only 3% of the population is foreign-born compared to 11% across America; high density of people (277) per square mile (compared with the national average of 80).
- Land area: 44,825 sq miles (just a little less than the size of England).
- Famous as the home of the Wright brothers, eight US presidents and astronauts John Glenn and Neil Armstrong.
- Served by the airports of Dayton, Columbus and Cleveland (in Ohio), Cincinnati (just over the Kentucky border) and Indianapolis (in nearby Indiana).

Part urban, part rural, Ohio has southern, Appalachian and north-eastern influences and contains a bit of everything American. It is a microcosm or generalism for the States as a whole. Some say it is *the* most American state; if you could shrink America into one state, Ohio would be it. Owing to its diverse socioeconomics and politics, many companies carry out test marketing here, using Ohio as a basis for the US in general. Columbus, along with Atlanta, Georgia, are considered to be the heartland of America, as they contain few extremists and a good mix of people; rural and high-tech members of the populace live side by side.

Geography and Climate

The Ohio River forms all of Ohio's southern and most of its eastern border, Lake Erie its northern. It has more than 43,000 miles of rivers and streams and 2500 lakes, and is a neat almost square-shaped state, measuring 225 miles east to west and 210 miles north to south. The countryside is rolling, with small rounded hills and valleys in the west (the Bluegrass region of Kentucky extends into Ohio) and more rugged terrain in the east (part of the Appalachian Plateau). Much of Ohio is flat, with large crop fields and straight roads. In south-west Ohio, where we were living, the area is very wooded, with trees everywhere lining the streets, breaking up the suburban landscape. It stays green in summer, despite the heat and sun. Its soils are fertile, particularly in the west, which is part of the great Midwest corn belt. It is rich in minerals. It is also one of the main shipping, trading and manufacturing states.

Official 30-year mean temperatures for Ohio range from 25°F (–4°C) in January to 72°F (22°C) in July. However, in reality lows of 10°F (–12°C) and highs of 100°F (38°C) can and do occur. There is roughly a 10° change either up or down from one month to the next, so the variations and extremes are much greater than we are used to in Britain. The summers can feel uncomfortably hot and when it rains it is often associated with a thunderstorm, with impressive sound and light. We planned our holidays with this in mind; a camping trip, sleeping under canvas, can be pretty uncomfortable in the height of summer, when even sleeping at home is difficult unless you have air conditioning and ceiling fans. Short trips in the car can be hell, especially if you have to park in the sun (because canny Americans have hogged all the shady spots). Investing in a car windscreen sunshade really makes a big difference and stops the steering wheel from burning your hands.

During winter, with an average of 20 inches of snow, there are plenty of opportunities for skiing trips, outdoor skating, picturesque country walks and getting snowed in. The local authorities are very organised, keeping roads clear with snow ploughs and salt lorries, and we never quite needed snow chains to get about. Local TV and radio channels alert you to school closures on heavy snow days, cancelled events, delayed buses and any other problems on the roads.

History and Today

The Iroquois who lived in Ohio more than 300 years ago called the river *O-hy-o* which means 'something great'. White people were first attracted to the area because of this great river they had heard about, hoping to find a route to China. They were explorers, not settlers. The first claim to the land was made by French traders, who lived peacefully with their neighbours, the Indians, and adopted their ways.

Contrastingly, the English, spreading westwards over the Allegheny mountains, brought their own lifestyle and viewed the Indians as savages. It wasn't until 1794, following defeat of the Indians and relative peace, that white settlers began to move to Ohio to live and farm, rather than simply trap and trade. Ohio was officially established in 1803. Cincinnati was the first most-westerly settlement on the Ohio River.

During the Civil War, the population of Ohio was torn in two – some supporting slavery, others abolition. Many slaves fled to Ohio from the South, and if you made it over the Ohio River you were free (as long as your owner didn't catch up with you). In 1833, Oberlin College was established as the first coeducational college in the world, admitting black people at a time when slavery was rife. Cleveland is famed as the first American city to have elected a black mayor (Carl B. Stokes) in 1967.

Ohio used to make all sorts of goods that millions of Americans relied on – TV sets, cash registers, steel, bicycles and glass, to name a few. Much of this manufacturing industry has now moved overseas, and unemployment is subsequently high in some areas. However, the state is still an important producer of tires, machinery, steel, tools, automobile components and processed food, along with aerospace and defence products.

The predominantly middle-class society of Ohio holds the virtues of honesty, steadiness, caution and thrift in high regard. In the 2004 elections, Ohio famously was the decider in the Bush–Kerry presidential run. While the East and West of America favoured the Democrats led by Kerry, the Midwest broadly voted for Republican Bush. Ohio was split: the south was conservatively Republican, the north liberally Democratic and middle Ohio was 50:50. After a very close-fought battle and controversial voting procedure, the Republicans triumphed. Of the eight US presidents originating from Ohio, all apart from one have been Republicans.

Local Wildlife

Much of what follows is based on our experiences of living in the Midwest. Depending on where in America you go, this may or may not be relevant (to cover the whole of the US, I would need to write another book). Nevertheless, what follows should provide a small insight into another country's wildlife.

Snakes

While fishing in the pond in our local park, we were treated to the sight of a fellow fisherman grappling with a 2-ft-long water snake, which he had just hooked. He proudly held it up for the kids to see and touch before letting it go at the far end of the pond. This snake was no danger to people and it was all very interesting, but I couldn't help feeling a little uneasy after that.

There are four deadly snakes in America: the copperhead, coral snake, cottonmouth moccasin and rattlesnake. A friend's dog dropped dead for no apparent reason, other than an encounter with a snake. So you are wise to check whether there are any poisonous snakes in your area (see *Useful Websites*). In reality, poisonous snakes are a vastly overrated hazard. You are more likely to be struck by lightning or die from a common bee sting than the bite of a snake. Of the 8000 or so people bitten by venomous snakes in America each year, only 15 at most die.

Snakes are mild mannered, docile and near-sighted. Despite initial worries, they will not rush up to you and start gnawing on your ankle. However, if you purposely handle or aggravate a snake, or if you inadvertently step on or right next to one, this may rattle its cage. Snakes love to sun themselves, so be a little careful where you walk. If you encounter one, just give it some space.

Skunk

The skunk is a member of the weasel family and there are four species of skunk in North America. The most common is the striped skunk. They eat mice, insects, grubs, fruit and carrion. Being primarily nocturnal and having poor vision, many skunk are killed on the roads by passing motorists; but don't, whatever you do, drive over a dead skunk – the smell will follow you around for days. Their musk is a pungent mixture of sulfur and alcohol, is strongly acidic and can cause a burning sensation to the eyes. (Incidentally, skunk urine is used in only the most expensive human perfumes.) Skunk use it in defence and it takes up to a week for a skunk to replenish its limited supply, so it does not spray on a whim. It will give warning signs first – stamping its front feet, hissing and/or growling, before spraying as a last resort. They can accurately spray up to 6 ft, and with the wind in the right direction this spray can cover a distance of 23 ft. So give them a wide berth.

You are very likely to get a whiff during spring, when males perfume the air as they come across real or perceived threats to their safety. They themselves may also get doused in a squirt by irritated females. Dogs often encounter skunks and may pay the inevitable consequences. To destink the dog, experts advise a mixture of 3% hydrogen peroxide (1 quart), ¼ cup of baking soda and 1 tsp of washing-up liquid (to degrease). Tomato juice is another traditional remedy. Failing that, take your problem to the pet parlour.

Groundhogs

Researching groundhogs on the internet, I was bombarded by Groundhog Day trivia, songs and poems, merchandise such as computer screen savers, sunglasses, party gear and even wallpaper. Americans appear to have gone wild cashing in on this strange part of their folklore. (For more about Groundhog Day see Chapter 13.)

In Ohio, after squirrels, groundhogs are the most common wild animal you see around. Weighing in at 2–4 kg, with some apparently reaching 14 kg (30 lb), groundhogs are hefty-looking animals. They defend their burrows and give a vicious bite to any dog silly enough to stick its nose in where it's not wanted. Also known as woodchucks and whistle pigs (down South), they belong to a group of large ground squirrels known as marmots, and are good tree climbers. They can live up to 6 years in the wild. They disappear into hibernation as early as late September, having laid down excessive fat reserves. Following hibernation, they have one litter in April/May. You usually see them in open country and along woodland edges; golf courses are a favourite, where they nonchalantly sit just out of shot of the average driver on the range.

Raccoon

My first sighting of a live raccoon was a bizarre experience. Towards the end of the day, while walking in a quiet spot in our local nature area, I spotted one grazing. The cute face in the tall grass looked just like one of the children's cuddly toys. It stared back at me for a while as we both froze, then carried on about its business, unperturbed. However, you are more likely to encounter raccoon dead than alive. Just as you see badgers and foxes dead on the roadside in Britain, in America raccoon, skunk and opossum are the usual road kill.

They eat virtually anything, including human garbage. They are prone to delving in rubbish skips, with often fatal consequences when they find they cannot climb out; I once found six raccoon dead and bloated in a park skip. Well, at least they died well-fed. They also tend to raid campsites, which we found to our cost. After a restless night being awoken by animal noises, we (or rather Jester) discovered that his dog biscuits had been stolen and the contents of a small bag of rubbish we had left out was now adorning the site. On another camping occasion, Jester began excitedly circling and barking up a tree at what we presumed was a squirrel. Some minutes later, we went over to have a look and discovered a baby raccoon frozen scared on a high branch. There was no way it was going to move while we were there so we all went off for a walk to give it time to disappear.

Raccoon are found almost anywhere in America and are so well adapted to humans that in urban areas they are considered pests. They do not hibernate during winter, but remain inactive for days if the weather is very cold. They are bold and easily identifiable by their bandit faces and stripy tails. Raccoon have no natural predators and populations can easily grow too large. Because they come into domestic areas, can be a nuisance to people and may carry rabies, they are hunted for sport and to control numbers. They were once hunted for their valuable fur, and Davy Crockett famously sported a coon-skin hat.

Chipmunks, Opossums and Squirrels

Busy gathering seeds and nuts and hoarding them away for the cold months, the chipmunk is a common sight in gardens. It has distinctive black and white stripes on its body, is extremely quick and agile, and enjoys cavorting and sunbathing. It has a loud chirping/clucking voice and noisily scolds intruders on its patch. We loved watching these little creatures in our garden, nipping out from under the decking, sitting on the children's garden toys, busily chewing nuts or playing with each other. Despite regularly putting food out, they were very shy and ran away at the first moment they sensed you were there.

The opossum is a strange-looking creature of the night, with a monkey-like tail, hairless ears and feet that resemble tiny hands. They are more often seen dead on the side of the road than alive. When threatened, the opossum gives an impressive act of a dead thing – with its tongue lolling out, eyes closed and completely limp body sprawled on the ground. Oscar material if ever you see it.

Red squirrels are not an endangered species, as they are in Britain. Flying squirrels are also prevalent. We had to call the pest control guy out to rid our loft of critters, as their scurrying was keeping the children awake at night. The traps caught six flying squirrels. These pretty nocturnal creatures are so small they can squeeze through the tiniest hole into your house, and are considered nuisances because of this.

Birds

Hummingbirds overwinter in Central America, then fly 600 miles or so across the Gulf of Mexico and up through Texas, before arriving in more northern states in late April onwards, just as spring wildflowers are ready to give up their nectar. They are the smallest birds in the world, weighing on average less than a copper cent, yet capable of flying as fast as 60 mph. They can beat their wings up to 200 times a second, enabling them to fly forwards, backwards, even sideways, and to hover, like tiny helicopters. Hummingbirds are attracted to bright colours, especially red, and sweet liquid. You can buy specially designed hummingbird feeders. However, because the males (in particular) are territorial and aggressive, you need to keep them apart by providing a couple of feeders (not just one, or they will fight over it). Fill with a sweet mixture of 4 parts water to 1 part sugar boiled for 2–3 minutes, then cooled. Feeders need washing once a week to keep them hygienic.

The dashing *cardinal* is the state bird of Ohio, the scarlet plumage of the males especially striking in winter against the white snow. The *northern blue jay* is well-known in eastern and central parts of the continent. It is a noisy, sassy bird that annoys smaller birds and teases cats. The *American robin* is much larger than our British variety. It is as big as a blackbird, with a red breast (though not as red as our robin) and fairly ubiquitous. It is a member of the thrush family, but homesick pioneers named it a robin. Male *red-winged blackbirds* have bright-red shoulder patches edged with yellow. They are migratory in the North and Appalachians, but permanent residents in the South and West, favouring marshy areas. The *English sparrow* is alive and well throughout the States. However, it is considered a pest owing to its penchant for eating large quantities of grain, and because it aggressively drives other birds from their nesting sites, is dirty and noisy.

Flying in a distinctive V-shaped pattern, *Canada geese* trek south at the end of the summer, having raised their young in the far north – in the Yukon, Canada and northern prairie states. They arrive in North America and take up residence for the autumn and winter wherever they can find a pool of water. In some public parks, border collie dogs are very effectively employed to terrorise the geese and stop them from settling and messing on the grassy areas. It is also not unusual for the traffic to be held up by a dithering flock of geese crossing the road. They make good eating and are easy targets for sportsmen.

Turkey vultures have a wingspan of nearly 6 ft and gregariously flock together. In some states, particularly in the South, they are protected by law because of the valuable job they do in disposing of undesirable carrion and garbage.

Conclusion

According to the Office of Immigration Statistics *Yearbook*, around 10,000 Brits become permanent residents in America each year. In those states without extreme weather, the climate alone is a good enough reason for some people to move here from Britain: you may choose to live in a sunshine state, with summers you can rely on; or if winter, snow and the great outdoors are more your thing, the Mountain states may be your preferred destination. Each state is different and individual, which is what makes travelling and living in America so interesting. Table 3.2 shows the origin of state names. I have included this because it evokes a sense of what the country might have looked like to the natives or first settlers and/or what significance it held for them. The different states also have their own descriptive titles or nicknames (see Table 3.3), and a particular designated bird, animal, fossil, gem stone, insect, tree, flower, etc. is assigned to each state. Often Americans like to use the nickname or symbol of their state; you see it on car plates, in sports team names and in the media. It gives a friendly impression, and denotes a sense of pride and individuality by the citizens of each state.

Table 3.2 Origin of state names (taken from www.infoplease.com, a website encyclopedia published by Pearson Education).

State	Origin of name
Alabama	May come from Choctaw meaning 'thicket-clearers' or 'vegetation-gatherers'
Alaska	Corruption of Aleut word meaning 'great land' or 'that which the sea breaks against'
Arizona	Uncertain. Perhaps from the O'odham Indian word for 'little spring'

Arkansas	From the Quapaw Indians
California	From a book, *Las Sergas de Esplandián*, by Garcia Ordóñez de Montalvo, c. 1500
Colorado	From the Spanish 'ruddy' or 'red'
Connecticut	From an Indian word (Quinnehtukqut) meaning 'beside the long tidal river'
Delaware	From Delaware River and Bay; named in turn for Sir Thomas West, Baron De La Warr
Florida	From the Spanish *Pascua Florida*, meaning 'feast of flowers' (Easter)
Georgia	In honour of George II of England
Hawaii	Uncertain. The islands may have been named by Hawaii Loa, their traditional discoverer. Or they may have been named after Hawaii or Hawaiki, the traditional home of the Polynesians
Idaho	Though popularly believed to be an Indian word, it is an invented name whose meaning is unknown
Illinois	Algonquin for 'tribe of superior men'
Indiana	Meaning 'land of Indians'
Iowa	Probably from an Indian word meaning 'this is the place' or 'the Beautiful Land'
Kansas	From a Sioux word meaning 'people of the south wind'
Kentucky	From an Iroquoian word 'Ken-tah-ten' meaning 'land of tomorrow'
Louisiana	In honour of Louis XIV of France
Maine	First used to distinguish the mainland from the offshore islands. It has been considered a compliment to Henrietta Maria, queen of Charles I of England. She was said to have owned the province of Mayne in France
Maryland	In honour of Henrietta Maria (queen of Charles I)
Massachusetts	From Massachusett tribe of Native Americans, meaning 'at or about the great hill'
Michigan	From Indian word 'Michigana' meaning 'great or large lake'
Minnesota	From a Dakota Indian word meaning 'sky-tinted water'
Mississippi	From an Indian word meaning 'father of waters'
Missouri	Named after the Missouri Indian tribe. 'Missouri' means 'town of the large canoes'
Montana	From the Spanish word 'mountain'
Nebraska	From an Oto Indian word meaning 'flat water'
Nevada	Spanish word for 'snowcapped'
New Hampshire	From the English county of Hampshire

New Jersey	From the Channel Island of Jersey
New Mexico	From Mexico, 'place of Mexitli,' an Aztec god or leader
New York	In honour of the Duke of York
North Carolina	In honour of Charles I
North Dakota	From the Sioux tribe, meaning 'allies'
Ohio	From an Iroquoian word meaning 'great river'
Oklahoma	From two Choctaw Indian words meaning 'red people'
Oregon	Unknown. However, it is generally accepted that the name, first used by Jonathan Carver in 1778, was taken from the writings of Major Robert Rogers, an English army officer
Pennsylvania	In honor of Admiral Sir William Penn, father of William Penn. It means 'Penn's Woodland'
Rhode Island	From the Greek Island of Rhodes
South Carolina	In honour of Charles I
South Dakota	From the Sioux tribe, meaning 'allies'
Tennessee	Of Cherokee origin; the exact meaning is unknown
Texas	From an Indian word meaning 'friends'
Utah	From the Ute tribe, meaning 'people of the mountains'
Vermont	From the French 'vert mont,' meaning 'green mountain'
Virginia	In honour of Elizabeth, the 'Virgin Queen' of England
Washington	In honour of George Washington
West Virginia	In honour of Elizabeth, the 'Virgin Queen' of England
Wisconsin	French corruption of an Indian word whose meaning is disputed
Wyoming	From the Delaware Indian word meaning 'mountains and valleys alternating'; the same as the Wyoming Valley in Pennsylvania

Origin of State Names. Infoplease.
© 2000–2006 Pearson Education, publishing as Infoplease.
3 June 2006 <http://www.infoplease.com/ipa/A0854966.html>.

Table 3.3 State nicknames (taken from www.infoplease.com, a website encyclopedia published by Pearson Education).

State	**Nickname**
Alabama	Yellowhammer State
Alaska	The Last Frontier or Land of the Midnight Sun
Arizona	Grand Canyon State
Arkansas	The Natural State
California	Golden State
Colorado	Centennial State
Connecticut	Constitution State (official, 1959) or Nutmeg State
Delaware	Diamond State, First State or Small Wonder

Florida	Sunshine State (1970)
Georgia	Peach State, Empire State of the South
Hawaii	Aloha State (1959)
Idaho	Gem State
Illinois	Prairie State
Indiana	Hoosier State
Iowa	Hawkeye State
Kansas	Sunflower State or Jayhawk State
Kentucky	Bluegrass State
Louisiana	Pelican State
Maine	Pine Tree State
Maryland	Free State or Old Line State
Massachusetts	Bay State or Old Colony State
Michigan	Wolverine State
Minnesota	North Star State, Gopher State or Land of 10,000 Lakes
Mississippi	Magnolia State
Missouri	Show-me State
Montana	Treasure State
Nebraska	Cornhusker State (1945) or Beef State
Nevada	Sagebrush State, Silver State or Battle Born State
New Hampshire	Granite State
New Jersey	Garden State
New Mexico	Land of Enchantment (1999)
New York	Empire State
North Carolina	Tar Heel State
North Dakota	Sioux State, Flickertail State, Peace Garden State or Rough Rider State
Ohio	Buckeye State
Oklahoma	Sooner State
Oregon	Beaver State
Pennsylvania	Keystone State
Rhode Island	Ocean State
South Carolina	Palmetto State
South Dakota	Mount Rushmore State or Coyote State
Tennessee	Volunteer State
Texas	Lone Star State
Utah	Beehive State
Vermont	Green Mountain State
Virginia	Old Dominion or Mother of Presidents
Washington	Evergreen State
West Virginia	Mountain State

Wisconsin	Badger State
Wyoming	Equality State

State Nicknames. Infoplease.

03 Jun. 2006 <http://www.infoplease.com/ipa/A0854968.html>.

Useful Websites

www.daylight-saving-time.com – daylight saving time.
www.enature.com – National Wildlife Federation; enter a zip code to find the wildlife in your part of the States.
wwp.greenwichmeantime.com – has a good map depicting the time zones of the USA.
www.srh.noaa.gov/data – National Weather Service.
http:/tycho.usno.navy.mil/zones.html – official Time Service Department time zone conversions.
www.usatoday.com – for a countrywide weather report.
www.weather.com – local weather forecast.

4 · Preconceptions and Reality

When asked to describe a typical American, most British people routinely respond with *loud*, *brash*, *fat*, *self-centred*, *friendly*, *easy-going*, *materialistic*, *generous*, *confident* and *proud*. This is based on both general conception and first-hand encounters. It is also, interestingly, how a large number of Americans describe themselves. In many respects the inhabitants of the United States are not like us. Their values and attitudes are different – some eye-poppingly over the top (antics on *The Jerry Springer Show* spring to mind), others traditional and grounded in family or religious morals. Moreover, each state in America has its own unique character. One of our American neighbours (another couple with young children) had recently moved to Ohio from California. Like us, they were finding things very different in their new part of the States. They remarked on the different attitude of Ohioans versus Californians (the former's friendliness), the odd food and of course change in climate. Even for Americans, the various states and regions have very different characters.

It's hard to say what the particular characteristics of any nation are. However, to get an idea of how Americans feel about their own country and their view of Britain, I devised a survey and sent it to a cross section of the community. I did the same for folks back home, to get an idea of their take on America and Americans. Although I sent the survey to roughly the same number of people on both sides of the Atlantic, it was noticeable how poorly the British responded in contrast to the Americans. This in itself I believe says something about the two cultures: one reserved and often suspicious, the other contrastingly open and helpful. In all, 28 Americans and 16 Britons gave me their thoughts on what they believe their trans-Atlantic neighbours are like. There are misconceptions on both sides, and I believe the answers form an interesting picture.

Common Preconceptions

Ask a British person his or her view of Americans and you are likely to get the following answers (all negative, I'm sorry to say):

- loud
- arrogant
- rude
- bombastic
- inward looking
- well-off without realising or appreciating it
- old fashioned
- their imaginations do not extend very far
- not well traveled, even within their own country
- physically an uncomfortable size; a case of big *not* being beautiful
- lacking in curiosity.

Ask Americans their views of their countrymen and women and you (surprisingly) get many of the same responses, though counterbalanced with positive, upbeat comments. Actually the Americans we encountered were on the whole friendly, helpful, welcoming and honest. They have genuine pride in and patriotism for their country, which may appear over-the-top to a more reticent British person, but which is at the same time admirable and refreshing. They are also very enthusiastic and proud of their children and their achievements.

They are fairly classless, and there is little difference in attitude toward the working class and rich. One American surveyed recounted an interesting personal story:

> 'I had an instance where I was waiting in line for a taxi at a rail station in Britain. I had given some space in front of me for two children to play and there were another six or more people behind me. And a lady stepped into the gap. I instructed her that the end of the line was behind the last gentleman. She asked me if in America ladies come first. She also told me that she had a 'title'. I wanted to tell her that in the US we gave people like her titles too, but I didn't think that was too friendly. After she got in her cab, the three British gentlemen behind me apologised and said that not all British people were like her. Now why couldn't they have said something when she was standing there?'

I think this anecdote reveals something about the different cultures.

The same American commented, 'I understand that the British think of us as cowboys. Not that we all ride horses, but that we shoot from the hip and make quick decisions'. This is probably a fairly accurate portrayal of how many British people view Americans. Yet, in a world where America has few allies, Britain has stood beside her, and Americans are eager to thank us for our military help and support in recent years. One American suggested, 'Ninety five percent of the time, Americans and the British are side by side in a world conflict. We may not always see eye to eye on everything or on how things should proceed, but we both want the same outcome'.

Some Personal Observations

From an early age, Americans are taught that anything is possible, and hence have a strong positive mental attitude and outlook on life. Compare this with our British viewpoint, which is often stuffy, grumpy and bemoaning. This aspect of the American character is very obvious in rural areas – less so in the cities. Outside of busy metropolitan areas, Americans appear to be laid back and nothing is too much trouble. I wish more British people were like this. On the flip side of this quintessential 'can-do' attitude, Americans can come across as rather simple in their outlook.

Herman Melville (1819–1891) was a famous American writer and poet. As long ago as the early 1800s, he had this to say: 'Let America first praise mediocrity, even in her children, before she praises...excellence in the children of any other land'. During television coverage of the Olympics, Americans' adoration for their own athletes at the expense of others was very evident. As you listen to the commentators bestowing the virtues of their own competitors and the crowd cheering, you begin to feel a little peeved. The foreign athletes in first or second place are often overshadowed by the patriotic reverence given to any American competitor who came even close to standing on the podium.

Most Americans are reluctant to offend and political correctness is rife. African-Americans call themselves niggers, but it is seen as derogatory if a white person uses the term. The gay fraternity are on the whole fairly nonplussed by the terms 'queer' and 'fag' when used amongst themselves. During Gay Pride Day in San Francisco, a much-heralded annual event, they use terms such as 'Dikes on Bikes', believing it better to use these name tags openly in an effort to reclaim them.

Americans are very concerned with their history (or lack of it). Beavercreek, where we were living, was little more than a scant collection of homes and farms 75 years ago, and had grown dramatically to become the sprawling, sophisticated suburbia it is now. It proudly celebrated its 25th year of being a city the year we arrived. It raises a smile when you see a business advertising that it has been family-owned or in operation for 30 years or so, or farm names with 'Established 1997'. Brits might think 'So what?' We are grounded in history; Americans don't have this, and they feel any and all historic achievements worth proclaiming. As a nation they are hungry for history. The majority of Americans hail from immigrant stock and love to tell you their ancestry. Many have traced their family line, and either aspire to or have already travelled back to their motherland (very often Britain). So they feel they have a link with and foster a certain fondness for 'the old country'. They also love to bring history alive by theatrically re-enacting events, as witnessed by their enthusiasm for renaissance festivals, battle reconstructions, site recreations, dressing up in old clothes and reliving significant events in their history.

Jim also noticed this attitude towards their background and history.

> Being a mass of immigrants, Americans value their original heritage perhaps more than any other nationality. Traditions and rituals are maintained flawlessly and performed with nationalistic pride. It is common, almost without exception, for Americans to describe themselves as something-American to establish the national derivative. It doesn't seem to matter how many generations have passed since the arrival of a family's first ancestors, the tag remains. Indeed, traits or habits are often blamed on the original nationality; this can include baldness, physique, eye colour, bluntness, religion and drinking habits. Interestingly, as Americans' knowledge of the world is poor there is an assumption that nations still act broadly as they did when their ancestors left those countries. Those Americans who do travel to find their roots are often shocked at how progressive their motherlands have become. But while Britain maintains a healthy regard for her history, she is not stuck in the past. Even if a little overdone sometimes, the preservation of traditions by Americans is impressive. However, while Scottish and particularly Irish traditions are common, the celebration of St George's Day is as muted as it is in England.

Americans like to chat about our Royal Family, in particular Princess Diana. On the whole, they view British people as much more refined, elegant, intellectual and clever than their own people. 'We must seem like absolute rubes!', an American friend once said to me. I believe this is partly due to our rather proper English accent, which they love (I wish I had a dime for the number of times I heard the comment, 'I just love your accent'). Also it is probably owing to the terribly dated British sitcoms and comedies shown on American television – the likes of *Upstairs, Downstairs* and *Fawlty Towers.* I guess I do sound a little like Sybil sometimes (apologies to Tim). Most of these shows are more than 20 years old and far from reality TV. Thank goodness Americans are not judging us on the basis of more modern-day British comedies such as *Harry Enfield* (The Slobs, Randy Wobbly Old Ladies, Dim Tim, etc.) and *Little Britain*'s highly dubious characters (Vicky Pollard, Daffyd and Bubbles Devere).

Results of the Surveys

And now to the surveys. Note: questions are shown in italics; below each question, I précis the results.

The American Survey

How well travelled are you outside of the USA? Which countries have you visited?
Less than half had visited Europe. The next most visited places were (unsurprisingly) Canada, the Caribbean and Mexico (with around 25% of respondents citing each of these areas, respectively), followed by Asia and South America. A quarter of respondents had never been outside the US.

Given the choice and inclination to visit Britain, where would you go?
Sixty percent said London, 57% Scotland, 42% Ireland and 14% Wales. Some mentioned the allure of Celtic music, beautiful countryside, laid-back fun and other things Irish. Many said they would like to visit because of family connections, to look up their ancestors. Museums and historic places were favourite attractions.

What if anything puts you off visiting, or even living in, Britain?
The expense of flying there, high cost of everything, awful food and missing American food were high on the list. Family constraints and the long journey were also mentioned. Warm beer, the weather, crummy stores, small hotel rooms, narrow roads, driving on the wrong side of the road and driving too fast were other put-offs.

What do you know about Europe?
Around 20% of respondents said 'Very little'. One commented, 'I know very little of the history – just some World War II type events'. A couple had studied a subject at university that included the history of Europe, or could speak another European language. Others were defensive: 'Most countries despise the US. They are civil, but you are better off pretending to be British than American. Europe is not very receptive to Americans'. Some mentioned the good train system for travelling around; others that Europe is ahead of the US in music and fashion trends. The kings and queens of England (Henry VIII and Elizabeth I in particular), Shakespeare and Irish music also got mentions.

Have you personally met any British people before?
About a quarter of those surveyed had work colleagues, and some had English friends

living in America. Others had family connections. A handful had met British tourists. A few said they had not met any British people before.

If so, what were they like? (please be honest)
Most said the British they had met were easy to get along with, friendly and polite, with a good sense of humour, quick to joke and laugh. Some thought our humour rather dry and sarcastic. Others find us stuffy and stand-offish. They feel we have the same work ethic as most middle-class Americans (i.e. are willing to work hard and get the job done) and that we work well in team situations. As well as being deemed to be more sophisticated and savvy, with a sexy accent, we are – on the whole – kind, generous, helpful and honest. 'They have the same ideas as us, just use different language', commented two Americans. We are also considered to be quiet, clean, well-kept and straight-laced. Conversely, others cited being brash, proud and opinionated as some of our faults. We are much more tolerant of nudity. We do not hug each other and 'no smiles' was another observation.

What preconceptions do you have about the country of Britain?
Approximately 30% of Americans think it rains all the time, that Britain is cold, dreary and foggy. Others mentioned the beautiful pastoral countryside and villages, rich in history and culture, which we respect and preserve. However, we don't know how to make coffee and have bad food, but on the upside have friendly pubs and 'cheeky birds'. Americans think that everyone in Britain loves (indeed is obsessed with) the Queen and Royal Family, who receive constant media coverage. Britain is thought to have less crime and a more liberal society. The British people are more proper and polite (personally I would disagree with the latter) and less preoccupied with looks and other superficial characteristics (though I think we are becoming more American in this respect). You can walk to where you need to go. However, on the downside, our cities are crowded and complicated, and we are less hospitable. Other quotes were:

- 'Britons resent the fact that America became independent of them and dislike the US.'
- 'There are two Britons: Londoners and everyone else. London seems faster and colder in personality; the rest is friendly and a little slower paced.'
- 'People in the south are well educated but can be a bit snobbish; people in the north are miners and less educated but lots of fun.'
- 'People are willing to take on tough duty and bear up cheerfully under stress (reference World War II); but also there is the rebellious, hard, weird, skinny, punk sort of attitude.'

Men in Parliament shouting poppycock, thick brogues and bobbies on bicycles are enduring British characters. One comment was, 'They all walk around wearing suits and ties and rarely dress down, even when working in the garden'. We probably have *To the Manor Born* to blame for that misconception.

On what are these preconceptions based?
Television and movies mostly. Specifically mentioned were British comedies such as *Monty Python, Red Dwarf, Are You Being Served?, Keeping Up Appearances* and *Benny Hill*; also *Braveheart*, broadcasts of Parliament sessions, *The World at War* series, James Bond, and films based on the novels of Jane Austin and Charles Dickens.

Name the four most famous British people you can immediately think of.
Tony Blair and Winston Churchill got the most mentions, followed by the Royal Family (in particular Princess Diana). Margaret Thatcher and the Beatles (notably John Lennon) tied next. Bono, Agatha Christie and James Bond/Sean Connery were other popular characters. Distinguished figures such as Charles Dickens, C.S. Lewis, Sir Arthur Conan Doyle, Shakespeare and George Wells were cited, as well as old royals such as Henry VIII, King George and even Napoleon(!). David Beckham, Simon Cowell and Craig Ferguson are modern-day characters. Twiggy, Queen (the pop group), David Bowie, Sid Vicious, Boy George and Jethro Tull are other famous Brits.

What do you consider are the main differences between the USA and the UK?

- Cars and driving: 'It is easier to drive in the US (less traffic and congestion)...Americans drive everywhere...Our public transportation system is not as developed as it is in Europe.'
- Space: 'I often feel that people who have never visited the US do not understand just how big it really is...We spread out a lot more – our properties and our waistlines!'
- Language differences (including accent).
- Culture and class: 'There's a lot of cultural jealousy that we (Americans) don't talk about. Americans *think* they are cultured, while British people *are*...Where people are educated in Britain is a factor in dividing the classes...In the US we are less reserved, more hedonistic...We are less likely to have visited another country, whereas Brits are more travelled.'
- History: 'The UK is much older than the US and has a greater sense of history and tradition. It values what has come before.'
- Americans are way too materialistic: 'We want to look the best, be the best, have the best...Everything has to be bigger, glitzier and newer...We are much more individualistic and preoccupied with ourselves...We are spoiled.'
- System of government.
- Health care: 'Britain has better, free health care.'
- Standard and cost of living: 'There is a lower standard of living and less debt in the UK.'
- America is an impatient country: 'We are more shortsighted; the UK sees things more long term.'
- Food and drink: 'We drink coffee, you drink tea...Britain is not known for its cuisine' (alas).

What would you say are the typical characteristics of an American?
The majority saw themselves as bold, innovative, go-getters; inventive and adventurous; competitive and passionate. However, they also viewed their average compatriot as loud and opinionated, rather self-absorbed and self-centred: 'We are blind to everything outside our world.' Most are hard-working and career minded; also heavy consumers and materialistic. They feel they are compassionate, generous and straightforward. 'We are quick to stand up and fight (not always a good thing)'; this aggressive nature some attribute to their frontiersmen origins. Surprisingly only three people mentioned that being proud and patriotic are strong American traits (yet I found these characteristics very evident). A couple said Americans are fat and lazy, and wasteful of time and money. Some mentioned blind ambition, shallowness and rudeness as typical characteristics. However, 'We are good people when the chips are down' and '...dreamers – we love the little guy beating the big'.

List what you particularly associate with your country.
More than 30% of respondents cited freedom, patriotism and diversity, respectively, as the main things they associate with their country; also a rosy optimism and the belief that anything is possible. Many mentioned opportunities, the American Dream and a high standard of living. Other associations include:

- Hollywood
- rock and roll
- cars, e.g. Chevrolet
- McDonald's
- baseball
- football (not soccer)
- cowboys
- overindulgence

What are the main problems of America (the country) and American society?
The biggest problem in most people's opinion was crime, in particular too much gun violence. Wealth inequality, the health care system and welfare were other bugbears. Government spending and taxes, corruption and its role in world events were concerns. A poor school system in cities compared to the suburbs, and lack of education for the poor and minorities were considered other negatives. Many Americans felt there was a lack of emphasis on the family and children; that career-minded Americans neglect their children, and there is too much reliance placed on school and television to help raise children. Also failure of marriage and family and high divorce rates were worries. Just trying to make enough money to pay the bills is a problem for many; people live beyond their means; lack ability to think long term; want instant gratification. 'We complain a lot when we have so much to be grateful for.'

Twenty percent mentioned racism, another 20% obesity and too much fast-food.

Drugs, drug-related crime, alcohol and pornography, a complete lack of moral values ('anything goes'), godlessness and diminishing civility were other issues. Pervasive marketing and advertising in society, and the media's influence on the ideas, beliefs and decisions of the American people were worrisome. Others cited:

- sexism;
- traffic jams;
- hurricanes;
- the war in Iraq;
- gas prices;
- a political system that doesn't respond to society's needs/problems (e.g. following the aftermath of Hurricane Katrina).

What are the great things about America?
According to Americans, what is the number-one great thing about America? Aretha Franklin sang it out loud and clear – 'Freedom. Freedom. Freedom!' Virtually every American surveyed gave this as his or her first answer. Next came diversity. After that, there were just a couple of mentions for each of the following:

- compassion;
- a 'can do anything' attitude and entrepreneurial opportunities;
- perseverance of the people, and a desire and capacity to pull together;
- our military;
- ability to take something from other cultures and reinvent it;
- high standard of living.

How important is religion?
Religion is very important (even a cultural necessity) to a surprising number of people – at least, surprising when looking at it from a British viewpoint. Only three out of all the respondents said that it was not very important to them.

What can America offer a British person moving here? (What benefits are there that a Briton does not already enjoy back home?)
You can see the world without leaving the country because of the diversity of geography, climate and cultures. America is a beautiful country to travel through. Americans enjoy more disposable income, have larger homes, bigger cars, enjoy better and more diverse food, with a large choice of ethnic restaurants, and all types of entertainment. Cold beer was another benefit cited. Hospitality and enthusiasm are other factors that are not as strong in Britain. 'In America, you have the chance to be stupid without standing out', said one survey respondent (I guess that's a relief).

The British Survey

In order to form an idea of how the average British person views life 'on the other side', I sent the following questions out. The survey was given to people visiting, moving to and already living in America.

What were your thoughts about the country of America before you arrived?
Most expected America to be large, overwhelming and spread out, with great diversity in all things; also lacking in community, rather impersonal and mainstream focused. Some mentioned great geography, good travelling and other opportunities. They expected America to be very clean and well-kept, with abundant good food, overcommercialised, quick-paced and most places nearly new. A lack of depth and finesse, with most impressive places typified by pure extravagance, were other preconceptions.

What were your thoughts about Americans before you arrived and/or after arriving?
One respondent commented that America's great ethnic diversity means it is nigh on impossible to define a typical American. Nearly all respondents, however, view Americans as insular/not worldly aware, despite some having travelled extensively; they are knowledgeable within their specific field but not outside of that, and stovepiped (not good at appreciating the bigger picture). Another observation was their relaxed, casual approach and helpful manner; they are seen as outgoing, with a strong positive outlook. This can also make them come across as loud and brash; they have an annoying habit of 'bar shouting', indeed being loud almost everywhere with complete disregard for others. They are liable to upset the locals when they are overseas, being overconfident and opinionated. They need to be seen as top dog. Nationalistic and fiercely patriotic, they are fed a filtered history that supports the 'America is Great' philosophy, leading to a superior attitude. They treasure their relatively short history.

A number of Brits commented that they are hard working, with a strong sense of purpose; they believe they can attain their dreams and are confident and self-assured. They respond well to success, but are easily deterred by failure and criticism; achievement is easier as the challenges they face are not as hard as those faced by people elsewhere. They are generally very tolerant of those who fail.

About 25% of respondents felt that Americans are overly image conscious (especially young girls) and superficial. 'I expected people would tend to be extreme, i.e. very fat or very thin' was a comment expressed by more than one person. Americans appear to be rich, e.g. with the latest camera hanging round their necks, but are far less concerned with status. It was remarked that they are often badly dressed. They are generous and genuine, and often desperate to be liked. Some felt Americans are difficult to get to know, and do not readily invite you into their lives. They are deemed to have a limited sense of humour.

What were your first impressions on arriving in America?
About 30% of Brits mentioned the big, boring roads, slow driving speed and slower pace of life. Also that there is so much space – 'from the air, the vastness of the coun-

try stretches out forever'. Some mentioned the interesting, attractive, well-kept homes and buildings, the fact that the American flag is flying everywhere – a nice welcome to America. Others noted the poor driving skills (e.g. not using indicators), the heat and humidity, and huge meal portions.

What were the biggest problems you encountered on first arriving?
Most people found the huge amount of administration and frustrations dealing with bureaucracy a big problem; also having to make decisions quickly without being able to fully consider and understand all the options. Understanding and navigating the road system was another issue. Children's schooling was a worry, because American schools are a year behind. Some military colleagues felt that British Embassy support could be better.

List what you particularly dislike about living in America
Having to drive everywhere takes some getting used to; no-one walks much and you are thought of as strange if you do. Also American drivers can be sloppy and lack consideration for other car users. Shop assistants tend to be rather dense and slow. Goods, etc. are sold exclusive of sales tax, and this addition of tax comes as a surprise. Commercial breaks on television were another irritation. The lack of individuality (the sameness of restaurants, hotels and such like) and good dark beer were other gripes.

What are the great things about America overall?
Most Britons commented that it is refreshing to find that children are welcome and catered for everywhere. Americans love good and plentiful food; restaurant service is usually excellent; there are easy and inexpensive facilities everywhere; and the quality and variety of food available in supermarkets is very good. The people are helpful and friendly; they speak to you, e.g. in queues. Shop assistants have a good attitude, rather than the 'I'm doing you a favour' routine you get in Britain. They are very customer focused in the service industry. You get a lot for your money (e.g. accommodation, cars, fun). There are endless shopping opportunities; garage sales are an absolute bargain. Other great things about America are:

- the entertainment possibilities;
- the changing seasons (more extreme than in Britain);
- little petty crime; the average American is law-abiding and much more honest, e.g. regarding pilfering;
- cleanliness;
- all the different cultures;
- good radio service;
- uncrowdedness, especially in state parks and the countryside generally;
- Americans are much more community focused (kids, sports, clubs, neighbours), and are proud of their culture and community;

- America has its own unique traditions, which the people fiercely uphold.

What are the main problems in American society? What if any concerns do you have?
Americans have a poor appreciation of the rest of the world and are ill-informed; they see the world with America in the middle and everywhere else lumped as 'foreign'. This lack of exposure to the international community results in naivety about how their good intents are perceived by others. The States is a wasteful society and there is less recycling; America has a lack of environmental care for the world outside the US, e.g. refusing to accept global warming is very short-sighted. Education levels of the average American seem low in comparison to Britain. Wealth inequality is another problem. Obesity and the effect on future generations was expressed as a concern by several respondents; also violence, and the fact that obtaining weapons is too easy. Overcommercialisation, e.g. of Christmas, was mentioned. Some found America over-regimented and prescriptive, with the religious right wing far too extremist. There is still strong colour prejudice. Also social security is a problem area, and health care is very expensive and not available to all.

What do you consider are the main differences (besides those described above) between the USA and the UK?
In America it is less of a structured, class-orientated society than Britain. Americans have respect for those who have achieved something, rather than for what you were born with; they do not feel limited by their background, whereas in the UK, people are seen as having ideas above their station. Americans have higher (often unrealistic) expectations and a much more positive attitude. They expect and need praise and require reinforcement (positive stroking). They have pro-active programmes for their children; the whole family gets involved, helps out, cheers on. People are more relaxed, happier, less grumpy and outwardly stressed. Americans are more willing to try something new.

On the whole, people dress smarter in Britain, but people with any wealth flaunt it: 'In the US, you can be worth a million dollars yet look like a slob and/or act like a down-to-earth person', said one respondent. 'Brits are definitely more reserved, but I think more sincere', commented another. The politeness of servers in American shops and restaurants is very noticeable and also that of teenagers. Religious commitment and open patriotism were also remarked upon. American news channels are very much US-based, with very little in the way of 'outside' interviews and stories; the British are more in-tune internationally. 'In the UK we are lucky to be able to travel to different places in a relatively short time – the States in comparison is huge.'

What can America offer a British person moving here? (What benefits are there that a Briton does not already enjoy back home?)
The majority cited greater opportunities and better facilities for sport, hobbies, shopping, etc.; also a better quality of life, cheap living and travel options – 'Our railways,

motorways and A roads are so clogged in comparison'. Next came America's national parks, good reliable weather, wide-open country and big cities (New York, etc.). The music and film industry were mentioned, together with theme parks.

Conclusion

> 'America lives in the heart of every man everywhere who wishes to find a region where he will be free to work out his destiny as he chooses.' Woodrow Wilson (1856–1924, President, and holder of the Nobel Peace Prize 1919)

This quote epitomises how Americans view their country, and the underlying ethos of the nation. It also tells us how important Americans feel their country is to everyone else – perhaps a rather overrated impression? Their limited world awareness adds to this somewhat unbalanced view of their own importance.

Americans have always been an optimistic and entrepreneurial lot, proud of their country and freedoms. On the surface, outside of their world, they often appear overly bold and brash, possibly due to underconfidence; and, as they indeed suspect, other nations view them somewhat disparagingly. I find this attitude towards them rather sad and cynical – sometimes more of a reflection on the person bemoaning them; why not look at their good characteristics, which I believe outweigh the adverse? Having had the wonderful opportunity to live in America, I hope we will take some of these characteristics back home with us – in particular their enthusiasm, openness, politeness and friendliness, and easy-going attitude. I believe we could use a lot more of this in Britain.

5 · Our New Country

Most Americans have not ventured far from the safety of their homeland, though many express a desire to visit other countries. In my survey (see Chapter 4), I asked the question *How well travelled are you outside of the USA?* A quarter of respondents had never been outside the US and less than half had visited Europe. In the Spielberg film *The War of the Worlds* (starring Tom Cruise), our hero, Ray, is speeding away from his first sighting of the machines that have come to take over the world, speechless and stunned by what he has just seen. His son Robbie is asking questions:

Robbie:	What is it?
Ray (aka Tom Cruise):	This came from someplace else.
Robbie:	What? Do you mean like Europe?
Ray:	No, Robbie. Not like Europe.

Steven Spielberg's joke is an appropriate one. Americans talk of 'London, England' and 'Paris, France', which sounds a little unnecessary to those of us who live in Europe and use the names without confusion. It was amusing to ask people where they thought we were from when they commented on our English accents. The majority said Australia. The most eye-raising response of all was, 'Gee, are you from Europe?' Thus 'Europe' seems to cover a multitude of unknowns.

Dave Barry (writer, humorist and winner of the Pulitzer Prize for commentary) has this to say about the reluctance of Americans to leave home:

> 'Americans who travel abroad for the first time are often shocked to discover that, despite all the progress that has been made in the last 30 years, many foreign people still speak in foreign languages.'

Owing to the huge diversity within their own country, the great variety of places, cultures and indeed climates just within North America, there is no real need to travel 9 hours or more on a plane for some lousy weather and bad food (in the case of Britain) and often rude foreign hospitality (in the case of many European countries). Why bother? Other countries can seem inhospitable, with language barriers and cultural differences often at odds with the States. This is one reason why many Americans are rather insular and prefer to stay at home. If they do travel overseas, it is often en masse; they seem to be more comfortable in groups. In fact, Erica Jong (American author and educator) stated that 'Solitude is un-American'.

The rest of the world does indeed seem rather a long way away, and infrequently touches people's lives in America. Often times I was asked to explain the structure of the UK and/or Great Britain, i.e. the relationship between England, Scotland, Wales and Northern Ireland, and how the European Community works. While Britain has close ties with and obligations to other countries in Western Europe, America is an independent nation and is really only concerned with itself and its citizens (on a general level). As one American friend put it, 'We don't have many neighbours'. Moreover, American politicians rely less on international organisations, such as the United Nations, in their 'War on Terrorism', and act more on their own, which has resulted in hostility and tensions between America and other countries around the world.

The following conversation Tim had with a young Japanese-American doctor illustrates the point that many Americans have rather a limited and blinkered view of world history too. It went something like this:

Doctor: So, you're in the military?
Tim: Yes, the British Air Force.
Doctor: Don't you guys have mandatory service?
Tim: No, not anymore. Conscription ended after the War.
(Blank look on doctor's face)
Doctor: So it changes quite regularly then?
Tim: No, not since the War.
(Doctor still looking blank)
Doctor: Do you mean the first or second Gulf War?
Tim: No, the Second World War.

Jim adds that:

> The average American's knowledge of geography is not bad, it's dreadful. A friend once drew the world according to an American in a comical fashion, with a large USA in the centre and small satellite countries floating around it. In addition to several 'ere be dragons' warnings, the map also identified Britain as the 'Olde World Theme Park'. It didn't seem possible that this was anything more than comical exaggeration, but the truth is alarmingly close. For a world in which Americans represent just one-eighteenth of the population, they have an inflated view of their impact upon it. Israel attacked Hezbollah in Lebanon in the middle of 2006 and this was the immediate headline on all news channels. Not 24 hours had passed before the stories started to slant to what this meant for America, primarily in terms of the rising cost of oil. That aspect

became the predominant feature and seemingly the reason for American involvement in brokering peace. Not only is the knowledge of the world outside America poor (the fact that approximately 65% of Americans do not own a passport is testament to this), but also there is a widespread assumption that everything America does is best. Certainly in many areas there is evidence to support this advantage, but it is not universal. For example, development of US cars has slowed in comparison with other countries to the point where the quality of Japanese rip-offs of stalwart American styles such as trucks make them much more attractive. American car-producing plants are closing and being replaced by onshore plants of Japanese companies, and this is the land where the automobile rules.

A Growing Population

Currently over 300 million people live in the United States. The net population increase is around 8500 every day (taking into account births, deaths, immigration and emigration) – equivalent to an additional 3 million or so new inhabitants every year; compare this with just 200,000 per annum in the UK. This represents one birth every 8 seconds, one death every 12 seconds and one new immigrant every 25 seconds. Thus there is a net gain of one new American every 12 seconds. America has a very volatile and young working population, with large numbers of immigrants crossing her borders every day. There has been a long-standing trend towards expansion of the population in the South and West, mainly from new immigrants. According to the 2000 Census, 1 in 5 Americans is foreign-born or a child of foreign-born parents. Los Angeles has the greatest number of foreign-born people in the country (mostly from Mexico), Miami comes second (with a Latin American – mostly Cuban – demography), and New York City third (though NY is uniquely diverse). America is still very much the land of opportunity for newcomers. 'No country is home to more foreigners than the United States', wrote Sam Roberts (editor, reporter and columnist for *The New York Times*, in his book *Who We Are Now*).

Among the industrialised nations, America stands out as the only one with such rapid population growth; most other nations are shrinking in this respect, with fewer new births. Hispanic people and blacks on average have a higher birth rate than whites, which accounts for part of the trend. Some see this population growth as an advantage America has over other countries, through greater economic and cultural power, because it makes for a more innovative workplace, generating more tax revenue, with a younger population who can take care of itself and its elderly.

> 'The contrast between youthful, exuberant, multicolored America and aging, decrepit, inward-looking Europe goes back almost to the foundation of the United States.' (*The Economist*, 27 August 2002)

While Europe is losing population, America is gaining. However, although the States has a large and growing population, it is spread out. The average number of people per square mile is just less than 80 – Japan has 835 people/sq mile, Germany 609, China 361, and England and Wales approximately 132. Table 4.1 shows some population figures taken from US Census data 2000. Among the states of America, Alaska has the smallest population density with just 1.1 people/sq mile. Contrastingly, Manhattan has 65,000 (1.5 million people squeezed into 23 sq miles).

Table 4.1 Population criteria (taken from the US Census 2000).

Population density	**People/sq mile**
North-East	330
South	115
Midwest	86
West	36
Average nationwide	79.6

Most heavily populated states (> 200 people/sq mile)	**Least heavily populated states (< 10 people/sq mile)**
Connecticut	South Dakota
Maryland	North Dakota
New York	Montana
Delaware	Wyoming
Florida	Alaska
Ohio	
Pennsylvania	
Illinois	
California	

Ten largest cities (in order of size of population)	**Cities with highest density of population**
New York	New York City
Los Angeles	San Francisco
Chicago	Chicago
Houston	Boston
Philadelphia	Philadelphia
Phoenix	Miami
San Diego	Los Angeles
Dallas	
San Antonio	
Detroit	

There are downsides to this rapid growth. Consumption of natural resources, sprawling towns and infrastructure, traffic jams and problems over border control are negative issues and consequences. However, some believe that it is prosperity that puts more pressure on resources than mere population growth – the rich use more water, energy and resources than the poor.

Different Attitudes

According to my experience, US citizens are more conservative than British (certainly I found this to be true in the Midwest and rural areas). Another English mother of an 8-year-old girl was warned about the perils of the girl taking her wet bikini top off in public. This appears to sexualize children as young as eight. Many public beaches provide changing rooms and expect you to use them. It goes without saying that topless sunbathing is basically taboo.

Watch groups monitor the media closely, on the look-out for potentially offensive instances of nudity and the use of swear words. In 2004 Janet Jackson caused a bit of a ruckus when she suffered what the media termed 'a wardrobe malfunction'. During her duet with Justin Timberlake in the Super Bowl halftime show, her right breast was exposed (albeit with a nipple shield still intact), and this sparked media controversy and uproar. J.J. was asked to make a public apology to the American public, and CBS paid a hefty fine. Congress raised the fine rate afterwards, and the incident ignited a new wave of protectiveness. Watching a clip on *America's Favourite Home Videos*, I was bemused to see a naked Barbie doll's private parts had been blotted out. Such attitudes seem overtly prudish and old-fashioned.

This character trait perhaps stems from those early Puritan settlers, who lived according to close-knit rules, in strict communities, where conformity with your group was considered of paramount importance. In addition, the hard-working, independent farming family shaped the basis of the American character. Show up at work, be on time, be responsible with money, work hard – these are core American values. However, concerning issues of morality, private and public attitudes are often confused. Americans can be both conservative and liberal – with hypocritical, lofty ideals versus reality. They like to conserve outward appearances, frowning upon changing a baby's nappy in public and men mowing the lawn with their shirts off, while some of their most popular female singers (Madonna and Cher spring to mind) parade around on stage in overtly sexual costumes. They dub potentially offensive words on television and in music, but blatantly advertise adult sex stores along many highways.

Despite this paradox, Americans can be very modern in their attitudes. Back in the 1960s, US culture took on the mantra of postmodernism, whereby what you *feel* is more important than what is in your head. The rather egocentric and wishful thinking of postmodernism fits the American culture well. The same is also true of the way things are going in Britain, but I feel we have a firmer grounding and slightly more realistic perspective on things. Gene Edward Veith Jr. (Culture Editor of *WORLD Magazine* and author of *Postmodern Times*) wrote:

> 'Postmodern religions do not require evidence of plausibility – liking something and wanting it to be true are the only criteria for their belief'.

Thus the statement 'chocolate is good for you' is something a postmodernist might say; you find what appeals to you and follow that. This is akin to the philosophy of Kabala (or Cabala), practised by Madonna, Ethan Hawke and Sir Ian McKellen (to name a few). I see postmodernist thinking as at the core of American life. With the power of mass-media and globalism, this ethic is spreading throughout the world, even to countries with deeply embedded traditional cultures; people there are dying to become American. Where America leads, others will follow.

My step-father, visiting us in the States, commented that Americans seem to *need* to present a materially orientated sense of order, as in a story book – that is, lacking reality. I know what he means. Americans love to dream and shape their lives beyond their reality – one reason for the high level of debt in American society (credit cards, school loans, mortgages, car loans, leasing, etc.). In our neck of the woods (southwest Ohio) I noticed how peculiarly law-abiding and openly patriotic the people are, and how (often frighteningly) neat and orderly they keep their homes, offices, countryside and other infrastructure. Planned communities are popular, with home-owners' associations imposing restrictive covenants, fees and fines on property owners in order to preserve the community feel of the town or development. Celebration near Disney World in Florida is one example, developed by the Walt Disney Company. Seaside, also in Florida, is another (incidentally, used for the filming of *The Truman Show*). The pristine, neutrally coloured homes are built close together, there are pavements to encourage walking, shops and businesses are located in a downtown area not far away, which is also the hub of community events, and many people use scooters or neighbourhood electric vehicles to get about. There are strict rules concerning how things should appear, including the style of house numbers, exterior paint colours, lawn furniture, lawn maintenance and what vehicles you are allowed to park out front. Chapter 10 on American homes goes into this more.

Moreover, Jim observes what he calls 'partioning' in American society:

> Life in the US is extremely partitioned. Activities must be conducted at the correct place with the exact equipment, clothing and style. Roads are for the exclusive use of cars driven by disinterested and slightly bored people immune from the consequences of poor judgement. Parking lots definitely fall into this idea of partioning; every establishment has its own. Even churches have exclusive car parks to accommodate cars for every seat in the church, even though the full capacity may only be used once a week. There is yet no limit in the provi-

sion of parking. It would be interesting to compare the number of parking spaces, miles of road, driving population and number of cars, either specific to a particular catchment area or even nationally. It would probably show an enormous untapped opportunity for greater use and efficiency. Stadiums are another case in point; for example, the Bengals Stadium in Cincinnati is used 11 times a year and is never used for anything other than Bengals games. Of course, financially this works as all those games are sold out. Nevertheless, does it make sense to have such an expensive and capable facility used so seldom?

Government and Politics

As politics is close to most Americans' hearts, a potted history and summary might help you converse on this subject.

History

Following the end of the Revolutionary War in 1783 and the cutting of ties with Britain, the then 13 states formed a confederation, with a written constitution known as the *Articles of Confederation*. A central government was formed, with specific powers to:

- mint coins (but not paper money) and borrow money;
- operate post offices;
- act on the country's behalf when dealing with foreign countries and signing treaties;
- declare war or peace.

This national government did not have as much clout as the individual state governments. As a representative and elective government, it put individual liberty above all else and constrained its leaders, by dividing up their power and operating a system of checks and balances in the form of the three branches of government – Congress, the President and the Supreme Court. Delegates from each state voted on major laws, which were passed if 9 of the 13 states agreed. This unusual system of government was a radical break from the normal governing structures of the time, which were based on monarchy.

Weaknesses in the Articles of Confederation resulted in their replacement with the *United States Constitution*. This document, ratified in 1789, forms the basis of America's whole system of government, politics and law today and divides federal (national) government into three departments: the Executive, Legislative and Judicial branches. In this way, each department acts as a watchdog over the others. However, the Constitution does not prescribe the form of government to be used by the states, which decide that for themselves.

Three years after the Constitution was ratified, following public unease over the powers of such a strong central government, with many fearing that their liberty would be curtailed, the *Bill of Rights* was added. This consists of amendments or additions to the Constitution and guarantees certain basic liberties, such as freedom of the press, religion and speech. The Bill of Rights is a dynamic document. 'Today we are still discussing what could be added, or taken away', commented one American friend.

The Division of Power

As discussed above, the government is organised into three branches:

(1) Executive
(2) Legislative, and
(3) Judicial.

The President heads the *Executive* branch of the government. He is head of state (like the Queen), head of government (like the Prime Minister) and also Commander-in-Chief (in charge of the military). The President appoints all the cabinet officers and many other offices within the Department of State, subject to Senate approval. Presidential elections are held in November, with inauguration in February. Two terms of 4 years each is the most anyone is permitted to serve as President.

The *Legislative* branch is Congress, which makes the laws. Congress is made up of the Senate and the House of Representatives, with two senators chosen by state legislatures from each state, and with House members elected directly by the people. Thus the Senate is somewhat akin to our House of Lords, and the House of Representatives to our House of Commons. Senators are elected for 6 years, Representatives for 2 years. Congress debates a new law (or bill) and if the majority of members approve it, it goes to the President. He either signs it and it becomes law, or vetoes it. The Legislative department can override this veto if two-thirds of Congress votes against it. It can also remove a president from office if he/she has committed a serious misdemeanour; this is known as impeachment.

The *Judicial* branch comprises a federal court system headed by the Supreme Court. The latter has nine members who are appointed for life, and rule on matters that relate to the Constitution. It has the power to give new interpretations to the Constitution, including those related to civil rights. The Judicial department reviews laws and may declare a law void if it believes the law violates the Constitution. Each state has its own unique legal system (which is why the death penalty for murder is enforced in some states but not in others), and all but one (Louisiana) is based on English common law.

The Political Scene

In one sense, the United States is rather like the countries of Europe; the diverse nature and separateness of the individual states creates many problems. There are differences between the federal and state structure of governing, each state having its own rules and regulations that differ from one state to the next. Moreover, each state is divided into counties, with *their* own powers, including setting the tax level payable in that county. The bureaucrats in Washington, DC, are likened to those in Brussels; they are viewed with suspicion and perceived to be lacking in understanding of the diverse lives of people in other states. That goes for the state politicians too, usually.

Despite the end of the Civil War, relics of unrest are still evident in the South, where many people feel that state rights should come before federal. The Dixie flag is still flying. This, together with the current debate concerning immigration, is one area where the States is not united. Up until fairly recently, there was generally solidarity of attitude and a somewhat blinkered patriotism, with people afraid to stand out as individuals for fear of being seen as unpatriotic. However, more often these days you hear people bemoaning their leaders. This is partly the result of greater media attention and changes in attitude. 'Our country is being led by a chimp; Blair seems more competent', commented one American. Another felt that 'Our two-party political system is driven by money'. The general American populace is becoming more suspicious and doubting of their leaders' abilities and intents.

The Two Main Parties

There are two main political parties – the Democrats and Republicans – and another two smaller and rarely mentioned parties – the Greens and Libertarians. Broadly, Democrats are idealists, favouring big government doing more things for the people (usually involving higher taxes) and looking at more short-term issues and problems (JFK was a Democratic president). Republicans are realists, preferring to take a long-term view and planning accordingly, favouring a tight-run, less bureaucratic government and fewer taxes (George Bush and Ronald Reagan are/were Republicans). The Republican Party is known as the Grand Old Party (abbreviated to GOP in many newspaper headlines).

During presidential runs, fundraising promotions are very much a part of the campaign. However, $4600 is the most the law will allow any individual to give to a single candidate. The news is hijacked by politics, with bickering between the two parties. Increasingly, the fight for power produces charges of corruption, spats over candidates' past conduct and innuendos concerning ethical and/or sexual persuasion. Senate and presidential races are often harshly personal.

Americans do not trust politicians any more than we do, and there is not much middle ground: 'I feel we are living under a dysfunctional democracy; we aren't participating in it and are not represented', one American surveyed said. Especially after the 2000 election, many view the electoral system (see below) as corrupt, and their leaders as marketing and money-orientated, self-interested and untrustworthy. A large number of Americans surveyed did not wish to identify with either side or simply felt confused by all the political jostling: 'I feel that neither the Democrats nor the Republicans offer something good anymore and see no sign of recovery yet'. As in Britain, to a large extent the economy affects how people vote at election time. Thus if the economy is strong, people will usually vote for the 'in' party. The question is 'How am I doing?'. If the answer is 'Fine', then there is no need to change things.

Lately there has been an increase in the importance of religion and politics; many people vote for a candidate or party according to their religious leanings. The Pew Research Center survey found that in the 2004 election, 71% of white voters who attended church at least once a week voted Republican. The Republican party also appeals more to the 'middle income and above' bracket. Interestingly, states that consume the most wine are more likely to have more liberal politics and social attitudes.

The Electoral System

The presidential electoral system is unique and complicated, and I will do my best to explain it. The President and Vice President are elected by the Electoral College – a group of electors chosen every 4 years to cast the electoral vote. The larger the state in terms of population, the more electoral votes and House of Representative seats that state commands. For example, according to the 2005 American Community Survey, the four most densely populated states – California, Texas, New York and Florida (in that order) – each have 55, 34, 31 and 27 electoral votes respectively. The four smallest states – Wyoming, Vermont, North Dakota and Alaska – have only three electoral votes each. The number of votes each state is allotted is based on the combined total of US senators and representatives that state has in Congress.

As a presidential candidate, you need at least 270 electoral votes to win (out of the 538 electoral votes available, divided among the 50 states and the District of Columbia). The electors are entrusted to follow the majority of their state's voter opinion when casting their vote, although in most states they are not required to do so. The large states are considered 'safe states' for one party or another and will be largely ignored by candidates touting for popularity. Small states with a small number of electoral votes will similarly be ignored as of little consequence in terms of adding up the numbers. Instead, candidates will concentrate their efforts on winning the 'swing states' – in particular Florida, Ohio and Pennsylvania.

Employing the electoral system of voting often means that the voting is off kilter. This was demonstrated in the 2000 election when Al Gore gained more individual votes in Ohio and thus held the popular vote, yet Bush won Ohio's electoral votes. Gore won the popular vote by about 500,000 votes, yet still lost the election. This is because each county in a state holds a certain percentage of the electoral votes for that state. Thus in any one county, if the popular vote for one candidate is 2 million and for another it is 1 million, the former candidate wins the county's popular vote and this is worth a certain percentage of the state's overall electoral vote. When all the percentages are added up, this might give a surprising result to who wins that state's electoral votes. A system based on adding up all the individual votes (popular votes) may give a different outcome in a close-run race. However, under the federal system of voting, the nationwide popular vote has no legal significance.

Voting in a leader using the Electoral College system is designed to prevent elections being won based solely on a heavy concentration of votes in a few areas. It thus avoids the sectionalism that is a problem in other geographically large nations such as the Soviet Union, China and India, and as was the case with the Roman Empire. It spreads the deciding factor so that one state does not have more say in who becomes President simply because it has a higher population density and those people voted in favour of a particular party/candidate. The Electoral College, instituted by the Founding Fathers of America, was and still is designed to safeguard against the nation's government leaders being chosen wholly by its citizens – the majority of whom are common people and thus not necessarily that well-informed politically.

Most Americans admit to not really understanding the Electoral College system and there is a big debate each election time as to whether to continue with it. America works on a democratic system, which needs an informed democracy to work – people need to know what they are voting for and why. Information available to the average citizen is unbalanced; the media distorts and overplays things, while the internet, although a boon in many ways, allows you to *choose* what you want to read. Furthermore, prosperity often breeds isolationism and a lack of concern for community issues; as people grow wealthier, they are often distracted from the political system and don't bother themselves with the issues of the day. In a recent survey, America ranked 139th out of 172 nations in the percentage of citizens of voting-age who turned out to cast a ballot in their country's elections. In the 2004 presidential election, only 64% of voters bothered to vote.

Patriotism and the Military

The Manifest Destiny was an early notion that Americans had a mission to expand and spread freedom and democracy; there was also an element of belief in Anglo-Saxon superiority. This idea still lives on today, with America's desire to use its military to spread and defend Western-style democracy. As one American put it, 'We try to police the world'. America has more forces stationed abroad than any other nation and spends nearly as much on its military than all the other nations put together. Americans are enthusiastic idealists with somewhat unrealistic expectations. Historical events are not necessarily portrayed accurately (in movies, on television, etc.) and often have a romantic bias, so how can you blame them? Memorials celebrate war and glorify human sacrifice rather than pitying it. As Mary McCarthy (American author and critic) in her book *On the Contrary* (1961) put it, 'The happy ending is our national belief'.

Americans are immensely proud of their country. They treat their military with reverence, George Bush declaring that, 'There is no higher calling than service in our armed forces'. Military-style hair cuts or buzz cuts are a very popular style for male Americans (though not so much on the West Coast). Servicemen travelling in full uniform have their hands shaken by members of the public, in support of their efforts in Iraq. Many airports have special USO (United States Organizations) lounges for servicemen and women and their families, where they can relax, watch TV, use the internet or make phone calls.

However, it has not always been like this. Back in the 1970s, Vietnam vets were largely ignored or else negatively stereotyped. Anti-war protesters spat on soldiers in airports, branding them as baby killers and walking time-bombs. Protesters felt that if you participated in the War, you were responsible for it, and support for the military was at an all-time low. The baby boomers represented a massive number of young people, who grouped together and rebelled against their parents' blind trust in the government, the failure of the War itself, and its effects economically and socially. People burnt their draft cards or absconded to Canada in defiance. The draft system hit the underprivileged in particular, which is why a huge proportion of the soldiers sent to Vietnam were black.

This appallingly poor attitude of the American populace towards soldiers in the Vietnam War has been recognised, and today war veterans receive respect and sympathy. Americans have learnt not to vent their disgruntlement on servicemen and women but on their government. There has been a change in attitude, and the military now receives impressive public support and enthusiasm. The organisation VFW (Veterans of Foreign Wars of the United States) is a prominent organisation. (Incidentally, 'veterans' is a term used for anyone who is ex-military.) There may be a hall near you where local, sympathetic people meet and provide help to military veterans in the community. They also actively campaign for donations. There is even a website that lists recently discharged veterans and their families who are seeking employment. Both veterans and active-duty members enjoy special rates at hotels, free entrance to public places such as local fairs and aquariums, discounted ski passes, etc. Veterans can still use the medical, sporting, social and other facilities on military bases, even though they have been discharged; indeed, many of them choose to retire and live close to a base just so they can take advantage of these valuable, free perks. If you are in the services (regardless of which country), always ask whether there is a military or government discount; you'll be surprised how often there is.

The US military is a voluntary vocation, with programmes to attract people to sign up, such as the opportunity to earn money towards college, as well as the lure of free medical facilities and other incentives (as mentioned above). According to the CIA's *World Factbook* (2005), the States has nearly 1.1 million men and women fit for military service. There are currently more women than men serving, and a disproportionate number of blacks. The US military was one of the first institutions to confront racism and segregation, and recently sexual discrimination. Job changes within the military tend to occur in the summer; suddenly everyone is moving and there is a flurry of house renting and buying. This must be costing the country a small fortune, as people are kept in post until it is convenient for them as a family to be moved (usually when the children start summer break).

The Midwest and South have a large number of military personnel, both serving and ex. Thus these parts of the country tend to be more openly patriotic than other regions. Each morning and evening, as the flag is raised on bases across the country, the American national anthem blares out, traffic stops and everyone observes a patriotic moment. In military cinemas, the national anthem may be played before the start of each film. Patriotism is a very obvious and important part of American life. The Iraq War has sparked an increase in public displays of patriotism and support for the military, with car stickers declaring 'I Support Our Troops But Not Our President' and licence plates proclaiming 'Support Our Veterans' or simply 'Support America'. Another revival in nationalism occurred after 9/11, with stickers announcing 'Proud to Be American'. Sport a sticker on your car in the UK saying 'Proud to Be British' and you risk having it scratched by some anti-establishment hoodlum.

Despite the country spending almost twice the amount Britain does on her military (in terms of percentage GDP), the American military machine is not as vast today as it was in Reagan's time. In my survey, one American felt that, 'We are spreading ourselves too thin militarily and skimping on our support of our fighting men and women'.

Icons of the United States

The American Flag or 'Old Glory' and Dixie Flag

When the Declaration of Independence was approved by the Continental Congress, the new republic needed a distinctly American flag. In 1777, Congress chose a flag of 13 stripes representing the original 13 states, and 13 stars representing a new constellation. Later it was declared that one star could be added for every new state that became part of the United States; the number of stripes remained at 13.

Americans fly their flag whenever and wherever, especially on patriotic holidays such as Independence Day, Veterans Day, Armed Forces Day and Memorial Day (when it is displayed at half-staff until noon and then fully raised); there is even a national Flag Day (on 14 June). In fact, Old Glory is proudly displayed outside many homes, businesses and offices and in other public places all year round. There is a Federal Flag Code that should be adhered to, which makes interesting reading (see *Useful Websites*). Among other flag etiquette rules, you must:

- place your flag in a position of honour;

- hang it either vertically or horizontally, with the stars at the top left-hand corner when you face the flag;
- not allow it to touch the ground;
- never allow any other flag to fly higher than the Stars and Stripes.

The Dixie flag, also known as the Rebel flag, Confederate Navy flag or Southern Cross, raises many contentious issues, and some schools and other public places have banned it. It was designed and first flown in Alabama in 1861 and was the flag of the Confederate states during the Civil War. It is still seen today in the South, flying on official buildings and elsewhere. It is also an emblem of the South's strong musical heritage – the blues, jazz, rock and roll, rockabilly, soul and country music. The Dukes of Hazard sported it on the roof of their car. Some see it as a symbol of repression that has been overcome and thus as a positive statement. Others, such as racists and extreme right-wing political groups, use it in a negative way.

The National Motto and Seal

The words *In God We Trust* appear on all coins and paper bills and constitute the national motto. The idea behind the motto is that the country is under the guidance of Divine Providence, which is leading the destiny of the nation.

The Great Seal of the US was adopted in 1782. It is used by the Department of State 'in the preparation, sealing and recording of Presidential appointees, on instruments of ratification of treaties and in the preparation and authentification of copies of records'. On one side is an eagle grasping an olive branch, in its beak a scroll with the Latin words *E Pluribus Unum* (one out of many). From its original political meaning 'from many colonies, one republic; from many states one nation' it has shifted to the contemporary 'from many peoples or nationalities, one people'. This expresses the fundamental nature of American society – its multicultural basis. On the other side of the Seal is a pyramid with the all-seeing eye of Providence and the year 1776 inscribed in roman numerals (the year of independence and signing of the Declaration).

The American Bald Eagle

The bald eagle is the official emblem of the United States. This 'king of birds' has been the symbol of freedom, strength, courage and military prowess as far back as the times of Babylon, Rome, the Middle Ages and the Byzantine Empire. In the late eighteenth century the new Americans deliberated and disputed over a national emblem, Benjamin Franklin favouring the wild turkey – which was a true original native of America, whereas the eagle was not. However, one species of eagle – the bald eagle – was found only in America and was unknown in Europe, and therefore was selected as the nation's emblem. It has a white head, and in Olde English, 'balde' meant white, hence the name (not owing to any lack of feathers).

Eagles were hunted in the past and are now rare. In 1967 a writer in a Los Angeles newspaper declared, 'If the bald eagle could speak, the national emblem might well complain that it is being deprived of life, liberty, and the pursuit of happiness'. These birds are now legally protected, but are still declining as they are shot by trigger-happy hunters mistaking them for hawks or poisoned by fish that have ingested insecticides. They are also under pressure owing to loss of their natural habitat.

The National Anthem or 'Star Spangled Banner'

The following four verses of America's national anthem were originally written as a poem by Francis Scott Key in 1814. They tell of an emotional moment in American history and Key's relief at seeing Old Glory still flying after a particularly vicious assault by the British.

'O, say can you see by the dawn's early light
What so proudly we hail'd at the twilight's last gleaming?
Whose broad stripes and bright stars through the perilous fight,
O'er the ramparts we watched were so gallantly streaming?
And the rocket's red glare,
The bomb bursting in air,
Gave proof through the night that our flag was still there.

O, say does that star spangled banner yet wave
O'er the land of the free and the home of the brave?

On the shore, dimly seen through the mists of the deep,
Where the foe's haughty host in dread silence reposes,
What is that which the breeze, o'er the towering steep,
As it fitfully blows, half conceals, half discloses?

Now it catches the gleam
Of the morning's first beam,
In full glory reflected now shines in the stream:
'Tis the star-spangled banner - O long may it wave
O'er the land of the free and the home of the brave!

And where is that band who so vauntingly swore
That the havoc of war and the battle's confusion,
A home and a country should leave us no more!
Their blood has washed out their foul footsteps' pollution.
No refuge could save
The hireling and slave
From the terror of flight, or the gloom of the grave:
And the star-spangled banner in triumph doth wave
O'er the land of the free and the home of the brave!

O, thus be it ever, when freemen shall stand
Between their loved home and the war's desolation!
Blest with vict'ry and peace, may the heav'n rescued land
Praise the Power that hath made and preserved us a nation.
Then conquer we must
When our cause it is just,
And this be our motto - "In God is our trust."
And the star-spangled banner in triumph shall wave
O'er the land of the free and the home of the brave!'

Ironically, the tune the anthem is set to (*To Anacreon in Heaven*) was a song written for a British drinking club. The music and words have been around a long time, but were only put together and officially declared as the national anthem by Congress in 1931. Most Americans only know the first verse (like us and our British anthem).

Uncle Sam

With stars on his hat and stripy red and white trousers, Uncle Sam symbolises the US government, just as John Bull represents England. He is based on a real person – Samuel Wilson, a New York merchant and patriot, who lived between 1766 and 1854. He rose from being a poor farm-hand, through enterprise and hard work, to the important position of supplying the army with meat. He was very popular in his community and devoted to his country. Affectionately, soldiers began calling their meat and many other army supplies 'Uncle Sam's', also declaring that they were in Uncle Sam's Army and on Uncle Sam's payroll. He thus came to personify America.

The White House

The White House is the oldest public building in Washington. All the US presidents have lived there, with the exception of George Washington, who helped design the

House but served his two terms as President in Philadelphia (seat of Congress) and New York (which in 1789 was the nation's capital). The White House was first lived in by President John Adams and his family in 1800. It was sacked and torched by the British in 1814. Extensive renovation work was undertaken between 1948 and 1952, though the House still retained its original exterior walls and historic floor plan. Today it boasts 132 rooms and 20 bathrooms. Each president and first lady adds his or her own design flair to the House.

The Statue of Liberty

At the historic main entrance to 'The Land of the Free', the Statue of Liberty shines her torch 15 miles out to sea. Gustav Eiffel designed the iron framework which was paid for entirely by donations from the people of France (with no government funding). The base was provided by donations from the American people. The statue represented two ideas: the spirit of liberty and the continued friendship between France and America. She was unveiled in 1887 and is thought to be the largest image created by man, standing 151 ft high. The book in her hand is inscribed with the date of America's independence – 4 July 1776 – and the broken chains at her foot symbolise the breaking of shackles. On the pedestal the following last five lines of a poem, *The New Colossus* by Emma Lazarus, are carved:

> 'Give me your tired, your poor
> Your huddled masses yearning to breathe free
> The wretched refuse of your teeming shore
> Send these, the homeless, tempest-tossed to me:
> I lift my lamp beside the golden door.'

The Wild West

The Wild West is part of America's heritage and has captured the imagination of people worldwide, largely through romanticised movies and literature. *The Great Train Robbery* (1903), essentially a western film, was one of the first moving pictures. Later, famous cowboy actors such as Gary Cooper, Roy Rogers, James Stewart and of course the Duke (John Wayne) became American icons. The movies were made to entertain, not to educate, and generally did not portray life as it really was, especially in regard to Indian hostilities. Despite this, the cowboy became a national folk hero and symbol of the American people.

The Old West was a hard, wild place to live in. During the 1830s, pioneers journeyed west in search of a better life over the next ridge. In 1848, gold discovered in California and silver in the western mountains spawned a rush of people. In 1862, the Homestead Act granted 160 acres to anyone who claimed a designated area of land for farming. The stipulations were that they had to build a house, cultivate the land and live on it at least 6 months a year for 5 years. Prairie land was difficult to cultivate and crops might take 2 years or more before they could be harvested, making the life of the homesteader a lean and difficult one. Heat, dust storms and harsh winters all added to the tenuous existence.

The cowboy era lasted only a short time (from the late 1860s to the 1890s), yet embodies the Wild West for most people. Cowboys rode the trails, herding horses and cattle across the plains. In 1869, the tracks of the Union Pacific and Central Pacific railroads joined together, and the East and West were now connected by railroad. This had an immense impact on western expansion. Railroads were essential in those days and few towns or businesses prospered without them. Ranching became easier as farmers were now able to transport cattle by rail.

Wyatt Earp was a highly reputed frontier marshal. He policed Dodge City in Kansas, then moved on to Tombstone, Arizona, a wild town full of outlaws and gangs. Wyatt, together with his two brothers and friend Doc Holliday, had a showdown with a group of outlaws at the OK Corral, famously and excitingly (though inaccurately) portrayed in the film *My Darling Clementine*, starring Henry Fonda. Following a 30-second gunfight, three outlaws lay dead, two scarpered, two Earps and Doc were wounded and Wyatt was the only man left standing. It was the stuff of legends.

Perhaps the most famous American outlaw was Jesse James. He and his brother Frank were members of a Missouri guerrilla group during the Civil War, on the Confederate side. After the war, they robbed banks, stagecoaches and trains. By attacking greedy banks and institutions, Jesse James in particular earned the reputation of an American Robin Hood and became a folk hero. There was never any proof that the brothers committed the hundreds of robberies attributed to them, yet their notoriety grew.

Billy the Kid (alias Henry McCarty) was another famous outlaw who roamed the Southwest. The facts of his life are sketchy, but it is said that he turned to petty theft at an early age because he couldn't handle cowhand work, being short and slight. He started stealing saddles outside brothels, then progressed to horses and mail, and joined a gang, on the run from the law. The Kid had a sunny nature, which endeared him to many people, but also a terrible temper. Despite his romanticised image, he was in reality a desperate teenager and cold-blooded killer. He made legendary escapes from the law and was finally shot and killed, at just 22 years old.

A bizarre incident in the history of the Wild West occurred at noon on 22 April 1890, when 10,000 or so people made a dash across the Arkansas and Texas borders into Oklahoma. The federal government had decreed that the former Indian Territory was now open to white settlement. The Indians who had been forcibly relocated to Oklahoma now found that the land that had been promised to them forever was no longer theirs – one of many broken promises by the white man. Native Americans inhabited North America as long ago as 100 BC, and proof of their civilised culture can be seen today in the ruined cities built into the rocks in Colorado. Then, as Europeans arrived and white Americans expanded westward, their lands and culture were subdued and systematically destroyed. Throughout history Native Americans have been very poorly treated by the white man, who stole their land, broke promises and treaties, starved them out by killing the buffalo (often simply for sport) and massacred Indians whenever they had the opportunity. Geronimo was a great Apache chieftain who led lightning raids into Arizona. He was eventually captured and spent the rest of his life as a prisoner of war, living on a reservation. Nowadays Native Americans are confined to reservations. They suffer from poverty, alcoholism and despair and have failed to assimilate into American society (Chapter 21 discusses this more).

American Heroes

What have Mark Twain, John Wayne, Paul Newman and Marlon Brando got in common? Well, throughout different eras in America's history, each has represented that quintessential American hero: an attractive male – strong, individual, a loner or outlaw. In short, a rebel who doesn't follow the rules. The cowboy is the epitome of this image. This great American hero is still a big ethic, especially as people's lives these days are so very structured. Who are America's heroes today? Americans idolise their sportsmen – football quarterbacks, baseball hitters, basketball stars. The famous 1920s and 30s baseball player Babe Ruth even has a chocolate bar named after him.

The British appreciate anti-heroes (for instance, buffoons like Mr. Bean), whereas American stories usually have a straightforward hero to root for. American films can be excruciatingly sentimental and over-the-top, as the hero of the piece fights off the bad guys and gets the girl, always coming out on top in a blaze of glory. Sylvester Stallone, Arnold Schwarzenegger, Bruce Willis and Harrison Ford often play such larger-than-life heroes on the big screen. Jim gave me his take on what it means to be the 'American Man':

> When you live in America, you get the feeling that American men have a need to be distinctive from their immigrant forefathers and to be uniquely American. This proves an interesting paradox given the zeal with which Americans also honour their roots. However, there are a number of things that now typify the American Man. From legends of Indian fighters, explorers, gunfighters and lawmen comes an amalgamated man who is larger than life. He is big, beefy, square jawed and magnanimous in the way he applies his seemingly limitless strength and bravery to achieve good. The personification of the American Man can be seen in the form of Captain America, a fearless trouble fighter in red, white and blue. The modern equivalent of the American Man comes with certain accessories, the most obvious being the large vehicle with an unfeasibly large engine. It is hard to understand why the lifestyle of American men requires each to have his own huge truck, particularly as it is sel-

dom that anything is actually seen in the truck bed. Nevertheless, practicalities are cast aside to maintain this manly image. Could it be that trucks are modern versions of the covered wagons that carried the original pioneers across the plains? Other toys beloved of American men include all manner of ridiculously powerful yard tools for harassing grass, trees and bushes; t-shirts a couple of sizes too small with hunting, fishing and shooting slogans; mugs the size of Watneys red barrels to hold an endless supply of coffee-flavoured caffeine; and a small armoury of guns for no other reasons than the Constitution allows it and you can't be a true American without the ability to start your own war. Sadly, few who possess the physique of Captain America match his virtuous ways. More commonly, those men who think of themselves as meeting the standard are overly boorish, particularly when lubricated with weak beer. Thankfully, most modern American men are sensible enough to veer away from the American Man standard and, while examples can be seen throughout the US, they are invariably found in hunting, fishing and shooting emporiums or bars without windows. Interestingly, Marvel Comics who invented Captain America recently had him killed owing to the parody of the impression of Americans around the world. There are rumours he'll be resurrected, but it may depend on the outcome of future opinion polls.

Commentators on American Life

Alexis de Tocqueville, a French social scientist, historian and political thinker, visited America in the 1830s. His famous work – *Democracy in America* – was a study of the political and social structure of America at the time. In it he stated:

> 'Picture to yourself, my dear friend, if you can, a society which comprises all the nations of the world – English, French, German: people differing from one another in language, in beliefs, in opinions; in a word, a society possessing no roots, no memories, no common ideas, no national character, yet with a happiness a hundred times greater than ours.'

De Tocqueville identified the characteristics of individualism, hard work and striving for advancement and monetary gain, together with a unique lack of class distinction, as peculiar American traits – and these still form the basis of American society today. It was a society based on free land ownership. Only in the South did the aristocracy prevail, owing to slavery and connections with the Old World. However, as rule by the common masses swept over the rich elite in America, it also meant that men of exceptional talent and intelligence were often blotted out – thus producing a rather mediocre middle way, according to De Tocqueville.

Alastair Cooke was another wonderful commentator on American life. Born in

Salford near Manchester, he became an American citizen in 1941, yet always retained his British demeanour and culture. During his career he worked for the BBC and *The Guardian*, hosted television shows including *Masterpiece Theatre* and *America: A Personal History of the United States*, presented the world's longest running radio series *Letter From America* (between 1946 and 2004) and wrote numerous books. His weekly essay on culture and politics in the United States – *Letter From America* – is perhaps what he is best known for.

A more contemporary writer, Dinesh D'Souza, comments that:

> 'America is the greatest, freest and most decent society in existence. It is an oasis of goodness in a desert of cynicism and barbarism. This country, once an experiment unique in the world, is now the last best hope for the world.'

This quote is taken from D'Souza's book *What's So Great About America* (2002); note there is no question mark at the end of the title, indicating that the author is making a serious case for America, the Great. D'Souza was born in 1961 in India and emigrated to the US. He served under Reagan and is a staunch conservative, intent on 'conserving the principles of the American Revolution'. He challenges left-wing beliefs through his many thought-provoking and critical books and lectures on subjects such as racism, American freedoms, feminism and social issues. *Wikipedia* (the free online encyclopedia) has a page devoted to him and his work, which readers may like to look up.

Conclusion

Today, Americans still love and value freedom, honesty and loyalty most highly. Their ultimate religion is freedom. However, over recent years, they, like many other nations, have become more materialistic and less tolerant of others (though I found the latter trait to be much less pronounced than in the UK). America is a youthful society, in which youth – not old age – rules and is glorified. Technology has given the young the edge. From fashion and the latest gizmos, to cars and homes, young people represent a huge market that marketers are eager to tap. As a result, society is becoming more concerned with individual needs and less with the good of the country as a whole. Americans are less supportive of decisions by their government and take less personal responsibility. That said, they have a strong human rights ethic. They prefer to *make* things happen rather than to *let* things happen, taking up causes around the world and reacting to them.

America has given many people the chance to prosper and enjoy freedoms and opportunities that are often unheard of in their countries of origin. The nation has produced more Nobel Prize winners (296), more billionaires (371), and more gold medalists (36) in the 2004 Summer Olympics than any other country. Being American – whether native-born or immigrant – means you are blessed with opportunities. There is also a much less rigid class system than in Britain. There is something for everyone in the great USA. Americans have a positive attitude that promotes enthusiasm; this vigorous and often simplistic character is somewhat at odds with British understatement and reserve.

Useful Websites

www.celebrationtowncenter.com – Celebration, Florida, the town that Disney built.
www.pewresearch.org – provides information on issues, attitudes and trends shaping America and the world. Look up publications by topic.
www.usflag.org – a website dedicated to the flag of the United States.
www.vetjobs.com – jobs for veterans.
www.vfw.org – official site of Veterans of Foreign Wars (VFW) of the United States.

6 · A Brief Travel Through American History

If you really want to get to know America, delve into some history and philosophy books. It won't take you long; you can read her whole story in one single book as her history basically only spans 500 years or so. I highly recommend *The Story of America* by Weinstein and Rubel. From discovery of the 'New World', the Pilgrims and breaking with the motherland (Great Britain), through Indian strife, slavery, Civil War and the Progressive Era to America's involvement in World War II, the Cold War and more recent terrorism threats, America is seen to be a nation of mixed people, yet dedicated to upholding the American ideals of democracy, human rights and free market economy.

People came to America to escape injustice and oppression (religious, social and political) and poverty. Except for the indigenous Indians and Eskimos who are the only true native Americans, everyone else is a descendant of a foreign national. Theodore Roosevelt (President between 1901 and 1909) stated that America is a nation of immigrants. Learning about the events that shaped this young country gives you a much better appreciation of America today and the values of the people. Having such diverse roots and ancestry, it is admirable how – out of this melting pot of cultures and nationalities – a people so patriotic and proud have arisen.

Early Explorers

America was inhabited for thousands of years before Europeans arrived. The Vikings were one of the first visitors from Europe. Around the year 982, Eric the Red founded a colony in Greenland, which existed for about 500 years. Columbus arrived in 1492, looking for an easier way to the Orient. Later in 1519 the Spanish explorer Cortez came in search of riches.

In 1492 Columbus set sail to cross 'the Great Ocean Sea'. Although an Italian, he was backed by Spain who gave him three ships with which to make the voyage. It took him nearly 3 months to reach land – San Salvador – which Columbus believed to be an outermost island of Asia. He was certain he had found the westerly route to the Indies. His search for gold and spices to take back to Spain was unfruitful. However, owing to the courage of Columbus and his sailors in crossing the unknown Atlantic Ocean, he is often credited with having discovered America, risking sailing off the ends of the earth in the process. In fact, he never set foot in present-day America, only getting as far as the islands of the Caribbean, including the Bahamas, Cuba and Hispaniola.

During the 1500s, Spanish adventurers or conquistadors came to America for gold, glory and God. Conquering Cuba, Mexico and the Caribbean, they moved northward, as far as Kansas. Led by Cortez, they destroyed the native Aztecs of Mexico in their efforts to convert them to Christianity. St. Augustine on the east coast of Florida is said to be the oldest European settlement in America. Later Spanish explorers claimed California, Arizona, New Mexico and Texas for Spain.

At the same time, the French were exploring Canada, the St. Lawrence River and the area of the Great Lakes. They were principally missionaries and fur traders, who integrated with and lived alongside the native Indians. They laid claim to a huge bite of the North American continent, across to the Mississippi River and down to the Gulf of Mexico. By 1750, around 75,000 French were living in North America.

The First English Settlers

The first English settlers arrived in 1585 and formed a colony on Roanoke Island, North Carolina. However, 3 years later the colony was found to be mysteriously deserted. In 1607 the English tried again and this time established the first permanent colony at Jamestown, Virginia.

Back in England, the Anglican Church was imposing its strict doctrines, ceremonial observances and hierarchy on the British population. Those who found it difficult to reconcile their beliefs with the Church's rituals and other 'popery' became known as Puritans (mostly hailing from East Anglia), and those wishing to withdraw from it completely were called Separatists. They were concerned that religious holidays were becoming parties instead of prayer services and that the poor and hungry were not being cared for. They did not agree with the political and religious trends in Europe. One group left for Holland, a place of tolerance in a Europe rife with religious dissension. These Separatists, or Pilgrims as they came to be known, feeling that Holland also did not offer them the freedom they sought, joined with London merchants to invest in a passage to the New World.

In 1620 the *Mayflower* set sail with 101 emigrants and crew, 35 of whom were Separatists. They arrived at Plymouth in Cape Cod, Massachusetts. Intent on creating a new godly world, free of the licentious people they felt were contaminating the Old World, they arrived in a desolate and unknown wilderness, too late in the season to plant crops. By the end of that first hard winter half the colonists had succumbed to death from sickness and starvation. Those that remained worked the land hard, realising that it held the key to their sustenance and survival. They were artisans and farmers, and were helped to learn the ways of their new land by some native Indians who chose to live amongst them. After a successful spring and summer they celebrated with 3 days of festivities, a holiday that became known as Thanksgiving.

They were a reserved and strictly ruled group, believing in diligence, thrift and sobriety; laughter was considered highly suspect. They were eager to possess the land, convinced they were chosen by God to create a new world, free from corruption; these characteristics ensured their survival and driving force. Thus they colonised the eastern seaboard of America. Table 6.1 details the years of colonisation and founding of the first 13 British colonies. The new inhabitants of America operated a form of democracy among themselves, but excluded women, slaves and the very poor from voting, and generally regarded the Indians as uncivilised and thus as enemies.

Table 6.1 Founding of the initial 13 British colonies.

Colony	Year founded	Founded by
Virginia (Jamestown, Chesapeake)	1607	Anglican settlers from England
Massachusetts (Plymouth, Massachusetts Bay)	1620	Puritan Pilgrims
New York (New Amsterdam)	1626	Dutch Reformed; followed later in 1664 by English
Rhode Island (Providence)	1634	Puritan group who left Massachusetts in order to freely practise their own religion
Connecticut (Hartford)	1636	Others from Massachusetts who wanted more freedom to govern as they wanted
Maryland (Baltimore)	1636	Catholics and protestants
North Carolina (Albemarle)	1654	Settlers from Virginia
South Carolina (Charles Town)	1663	Europeans, especially English newcomers
New Hampshire (Rye)	1664	People from Massachusetts who left there for political and religious reasons
New Jersey	1664	Swedish and Dutch Quakers and Reformists
Pennsylvania (Philadelphia)	1681	Quakers led by William Penn
Delaware	1682	Quakers
Georgia	1732	English, to quell Spanish usurping

The Eighteenth Century

By the mid 1700s, Britain was the dominant colonial power in North America, overshadowing the other nationalities that had made America their home (predominantly French, Spanish, Dutch, Swedes, Finns, Swiss and Africans). This 'New England' was a melting pot of cultures and produced a new countryman, shaped by the harsh environment – an 'American'. This new breed of people developed an outlook that was born out of facing troubles, independent of their homeland, and with respect for each other, regardless of social status. Frontier living was embraced by hardy, independent, Christian farmers and their families, who initially banded together in small communities to survive in the wilderness. Most were of English descent, later joined by Scots, Irish (fleeing the potato famine) and a significant number of Germans. The Irish settled mostly in the cities and dug canals, lay rail track and built roads. The Germans were largely farmers.

During 1756 and 1763 Britain was at war with France and India and soldiers were stationed in America to fight the French on American soil. This was known as the Seven Years' War (and, in America, as the French and Indian War). In 1763, France ceded Canada and her possessions east of the Mississippi to Great Britain. In an effort to share the cost of this war and offset the burden on British taxpayers, the British government increased the colonists' previously light tax-burden. The colonists had up till that point been proud to be part of the British Empire, respecting her laws and being loyal to the King. After all, she was 'the mother country'. However, the new taxes, in particular the Stamp Tax, and other impositions caused furor throughout the colony as the people protested their rights as free men, rallying against 'taxation without representation'.

Resentment over British injustice concerning taxes and harsh punishments for rebelliousness reached a head with the Boston Tea Party in 1770. England insisted on bringing over red-coated soldiers for the protection of the colonists, who felt they could protect themselves. Many of these soldiers were former felons, underpaid and ill-treated, and they taunted and abused the 'Yankees', singing bawdy songs such as *Yankee Doodle* on the Sabbath. When three British ships loaded with tea would not turn back from Boston, patriots dumped the cargo into Boston Bay – as a lesson to the British that they were not wanted there. Instead of recalling the redcoats, Britain sent more and squeezed the port by passing unjust trade acts. Tensions mounted.

Open warfare eventually erupted, with the American War of Independence (what Americans commonly refer to as the Revolutionary War) beginning at Bunker Hill, just across Boston Bay, in 1775. In 1776, America's greatest men at the time (known as the Committee of Five) gathered to sign the Declaration of Independence, a document composed by Thomas Jefferson, then a young Virginian and later America's third President. The signing took place in Benjamin Franklin's home city of Philadelphia, which was the richest and most populous city in America at that time.

The Declaration contained, among other things, those immortal words 'all men are created equal' and are entitled to 'life, liberty, and the pursuit of happiness'. The document made a case for independence of the colonies from Great Britain by listing their grievances against the King. Most Americans agree that this is the most influential document in their history, representing their cherished liberty. The Declaration's inspirational words have been used by people throughout the world in struggles against oppression. It upholds individual liberty, stating that a person's position should not be determined by his or her birth, title or rank but by his/her ability, talent and enterprise.

Also in 1776, the Constitution was drawn up, comprising seven Articles laying out the formation and duties of an independent US government (formed of three branches – legislative, executive and judicial). This document was never meant to be set in stone, and since then has been amended many times.

George Washington led the colonists in war against Britain, serving as President. He financed much of the war himself, buying and maintaining the troops. The people wanted to crown him as king, but in the end he had the strength of character to walk away from it. Meanwhile, overseas, Benjamin Franklin (statesman and one of the Founding Fathers), feeling betrayed by the British government, whipped up support for America in France.

In 1778 France declared war on England, shortly followed by Spain and Holland. Without France's military and financial aid, the colonists may never have defeated Britain. For 8 years, the bloody war raged. In 1781, a combined French/American army captured a large British army led by General Cornwallis at Yorktown, Virginia. Cornwallis's surrender brought to an end any further serious British military efforts. British Prime Minister Lord North resigned, and his successor, Rockingham, began the peace process. Finally, in 1783, the Treaty of Paris recognised the independence of the new United States of America.

In the years that followed, the colonists, now free of British rule, struggled to find their way. They suffered from social problems and economic depression, as well as interstate rivalry and foreign unrest. Their ideals of liberty and equality for all were in sharp contrast to the reality of slavery, which existed in all 13 states. Slaves brought to America from Africa made up 20% of the population and comprised the labour force on which much of America's prosperity was based.

Back in 1775, at the start of the Revolutionary War, the Quakers formed the first anti-slavery movement, and support for abolition grew as Negroes fought with whites during the War. Slavery was forbidden in the Northwest Territory (all land west of Pennsylvania and north-west of the Ohio River) and it was outlawed in Ohio in 1803. Ohioan Quakers formed the Underground Railroad, used by some 75,000 slaves as a route north to freedom. This loosely organised network of people used railroad terms to describe the guides, safe houses and routes to freedom. The most heavily travelled route went through Ohio, Indiana and western Pennsylvania.

The Bill of Rights in 1791 comprised the first ten important amendments to the Constitution, including freedom of religion, speech and the press, the right to assemble and petition, to bear arms, to justice and a speedy jury trial. However, despite sounding honourable, the slavery issue was swept under the carpet; the 700,000 or so Negro slaves living in America at that time were simply ignored.

The Nineteenth Century

During the years that followed, explorers Lewis and Clark, backed by President Jefferson, continued expansion west into unknown territory. The President declared:

> 'The object of your mission is to explore the Missouri River, and such principal stream of its, as, by its course and communication with the waters of the Pacific Ocean...may offer the most direct and practicable water communication across this continent for the purpose of commerce.' (Thomas Jefferson, 1803)

During 1804–1806, Lewis and Clark undertook the first overland expedition to the Pacific coast and back – a journey that would take them 28 months. As cartographers, naturalists and ethnologists, they wrote extensive journals, recording everything they found on their exploration of the western territories. Their expedition encouraged further exploration and settlement by whites.

In 1812, America again went to war with Great Britain, this time over the following issues:

- Britain and France were interfering with US ships and trade.
- The British were arming Indians in the Northwest Territory, who were attacking settlers.
- There was argument over who should preside over Canada.

The British were successful in capturing and burning Washington, DC. However, they lost the war overall and were forced to sign a peace treaty in 1814, promising to recognise US boundaries and to no longer interfere in the Northwest Territory. A little later, in 1823, the then-president, James Monroe, drew up the Monroe Doctrine, which effectively told European politicians to keep out of the Americas. The Doctrine restricted other European nations from forming territories in the American continent and ostracised the US political system from those of Europe.

The Mexican War of 1846–1848 arose over a dispute concerning the border country in the state of Texas. Texas had formerly belonged to Mexico. Following an influx of white Americans into this territory, who then proceeded to set up their own government, Mexicans attempted to retain control. Mexican soldiers gained a brief victory at the Battle of the Alamo. This was quashed a month or so later by American troops, who forced the Mexicans to sign a treaty that signed over independence to 'the Lone Star Republic'. Ten years later, in 1845, Congress decreed Texas a US territory.

Mexico opposed this and the drawing of the southern boundary. As a result, America declared war on Mexico. Following a mighty American victory, Mexico was forced to concede her territories of Utah, Nevada and California, and parts of Wyoming, Colorado, Arizona and New Mexico.

There followed a period of renewed American confidence and expansion. Trade all but ceased with Britain, allowing homeland industry to flourish. Explorers and settlers pushed the US frontier (the boundary between wilderness and settled land) further and further west. This was the era of the pioneer. Initially people arrived by horse and wagon, and some by water. Later, between the 1850s and 1870s, the railroad system came into being. The Homestead Act of 1862 granted government land to those who would farm and live on the Great Plains, and prompted further expansion. Bloody battles with native Indians ensued. However, by the end of the century, the frontier had virtually disappeared.

Civil War (1861–1865)

Old versus new;
South versus North;
local versus national;
crops versus machines.

Before 1861, the US was made up of 13 separate states, each, on the whole, with its own rules and regulations. Some felt a single central (federal) government was necessary in order to unite the states, whereas others wanted to stay separate and decide their own rules, for instance with regard to taxation, commercial issues and whether to support the institution of slavery or not. The dispute over the right of states to secede from the federal Union was becoming more and more heated, with the South worried that the federal government based in the North was growing too powerful.

The States' Rights debate was comprised of several issues. The South was based on subsistence agriculture, plantations and export crops (principally cotton and indigo to Britain). Free slave labour contributed to the wealth of white southerners who felt the Union had no right to stop those keeping slaves and expanding slavery into new territories; they were also disgruntled at having to pay taxes to the federal government, instead wanting to keep this money within their own states. The North was rapidly modernising, with a factory-based commercial market economy. Industrious entrepreneurs and hard-working individuals saw a moral and political problem with the free labour and unfair competition of the South.

In 1861 things reached a head. Just before Abraham Lincoln, a staunch opponent of slavery, took office as President, seven southern states declared themselves separate and formed the 'Confederate States of America', with their own senate, army, capital city (Montgomery, Alabama), flag (the Dixie flag), constitution and president

(Jefferson Davis). The ensuing civil war was fought by these pro-slavery Confederates on the one side and Union nationalists on the other.

Throughout the country, feelings were divided. Virginia was so confused it split to form a separate state – West Virginia. Kentucky was the homeland of both Lincoln and Jefferson Davis (they grew up just 100 miles apart) and as such was a state divided by loyalties. Ohio was also split – southern counties had ties with Kentucky (family, cultural and economic) and slave states south, while northern counties were anti slavery, having their populations' roots in New England.

Unionists outnumbered Confederates by about 3 to 1 and were in a much stronger position. The North had money, factories and railroads and 22 million people (albeit including thousands of immigrants who felt no compunction to fight). The poor South had only 9 million people, 4 million of whom were slaves. Yet the Confederate army scored early victories, blessed with brilliant generals, headed by General Lee, who were far more adept than the Union's military leaders. However, another advantage the Unionists had over the Confederates lay in the fact that the South relied heavily on trade; so the North simply blockaded the ports, cutting off imports to the South.

The Battle of Antietam in Maryland marked the turning point in 1862, with heavy losses on General Lee's side. It was the bloodiest single 12 hours in American history, with 23,000 dead or wounded (nine times more than those killed or wounded during D-Day). The Battle of Gettysburg in the following year was another crucial point in history; if the Confederates had won this battle, Britain who was backing them would have recognised their independence from the Union and we might never have had a *United* States of America.

Another 2 years of bloody fighting continued before the Confederates finally surrendered. An estimated 95,000 Confederate soldiers died in the war and 35,000 Unionists. Following the North's victory over the South, ending with official freedom for all the nation's slaves in the form of the 13th Amendment (ratified in 1865), President Lincoln proclaimed the last Thursday in November a national Thanksgiving holiday. He was assassinated 5 days later by a southern sympathiser.

Native Americans

> 'A Native American grandfather talking to his young grandson tells the boy he has two wolves inside of him struggling with each other. The first is the wolf of peace, love and kindness. The other wolf is fear, greed and hatred. "Which wolf will win, grandfather?" asks the young boy. "Whichever one I feed", is the reply.'

This Native American proverb sums up the situation between the native peoples of America and the Europeans who came to the new land. From the beginning of America's history up to the 1930s, the white man has treated the Native American abominably. It is estimated that 10 million Indians inhabited America before European colonists arrived. Tragically, nearly 90% of the population that once lived along the eastern seaboard was wiped out by diseases the Europeans brought with them, such as smallpox, measles and the common cold.

Initially the natives granted all the land the colonists wanted, exchanging food and knowledge for the Europeans' horses, guns and sugarcane. The American Indian expressed reverence for the land by linking his life to the forces of nature and was not afraid of the savage wildness of the western plains, as were Europeans. As the white man began to lay claim to more and more land – clearing forests, shooting game that the Indians depended on for food, and taking whatever he wanted, often forcibly, using guns – the Indians banded with the French against the colonists in what became known as the French and Indian War (1754–1763). However, white (predominantly British) settlers reigned supreme, wresting most of North America from the hands of the French, and continuing their expansion of the continent. The French sold the Louisiana Territory (Middle America) to the Americans, much to the chagrin of the native Indians, who felt the land belonged to them.

Daniel Boone was a famous pioneer who lived between 1734 and 1820. He discovered a way through the Appalachians (the Cumberland Gap) into the virgin land of Kentucky, thus breaching the western frontier. Native Americans who had inhabited this vast continent for hundreds of years were pushed further and further west as more settlers arrived. The new settlers made the Indians many promises, but rarely kept them. They stripped the plains of buffalo, which the Indians relied on for food, shelter and clothing, and forced them to move to more inhospitable areas. Thus 'the white man' came to be the enemy of the Indian. Rugged, sunburnt cowboys, herding cattle from the fattening ranges in Texas to the booming markets in the north, braved the hazardous plains, fighting off Indians as they went. The legend of cowboys and Indians was born. A one-side battle was fought, with rifles versus tomahawks. White settlers, ranchers and miners forced Native Americans off their ancient lands, though not without difficulty. The Apache and Sioux tribes in particular were fearsome warriors. Many battles took place, some of which were won by Indian tribes.

Over the years, the US government persuaded some chiefs to sign over their lands peacefully by offering payment or new lands to move to. However, such agreements were often dishonest or not recognised by white settlers, who laid claim to the Indians' land. In 1830, the Indian Removal Act granted the US government the power to move tribes. Some, especially in the Great Plains and South West, fought back, resulting in what came to be known as the Indian Wars. According to US Census Bureau estimates, 45,000 Indians and 19,000 whites lost their lives during these wars, including women and children, as frontier fighting was brutal and indiscriminate. By 1846 Americans stretched 'from sea to shining sea', spurred on by the 1849 California gold rush. Following the discovery of gold on Indian land, the government, which was broke after the Revolutionary War, deliberately encouraged gold-hungry whites to slaughter the buffalo and starve the Indians out.

The 1876 Dakota gold rush sparked the Battle of Little Big Horn, during which General Custer was killed in an onslaught with Sitting Bull. Apache chief Geronimo was the last famous chief, captured in 1885. The final battle between Native Americans and whites was fought in 1898 at Leech Lake, Minnesota. By 1900, the US government had forced all Native Americans to move to reservations. However, this did nothing to end the whites' lust for land, and by 1934 the Indians had been deprived of a further 86 million acres. They were not even recognised as citizens until 1924. The largest community of Native-American speakers (140,000 people) lives on the Navajo reservation, covering an area of 16 million acres, most of which is in Arizona.

For more on the conflict between Native Americans and non-native Americans, see Chapter 21.

Black Americans

Twelve years after the first European settlers arrived in America, the first African slaves were brought to the New World. The plantation system, implemented by the English, subsisted on the backs of African slaves. Captured by Dutch traders, mostly from along the West Coast of Africa, Africans were transported to the early American colonies to provide the labour and also often the expertise required to work the southern plantations. They provided vital knowledge of indigo (used in the dyeing of wool, especially in demand for dyeing British naval uniforms), cotton and rice production, iron-working, boat building and cattle rearing.

A great many Africans died on route to the colonies in the awful conditions aboard the slave ships. Some were offloaded in the West Indies and sold into slavery; the rest continued on to America. Approximately 25% of all Africans passed through the port of Charleston, South Carolina, or landed on Sullivan's Island, just offshore. Not all Africans who came to America were slaves. Some came as free men and worked as blacksmiths, cobblers, and wheelwrights and in the building trade, and became wealthy citizens.

By 1850 the slave population in America had reached 3 million. The South was exporting more than a million tons of cotton each year to England's textile mills. While the economy of the South was based on slave-worked plantations, the North was becoming more industrial and urbanised, and the contrast between the two grew. Abolitionism became a multi-ethnic, international cause. The Republican party started out as the antislavery party. Frederick Douglass (a slave himself, later a freeman and staunch abolitionist) helped convince Abraham Lincoln that slavery needed to be destroyed, rather than slaves simply shipped back to Africa.

The slave trade continued until 1865, the end of the Civil War, when technically all black Americans were freed. However, owing to the antebellum Reconstruction period and disagreements over the Constitution by some southern states, in reality this freedom was often not acknowledged. African-Americans were not given full rights as citizens. 'Black codes' in some southern states decreed that former slaves were not allowed to vote, serve on juries, testify against whites in court or join the state army.

Following emancipation, many former slaves moved north to work in the cities and take advantage of the free education offered there. Those remaining in the South often subsisted on farms in black communities, with their own churches and schools – owing to the unwelcoming attitude of the generally white population. The African-American proverb 'You've got to work twice as hard to get half as far as a black person in white America' sums up the situation.

The notorious Ku Klux Klan (KKK) was founded in 1865, a time of southern lawlessness. Members wearing white portrayed the avenging ghosts of slain Confederate soldiers. Their aim was to intimidate blacks and sympathetic white Republicans. From its roots in Tennessee, the organisation quickly spread. Unperturbed, the government passed the 14th Amendment in 1868, guaranteeing former slaves citizenship, and the 15th Amendment in 1870, giving them the right to vote and hold political office. The KKK was officially banned by Congress and mercifully died out by the early 1870s. However, legislation actually did not have much effect, and by the late 1870s, things had reverted. Blacks were denied the vote through devious twists in southern state laws.

Racial tension lasted for nearly a century more. In 1915, the KKK enjoyed a resurgence, fueled by superpatriotism following World War I, with people worried about losing America's small-town Protestant values; some also credit its revival to the controversial and popular movie of the time, *Birth of a Nation*. As hostility towards immigrants and economic tensions rose, so did membership of the KKK, which vented its aggression on Catholics, Jews and especially blacks, who suffered the worst segregation and violence. Southern states and even some northern areas practised segregation and discrimination. Among other things, they segregated passenger shipping, dining facilities, drinking fountains, colleges, movie theatres, housing and employment.

During the 1950s and 1960s, blacks began to rebel against the segregation laws by defiantly occupying front seats on buses and sitting in 'white only' restaurants. In 1955 the Civil Rights movement began. The early 1960s were a time of idealism and hope for many. In 1963, 200,000 people rallied in Washington at a meeting at which Reverend Martin Luther King Jr preached for passive but unrelenting resistance to black segregation and discrimination and urged for non-violent protests. It was here that he gave his immortal speech:

> '...I have a dream that one day this nation will rise up and live out the true meaning of the creed – we hold these truths to be self-evident that all men are created equal'.

Shortly afterwards, he was killed, before the new Civil Rights Bill realised that dream. The Bill gave the right to vote to *all* Americans and outlawed segregation. Yet, even today, there are parts of the States, especially in the South, where blacks are discriminated against and treated unfairly. This seems to be a legacy America still has to break.

Immigration

America has always been a land that people have flocked to. In the beginning, this vast continent of unmapped wilderness attracted the French, Dutch, Germans, Swedes, Danes and Finns, besides English, Scottish and Irish people. Under the new lawgivers, anyone coming to America could look forward to being a landowner. Indentured servants worked off the cost of their passage over a period of 4–7 years and then received a suit of clothes, tools and 50 or so acres of land. Their prospects were hugely improved compared to that of the average poor London family.

More Europeans arrived between 1820 and 1870, including the Irish escaping famine. Immigrants from China came in their thousands during the 1850s and from Japan in the late 1880s, settling along the West Coast. In just 20 years, between 1880 and 1900, about one-third of European Jews emigrated to America, most settling in New York. At the peak of the influx, at the end of the 1800s, up to 10,000 people a day passed through the processing centre in New York.

As well as religious freedom, people were lured by prosperity and free education, the latter being seen as the key to tomorrow. After World War II, a law restricted the number of immigrants, thus reducing the flood to a trickle. In 1965 the law changed again to permit more Asian and Latin American people to enter the US, including thousands from Vietnam.

The Twentieth Century

I have not included much historical detail on the last century, because most readers will be familiar with it, and indeed will have experienced more recent events. What follows is a brief description of the decades and some notable events.

Following the Industrial Revolution between 1850 and 1900, the Roaring Twenties was a time of boom, rebellion and stock market investment. The 1930s conversely saw the Great Depression (a national and world phenomenon). The stock market crashed, banks closed, businesses collapsed and crop prices plummeted. By 1932 1 in 4 Americans was unemployed, and without welfare or social security things looked bleak. For the first time in history, America lacked hope for the future. The new president, Franklin Delano Roosevelt, dealt with the dilemma by proposing a plan called the New Deal. He established the Works Progress Administration (WPA), which gave jobs to the unemployed – building city pavements, paving rural roads and painting murals on public buildings – and successfully began to turn things around.

Following World War II, much of Europe and Asia was left in tatters, economically, physically and socially, whereas America emerged relatively unscathed. This fact formed the basis for the economic boom of the 1950s. Americans excelled in producing appliances to make life easier. Then followed the Atomic or Space Age in the 1950s. The Soviet Union launched Sputnik I, the world's first artificial satellite, and the race was on between the United States and the Soviet Union. During the 1960s and early 1970s, civil rights and the Vietnam War were uppermost in most people's minds. Then followed Reaganomics and the Information Age, with the rise of personal computers, the internet and the digital revolution. The 1990s saw the dot.com bubble burst. As we live through the first part of the twenty-first century, it is terrorism and Middle Eastern dissent that preoccupies Americans most.

Notable Dates

1900–1917
The Progressive Era (highlighting social reform, Prohibition, women's suffrage and government corruption).

1917
America enters World War I after German U-boats sink numerous unarmed American ships, as well as the Lusitania, an unarmed British passenger ship, killing 1200 people, more than 100 of them Americans.

1920
President Woodrow Wilson establishes the League of Nations. However, the US, intent on a policy of 'isolationism' and despite Woodrow Wilson's involvement, never joined the League. The 19th Amendment granted women suffrage, or the right to vote.

1929
Stock market crash and start of the Great Depression.

1941
Attack on Pearl Harbour. America enters World War II.

1945
Bombing of Hiroshima and Nagasaki. Roosevelt, Churchill and Stalin form the United Nations, with its HQ in New York.

1949
NATO is formed.

1950–1953
The US intervenes over communist North Korea's invasion of the non-communist South.

1961
US invasion fails to free Cuba from dictator Fidel Castro.

1962
The Cuban Missile Crisis – America insists that the Soviet Union removes its nuclear missiles from Cuban soil.

1964
Bombing of North Vietnam begins and US military forces are sent to the South.

1966
The Civil Rights Act makes segregation of African-Americans illegal in all businesses open to the public.

1969
US astronauts Neil Armstrong and Edwin Aldrin land on the moon.

1973
Peace agreement ends the Vietnam War, at a cost of 58,000 American lives.

1974
Nixon resigns over the Watergate scandal.

1979
Hostages from the US Embassy in Tehran, Iran, are freed after 444 days.

1980–1988
The Reagan years – a period of prosperity, but also increasing government debt.

1989
Iraq invades Kuwait.

1991
Dissolution of the Cold War between the United States and Russia. The Gulf War begins, lasting 6 months (345 American troops killed, 1000 wounded, many more suffering from Gulf War Syndrome).

1992
President Clinton takes over from George Bush.

2000
George W. Bush becomes President.

2001
Terrorist attack on the World Trade Centre. The US invades Afghanistan and overthrows the Taliban regime, which was supporting and harbouring bin Laden.

2003
Iran–Iraq War. The US invades Iraq, prompting anti-American sentiment with this unpopular action. Tony Blair is virtually Bush's only major international ally in this.

2005
Hurricane Katrina decimates New Orleans.

2007
Thirty three students killed in Virginia Tech campus shooting, the deadliest shooting rampage yet in America.

2007 also saw a visit to Virginia by Her Majesty Queen Elizabeth, in commemoration of the anniversary of the founding of Jamestown, the first permanent English settlement in the Americas. Virginia is the most English of the colonies (according to locals) and a hotbed of royalist support in America, with a large mural portrait of Princess Diana on one town centre building. Our local *Dayton Daily News* described the Queen as:

> '...dressed in a long lavender coat trimmed in pink, with a matching oversized pink hat trimmed in lavender. She wore a large diamond brooch shaped like a bow, along with triple-strand pearl necklace and pearl earrings. She wore sensible black shoes and carried a patent handbag'.

Some things never change.

Conclusion

George W. Bush, in his 2001 inaugural address, stated that:

> 'America has never been united by blood or birth or soil. We are bound by ideals

> that move us beyond our backgrounds, lift us above our interests and teach us what it means to be citizens'.

Early colonists were adventurers, profiteers looking to strike it rich, and people willing to take risks and make sacrifices to improve their lives and those of their families. Since then, generations of immigrants have been drawn to a better life in America. Entrepreneurship and opportunism are lasting characteristics of America's citizens. Most Americans today are proud, patriotic people, advertising a love for their country on car bumpers and buildings, their beloved flag flying year-round in front yards and communities. Despite the odd grumble (usually political), they are enthusiastic and devoted citizens.

The Declaration of Independence and the Constitution were a unique philosophical and political concept, founded on admirable beliefs which are still fiercely upheld today. Children as young as four learn the Pledge of Allegiance:

> 'I pledge allegiance to the flag of the United States of America
> And to the Republic for which it stands,
> One nation under God,
> Indivisible,
> With liberty and justice for all.'

Margaret Thatcher once stated that 'Europe was created by history. America was created by philosophy'. The UK has hundreds of years of tradition; in comparison, the US has yesterday. America was and continues to be a social experiment. Americans cherish their relatively short history and their philosophy. Yet they are still evolving, still experimenting, perhaps unlike any other nation.

Useful Websites

http://www.bbc.co.uk/dna/h2g2/A1081180 – a BBC-run site; a guide to life, the universe and everything; this page is on immigration.
http://www.house.gov/paul/constitution.html – the full text of the United States Constitution.
www.nationalgeographic.com/lewisandclark – National Geographic Lewis and Clark interactive journey log.
www.nps.gov/history/nagpra/documents – location of Indian Reservations in the continental United States.
www.pbs.org – tons of great information is on this site.
http://usinfo.state.gov/products/pubs/constitution/bill.htm – Department of State website on the Bill of Rights and Amendments I–X of the Constitution.

Wikipedia:
Civil Rights Act of 1964

7 • A Not So Common Language

George Bernard Shaw joked that England and America are two countries separated by a common language. A quote from our local newspaper illustrates this, with the headline, 'Thrown margarita glass misses officer, who writes up tosser'. Case in point. Today the American language has superficial similarities with English, but borrows from all the immigrant languages that impacted on the USA's development.

With regard to language in the New World, British colonists originally led the way. However, owing to the mix of nationalities arriving at America's shores (notably the Dutch, Germans, French and Scandinavians), a form of English that was different from the mother tongue developed and the new settlers began to use their own 'American English'. Nineteenth century immigrants from China, Italy and Ireland, as well as Jewish communities brought new words with them, further adding to the mix. All these impacted on the newly adopted American English language. However, Spanish still held sway in the South-West, while Native Americans fought to retain their unique language. Fifty two languages that were formerly spoken in America have since died out.

In 2000, the US Census Bureau found that:

- 20% of US residents (47 million people) speak another language at home;
- 55% of these people said they speak English as a second language very well;
- Spanish is the second most commonly used language (28 million Americans speak it), followed by Chinese (2%), Korean, Vietnamese and Tagalog (spoken by Filipinos);
- French, German and Italian are spoken by around 1 million American citizens, respectively.

More than 20 US states have adopted English as their official language. However, there is much debate over whether this is right or not, and whether other states should come on board and make English the official language of the USA.

The Written Word

The first American dictionary – *An American Dictionary of the English Language* – was published in 1828. It was written by Noah Webster and took him 27 years to complete. Webster was a political writer, editor, textbook writer, lexicographer and, above all, a spelling reformer. He believed that English spelling laws were needlessly complex, having been hijacked by the British aristocracy. He followed the 'rule of speaking' and simplified American spellings. Moreover, as westward expansion continued, new phrases and words were needed to describe the unfamiliar things the new settlers were discovering. Webster's dictionary was the most popular American book of the time and helped to standardise the American language. Punctuation and spelling differences between American English (AE) and British English (BE) have evolved as AE has rationalised, with AE words spelt more how they are sounded: some examples are center, favor, defense, traveler, dialog, maneuver, judgment, plow and tire, to name a few. Hence AE spellings often make more sense than their BE counterparts.

The world's first TV game show is said to have been a show called *Spelling Bee*, broadcast by the BBC in 1938. Spelling bees originated in America and are today known throughout the world. A 'bee' is any social get-together where a specific activity is carried out; so, for example, you get quilting, sewing and spinning bees. In a spelling bee, competitors vie to see who can spell the most number of words correctly.

Besides different spellings, Americans appear to have some strange grammatical rules. They have a way of shortening headlines in newspapers, which makes them read oddly and often incoherently, until you get used to the idea. The following examples were taken from local and national American newspapers:

> 'Presidents' letters speak of love, more.'
> 'Meet some of the people, organizations working to keep local children, teens on the right track.'
> 'First windmills appear in France, England.'
> 'Jobs, education fuel Asian population growth.'
> 'Attacks kill eight US troops, European journalist.'

This appears to be taking the English grammar rule of using a comma in place of 'and' a little too far for sensible comprehension and flow of English. Such flaunting of the grammatical rules makes reading newspapers rather disjointed and hard work.

Dates are another area that cause problems if you are British. The American way is to put the month first, and the day of the month second, e.g. 01/12 means 12 January not 1 December. Alternatively they would write or say January 1st, never 1 January.

A Strange Manner of Speaking

Americans love to make up words. Some words you won't find in common usage in

Britain (at least not yet) but which Americans use freely include solutionalize (to solve), incorrections, objectified, analyzation (analysis), irregardless, disrespecting (as a verb), redistricting, repurpose (as in to rearrange, e.g. a cupboard), rightsize (when talking about laying off employees), deselect (to discharge a trainee during training), dehire, cosmeceuticals (cosmetics/pharmaceuticals), and warm fuzzies and pricklies (often used in business and school when talking about something that is good or bad, akin to our carrot and stick). They also have a habit of being rather long-winded, for example:

'Participating in the electoral process' means voting.
'Do you have a motion discomfort bag?' refers to a sick bag.
'No accident related activity' means no accidents.
'A downward income adjustment' is a pay cut.
'Below normal in the temperature category' means sub-normal temperature.
'Follow the directional signage' means follow the signs.

Moreover, Americans like to give people titles that sound grander than our British version, e.g. chief meteorologist for weatherman, administrative associate for secretary, office manager for admin clerk, senior marketing engineer for customer service, inventory controller, specialist or technician for shelf stocker, domestic hygiene specialist for cleaner, even domestic engineer/household manager or stay-at-home mom for housewife (which is a very uncool word in America).

Turn the tables and you find that Americans are often equally bemused by our use of English. In shops, offices, restaurants and other public places, I was often looked at blankly and asked to repeat or rephrase questions. I felt like a foreigner speaking a strange language. However, often it is not the words but rather the English accent that blows them. Below is a conversation Tim had with a shop assistant in a department store. It went something like this:

Customer Tim: Hello, can you tell me where the irons are?
Shop assistant: The what?
Tim: The irons.
Met with a blank look
Tim: You know – an iron?
Still blank. Tim starts to make an ironing motion
For ironing?
Now ironing away vigorously
Um…for pressing clothes?
Shop assistant: Oh, it's your accent. Do you mean 'ironing'?
(She says it just the same way)
Tim: Yes. Ironing. Er, sorry about that.
Shop assistant: Oh no, it's lovely. I just love your accent. Yes, the irons are over there.

Whether she was flummoxed by his good looks or unexpected English accent, we will never know; however, I maintain it was the accent. Within one minute of meeting and greeting a stranger, I can virtually guarantee you will hear the immortal words, 'I just love your accent!' This is usually followed by the question, 'Where are you from?' To this you can answer England (if appropriate) or Australia, depending on how facetious you are feeling; you can get away with either. (Tim was also suspected of coming from North Dakota, so he sometimes posed as a North Dakotan just to see how far he could go with the conversation.) You may then be treated to a potted history of your new acquaintance's roots if their descendants came from Britain, as is often the case. You might be told that they have been to London or, failing that, haven't been to Britain at all, but would love to go. Either way, you start feeling a little bit 'special' and cultivating that Great British accent, which most Americans seem so rarely to hear spoken in person.

American English Versus British English

Whole books have been written on the subject of how American English (AE) differs from British English (BE). AE is not a corrupt form of BE, as many people think. Originally, Americans borrowed words from Native Americans for the flora and fauna they found, and to describe the topography as they explored their new world. Later, they devised their own words, in particular as transportation developed, which is why many AE words that relate to the railway, roads and cars differ from BE. AE sometimes favours more complex words over the shorter BE forms, e.g. transportation versus transport; to burglarize versus to burgle. Some words are used in both AE and BE but have meanings or uses that are dissimilar. For example: in BE, 'Yank' means any American, whereas in AE it means someone from the North-East; 'slated' in AE means 'planned' (as in 'Fair slated at county park'), whereas in BE it means severely criticised.

Some other examples of irregularities between AE and BE are given in Table 7.1 and elsewhere in this book (see the table lists of terminology at the end of some of the chapters). Besides the obvious differences like 'iron' and 'iron' (only kidding), there are other subtle and not so subtle ones. Mum and Mummy is *always* Mom, Mommy or Mamma in AE (mummy in AE refers to an Egyptian in a wrap). Walk into a stationery shop and ask for a rubber and you'll be stared at incongruously ('Why is she asking me for a condom?', the shop assistant will be thinking). Go into an art museum in America and you'll find an art gallery. Ask the way to the county show and you'll be looked at blankly (the word is 'fair' not 'show'). Our local sporting and events arena was called the Nutter Centre (after a Mr Nutter), which always raised a giggle with us. Certain linguistic differences also sound very strange to a British person. 'Different...than' is one example that is correct American usage but just sounds plain wrong. 'Gotten' as the past participle for 'to get' is another. 'Normalcy' meaning 'normality' and 'weatherization' meaning 'weatherproofing' are a couple more examples.

Table 7.1 Some more examples of differences between American English and British English.

American English	British English
Bangs	Fringe (hair)
Bathroom, restroom, washroom	Toilet
Intimate apparel	Underwear
Last name	Surname
Locker room	Changing room
Lost and found	Lost property
Mom-and-pop run	Small business
Napkin	Serviette
Native American	American Indian
Potato chips	Crisps
Purse	Handbag
Running shoes, sneakers, tennis shoes	Trainers
Seeing eye dog	Guide dog
Sherbet	Sorbet
Soda	Any soft fizzy drink
Stroller	Push chair, baby buggy
Sweats	Tracksuit
Teller	Cashier
Traffic circle or rotary	Roundabout
Underpass	Pedestrian subway
Undershirt	Vest
Utility pole	Telegraph pole
Valance	Pelmet
Vest	Waistcoat
Wallet	Purse
Washroom	Toilet

Little yet important differences between AE and BE can bring about some funny and often embarrassing situations. For instance, 'pants' often causes some British snickering, as it means 'trousers' in AE (from the French word *pantaloons*), not underwear. Conversely, think twice before announcing that you need to take your jumper off because it's so hot, as jumper in AE means dress (pinafore); instead you should say 'sweater'. For a while I was under the deluded impression that a 'tent sale' meant just that – a special sale of tents (actually it means a sale of items held under a tent, so it could mean absolutely anything). A 'scheme' in AE means something sinister (so a 'government scheme' takes on a whole new meaning in American English). It is quite common for Americans to announce without embarrassment that they need to 'go potty' when stating their intention to go to the toilet; they even use this term with their pets, e.g. 'I'm just taking Bruno to go potty'.

Regional and Cultural Differences

American English is coloured by the dialect of many cultures, and within America regional dialects remain strong. There is a linguistic divide between North and South, with southern accents perceived as bad English. Southern coastal or plantation speech is losing out to its 'country' neighbour, both of which are scorned by northerners.

On a simple level there are four American dialects: New England, Southern, Western and General American.

- *New England* dialect owes its roots to Puritan East Anglian settlers and is usually thought of as extending as far south-west as the Connecticut River. This northern coastal dialect is separated from southern coastal speech by the Potomac River.
- The greatest population and therefore largest body of speakers is in the South, where the *Southern* accent has not changed much owing to the population remaining fairly static.
- The West Coast speaks many languages. The *Western* accent has been coloured by immigrants and Americans travelling west during the gold-rush era.
- West of the Appalachian Mountains you find *General American* or Midland speech, which is considered to be 'normal' American speech. The Ohio River is traditionally seen as the boundary between the Midland and Southern dialects. Midland speech can be divided into North Midland (north of the Ohio River) and South Midland (which extends south-west towards California; the sound of CB radio and country music).

Researchers say it is impossible to count the number of regional dialects in the States, owing to the country being made up of such a mix of diverse peoples. Some of the main recognised dialects are described below:

- African-American English
- Appalachian/Smoky Mountain
- Cajun
- Californian
- Midwestern
- New York City
- Southern
- Spanglish
- Texan

Spanish-influenced Chicano and North Carolinian Lumbee are other regional dialects. In the Pacific North West, west of the state of Mississippi, people use a form of speech known as 'up-speak', which makes statements sound like questions. In Pittsburgh and western Pennsylvania, Pittsburghese is spoken, which is similar to Appalachian speech. It is a form of Midland dialect coloured by Scots-Irish settlers. Boston speech is another anomaly. Bostoners talk fast and with a thick brogue, much like New Yorkers; President John F. Kennedy had a strong Boston accent.

African-American English

The speech known as African-American English is distinct from 'white' AE. It has developed separately, owing to blacks living independently and indeed often being segregated from mainstream America. Both grammar and sound are different. This separation of speech serves as an enduring divide between the two societies. The rap or hip-hop culture also has a strong influence; here, the black community has taken the lead and in its way has become intrinsically segregating, using language to demarcate.

Colloquially known as Ebonics (from 'ebony' and 'phonics'), speakers of African-American Vernacular English are often deemed uneducated and of low intelligence, owing to the peculiar grammatical rules and pronunciation of Ebonics, e.g. 'She ain't gone nowhere', 'They be gone', 'Don't nobody know where she at'. Ebonics evolved from the diverse languages of African slaves coming to America, who had to find a way to communicate among themselves. A pidgin (mixture of two or more languages) resulted, which then developed into creoles, like the Gullah of South Carolina and Georgia. Owing to the continued cultural differences between blacks and whites, Ebonics has thrived and is today a form of legitimate speech.

Appalachian/Smoky Mountain

Appalachia is roughly the size of Britain, with 20 million or so inhabitants, and is an undeveloped, mountainous area. The soft, lilting quality of 'mountain talk' has its roots in the local culture and traditions of this rural region. It is a very distinct dialect both socially and linguistically, and sounds rather uneducated and unsophisticated to most people, e.g. 'She ain't been here', 'She don't know no more'. With its colourful and twangy phrases such as 'I fell in the river and got to a-slipping and a-sliding', it hails from the speech of a diverse group of white, black and Native American people.

Cajun

Below the Mississippi River, in southern Louisiana, Mississippi and Texas, Cajun is spoken – a mixture of English, French and other influences. Cajuns are descendants of French people who settled in Nova Scotia in the early 1600s. France and England periodically fought over the territory, until at last the English won possession. It was decreed that all persons of French ancestry must pledge allegiance to Britain. Those who refused were deported to other states, where they were ostracised by Protestant English and forced to live in isolation. This resulted in preservation of the old French language of the 1700s. Gradually over time, this was diluted with English until we have the Cajun dialect of today. Cajuns talk fast and clip their vowels. The dialect is still stigmatised by the Anglo community.

Californian

California is a new state so it lacks the depth of dialect of other parts of America. With a population of nearly 34 million, only 46.7% are white. There is a large Latino (32.4%) and diverse Asian-American population. Young, white Californians use West Coast surfing, skate- and snow-boarding slang, with phrases such as 'Rad' (short for radical), 'Full on', 'Right on' and 'Off the wall'. They use 'like' instead of 'um' or 'er' and to mean 'unquote', e.g. 'Yo, dude. I'm like totally wasted.' 'Yeah. It's like what happened to yesterday?' The cult TV show *My So-Called Life* and the film *Clueless*, based on Californian teen talk, spawned 'Valley Girl English' (which has now spread to most other states), with popular phrases such as 'You guys', 'That's *so* not me', 'As if!' and 'Whatever'. With the advent of MTV and the intense promotion of popular music, this form of teenage lingo that originated in the West is pushing the limits. With its constantly changing specialised vocabulary, many adults have difficulty understanding it.

Midwestern

The Midwest comprises the north-central and north-eastern inland states of America. It is considered by many Americans to be the sociocultural centre of the country. The Midwestern dialect is said to be accentless, compatible with the view that Midwesterners are rather boring and nondescript and lacking in culture. It is the accent preferred by many television and radio stations. The Great Lakes region has a Canadian influence; parts of Michigan have Dutch connotations; and western Wisconsiners and Minnesotans have a strong Scandinavian accent.

New York City

Residents of northern New Jersey, New York City and its suburbs have a peculiar dialect, evolved from Dutch settlers. It is spoken in the main by middle and working class European Americans and is characteristically loud and fast. New Yorkers like to talk and fill up natural silences in conversation with incessant speech and interruptions, which to a non-New Yorker may seem rude, and lead to misunderstandings. They love to tell stories, talk to strangers and butt into conversations, especially to complain vociferously about something. Machine-gun questions do not help the negative stereotype. They don't mean to be unfriendly or intimidating, but sometimes come across that way. The New York City accent is one of the most recognisable American accents and is spoken by many famous movie stars, such as Bruce Willis, Danny DeVito, Woody Allen and Bugs Bunny.

Southern

Coastal southern speech can be traced back to West Country English and African slaves. It drops the 'r' after a vowel, before a consonant and before a pause, and thus is known as an '*R*-less' dialect. It is interwoven with the redneck culture and country music sound – country singers are expected to imitate it even if they are not native southern speakers. However, generally it attracts a stigma. Common grammatical turns of phrase include 'I'm a-fixin to leave. Wilma, fetch me that there coat and give me them gloves'; 'We got to talking and he said he don't catch nothing from that there lake, but I'm gonna catch me a big un'. There is great variation in the dialect between regions in the South and between old and young people. Some famous southern speakers are Jimmy Carter, Bill Clinton and Elvis Presley.

Spanglish

Further south and westwards, the language is a mixture of Spanish and English. There are many varieties of Spanglish depending on the origin of the people, and it varies from one region to another. Hispanic Americans have become more widespread than African-Americans in this region and heavily influence the English. Indeed, in states bordering Mexico there is a silent usurping of AE by Spanish. Many newly arrived Latinos in America do not speak any English at all; their children live in a bilingual environment and are caught between two worlds – which is where Spanglish originates.

Texan

The Texan drawl is slow and laconic ('Y'all'), combining two southern dialects: Appalachian or true 'country' and plantation. Texans use lots of metaphors and similes, spicy phrases (for instance, 'the short and curlies') and a flamboyant style. To avoid swear words they use their own particular lingo, such as 'Dag bum it!', 'Dag blame it!' or 'Dag nab it!' Texas is the home of isolated ranches, cowboys, oil, modern cities and President Bush. The Spanish language predominated before English settlers began to move into the area from the 1820s onwards. The Mexican Revolution pushed out the Mexicans, who were replaced with people from southern states and large numbers of Europeans. Since 1990, there has been a huge Mexican influx. More than half the population growth of Texas is due to immigrants. Approximately 30% of Texans live in the San Antonio, Houston, Dallas/Fort Worth area. Thus there is a significant rural–urban linguistic split forming.

Humour

Americans have quite a different sense of humour to us. Often only those Americans who have travelled and been exposed to Europeans, in particular British people, understand our rather facetious humour. Humorous sarcasm and cheekyism are not as common in the States as they are in Britain. If you make a joke about something, you are never quite sure if they have got it; sometimes it is best just to keep quiet. British slang terms and personal references used in British comedy can be puzzling to Americans. Our puns don't easily translate; our nonsense, satire, understatement and irony often go undetected. One American friend suggested that American humour is less sophisticated and more prudish. Some British comedies that are popular on American TV include *Last of the Summer Wine*, *The Benny Hill Show*, *Fawlty Towers*, *To the Manor Born*, *Jeeves and Wooster*, *Keeping Up Appearances* and *Don't Wait Up*.

US sitcoms are often kinder than British ones, as the audience laughs *with* rather than *at* the characters, e.g. the TV show *Friends*. American humour is generally gentler than ours. It often parodies stereotypical Americans, e.g. southern people and rednecks, who are portrayed as unsophisticated, rural and very conservative, with gun racks on their cars and the Confederate flag hoisted (Jeff Foxworthy specialises in this). Chris Rock and Eddie Murphy poke fun at blacks, but it is taboo for a white person to do so. Richard Pryor was a pioneer in black comedy.

Other famous American comedians include Bill Cosby, Adam Sandler, Steve Martin, Bill Murray and Roxanne, to name a few. Jerry Lewis is a national hero in France, with a huge following. Ellen DeGeneres and Jerry Seinfeld are popular for their observational and stand-up comedy. *Seinfeld* was the most successful sitcom in American TV history (it went off the air in 1998). Seinfeld says he was inspired by the 1950s sitcom *The Abbott and Costello Show* and is now doing stand-up performances. Jim Carrey undertakes physical comedy. Robin Williams is an example of an improvising, physical and stand-up comedian. Will Ferrell is a comedian turned actor, popular with high-school kids.

Saturday Night Live is hosted by a different famous person each week (usually an actor), with live sketches by unknown comedians. The show has spawned numerous, famous comedians, and is a long-running success. Many stand-ups now have their own shows, e.g. George Lopez. Talk shows featuring an introductory 5-minute stand-up routine are also popular (cue David Letterman and Jay Leno). The improv scene is big in America, especially in New York City and Los Angeles, with people paying to go to comedy clubs. Cable TV has a Comedy Central channel.

Many American sitcoms use toilet humour to raise a laugh, e.g. *Beavis and Butt-Head*, *The Simpsons* and *South Park*. Movies such as *Dumb and Dumber* are in the same vein. *The Simpsons* satirises American culture, society and even television itself, basing itself on a parody of Middle-American values and lifestyle. It is the longest running animated series in US television history. The second longest-running sitcom is *South Park*, which also ridicules American culture and, in particular, current events. Many films and TV series designed for children are also very funny for adults, with underlying humour for the grown-ups (or not so grown-up as the case may be). Films such as *Shrek*, *Madagascar* and *Ice Age*, and TV programmes like *Sponge Bob Square Pants* and *Jimmy Neutron* are a combination of satire, low-brow humour and plain good fun.

Common and Not-So-Common Phrases

Table 7.2 lists some slang words and phrases that you may not have come across before; you don't want to get bent up having a snow job done on you or be treated like you've just got off the boat.

Table 7.2 Some American slang words and phrases.

American slang	Meaning	Examples
Bad	Intense	'That movie was bad' (so it could mean intensely good!)
Bent	Angry	'Don't get so bent out of shape'
Bombed	Intoxicated	
Clip	Cheat	'Be careful they don't clip you'
Do a snow job on	To deceive	
Flaky	Unreliable	'She's a flaky worker'
Pure gravy	Easy money	'The job is pure gravy'
Grungy	Dirty	
Hip shooter	Talking without thinking	'He's a bit of a hip shooter'
Just off the boat	Naïve	
Narks	Drug police	
Rinky-dink	Inferior	

The American habit of saying 'Have a nice day' can grate on some British nerves, because it is overused and can sound insincere. Personally I think it is better than no comment at all at the conclusion of a service. Another common saying is 'You're welcome' whenever anyone does something for you. It's a nicer way of saying 'That's OK' or better than simply saying nothing, the usual British responses.

A Brit who ran a marathon commented on the great experience but also on being irritated by the succession of bland 'cookie cutter' (same) phrases of congratulation. After thousands had welcomed him over the line with 'Way to go' and 'Good job', he claimed that the effect of these phrases weakened and eventually reversed. It's not that Americans lack vocabulary or intelligence, but they have unknowingly – or maybe knowingly, who knows – developed a verbal efficiency in the form of stock phrases. Consequently, for each type of occasion there are one or two phrases that are appropriate. Initially, the use of the stock phrase can be as charming as discovering a new language. Some of the phrases have been chosen to sound clever and 'cool'; but after prolonged exposure they just become irritating. With Britain's increasing reliance on American TV programmes and use of text and e-mail as communication forms, we should expect similar language development – if that's the right description – in the UK.

Americans often use 'Sir' or 'Ma'am' when addressing another person, especially someone they don't know. Youngsters are encouraged to call you Mrs or Miss even when they know you quite well, e.g. 'Ask Mrs Musk/Miss Julie if you can have a drink'. They are also very politically correct and have developed appropriate terminology. Thus stewards and stewardesses are called flight attendants, mail men or women are mail carriers, the handicapped are differently abled or physically challenged, coloured people or blacks may be called people of colour, and pets are animal companions.

Most Americans are polite and courteous. Indeed, when forced into close proximity with the potential for accidental collision, a well-mannered 'Excuse me' is often heard. However, this can give you a false sense of security, leaving you vulnerable to less well-mannered versions. In stressful situations – supermarkets are fine examples – you may find yourself charged down by wild women and, as you're rudely cast aside, barked at with 'Excuse ME!'. Generally you'll only recover your wits once the danger of collision has passed so all you can do is direct a hurt glare to a rapidly receding behind – normally a target of some substance. In these situations the 'Excuse me' is actually a substitute for 'Get out of my way', which is what the deliverer actually wanted to say, but she somehow managed to maintain some restraint. The majority of abusers of 'Excuse me' are women, as they are best equipped with the piercing voice and indignant body language that gives the impolite version of the phrase its bite. However, should you be unwise enough to force a change of direction to a trolley-wielding harpy, then you'll face the full megaton-tipped 'EXCUSE ME!', delivered with eye-watering precision and sting. It is not that the deliverers of these barbed phrases mean harm, but it's the most aggression that good members of society can allow themselves without drawing blood. The normally respectful terms 'Sir' and 'Ma'am' are also frequently mistreated by irritated individuals. Given an injection of vitriol, use of these otherwise respectful words means, 'I want your attention, and I will not be ignored'. Another common use is to add them to disagreeable statements, as if a respectful closure makes them unquestionable.

Some words that British people use are foreign to the average American. They rarely use 'mate' as in 'Hello, mate'; instead they might say 'dude'. The word 'untidy' raises quizzical eyebrows, e.g. instead of 'My car is very untidy' they would say 'My car is a mess' or 'My car is a wreck' (which could be misleading). A few other British English sayings that are anomalous are 'sorted out' (as in 'We must get this room sorted out'), 'snogging' and 'quite nice'.

Conclusion

American English has its own spellings and terminology, often different from British English. This was brought home to me on my first week of arriving in the States, when we went out to an Italian restaurant and I ordered my favourite pasta dish – spaghetti à la marinara – looking forward to a big plate of seafood pasta. Instead I ended up with plain old pasta in tomato sauce – the American version of spaghetti à la marinara (I thought the price was too good to be true).

Linguistically, America is one of *the* most diverse countries in the world. An amazing 336 languages are claimed to be spoken or signed there, 176 of which are indigenous. According to US Census data, nearly 34 million US residents are foreign born, and 11 million are not fluent in English (most living in California, Texas, New York, Nevada and Arizona). Both American English and British English continue to influence each other, and many Americanisms are now common in British speech. As part of the American spirit, American English is becoming more informal, flaunting the rules of grammar and syntax and becoming ever more inventive. Many Americans take pleasure in their colloquialism, slang and adaptations to their language.

As an adult, you will probably not lose your English accent, no matter how long you stay in America. However, children are another matter. William picked up the American drawl within weeks of arriving and there was no holding him back. However, it took about 5 months before his younger sister, Rosie, developed the twang. It was funny hearing her say things like, 'Oh, mayn, my paynts are wet, darn it' – meaning she'd got her trousers wet, of course.

Useful Websites

www.about.com – has a useful page under 'American English', giving equivalent British expressions, and vice versa.

www.pbs.org/speak/seatosea/americanvarieties – varieties of American English.

8 • Education

The American schooling system is different from the British system, partly because, in America, schooling does not formally begin until age 6, whereas in Britain children enter school at 5, and even some tender 4-year-olds start as rising 5s. In the States, education is compulsory between the ages of 6 and 16 or 18 (depending on where you live). American children start school in the autumn *after* their sixth birthday (in Ohio, for example, children must be 6 on or before 30 September to start that year). The school year begins in late August/early September and goes through to mid June (dates vary according to school district).

Terms Used in the American Education System

Some toddlers start in *pre-school* at around 3 years old. Our daughter Rosie went to an all-day one which offered 2½ hours' basic academic tuition in both the morning and afternoon; the rest of the day was structured play and activities. Children may then progress to *pre-kindergarten* class. However, many children do not go to any kind of formal school/class until they enter *kindergarten* at age 5 or 6. Ninety five percent of American children attend kindergarten.

School proper starts at age 6 when children go to *elementary* school. The years are called *grades.* The UK equivalent of primary and secondary education is often termed *K–12* in the US (K for kindergarten and 12 for 12th grade). Some areas have *middle school, intermediate school* or *junior high*; this provides a bridge between primary and secondary education for 7th–8th grades. *High school* is for the teenage years. If all this sounds rather confusing, it is. It is difficult to make a direct comparison between the British and American schooling systems because of the different terminology and division of ages, which can also vary according to state. Table 8.1 is my attempt to provide a basic comparison.

Table 8.1 Terminology used in education.

American term	Equivalent British term	Notes
School years		
Pre-school	Nursery, crèche	Children 4 years old and younger
Pre-kindergarten	Reception class, rising 5s	Children aged 5 and less
K–12		Kindergarten through to 12th grade (age 18)
Kindergarten	Year 1	Children aged 5–6
Grades 1–6, elementary school	Years 2–7, primary or junior school	Children aged 6–11
Grades 6–8 (and sometimes 9), middle/intermediate/ junior high school	Years 8–9, secondary school	Children aged 11–14
Grades 9–12, high/senior school	Years 10–13, upper school/sixth form	Children aged 14–18
Freshman	Fresher	First-year college or high-school student
Sophomore	Undergraduate	Second-year college or high-school student
Junior		Second year
Senior		Third year
Fraternity/sorority terms		
Greeks		Members of societies
Greek week	Rag week	
Frat house		Houses owned by Greek societies
Honor societies		Undergraduate societies that recruit students with high grades
Rushes		Recruiting of new society members; often involves initiation rites
General terminology		
Brown bag lunch, sack lunch	Pack lunch	
Grade	Class or form	
Recess	Break	
School	School or college	Any institute of education

Semester	Term	Usually there are two semesters: fall (late August to Christmas) and spring (January to May/June)
Summer school		For college students, who need to catch up/redo their studies

Universities offer a wide range of undergraduate and postgraduate degree courses (Post Doctorate, Doctorate and Master's degrees), with faculties undertaking research. *Colleges* offer only Bachelor and Associate degrees. Students are said to *major* in a particular field of study in order to obtain a degree. They then select courses in that major that add up to a degree programme. *Freshmen* are first-year students in college, universities or high school. *Sophomores* are second-year students. The word comes from the Greek *sophos* meaning wise and *moros* meaning foolish. A *middler* is a third-year student in a college that offers 5 years of study. *Juniors* are students in their penultimate year of study. *Seniors* are in their last year.

Students receive academic *grades* and *points* for every exam, paper and course they take – according to their peers. Thus this cannot be compared with the British system of GCSE exam results, or indeed very well with the grades of similar students in other US schools, because there is no standardised system across the country. Table 8.2 describes the levels of grading. A *grade point average* (*GPA*) is calculated overall. Students wanting to go on to higher education outside their state normally sit a *SAT* or *ACT test* (see below) to demonstrate mathematical and verbal skills. It is generally accepted that American colleges have lower admission standards than British ones.

Table 8.2 The academic grades and points system in the United States.

Points	Grade	Standard
4	A	Very good
3	B	Good
2	C	Average
1	D	Poor
0	F	Fail

Your Schooling Options

Based on statistics from the 2000 US Census Bureau, and according to Sam Roberts (author of *Who We Are Now*, 2004):

- more than 52% of 3- and 4-year-olds attend pre-school or pre-kindergarten;

- 60% attend all-day kindergarten;
- 1 in 10 children go to private school;
- 1 in 50 are homeschooled;
- half of all college students are 25 years old or more;
- 87% of native-born Americans aged 25 years plus have a high-school diploma.

Across America, there are concerns over racial disparities in schools, which seem to be an intractable problem of American society. For instance, in the South, public (i.e. free state) schools, though officially desegregated, are often full of children from minority families, whereas those whose parents can afford it go to privately funded schools. In the North, inner city schools tend to be dominated by children from low-income families, those with money having moved out to the suburbs, where they send their youngsters to predominantly white schools.

Public Schools

Approximately 80% of elementary and secondary schools are publicly funded, i.e. free. Attendance at public schools is catchment-area driven, and you will need to have either purchased or signed a lease on a house before your child can attend the local school. However, determining which *is* your local school can be tricky. It is not unheard of for children on one side of the street living in odd-numbered homes to go to one catchment school and for those on the other side of the street living in even-numbered homes to go to another. Look up the town/city you are going to on the internet to find information on your options.

Public schools are controlled and run by school boards, who are reliant on local taxes for funding, and so resources vary accordingly. Class size is also highly variable, and can be much larger than in Britain. A school voucher system is being debated, whereby parents can receive a refund of taxes paid, to put towards the costs of paying for private or homeschooling. While this would appear to be fairer for parents who want to homeschool or send their children to private schools because they are concerned about the standard of their local public schools, it could adversely affect the public sector by drawing funds away – thus creating a vicious circle.

Charter Schools

Charter schools are privately run, licenced alternatives to state schools. They are publicly funded by taxes, but operate outside the direct control of the conventional school district. Charter schools aim to offer smaller classes and a more specialised and greater choice of curriculum. Some practise non-classroom-based activities for part of the school term (e.g. homeschooling, distance learning or independent study), thus involving much more parent participation. Thirty seven American states operate charter schools, and California and Arizona have the most.

Private Schools

Private schools include church-affiliated schools, non-profit independent schools, and for-profit private schools, and approximately 1 in 10 school-age children attends a school in this sector. A third of all private schools are Catholic. Some churches partially subsidise their schools and thus charge less than other private schools, which is perhaps one of the reasons why half of all private school pupils are in Catholic schools. The National Association of Independent Schools (NAIS) represents non-sectarian schools.

If you can afford it, a private school is especially appropriate if you are living in America for only a short time. Because American children do not start schooling until they are 6 years old, your child may have to take a step backwards when he or she starts school in America. Both public and private schools prefer to slot new children in according to age, though private schools may be more willing to assess a youngster to see if he or she could cope with being in a higher grade/year. Even if not, the smaller class size (sometimes as low as 10 children to 1 teacher) in private schools mean that your child should receive much more individual attention than in a public school.

The Montessori system of educating children is popular in America, and the States has 1100 of these schools (compared with just 45 in the UK). Visit the websites listed at the end of the chapter to find out more about the Montessori system.

Military Academies

There are still a number of military service academies in America, mostly in the South. They require students to be nominated by a member of Congress, and thus restrict admissions to those who can show their worth or merit. They are not necessarily run by the armed forces, but may be a middle, high school or tertiary-level college – private or publicly funded. The guiding principle is that they favour military-style education, discipline, hygiene and tradition.

Homeschooling and 'Unschooling'

Homeschooling is another option, popular in America. It usually involves a group of parents banding together to school their children in their own homes, or parents may opt to homeschool on their own. Special programmes are offered for homeschoolers by the authorities and local organisations, for instance science days at state parks, craft workshops and natural history classes at museums. There are online public education programmes and curricula, and an extensive parent homeschool network, with parents able to swap resources, e.g. books. Two magazines on the market are aimed specifically at homeschoolers: *Homeschooling Today* and *Home Education.*

If you choose to homeschool, you will not receive any refund of taxes or government help – it is your choice to opt out. States vary in the recommended criteria for homeschooling. In Ohio, you need a high-school degree to teach your children. You must notify the school district and agree to teach a set number of hours a year (approximately 900). At the end of the year, you have the choice of either showing a portfolio of your child's work to a certified teacher or getting him or her to take a standardised test, or you may come up with some other way of showing you are working to standard. In Ohio you are not told which curriculum to use; you can purchase all or part of a specific or across-the-board curriculum, whichever you prefer. Some come with a built-in test.

Homeschooling involves a lot of self-discipline and motivation, not to mention a great deal of time spent with your children, so it is not for everyone. Some parents make the choice based on religious beliefs, or because they want to cherish time with their children; others because they are concerned with the poor quality of their public schools or rather lax morals. One friend felt that, 'Proficiency tests are killing schools, as the kids have to pass them for the school to get funding. They have to take a test every year, so teachers teach a list of facts and kids are taught to memorise the answers'.

Unschooling (also termed natural or discovery learning, child-led or child-directed learning) is another non-traditional method of education. Parents provide the environment, resources, support and instruction (when asked) based on a child's curiosity and wish to learn about a subject. Parents act as 'facilitators', allowing their children to choose what they want to learn and when. Standard formal education, e.g. learning to read, may not start until the child expresses enough interest and is ready to learn. It is a very child-directed form of education, with no set structure. Such freedom for children to choose what they want to learn and when sounds a bit dodgy to me; I can imagine my two choosing the television and computer for their 'education' most of the time. It's an interesting idea, but is it workable?

Studies have shown that (rather surprisingly) homeschooled and unschooled children do well if not better than their formally educated peers. Christine Foster, writing in the *Stanford Magazine* (November/December 2000; see *Useful Websites*), has this to say: homeschoolers

> '...have the spark, the passion, that sets the truly exceptional student – the one driven to pursue independent research and explore difficult concepts from a very early age – apart from your typical bright kid'.

Despite not having any recognised grades or qualifications, homeschooled children are able to bring these qualities with them to college, and as a consequence of their special motivation and experiences, often do very well. The National Home Education Research Institute estimated that in 2000, 1 in 33 school-aged children were homeschooled (approximately 1.7 million), and this figure appears to be growing.

Starting a New School in America

Below are some other things to contemplate when starting a new school in America:

- Check with your prospective school regarding medical issues. In America, children need to have received, or at least started, a course of hepatitis B vaccinations, and there are other differences in vaccination requirements and schedules for children coming from other countries, even Britain. See the section *Coming to America: Taking Care of Your Health* in Chapter 18.
- Most schools do not impose a uniform rule, apart from some private schools.
- It is usual to have to bring your own stationery, and at the beginning of the school year you will be given a long shopping list of back-to-school items, including pens, paper, folders, glue, scissors, paints, crayons, etc.
- Given the earlier start afforded by the UK educational system, you might discuss with your prospective school whether your child could move up a year, especially if he or she has good school reports to back this idea up.

School Holidays

Because the US Constitution separates church from State, in public schools assemblies for religious purposes and formal prayer are outlawed and schools are not allowed to honour religious customs. This is why there is no Easter break; instead, Americans have what is called spring break, usually sometime in March (timing varies according to state). They also do not have half-terms, so the autumn/winter term is rather a long stint through to Christmas, with only a few days off for Thanksgiving at the end of November. However, they make up for it in the summer, when schools may be on vacation for anything from 9 to 11 weeks. Some parents find this too long – with the children forgetting what they've learnt and getting out of learning practice. It is also a long time to keep them occupied and entertained, and consequently many parents are itching for the children to go back to school come the beginning of autumn. This is one reason for the importance of summer school or camp.

When kids who do not make the passing grade need extra tuition they go to what is called summer school. Summer camp, on the other hand, is geared up to fun and perhaps teaching specific skills, for example tennis lessons, swimming, baseball, nature studies, dancing, etc. Children can learn self-defence, fire and road safety, or do community service. Other activities are wholly entertainment orientated, focusing on fun and social time with other kids, e.g. fishing, canoeing, field trips, arts and crafts, themed weeks – the list is endless. Charges are usually by the week and very reasonable. Summer camps are also popular with teenagers; for some it will be the first time they sleep away from home. Counsellors look after the children, organise activities and usually sleep and stay with their groups. It is a popular summer job for high-school and college students. The pay is often less than the minimum wage, but food and lodging is usually free. The YMCA and Boy Scouts offer great summer camp programmes. 4-H (which stands for Head, Heart, Hands and Health) is for 5- to 21-year-olds and largely centred on agriculture.

There are also many free events going on during the summer, so there is no excuse for the kids to get bored at home, so long as you are willing to act as chauffeur. Check your library for their summer reading and activity programme. Local nature areas, parks and museums usually have plenty of planned, free events for children also.

Curriculum Issues

Children have to undertake annual state assessment exams, required under the No Child Left Behind Act. The curriculum in America's schools is decided largely at local and state level, and can vary between districts. In elementary schools, social studies and science are often not well developed. Children are taught local, state and national history and geography, and little about the world outside America (is there anywhere in England besides London?). They usually receive all their lessons from one teacher. In middle school, they begin to be taught by a number of different teachers and can sometimes choose one or two classes as core subjects; these are known as *electives*. However, it is not until high school that students are given more control over their education, with most specialising in electives during their second year.

To obtain a high-school diploma, typically a student must study and pass in the following subjects:

- English – 4 years.
- Math – usually 3 years.
- Physical education – at least 1 year.
- Science (biology, chemistry and physics).
- Social science (economics, government and history).

Some schools also require students to study a 'health' course, incorporating first aid, anatomy, nutrition, sex and birth control, and alcohol, smoking and drug-related issues. Some make teaching a foreign language or the arts a mandatory part of their curriculum.

Usually high-school students in their third year (11th grade) sit the SAT Reasoning Test (Scholastic Aptitude Test) or ACT (American College Testing), or both, in order to go on to college. The SAT is 'a measure of the critical thinking skills needed for academic success in college' whereas the ACT tests students' 'general education development and their ability to complete college-level work'. SAT versus ACT is usually viewed as aptitude (to evaluate innate ability) versus achievement (gained during high school), though the distinction between the two is hazy. The SAT has been around since 1926 and has been the test of choice in East and West Coast states. The ACT came in in 1959 and is favoured by the states geographically in between. However, nowadays the ACT entrance exam is accepted by every 4-year college and university in America that requires a test. Despite this, geography still determines which test most students choose to take.

Many students participate in extracurricular activities, though in the public sector the number of activities offered depends on funding; some schools charge students for any extra activities they want to do. America is fairly unique in the way it promotes high-school sports. Football and basketball are especially popular and attract huge crowds and enthusiastic followings, with significant media attention, while at the same time providing major funding for some school districts. Other highlights of school include cheerleading, marching bands, drill teams, homecoming, and pep rallies before sports events. The school prom for juniors and seniors held in May (around graduation-time for seniors) is the big social event of the year. It evolved during the 1930s, when high school was the peak of education. Often by then, couples were already engaged, some even married. If not, there was, and still is, a great deal of date pressure. Kids dress up in tuxedos and gowns, the boy is expected to buy his date a corsage, and a limo might be hired to take them to the dance. It's a bit like a mini wedding. Couples often go out to dinner first, and then to the dance, where finger food and punch is served (no liquor, though a bottle or two may be surreptitiously added to the punch bowl). Teachers act as chaperones. Despite this, terrible accidents (usually involving driving) frequently occur on prom night.

Higher Education

Post-secondary or higher education usually encompasses 4 years of a student's life (more if they flunk some of the course and have to stay on). Though America ranks low in her standard of primary and secondary education, she excels in the later years of training (ages 18 plus), having at least 22 of the top 30 universities in the world. This is why huge numbers of foreign students are attracted to studying in America.

The top eight private institutions of higher education make up the Ivy League (also called the Ancient Eight or Ivies), so termed because of the ivy that grows on many of their historic buildings. They are:

- Brown University (Providence, RI)
- Columbia University (New York, NY)
- Cornell University (Ithaca, NY)
- Dartmouth College (Hanover, NH)
- Harvard University (Cambridge, MA)
- Princeton University (Princeton, NJ)
- University of Pennsylvania (Philadelphia, PA)
- Yale University (New Haven, CT)

The Ivies were originally part of an athletic conference, with their sports teams playing competitively against each other. 'The Big Three' refers to Harvard, Yale and Princeton (commonly abbreviated to HYP), which originally dominated college football. Nowadays, the term Ivy League denotes academic excellence and social elitism. Harvard University is the oldest university in America (founded in 1639). It is ranked as the number-two dream school by US college applicants, New York University (the largest private university) being number one (*Princeton Review*, 2005). The Ivies are highly selective in their admissions. All were founded by religious societies and are now privately owned and controlled, though they may receive federal or state funding for research projects. Both collaboration and competition between them are high.

Besides these top private schools, there are also the Public Ivies (for instance the Universities of California, Michigan and Virginia), the Little Ivies (a handful of liberal arts colleges) and the Seven Sisters (all-female institutions). Each state also has its own non-profit public university system, the largest being California State University (CSU) and the State University of New York (SUNY).

Whichever American university you go to, the experience doesn't come cheap. Typically, out-of-state students have to pay higher rates to attend another state's university (similar to private university rates), though after the first year they may then be regarded as resident. Tuition fees range from $5000 per academic year for state residents to a whopping $40,000 for out-of-state residents. Dwindling state funding has resulted in a 14% hike in tuition rates at public high schools compared to 6% at private schools (according to College Board figures, 2002–2004). Living expenses are extra – anything up to $12,000 per academic year. Most students rely on student loans and/or scholarships to pay their way through university. It also costs a small fortune to graduate – what with the obligatory cap and gown, newspaper announcements, a framed diploma, class ring, yearbooks, jacked-up hotel prices, river cruises and buffet dinners; some schools even charge graduation fees. Despite the high costs involved in obtaining a university education, it is usually worth it, as the US Census Bureau reckons that graduates earn at least $200,000 more in their lifetime than non-graduates.

If you can't afford the often exorbitant fees charged by colleges and universities, your local community college may be the next-best option. They have an open admissions policy, and generally attract low-income students, as well as many older people seeking a vocational qualification in order to boost their income. However, an estimated two out of three students leave without a degree, mostly because they have outside pressures, such as children or work. If you have good grades, after 2 years at a community college you can transfer to a more expensive state university for the last 2 years.

Fraternal organisations, sororities, reunions and alumni (the network of past students who like to keep in touch with their old school or college) are very popular in America; just take a look at the listings in the *Yellow Book* (*Yellow Pages*). At times, whole pages in our local paper were taken up with area reunions. Fraternities and sororities are very much a feature of American colleges and universities, and may be categorised according to:

- Gender – fraternities (from the Latin *frater* for brother) may be all-male or mixed sex; sororities (from the Latin *soror* for sister) are all-female.
- Religion.
- Culture or ethnicity, e.g. African-American fraternities. There are also multicultural frats.
- Purpose – social, professional, community service, charitable, etc.
- Size – local or national.
- Era – according to when the organisation was founded.

Groups are usually identified by two or three Greek letters, e.g. Phi Beta Kappa (considered to be the oldest Greek-letter student society in America). In student towns, Greek letters on the front of community houses indicate which group is based there. Hazing (ragging) has caused controversy, as freshmen students are subjected to humiliation and abuse, and are often forced to undertake dangerous stunts in order to be accepted into the society (witness the film *Animal House*). Many schools are now cracking down on this practice.

Problems with the American College System

The PBS-produced television documentary *Declining by Degrees* (2005) paints a very dire picture of America's higher-education system. Numerous issues of concern are raised:

- 1 in 4 freshmen don't make it to their second year.
  Rising costs means many students struggle to pay for their tuition and living expenses while at college. An estimated 20% have a full-time job while trying to be a full-time student, and 68% work at least 15 hours/week. It is therefore little wonder that so many drop out of school due to pressure of commitments. Those on low income or who are unwilling to take out a loan are thus often discriminated against owing to the high costs associated with college. The government's social contract, which was originally put in place to aid those who couldn't afford to go to college, clearly isn't working.

- 1 in 2 students leave college or university without graduating.
  Many students are disappointed by their experience of college or university. Graduates from high school are freely admitted to public colleges in their home state, which means that the size of the first undergraduate year can run into thousands. Faculty staff are under a great deal of pressure. With first-year class sizes often running at 200–300 students per lecture, it's no wonder teachers don't set

weekly papers. (Imagine reading and grading that amount of papers each week.) They do not have the resources and time to cope with this number, so something has to give. Thus young people go unchallenged, are discouraged and often drop out. There is often no attendance register, and the lecturing style of teachers is off-putting, with very little personal interaction.

- Employers are finding that graduates lack necessary basic skills.
  Many campuses are so large and anonymous that half the students get away with studying 15 hours or less a week, don't do the homework reading and simply turn up for the lecture, yet still find they can pass with reasonable grades; there is little incentive to do more.

- Grade inflation
  Teachers who mark firmly and fail students get a bad reputation and do not fulfill their graduate quota. Thus grade inflation is a problem, and minimal effort is often all that is required to pass.

  Another reason for grade inflation is that university budgets are based on the number of students who enroll, see out the course and graduate with reasonable grades. So universities often offer scholarships to the more clever high-school graduates (national merit scholars) in order to boost their own reputations of producing high-quality graduates. Universities are also pressurised to maintain their ranking, e.g. by publications such as *U.S. News*, which prospective students rely on heavily when deciding where to enroll.

- Increasing importance of non-educational facilities.
  Recently, establishments of higher education have had to fundraise as they cannot rely as much on state support as in the past. Schools operate in a highly competitive market and campuses have to sell themselves – perhaps by building new, state-of-the-art facilities, such as plush student halls, food courts that rival those of shopping malls or swish fitness centres. It is hard to see how this raises educational standards. Often college sports are overemphasised and sports students given unfair advantages, e.g. full athletic scholarships and being allowed more time to play sport than attend classes. College sports create a huge amount of revenue for the faculty and are very commercialised (e.g. with sponsorship); coaches earn big pay cheques.

The Yellow Bus

School transportation is usually provided by the famous yellow bus. Around 440,000 of these distinctive vehicles bus 25 million children to and from school each year, which represents just over half of all K–12 students. Ask your school about putting your child's name down for the bus. If a pickup is not available near your home, the cost of transport to/from school may be reimbursed by the county council.

Conspicuous canary-yellow is the colour of all school buses throughout the US and Canada (officially the colour is known as National School Bus Glossy Yellow). It was chosen for safety reasons, as black lettering is easier to see on dark mornings on this bright yellow background. The school bus is a very specific type, distinct from all other buses, with 45 construction standards, including colour. Very few have seat belts, though lap belts are required in California, Florida, New York and New Jersey. Some modern ones have the luxury of air conditioning, but it is more usual in hot weather for the driver to simply leave the door open. The seats are also pretty uncomfortable. The younger kids are well looked after by the older students and bus bullying is rare.

The buses generally collect children direct from their homes and drop off at the myriad schools in the area. Sometimes a change of bus is needed, which extends the journey. Schools generally start earlier than in Britain, at around 8 a.m., so you will have to get used to an earlier routine. Finishing time is around 3 p.m. You feel very safe around the buses, as they stop in the middle of the road with their lights flashing and their stop arms barring any would-be passing motorists. Indeed, it is a serious misdemeanour to pass one (see Chapter 11).

You can buy a second-hand school bus for around $5000. People use them for hauling, in demolition derbies, as storage units, workshops or mobile stores. Schoolies or skoolies are school bus enthusiasts who convert them into motor homes or RVs, or simply restore them. Some old buses are shipped to Latin America and Africa for public use there.

Security at School

In 1999, 12 students and one teacher were shot and killed and another 24 wounded when two teenage boys, angry at society, opened fire at Columbine High School, Colorado, before committing suicide. In 2007, another student shot dead 33 people at Virginia Tech. As a consequence, many schools have implemented plans to protect their communities in the event of a school shooting. Measures include:

- zero tolerance of weapons and threatening behaviour;
- new anti-bullying policies;
- installing metal detectors;
- security guards;
- computer-generated IDs;
- see-through backpacks;
- door numbering – to assist public safety officers in responding to incidents.

There are also strict rules about collecting children from school (owing to incidences of child abduction). At William's school – a suburban, independent, lower school (for ages 6 and up) – we were given a name card to display on the car windscreen, alerting someone standing at the school gate that we were there to collect William. The school attendant then relayed the name via walkie-talkie to the hall where all the children were waiting to be called. The children were then escorted out to the pick-up point and another person ensured the child got into the right car. It was quite a rigmarole, and you could be waiting some time in the parents' queue, but I could understand the precautions. Schools are fearful of the legal aspects of handing a child over to someone without pre-arrangement for pick-up, so they devise systems to ensure you are identified and authorised.

You may also be given a photo identity card for your child, for you to complete with his or her vital statistics and keep in your purse or wallet. In the horrible event that you lose your child, you can whip out the card to show the authorities immediately. Even if your school doesn't supply such a thing, it is a sensible item to have just in case. There are far too many cases of child kidnapping these days.

Attitudes Towards Children

Americans are almost French-like in their emphasis on the family and associated values. At Christmas, it is very common to receive photo cards from American friends, with their little angels (children) pictured in charming poses, rather than a traditional shop-bought card with a Christmas tree or snowy scene.

King Edward VIII is reputed to have said, 'The thing that impresses me the most about America is the way parents obey their children'. Some parents in America treat their children more like friends. *The Brady Bunch* was a popular TV sitcom on the air between 1969 and 1974. It centred on a fictional happy family of three girls, three boys, mum and dad (on their second marriages) and housekeeper. This depiction of a harmonious family influenced many prospective parents growing up in the early 1970s and later (as repeat episodes were broadcast). Praise and 'positive stroking' are now the norm, and American children seem to have much more freedom to do what they want than children of other nationalities. They expect constant attention and confidence boosts (as do many American adults). It is rare to hear parents chastising their children in public; they usually talk around the issue, rather than being negative. I was often surprised to hear parents trying to reason with their unruly children and cajole them into good behaviour, when I would have given them a simple 'No', followed by some kind of threat or ultimatum if they persisted. I'm not sure which is best, but it does appear to me that children in America have the upper hand.

Another observation is that children are often allowed to stay up late. Many children's events do not start until 7 p.m. and may run on as late as 10 p.m., long after my two youngsters had been resigned to bed. Keeping young children up till 8 or 9 o'clock so that dads working late get some time with their little ones at the end of the day is common in many families. When do parents get their personal time, I'd like to know?

The upside to this emphasis on children is that most Americans are extremely child-tolerant. Children are welcome seemingly wherever you go. Finding places to eat is a doddle; they are nearly always seated with free colouring paper and crayons and can select from their own menu. Drinks come in snazzy spill-proof cups, which you can keep and even ask to take away a refill in. In places like McDonald's there are free play areas, all for the price of a coke (if that's all you want to run to). Out and about, children are often treated to free stickers, balloons and sweets. At a drive-in bank while depositing a cheque, I was surprised to find one dog biscuit and two lollipops returned in the shuttle, much to the delight of the small two- and four-legged occupants of my car.

Even on golf courses, where you might expect a certain amount of adult stuffiness and decorum, children are not seen as anti-golfers or frowned upon. Tim regularly took William and Rosie to local courses, where other golfers welcomed them and were happy for them to come along on a round of adult golf. I cannot imagine taking a 4-year-old to a public golf course in England without some negative comment or looks of annoyance. It is just not done. The same is true of many public places in Britain, e.g. restaurants, pubs, libraries and other 'precious' adult domains. They are just not used to tolerating children or allowing them their own space; neither are they geared up to entertaining them. In America, you can pretty much go anywhere with children. That is one aspect of American living we particularly appreciated.

Personal Findings

If you are a family moving to America, your children's schooling is one issue you will have to resolve. We were quite concerned how our two youngsters would fit into and out of the American schooling system. William was 5 when he arrived in America, with a year's reception class grounding under his belt. We were able to send him to a good independent school with a teacher:pupil ratio of 1:14, which I think lessened the impact on his transferring between the American and British systems.

There was a slight regression for Rosie, our 3-year-old. She continued to go to a pre-school much like the one she had attended in England. However, come 4 years old, when she would normally be starting school in the UK as a rising 5, she had to continue in pre-kindergarten class. In pre-K, children are only formally taught for 2½ hours each morning and afternoon; the rest of the day is spent playing. Moreover, it is state law in Ohio that all children up to the age of 5 who attend day classes have at least an hour's nap during the day. We had weaned Rosie off day-napping, so this was a retrograde step for her.

Another noticeable difference between our schooling experiences in England and America was that American children are taught non-cursive writing to start with, only progressing to joined-up handwriting in Year 2. William had developed a lovely cursive style in his first year in English school, and then unlearned it in America. On our return, we had to work to get his handwriting back into the cursive style. Another difference was that they weren't taught their letters by phoneme (i.e. sound); instead they learnt to say the name of the letter. This made it harder for Rosie to read words, as she had not been taught to sound out the letters.

Throughout America, Spanish is taught as a foreign language right from the start (whereas in England, French is introduced into the curriculum a little later). At William's school, they focused on a couple of subjects for weeks at a time, then switched to others, rather than splitting the day up with many different subjects. That way, the children could concentrate on a few topics at a time, enjoy a deeper immersion, carry out long-term projects over several weeks and really get to grips with a subject, rather than chopping and changing. Also sharing was an important aspect of class time, with children allowed to bring in something interesting from home to share with their class mates each week (but no toys).

Conclusion

Education in America is state-governed, which is why standards and regulations vary. Of all the developed nations, America has the highest dropout rate from school. The decline in the nation's literacy is also causing some concern, as the rate of literacy is lower than in most other developed countries. America spends far more per pupil than any other nation, yet the education of youngters from age 6 to 18 is recognised as being mediocre. American students are inferior in terms of performance compared with students of other nations. In particular, the US ranks below average in science, maths and problem solving. Teaching in geography is also reported to be lacking. In a study of the maths proficiency of sixth formers from 15 different countries, the US came twelfth in geometry and calculus and fourteenth in advanced algebra. Hong Kong and Japan were the leaders, followed by England and Wales in third and fourth position in all three subjects. A college education has always been considered a highway to the middle classes; however, with record numbers dropping out or flunking, the future may not be so bright for many of America's young people.

In 2001, the government passed the *No Child Left Behind Act.* Now all students in primary and secondary education in the States must sit an annual test to ensure they are not falling behind their peers. However, the President does not appear to be overly concerned:

> 'To those of you who received honours, awards and distinctions, I say well done. And to the C students, I say you, too, can be president of the United States'.

These words capitulate the American ethos of anything is possible; it doesn't matter who you are, or how well you do at school, you can achieve success in life. American children are overloaded with encouragement and praise, for every small achievement. I wonder that this perhaps breeds big egos and overconfidence – which, some would say, are common American characteristics. However, compare this with Britain, which has been branded by UNICEF as the worst country in the developed world in terms of children's sense of their own well-being. Antisocial behaviour, youth violence, drink and drug cultures, and loutish attitudes are commonplace in Britain. Refreshingly, America's youth do not seem to have gone down this road so much. Surely this says something about America's family values and youth-centred approach?

Useful Websites

www.asd.com – American School Directory, a subscription-based listing of K–12 schools across the States.
www.amshq.org/schools.htm – American Montessori Society schools throughout the US.
www.montessori-uk.org – Montessori Society AMI (UK).
www.standfordalumni.org/news/magazine – features a good article on home-schooling and unschooling (key in 'unschooling').
www.unschooling.info – some of the posts are particularly interesting; it made me realise how much more proactive we could be in our children's education.

Wikipedia:
College and university rankings – for a discussion on the ranking system in the US.

9 · Systems and Services

This chapter offers practical information, advice and tips on how to get up and running in America (with regard to communications, being switched on and financially organised).

The Postal Service

The United States Postal Service (USPS) is generally praised by Americans, who consider it to be one of their most efficient public services. I'm not so sure, having had variable experience with the service, especially with regard to the delivery of mail.

Our house, like many in America, had a stand-alone mailbox at the end of the drive. This is so that the mail carrier, arriving in his or her white, righthand-drive postal van, can do everything from the comfort of a padded seat with a roof over his/her head. It makes delivering the mail a quick and labour-saving job. Pity our British postmen and women who have to trudge up drives, carrying a satchel of mail, putting up with barking dogs and pouring rain. I'm not sure the American system would work in Britain though, as I can see these boxes being a target for vandals and young hoodlums; this is not generally a problem in America as it is a federal offence to tamper with mail. If you don't have a box at the kerb, the mail is delivered to a letterbox usually in the front door. Packages or oversized envelopes are also left at the front door if they won't fit in the box. Courier and USPS delivery services don't bother leaving an alert card, so if you use the garage or a side door to come and go by, be sure to check occasionally, or it may be days before you discover a soggy package sitting on the front door mat.

The house mailbox acts as both a pick up and delivery point for mail. The metal arm on the side of the box in the upright position acts as a small red flag to indicate you have mail to 'uplift'. If you don't feel comfortable leaving mail in your box (particularly sensitive matter), then use the dark blue post boxes, found outside offices, supermarkets, on a main street or corner, or at the post office; they may look like rubbish bins but are in fact mailboxes, so long as they sport the postal service logo. In

America they are not nearly as commonly found in residential areas as in Britain.

If you are away from home for any length of time, pick up a yellow card at the post office entitled 'Authorization to Hold Mail', complete and return to the cashier or leave it in your mailbox for pick-up. This will stop mail being delivered while you are away. You can hold mail for a minimum of 3 but not more than 30 days.

The website www.usps.com is a convenient way to take care of most mailing needs from home. Once logged on, you can order stamps, envelopes and other stationery, calculate postage and organise free carrier pick-up. Many post offices in America keep very good hours (our local one stayed open till 7 p.m. on weekdays and 4 p.m. on Saturdays). Also if there is an automated postal centre (APC) machine, this saves you having to queue for counter service; these machines are often available outside normal working hours – any hour of the day, any day of the week.

There is only one class of internal letter mail – first class – which is a standard rate. At the time of writing, this was 41 cents, which is roughly equivalent to British second-class. In order to qualify for this, your letter must:

- weigh less than 1 oz. For each additional ounce it costs another 24 cents;
- measure not more than 6⅛ inches tall and 11½ inches wide. As with paper, standard-sized envelopes are smaller than in the UK, so if you are sending domestic mail, watch that you are not using an oversized UK envelope or you will pay extra for this;
- postcards are cheaper to send at just 26 cents.

Other options are:

- *Priority Mail* – delivery takes 2–3 days for any item weighing 70 lb or less, to any US destination so long as your item fits inside one of the special flat-rate envelopes, available at post offices. Flat-rate boxes are also available.
- *Express Mail* – offers a money-back guaranteed overnight to 2-day service including tracking, proof of delivery and insurance.

On all mail (domestic and overseas) you should write or affix your name and address on the front of the envelope in the top left-hand corner so that it can be returned to you if undeliverable. You can either buy (very cheaply) sticky address labels for convenience or use the free sheets that come in the mail – sooner or later you will start to receive mailings from charities asking for donations, with the advantage that many of them include free sheets of labels with your name and address printed on.

The USPS preferred way of addressing an envelope or package is as follows:

ELMER FUDD
23 MAPLE CT APT 4
ANYTOWN
CA 99887-7665

Use the two-letter abbreviated state name (see Table 9.1). The zip code (same as our postcode) consists of nine digits, with a dash after the fifth digit. Often the dash and last four digits are left off, but strictly speaking you should include them.

Table 9.1 State abbreviations.

Two-letter abbreviation	State
AK	Alaska
AL	Alabama
AR	Arkansas
AZ	Arizona
CA	California
CO	Colorado
CT	Connecticut
DC	District of Columbia
DE	Delaware
FL	Florida
GA	Georgia
HI	Hawaii
IA	Iowa
ID	Idaho
IL	Illinois
IN	Indiana
KS	Kansas
KY	Kentucky
LA	Louisiana
MA	Massachusetts
MD	Maryland
ME	Maine
MI	Michigan
MN	Minnesota
MO	Missouri
MS	Mississippi
MT	Montana
NB	Nebraska
NC	North Carolina
ND	North Dakota
NH	New Hampshire
NJ	New Jersey
NM	New Mexico
NV	Nevada

NY	New York
OH	Ohio
OK	Oklahoma
OR	Oregon
PA	Pennsylvania
RI	Rhode Island
SC	South Carolina
SD	South Dakota
TN	Tennessee
TX	Texas
UT	Utah
VA	Virginia
VT	Vermont
WA	Washington
WI	Wisconsin
WV	West Virginia
WY	Wyoming

Sending Mail to the UK

External mail (non-domestic) is charged according to weight; the size of the envelope or package doesn't matter. When addressing mail destined for home, write ENGLAND as the country name, not the UK or Britain. Also remember to affix a blue airmail sticker. At the time of writing, a postcard cost 75 cents and a letter weighing less than 1 oz cost 84 cents. You can check the weight and buy a sticker stamp using one of the automatic USPS machines inside the post office. If you have many letters to send at once, it may save a few pennies if you put UK second-class stamps on the envelopes and stuff them inside a large envelope addressed to someone who wouldn't mind popping them in a post box back home.

Parcels must be dealt with at the counter. For everything other than a letter, flat sized envelope or card, you should fill in a Customs Declaration and Dispatch Note, listing the contents of your package, which is then stuck on the parcel. The smaller green Customs Declaration CN 22 form is used for some printed matter and documents. It is a good idea to place a card with the name and address of the recipient inside the box, in case the label on the outside becomes detached.

If sent by Global Priority Mail, your package should arrive in 4–6 business days; if by Global Airmail, allow 4–10 days. At Christmas time, if you want to send your cards and presents by Global Economy (surface) mail, you need to pack them off at the beginning of November. Surface mail is the cheapest and slowest method of sending mail, especially good for bulk items you don't need delivered quickly.

Receiving Mail from the UK

Opt to have mail redirected from your last UK home for as long as possible (you can pay for up to a year, and then renew for another year). This may seem a little excessive, but it makes sense for a couple of reasons: if you have tenants in your house, they will not be bothered by mail addressed to you; also they cannot gain access to any important personal information that such mail may contain. It is not unusual these days for credit card companies to mail out blank cheques, and there have been cases where tenants have gone on a spending spree with cheques addressed to the hapless landlord. Moreover, there will always be some organisations that you forgot to give a change-of-address to, or that have you on their mailing list unbeknown to you. Thus it is safer all round if you take out an extended period of mail redirection, to catch these.

In addition, it could save you money if you are canny. Anyone can post something to you (a letter, parcel, magazine, etc.) using your old UK address, applying UK postage, and it will be forwarded to you in America, albeit slightly delayed as it follows a circuitous route. Having paid for extended mail redirection, you and yours might as well use it to your benefit.

If you do not have mail redirection on your old address in the UK, then folks back home will have to use your US address. Airmail letters are priced according to weight; they cost a basic 30 pence up to 60 g, then the price goes up in increments, up to 2000 g. Delivery should take up to 5 working days, but I have known mail from the UK to take much longer; then again, letters sent from England on a Friday have spookily arrived in my American mailbox by Monday, so you never can tell. Surface mail costs half the price of standard airmail but takes up to 8 weeks. On parcels, the sender may need to write 'Small Packet' on the front top left-hand corner and attach a customs declaration. It is also a good idea to obtain a Certificate of Posting in case the item goes astray.

If you are in the military, friends and family in the UK can use the all-in-one letter and envelope know as the Bluey, available free from post offices (just add a first-class stamp). No enclosures are allowed. Address as follows:

For military personnel and families based outside Washington:
Rank and Name
Your mailbox number
BFPO 2

For those based in Washington:
Rank and Name
Department
BFPO 2

BFPO 2 is the British Embassy in Washington, DC. People back home can send any mail to you at that address and it will only cost them normal UK postage. Mail comes into the Embassy, finds its way to your mailbox and then is periodically posted on to you at no extra cost. There is also HM Forces Special Delivery, which is the same price as normal first-class UK mail. Use your military address for UK magazine subscriptions and pay the normal UK rate, rather than extra for international delivery.

The Telephone System

The telephone system in America is very definitised; you pay for most things, even emergency calls. One great thing about it, though, is that local calls are free. However, as soon as you phone outside the local area, this is classed as a long distance call, which can be expensive. Any number that does not begin with your area code or is prefixed by a '1' is considered long-distance. You may be surprised to learn how short a geographical distance there is between 'local' and 'long distance'.

To set up a phone service, you may be asked to pay a deposit, refundable after the first year. You will have to choose a carrier (or different carriers) for local (within your area code), local long-distance (within your state), long-distance (within the US) and international calls, and it is wise to review this periodically to ensure you are getting the best deal. You are not tied to the telephone company you set up with for local calls, and you may find it more economical to go with a separate provider for long-distance calls.

It is also possible to sign up with one long-distance carrier but to use other access numbers to ensure a good rate to the UK, e.g. a '10-10' number. There is hot competition between companies, so do not be afraid to negotiate a deal that suits you. At the time of writing, AT&T was the largest provider. Competitors include MetroPCS, Nextel, Sprint, T-Mobile, Verizon and Wireless. Time Warner provides telephone services as well as cable TV. Beware, though, of some cheaper suppliers who use low-quality lines (when you phone the UK, no-one may be able to hear you). Others offer cheap monthly plans but charge high fees for setup, directory enquiries and changes to your plan. There are no standard cheap rates according to the time of day you are calling, as in Britain; instead it depends on the package you opt for. Investigate other providers of cheap telephone calls, e.g. Skype and Rebtel.

Many American businesses and charities use telesales personnel. When you are first issued with a home phone number, ask for it not to be listed in the phone book; this shields you from a lot of unwanted sales calls from both bona fide and downright dodgy sources. However, when dealing with telemarketers, spare a thought for the poor soul on the line who is trying to win your interest. One former sales manager complained that while the English listen and then say no thanks, Americans were often stupid and abusive. So be firm but keep up that British politeness in declining their offer. Also do not divulge any personal information unless you initiated the call. Use caller ID so you can cherry-pick your calls and avoid nuisance callers.

Another way to avoid telesales calls is to register your number as a 'no call number' with the National Do-Not-Call Registry. This is a nationwide registry run by the Federal Communications Commission, which applies to most telemarketers, though certain, non-profit organisations are exceptions. Your number remains on the registry for 5 years, after which you must re-enter it.

Table 9.2 lists some US telephone numbers and prefixes and describes what they do. US telephone numbers consist of eleven digits if they include an area code (1-xxx-xxx-xxxx) and seven digits if they are within your area code (xxx-xxxx). The country code for the UK is 011 44, then drop the first zero in the area code, and follow it with the telephone number. The country code for the US is 001, followed by a three digit area code and then the telephone number. UK 0800 numbers often do not work States-side, and you may also have trouble with 0845 and 0870 numbers (try omitting the initial zeros). This is why, in advance of moving, endeavour to obtain international dialing numbers from the companies and organisations you call regularly, e.g. UK banks and building societies. Otherwise you will be frustrated trying to get through to them. I know, I've been there.

Table 9.2 US telephone numbers, prefixes and symbols.

Number/prefix	Description
0	Operator
1	To dial a number outside your area code
011	International access
1-800-COLLECT (1-800-2655328)	For collect (reverse charge) calls within the States
311	Non-emergency police
411	Directory enquiries
511	May get you through to road and traffic information
800, 855, 866, 877, 888	Toll-free numbers
900	Special rate – a recorded message should tell you what the charge is
911	Equivalent to our 999 – for emergency police, fire or ambulance
*	Asterisk or star
#	Hash, number sign or (incorrectly called) pound sign

To make a call from a public phone, you will either need a pocketful of quarters or a prepaid phone card (available, for instance, from AT&T, GTI or MCI, and often rechargeable). You will normally be asked for a minimum fee of one quarter, even to phone the operator or toll free, but the machine should spit the coin back at you after you hang up. If you don't have coins or a card on you, you can always try phoning collect. Most American motels do not charge a premium for calls made on the room telephone, as in the UK, where such calls can be prohibitively expensive because the hotel whacks on its own charge. Where US hotels do impose a charge, you may be able to dial your preferred long-distance carrier first and go through them in order to keep the cost down.

Cellulars

Most people these days have a mobile phone (known as a cellular in America). Cellulars tend to be expensive and most phone deals do not cater for the low user. Your local mall may have a number of shops selling cell phones and services. Monthly cell-phone plans look good initially; however, by the time you've added on taxes and surcharges, text-messaging fees (sometimes 10 cents per message), or surcharges for exceeding your minute allotment (possibly 45 cents a minute), you won't be feeling so pleased with yourself. Shrouding the true cost of products and services is commonplace as companies compete to attract customers with low upfront prices – and this doesn't just occur in the telephone market.

Mobile phones are a fact of modern life, and anybody who is anybody has one, but people can get pretty silly with their phones. We saw one important-looking person striding across the parking lot yelling into one phone while clutching another to his ear. Ten-year-old boys ride along on their bicycles no-handed, busy texting their friends or chatting away; most motorcyclists (sensibly) pull over. We lost count of the number of times we cursed bad drivers, who turned out to be on the phone – completely oblivious to other traffic. In America it is not an offence to make a call while you are in charge of a vehicle, and people frequently do.

Internet and Television

Most television and phone companies also offer internet connection services. You pay a monthly set charge when you sign up with a provider, but as local calls are free you do not pay for your time online. Netzero and SBC Yahoo DSL are popular, low-cost providers.

There are no such things as TV licences in America; you simply pay for a package of channels according to choice. There are 2218 broadcast stations throughout America, so investigate the channels that are available in your area and what's included in the different tiers before deciding. You can view terrestrial TV free of charge with an antenna, and this gives you six basic channels plus a couple of regional stations advertising events and places locally.

The six national networks are ABC, CBS, Fox, NBC, UPN and WB. Cable TV supplied by Time Warner Cable offers over 275 channels, requires no specific equipment and does not tie you into a specific contract. It comes with the option of a built-in DVR (digital video recorder), allowing you to record and pause live TV without the use of videotape. You can rent movies on demand, enjoy dozens of commercial-free music videos 24 hours a day, take out a digital sports package, etc., according to individual preference.

We opted for a Basic Tier package (the minimum cable service you can subscribe to) which gave us the first 26 or so channels. Of these, three were shopping, two religious, two government access, a couple educational and public, one was Time Warner and the rest were local and commercial broadcast stations. Not a bad deal for $13.29/month. The next tier up is the Classic Tier, which gives you 78 channels for around $51/month.

The list below offers some help in deciphering what the different channels offer:

- ABC – American Broadcasting Company: family, news and sports; franchised and therefore local;
- AMC – American Movie Classics;
- BBC America – best in British TV;
- CBS – news, sitcom, drama, children's viewing, sport;
- CNN – Cable News Network;
- ESPN – sports;
- HBO – Home Box Office: see below;
- HGTV – creative ideas, helpful hints and professional advice;
- Lifetime – for women;
- MTV – music television, aimed at teens and young adults;
- NBC – National Broadcasting Company: news, sport, sitcom;
- PBS – Public Broadcasting Service: see below;
- Nickelodeon – children's viewing;
- QVC – Quality, Value, Convenience: home shopping;
- Spike – aimed at young males; action movies, shows, babes, gaming;
- TBN – Trinity Broadcasting Network: the world's largest Christian religion TV network, with 5 million US householders tuning in each week;
- TBS – sports and variety, with a focus on comedy;
- TCM – Turner Classic Movies;
- TNT – Turner Network Television: sports (including NBA games and NASCAR), high-action movies and old TV shows.

CNN, Fox News and MSNBC provide 24-hour news coverage. Local and national news is usually broadcast on other network stations at around 5 and 11 p.m. EST. *60 Minutes* (on CBS), *20/20* (on ABC) and *Dateline* (NBC) provide investigative reporting. The three traditional commercial TV networks are ABC, CBS and NBC. Premium cable and satellite services include CBN, CNN, ESPN, HBO, Lifetime, MTV, Nickelodeon, Showtime, The Learning Channel, The Movie Channel, The Weather Channel and VH-1.

HBO on Demand offers more than 100 different titles each week, with new shows added on Mondays, in case you're getting jaded. You can tune in to over 40 movies at any time, and more than 20 different kids' titles each month. It provides *World Championship Boxing* and *American Undercover*, as well as series like *Sex and the City*, *Six Feet Under* and *The Sopranos*. HBO is expensive to subscribe to, but it does allow you to see original full-length TV movies, feature films and some popular original series.

Leo Anthony Gallagher (American stand-up comedian) joked, 'Don't you wish there was a knob on the TV to turn up the intelligence? There's one marked "Brightness", but it doesn't work'. PBS is a non-commercial television broadcasting station offering quality programmes (documentaries, cultural and public affairs) and educational services, both on TV and online. It is funded by members of the public, charity contributions and miniscule arts funding. Its *American Experience* is America's longest running and most-watched history series. *Nature*, which airs September to May, and *NOVA*, its science and documentary series, are very good. Other series include *Frontline* (public affairs) and *American Masters* (biographies of America's cultural artists). Check out the PBS website for what is showing and how to sign up for email alerts to keep you informed according to your particular interest. Jim Lehrer's *News Hour* report is another good programme. It takes one or two of the main news stories and talks in depth about them. It is shown on PBS every night (between 6 and 7 p.m.) and aired on radio.

BBC America (on channel 115, in our area at least) gives you BBC News and Sport, BBC Kids (for instance *Rosie and Jim*, *The Shiny Show*, *Binka* and *Andy Pandy* and such like), and a plethora of other great (and not so great) British viewing such as *Sharpe's Honour*, *Footballers' Wives*, *Little Britain*, *The Vicar of Dibley*, *Hamish Macbeth*, *Bargain Hunt* and *Cash in the Attic*, *The Avengers*, *Bad Girls*, *Hex*, *The Kumars*, *Changing Rooms* and *Ground Force*. Online you can read and view *All About Britain*, which has a travel-selling section, *Ask a London Cabby* and *The Royals*. You can also pay a monthly subscription to EchoStar's DISH Network to keep up with *EastEnders*.

Electricity Supply and Appliances

The utilities of fuel and light are deregulated and a shambles. New accounts are required to pay a deposit, the amount of which varies according to the average usage of the former occupants of the house. So if the former owners or tenants were high users, you will have to cough up a larger than average deposit. This money may be refundable after one year or alternatively not until you move out of the house; it just depends on your address. You may also be asked for a hefty deposit simply because you initially have no US credit rating. Once signed up, you are billed monthly for usage.

Fitting an electronic timer can give you big savings on your utility bills. Also it is a good idea to invest in a surge protector to prevent damage to your computer or electronic equipment from a thunderstorm power surge. In the Midwest, lightning season lasts from mid-April to mid-September and can be pretty spectacular. When buying a protector, ensure it conforms to UL 1449 – the standard for transient voltage surge suppressors. Some have added phone line protection.

Most UK appliances need a voltage converter/transformer to convert to American 110 V supply and adapter plugs to fit US sockets (which are two pin). You can buy this equipment cheaply online through a company called Voltage Converters. British TVs and video recorders use a different frequency, so unless they are designed for dual use, there is no point bringing them out to America with you. Moreover, do not be tempted to buy too many US DVDs; they won't work on your system back home in the UK (American DVDs are group 1, whereas most UK players only play group 2).

Extended warranties on electrical items are sold aggressively by salespeople on commission. In reality such add-ons offer little benefit to the consumer. In any case, if your small electrical gadget breaks, you will probably look at replacing it with a newer model rather than going to the hassle of sending it off to be repaired.

Money, Banking and Finance

America and Canada both use dollars and cents, but their currencies are quite separate. Table 9.3 lists US currency in circulation. Early traders sold buck skins for a dollar in eastern markets, and this is how the dollar got its name as 'a buck'. Notes are

Table 9.3 US currency.

Currency	Design on front	Design on back
Coins		
1 cent (a penny)	Abraham Lincoln	Lincoln Memorial
5 cents (a nickel)	Thomas Jefferson	Monticello
10 cents (a dime)	Franklin D. Roosevelt	Olive branch, oak branch and torch
25 cents (a quarter)	George Washington	Eagle*
Notes		
$1 (a buck)	George Washington	Great Seal
$2	Thomas Jefferson	Declaration of Independence
$5	Abraham Lincoln	Lincoln Memorial
$10	Alexander Hamilton	US Treasury
$50	Ulysses S. Grant	US Capitol
$100	Benjamin Franklin	Independence Hall, Philadelphia

* Each state has its own design of quarter (called State Quarters), which some people like to collect.

often referred to as 'green' (e.g. 'Give me some green') because of the colour of the paper used. Dime comes from the French word *dixième* for a tenth. Cent comes from the Latin *centum* meaning one hundred.

Most prices in America are quoted exclusive of sales tax, which varies from state to state, and even between counties. Merchants charge customers a combined rate of state tax plus local tax. Alaska has the lowest combined state/local average tax rate (1.15%), while Washington, DC, and New York have the highest (8.45 and 8.25% respectively). In other states it ranges between 5 and 8%. Rates also vary according to the type of product or business. Tangible personal property is everything other than real estate that has a value by itself (i.e. all goods, chattels and other articles of value) and is taxed. Food, pharmaceuticals and agricultural products are normally exempt, and so are most services.

If possible, open a bank account before you leave the UK and deposit some ready cash in advance of your arrival. Opt for an account that allows online bill payments (see page 374). The main big banks are listed below, but see the Google website cited in *Useful Websites* for a full listing of what banks operate in your state:

- Bank of America is a nationwide bank.
- Chase (who we banked with) is the largest banking company in the States.
- Citibank is one of the largest banks in the world.
- First USA has offices in both America and England.
- HSBC and MBNA have branches in both the UK and the US, which may make your financial transition easier.

Many US banks need to see a Social Security Number before they will allow you to open an account, which is another reason for applying for your SSN as soon as you arrive in America.

Bring some US dollar travellers' cheques with you to avoid having to carry wads of cash; most places in the States accept them. Buy them in the UK using a building society cheque rather than a credit card if you can, to avoid commission charges. It costs 1% of the amount purchased to buy them and there is no charge for using them. Beware of withdrawing cash in America using a UK-based credit card because this incurs a fee of up to 4.75% of the amount. Using a debit card is cheaper, at around 2%.

The American banking system is different to the British and rather archaic. It is not straightforward (or even possible in some cases) to set up direct debits or standing orders for automatic payments. This is one area where American banks are behind the times. Some branches will not accept cheques drawn from outside their state, though if you are a customer of that bank, there is less likely to be a problem. Also, owing to identity fraud, you will usually be asked by counter staff to show some form of identification (for instance your state driving licence) before they will allow you to transact. You may be charged for cash withdrawn at banks and ATMs when you are out of state, and sometimes locally. The average ATM fee for non-bank customers is around $1.60.

When cashing a cheque in a bank, even your own, you will be asked to produce identification. This is because cheque theft is becoming more prevalent. When writing a US cheque, the cents are written in numerals over 100, e.g. $12.75 would be written as 'Twelve and 75/100'. Cheques are not accepted unless they have your name, address and account number printed or written on the front. There are no cheque guarantee cards, so if your cheque bounces, the retailer will use the address on the cheque to find you. Bouncing a cheque in America is considered to be a very serious misdemeanour, and it is even illegal in many states to go unexpectedly overdrawn. At the very least, it will dent your creditworthiness.

Some places state that legal tender is not accepted. This means that you can only pay with a credit or charge card or by some prepaid method. Not having cash on the premises obviates against burglaries. Banks charge for issuing cheque books, so where possible use credit card or electronic payments. It may be possible for your bank to send cheques to third parties on your behalf free of charge; just go online with the third party's details and click a button to send the payment.

Credit Issues

You need a credit rating in order to sign up with utility companies, buy a phone, a car, get a loan, etc., but you cannot get a credit rating until you start to pay bills, buy things, and so on – it is rather a Catch 22 situation. You will probably find that your UK credit history is useless in America. Thus obtaining a US credit rating can be tricky and this may make things difficult for you at first. Equifax may be able to help supply you with a credit reference that is recognised in the States. You can also build up a history by any of the following means:

- Apply for in-store cards and make purchases with these.
- Avidly use any American credit card you are offered – for everything.
- Apply for a small loan at your local store or bank.
- Pay your bills on time.

It took about 3 months before we had built up sufficient history to be offered credit cards without restriction.

Many credit issuers now charge as much as $39 for late payment and $35 for going over your credit limit. Moreover, they have reduced the payment window deadline, in an effort to catch more late payers. On top of this, expect to pay interest rates as high as 31% on your outstanding balance. Money from fees represents a big chunk of credit card companies' income. As mail delivery can be unpredictable, you may prefer to pay your credit card bills online or over the phone, to avoid cheques being received past the due date. If you do incur a charge, try sweet-talking your way out of it – offering valid excuses for the oversight and suggesting that you do not really need their credit card anyway. They may waive fees just to keep your custom.

One thing to watch for, particularly with car hire companies, is the blocking-off of credit on your card. If you give them your card by way of a deposit, they may block this amount off, reducing your line of unused credit for the duration you are renting the car. This can have embarrassing consequences if you do not have a very generous credit limit on your card, or it is the only one you rely on.

Once you have a home address, you will be inundated with 'free' or easy pre-approved credit cards. Be careful of these offers, as some are scams. Those that ask you to call a telephone number beginning with 900 may simply be making money out of your call, without actually sending you anything in return. Every other day, we received an invitation in the post to take out yet another card. The average American possesses at least five different credit cards, and there seems to be an unending supply of credit from finance companies. Young people in particular can qualify for more credit than they can handle; even our 5-year-old, Rosie, was offered her own credit card (scary). Once you have built up a credit history, you may receive invitations from credit repair companies offering to clean up your credit history for a fee, yet you can do this yourself for free by contacting the credit bureaus direct. So be careful and don't get caught out. Also, always shred any paperwork that has your name and address or other personal details on, as identity theft is rife.

Weights and Measures

America still uses the old Imperial system of weights and measures. Road signs are in miles, petrol pumps dispense petrol in gallons, fruit and vegetables are sold by the pound and house plots are measured in square feet. However, the American Imperial system is based on the system that was current at the time the American colonies became independent, i.e. it is based on the old English system of the 1700s. This accounts for the slight discrepancies between American and English Imperial measurements. If you are a cook following a recipe, it may be a good idea to invest in a set of American measuring devices to avoid disasters in the kitchen. The government is encouraging a switch to the metric system, but it is a voluntary process and not proving popular. Table 9.4 lists some common units of measurement and their SI equivalents.

American clothing and footwear sizes can be a complete mystery to a foreigner, and very haphazard. American sizing seems to be two sizes smaller than British – a happy prospect for most women. Women's shoe sizes work in the opposite way, going up a couple of sizes. Men's shirts, coats and suits are the same size as back home. Children's sizes are a minefield. The Wikipedia website (see below) has charts that might be helpful.

Table 9.4 Some US weights and measures and their British equivalents.

US unit	Division	SI or British equivalent
1 cup	8 fl oz, 16 tbsp or 0.5 liquid pint	240 ml
1 liquid quart	2 pt	946 ml
1 pt	16 fl oz	20 fl oz
1 gallon	4 qt or 128 fl oz	3.785 l or 0.833 British gallon
1 stick	4 oz	115 g

Useful Websites

www.annualcreditreport.com – to obtain a free US credit report.
www.bbcamerica.com – BBC America.
www.bfpo.org.uk – British Forces Postal Office.
www.fcc.gov/cgb/donotcall – National Do-Not-Call Registry.
www.ftc.gov – Federal Trade Commission; among other things, gives details on scams, identity theft and how to stop telemarketing calls.
www.optoutprescreen.com – Consumer Credit Reporting Industry; to opt-in or opt-out of offers of credit or insurance.
www.pbs.org – to see what's showing on PBS.
www.socialsecurity.gov – official website of the US Social Security Administration.
www.timewarnercable.com – key in your zip code to find out what's available in your area.
www.usps.com – United States Postal Service.

Google:
'Banks and institutions, North America' – select Google Directory and click on a particular state to see which banks operate there.

Wikipedia:
Sales taxes in the United States – rates of sales tax in each state.
US standard clothing size – for men, women and children.

Terminology

American term	Equivalent British term	Notes
Antenna	Aerial	
Bill	Bank note	
Busy signal	Engaged	
Charge account	Credit account	In a store or shop
Checking account	Current or cheque account	
Collect call	Reverse charge call	
Cord	Electrical lead or flex	
Direct drafting	Direct debit	
Ground electrical	Earth	
HVAC		Heating + ventilation + air conditioning
Jack, outlet	Socket	
Lead	Cable	
Line chord	Mains lead	
Power outage	Power cut	
Pre-authorised payment/withdrawal	Direct debit/standing order	
Savings and loan	Building society	
Teller	Cashier	
Zip code	Post code	ZIP = Zoning Improvement Plan

10 · There's No Place Like Home

'America is so vast that almost everything said about it is likely to be true, and the opposite is probably equally true.' James T. Farrell, American novelist

Coming from such a relatively small place as England – which is barely the size of the state of New York – America's vastness hits you straight away. Not only is the country huge, but also the living is much more spread out. Outside of the cities, in middle-class areas extensive homes occupy great plots of land, grassed and open. The recurring cry from William and Rosie on first arriving in America was, 'Look, Mummy, there's another play park'; in fact, they were just pointing out the elaborate equipment in yet another back yard. It made our sandpit and small garden at home in Dorset pale into insignificance.

If you are looking for some serious space, head for Wyoming, Montana, North and South Dakota and Alaska – the least populated of all the states. Conversely, the north-eastern coastal states and Florida are some of the most heavily populated. The suburbs are the place to be; nearly every large metropolitan area across America is losing residents, especially middle-class people, who are moving out in search of bigger homes and more space in surrounding areas. Some states and cities are seeing many more residents move out than others (in particular the District of Columbia, North Dakota, New York state, California and Illinois, and the cities of New York, Los Angeles and Chicago), while others are gaining people (Nevada, Arizona, Florida, Georgia, Utah and Idaho).

A large home is central to the American dream and what most people aspire to. These days at least 2 in 3 Americans own their own home, but there are racial and ethnic differences; the 2000 Census found that 72% of whites but only 46% of black and Hispanic householders own their home. In 2002, there were 116 million housing units in America. Of these, 3.6 million are temporarily vacant (used for recreation or as vacation homes), mostly in the north-eastern states of Maine, New Hampshire and Vermont.

The median sales price across the country in 2000 was $119,600 (US Census data); by 2005 it had increased to $208,000 (according to the National Association of Realtors). Expect to pay higher prices on the East and West Coasts. The largest and most expensive homes are generally in the North-East (particularly the Boston–New York–Washington area), Hawaii and California; the smallest (though by no means less expensive) homes are in the West; the cheapest are in the rural South (for instance, Georgia and North Carolina), Iowa and Oklahoma. Highest annual increases have been seen in Nevada, Hawaii and California. The greatest concentration of renters is found in Jersey City (New York), New York City, the Los Angeles–Long Beach area, San Francisco and Bryan-College Station (home of Texas A&M University). Table 10.1 lists the 10 most expensive places to live in America; half are in California.

Table 10.1 The ten most expensive places to live in America (US Census Bureau 2000).

Ranking	City (state)
1	Cambridge (MA)
2	San Francisco (CA)
3	Pasadena (CA)
4	Los Angeles (CA)
5	Fort Lauderdale (FL)
6	Berkeley (CA)
7	Stamford (CT)
8	Honolulu (HI)
9	Atlanta (GA)
10	Fremont (CA)

Housing Styles

The first log cabins were built around 1683 by Swedish immigrants coming to Delaware. Things have changed a lot since then. Today there are many styles of American housing, ranging from the magnificent showpiece to the lowly mobile home.

First a word on terminology:

- A condo or condominium is a block of flats or apartments; see below.
- Detached condos are single family dwellings. A homeowners association cares for the exterior of the dwellings, yards, etc. It is the preferred style of housing in planned neighbourhoods and gated communities.
- Duplex means semi-detached.
- Triplex is a three-unit dwelling.

- A modular home is constructed on an indoor assembly line, then delivered to its intended site; see discussion below.
- A town house is a terraced home or row house, comprising three or more houses in a row sharing a party wall.
- A tenement is a multi-storey apartment building, usually found in older parts of large cities, e.g. New York. The building is owned by a single entity and rented out to many. A tenement is a basic, inexpensive apartment and often implies a run-down building.
- A ranch bungalow is a single-storey or one-and-a-half storey house, usually with basement and garage. On one side are the bedrooms; on the other 'public' side are the living rooms (kitchen, lounge, dining and family rooms) as well as the garage.
- A prefab is where the main structure is prefabricated. They were very popular after World War II.
- A mobile home or manufactured home is a trailer-style home set on a park (see discussion later).
- A realtor is an estate agent.
- A lot is a plot of land.
- The yard is what we call the garden. In America it is any part of the property not covered by buildings.

Condominiums are individually owned flats, other portions of the property being commonly owned (e.g. hallways, recreational facilities). Owners pay a monthly or yearly building maintenance fee to upkeep the buildings, infrastructure and grounds. They usually have free use of a clubhouse, pool, etc. Condos are cheap to buy and are secure communities. They are especially popular with single working people, retirees who like to travel, and those who do not want the upkeep hassles of a home and garden.

Modular homes are very popular in America because they are cheaper than conventionally built homes. Designed on similar plans and to local codes and standards, these preconstructed dwellings are put together on factory assembly lines indoors, which keeps the cost of materials down. They are delivered to your plot and can be assembled in a matter of hours or a day. They can be built on any number of surfaces, e.g. slabs or stilts (in flood-prone areas).

Prefabricated homes are an amalgamation of panelised and modular building systems and can mean either. The word 'prefab' is used more as a stylistic term than referring to a particular construction method. Outlets for prefabs and modular homes are everywhere, with show houses conspicuously placed alongside main roads and motorways. In my view, they look a little like children's playhouses – simple in design and slightly unreal looking.

Private Housing Developments

Private housing developments or gated communities are for the relatively rich. They are a new thing, of the last 15 years or so, at least in Ohio. To protect themselves from 'others', the new-rich aristocracy have enclosed themselves in self-contained communities, reminiscent of a country club. There they enjoy planned community entertainment, a menu of activities including swimming, fishing, golf and tennis; even piped-in music (elevator style) fills the air. Tudor mansions overlook mock castles complete with moat, which sit next to lakeside homes, the whole effect beautifully set off by landscaped gardens and carefully planted trees. Not only do the homes in these communities cost a premium, but also you usually have to pay exorbitant monthly or quarterly fees to the homeowners association for the privilege of living there.

Similar new developments for the middle classes are in demand. Some are advertised as collections of unique villages, carefully designed and planned. Galveston beach town in Texas is one such community, typical of the New Urbanism movement that is sweeping America. Designed by the same company that created Seaside in Florida (said to be the first planned community, where *The Truman Show* was filmed), Galveston is promoted as having the following advantages:

- walkability;
- a traditional neighbourhood development;
- it reclaims community values;
- it is listed in CNNMoney.com's *Best Places to Retire.*

On similar planned developments elsewhere in the US, single family homes may be built on small plots side by side. The gardens are totally open plan, with no visible boundaries between neighbours. Most have double garages – the most prominent feature of the houses (a space alien seeing this collection of residences would quickly realise that the car is all-important to the inhabitants of this part of Earth). The grass is mown to a uniform height, perfectly green and weed-free, the mail boxes all look the same, the pavements and drives are spotlessly white, and there is not a fallen leaf or twig in sight. A few carefully planted, new trees are all that break up this uniform world. There are no open windows, even on warm days; instead, air-conditioning units provide a background hum. There are no toys or children's play things out on the drives or front lawns, no washing fluttering in the back yards. The community seems strangely devoid of life and movement. It is a distinctly conformist culture you have entered into.

I plucked up courage to enter a show house on one of these new developments. It was as immaculate inside as out, richly furnished, with hard wood flooring and soft pile carpets. Open plan, with tall windows to let in plenty of light seems to be the preferred style. The kitchen is an open affair, hived off from the dining room and lounge by a dividing counter – very sociable for the hostess and/or chef. I asked the sales representative to explain the rules of the community to me:

- You cannot park certain vehicles, for instance worn-out cars, on your drive or in the road, and trailers and boats must be stored away, out of sight.
- No junk or rubbish should be left out.
- Satellite TV dishes cannot be larger than a certain diameter.
- If you build a storage shed, it must match the home.
- You are not allowed to erect a fence or plant a hedge in the front yard; the front must be kept open plan and uniform with the rest of the houses.
- You can erect a fence at the back, but it must not be higher than 4 ft, so that it doesn't obscure your neighbour's view.
- If you install a swimming pool, it must have a 6-ft-high fence around it, for safety reasons.
- Houses must be separated by 20 ft of open grass, and homeowners are not allowed to build anything on these side areas.
- Most communities set a limit on the number of animals you are allowed to keep, e.g. usually two dogs.
- You cannot run a commercial business from the home.

The homeowners association imposes these covenants and restrictions in order to 'protect' homeowners. Residents pay an amount each year to the association, which may undertake front-yard grass cutting, sign maintenance, clearing ice and snow from pavements, and generally keeping the front appearance of the properties looking smart. Sometimes everything can look so much the same that it is difficult to find your way out of the housing development because there are so few distinguishing features.

Assisted living for groups of senior people in carefully planned settings is a popular option which is highly developed in America. It allows older people to retain their independence, to live safely and securely in a social community, maintenance free. It also gets round the problem of what to do with your old folks. There are also gay retirement complexes, where aging lesbians and gays can live together in friendly communities. Many developments have on-site wellness centres, beauty parlours, dining rooms, banks, convenience stores and pharmacies. They may provide transportation into town, on-call nursing staff and round-the-clock emergency assistance, library and community rooms for social opportunities, as well as classes, field trips and organised daily activities. Many have controlled access to keep the area private.

Big Is Beautiful

On first impressions, American homes may appear to be luxuriously laid out and equipped, but in reality the materials used in new buildings are often cheap and the houses not made to last (perhaps understandable in regions with severe weather, e.g. hurricanes or tornadoes). The newer the house, generally the cheaper the materials used, with perhaps more concern for appearances than substance. In our suburban neighbourhood, there were very few terraced or semi-detached homes – most were detached. Many homes have elaborate porches-come-entrance ways, with decorative pillars and columns, which look pretentiously grandiose in our reserved British eyes. One American friend remarked on the recent trend for everyone to desire a mansion. Sunken baths, large vanity units, walk-in dressing areas, open plan spacious rooms, sink waste disposal, double garages with electric doors, decked verandahs, swimming pools, even fishing lakes are quite normal in some areas.

Outside of the cities, housing is not generally constrained by space, unlike in the UK. Some zoning laws even prevent you building on small plots. According to the US Census Bureau, the average one-family home has the following vital statistics:

- a generous floor size of 2200 sq ft;

- a lot size of 17,000 sq ft or so;
- more than 50% are set on two or more floors;
- the average number of rooms is 5.8; 1 in 4 have 7 rooms;
- 33% have 4 or more bedrooms;
- 54% have 2.5 bathrooms.

Two- and three-car garages at 600–900 sq ft are the norm (which is the same area an entire average family home took up in the 1950s). These garages are often used to store excess stuff, while the car sits out on the drive. Incidentally, there are more cars on the road than registered drivers, so make that two or three cars on the driveway. Homes have become a conspicuous symbol of consumption. The trend for what has been variously termed *McMansions*, *Starter Castles*, *Gable-opolis* and *Beltway Baronial* began in the late 1980s; these are all rather derogatory terms used to describe the vast developments of swanky, oversized homes, made from the same cookie cutter. 'Parachute homes' is another name, because they appear to have simply been dropped in from somewhere else. In certain areas, old houses (even historical ones) are difficult to sell as most people want new. Perfectly functional homes are bulldozed to make way for newer, bigger and better. As my American friend Betty commented, 'New homes costing three to four hundred dollars apiece are appearing all over the place in our locality. Where are all these rich people coming from?'

They are coming from the middle and upper-middle classes, who are fueling the demand for large homes, often without gardens but simply grassed all round, and set on housing estates – often herded together in partially self-governed gated communities. Many of them are in lakeshore and golf-course communities. The term McMansion comes from similarities with the McDonald's fast food chain, as they are seen as culturally ubiquitous, bearing no appreciation for or resemblance to local or regional architectural styles, but simply mass produced for broad appeal. The most popular styles are faux French chateau, English Tudor and Jacobethan, half-timbered European, classical and neoclassical.

McMansions have been criticised as having negative effects on communities and nature. Homes are grouped together on landscaped sites, heralded as 'Oak Ridge' or 'Cinnamon Heights' – without a single oak or cinnamon tree in sight, these natural beauties having been ripped out during the development stage. Odd spellings such as Hunter's Pointe and Heatherwoode conjure up continental sophistication. The accent is on the visible frontage of the house, and so ornamental features are high on the list of must-haves.

They often incorporate huge garages, for three or more vehicles, which also house work areas, storage rooms and covered areas for the lawn tractor, golf cart, boat or RV. Exterior lights are sometimes used for grand effect, invoking light pollution as another criticism. The interior lighting is complex and the audio system usually sophisticated. There may be separate rooms for games, music, home theatre, a home office, library, bar, even a room solely for the family dog. The large number of infrequently used rooms leads to excessive consumption in furnishings and wastefulness (or luxury in the homeowner's eyes). There are often as many bathrooms as bedrooms, and spa-like features in the master bathroom. The large and numerous windows and high ceilings, which are a common style of these homes, mean higher heating and cooling bills and are thus environmentally wasteful.

I appreciate that I have painted a rather scathing description of these Frankenhouses (which, incidentally, is not my own term but one in popular use). Someone else has described them as Colonial Reproduction of Amended Periods (C.R.A.P.). However, they are very much a feature of new America. I was privileged to visit a couple of these privatopias when dropping my children off for playtime at friends' homes. Having negotiated the private drive and bridge, and asked permission to enter at the electric gates, I drove past the neighbours' Taj Mahals in awe, and wound my way up to the dizzy heights of the friend's monster pad. Inside I was treated to a tour of the house, involving more rooms than the occupants possibly knew what to do with. I came away with a feeling of unease – having lost myself twice on the way to taking Rosie to the bathroom – and pity at the wastefulness and coldness that the family called home. The children's voices echoed round the house, bouncing off the hard floors and high ceilings, lost in the maze of interconnecting rooms. How could you ever keep track of your family (perhaps that was the idea)?

Jim also comments on the 'big is beautiful' idea:

> American cities are spreading outwards and houses have grown due to an underlying affluence, to the point where they are two to three times the size of the average British house. The space is very nice to have, but imagine the cost of heating and cooling. As city populations increase and people can afford grander houses, additional communities grow up on the outskirts. These communities then become cities (defined as having a population of at least 25,000) in their own right, the housing typified by the mini-ranch, a property excessive in proportion to the number of occupants (a friend of mine had a 4800 sq ft mansion for him, his wife and occasionally visiting three children – oh, and the dog). Such homes have large yards so that on initial inspection they don't look excessive; and they say an Englishman's home is his castle! In some places, major city suburbs for example, land is not so plentiful and is inevitably already built on. So, the trend is to replace older houses with newer, bigger and grander ones on the same plots. These McMansions, as they have become known, look extremely out of place compared with their older neighbours due to the lack of proportional space around them. Indeed, so tightly are they packed that the effect is similar to the average British street.

External Appearances

Houses are sometimes numbered using a co-ordinate system, with numbers allocated one for every 25 ft of frontage. This explains why in rural areas with fields between plots, house numbering may seem bizarre; for example, the next house number after 550 may be 1050 if there is 500 ft of frontage plus open space between the two homesteads.

In the suburbs of Beavercreek, where we were living, most people took a great deal of pride in their homes and surroundings. Many had a porch, with the traditional rocking or swinging chair, decorative homely touches and plenty of fairy lights. Many were obviously patriotic, with red, white and blue painted mailboxes, flower displays, ribbons or the revered flag, and had a 'Welcome' sign by the front door. Front gardens were usually neat and open-plan, one running into the next, with no fences, hedges or other discernible borders. Some homes had 'invisible fences' to keep the dog in without obvious fencing; a batteried collar produced a shock if the poor animal reached the invisible end of his tether. So if some barking beast starts running across the lawn towards you, try not to be too alarmed; the invisible fence should stop him in his tracks.

On newer housing developments, where similar-looking homes sit on small open plots, butting up against neighbours, there is a strong whiff of conformity. People there seem to like to show off their tiny yards as if they were something out of *House Beautiful.* They titivate their lawns, drives and front porches, and 'weed whack' (strim) anything that dares grow unplanned. Edges are clipped, drives are leaf-blown and beds are mulched – nothing is out of place. I feel sorry for the wildlife that has to traverse these huge swathes of mown grass without a bump or rogue blade of grass to break it up.

Virginia Scott Jenkins, in her book *The Lawn: A History of an American Obsession* (1994), said that, 'American front lawns are a symbol of man's control of, or superiority over, his environment'. This sounds pretty noble, but ask Tim for his feelings on the matter and he'll give you a different view; our modest plot occupied him and the lawn mower for more hours than he cares to add up. Other people pay to have their lawns maintained. Lawn care is big business, with a heavy dependence on chemicals and watering; in some areas, 50–70% of residential water is used to keep lawns green. It is not unusual for homeowners to employ a professional firm to come regularly throughout the growing season to weed and feed the grassed areas around the house. Some homeowners spend hours at the weekend on their ride-on mowers (which incidentally cost around $2500, much less than in the UK), often with a can of something in one hand and the other hand barely twitching as they drive slowly up and down their immaculate plots. One neighbour was religiously out at 7 a.m. three times a week cutting his front lawn during the season. Jim's neighbours were not much different:

Sitting on the deck overlooking the yard, sipping cool drinks and watching our young girls play could be both a wonderful experience and one of immense but fleeting significance in our lives. However, rarely could these important moments be enjoyed without the constant, unignorable and irritating drone of petrol-engined tools being used to harass the greenery of adjacent yards. One might assume that the incessant noise could only be achieved with careful prior planning and precise timing. However, it became evident that the constant whining was achieved simply by the accidental overlapping of many tools being used. Americans view yard-work (gardening) not necessarily as a pleasure or pastime but as a profession to be honed over many years of dedicated practice. Added to this prowess is a rather obvious one-upmanship of tools. The best are proudly exhibited as often and as observably as possible but in a way that just dodges being brazen. Unkindly, we developed the view that a few men used yard-work as a distraction to avoid getting involved in more family-orientated activities. Some men would labour in their yards just long enough to provide a convincing reason to collapse on the couch for several hours afterwards, conveniently when a particular sports game was on the TV. Others saw it as an unquestionable civic duty and one that had to be achieved on schedule at all costs. This schedule could be as aggressive as every 4 days, resulting in the grass being not so much cut as groomed. The result of all this pastoral activity made the neighborhood a pleasure to look at, even if the relentless noise sometimes made it difficult to live in.

All this had the effect of making me feel a touch defiant. Fortunately for us, our immediate neighbours were not yard Nazis, so we were able to retain some sense of living with nature among us. Grass grew slightly longer on our side of the street, weeds were allowed some leeway, and fallen leaves – well, I think they are beautiful in themselves, so they hung around our plot longer than most other yards, which were swiftly denuded. Check with your neighbours, though, and you may find it is illegal to let your grass grow more than a certain number of inches high. If you plan to be away for more than a couple of weeks in the spring, you might need to ask a friend or neighbour to cut the lawn for you. In some neighbourhoods, if your grass gets too long, the city comes and puts a large yellow sign in the front garden warning you to do something about it or else. This is meant to embarrass the homeowner, and usually has the desired effect.

With all that grass you would expect to see children kicking about or some other use being made of the area. There may be a basketball hoop on the side of the drive, but that's usually about it. It seems such a waste of valuable space; but then we see it from a British perspective, where for most people space is at a premium and you try to maximise your living area. In our part of Ohio at least, it is obviously not an issue.

The front of most American's homes is really only for appearances and for coming and going in the car. In the front yard, homeowners put on a show; you may see all manner of decorative frills and (often) tacky garden paraphernalia. At certain times of the year, in particular at Halloween, Thanksgiving and Christmas, many are transformed into spectacles – some wonderful, others totally over the top.

With such huge boundaryless gardens (both front and back), drifting into neighbours' plots, open for all to see, outdoor privacy for the occupants does not seem to be all that important. Streets often have no footpath or pavement bordering them; the lawns simply end at the road. As a pedestrian you have to walk in the road, but passing motorists are usually considerate and slow down when they see you. (However, I still found it rather disquieting to be in that position, especially with two young children and a dog in tow.) Many homes are strangely quiet and closed up, exuding an air of unoccupation. Even during the day, blinds are drawn, invoking secrecy; curtains are a rarity. Whether homeowners hide behind their blinds for security or prefer to live in semi-darkness, perhaps because the television is on, is uncertain. Interiors are often dark in any case, shadowed by the porch overhang or elaborate frontage. Having a semi-outside/inside living area in the summer in the form of a porch, for entertaining or just chilling out on a balmy evening, sure has its attractions, but makes indoor living a little closed and dark.

Jim's neighbourhood was pretty similar to ours, and his remarks are a little more positive:

> Looking down a typical American suburban street, more commonly known as a neighbourhood, you get a sense of space. Houses are set back from the road and front yards are simple and elegant, though this is achieved with some effort. It is not uncommon to find local bylaws (or city/neighborhood ordinances) dictating the maximum length your grass is allowed to grow. Moreover, few American yards are protected by fences. The absence of boundaries, combined with great swathes of well-cut grass, trimmed bushes and a large number and variety of trees opens the typical street into a vista of pastoral calm. While the average British street is beleaguered with the disorder of flowerbeds, unmatching, disfigured and alarmingly coloured fences and walls, the American neighbourhood street is uncluttered, mellow and aesthetically agreeable. The inefficient use of space might seem arrogantly wasteful to Brits, but there is no doubt about its positive effects. The open spaces allow greater visibility of wildlife and it is not uncommon to see animals like raccoon, deer, possums and chipmunks in seemingly built-up areas. With around 2% of the land given over to yards, a large proportion of the fuel used in the USA goes on yard work. As fuel becomes scarcer, and prices inevitably increase, it will be interesting to see if yards decrease in size or if some areas are allowed to go fallow.

The Other End of the Market

In poorer neighbourhoods and states, especially in rural areas, things can be quite different. Here you see many prefab and mobile homes, perhaps raised up on blocks (no foundations). Some are well kept, while others spread their junk out for all to see, obviously caring nothing for appearances. Front yards are often strewn with toys, rusting cars and appliances, giant satellite dishes, porches piled high with old seats and settees and what look like bags of rubbish; they do not appear to care for their possessions, leaving things to deteriorate outside and visually and physically polluting the environment. Tacky artificial frills, plastic animals and dubious-looking statues decorate some front yards (garden would not be the right word here). As Henry Louis Mencken (American humourist and critique of American life, 1880–1956) once said, 'Nobody ever went broke underestimating the taste of the American public'. These untidy homes often sit slap bang next to pretentious home estates, proudly advertising themselves with their white corral fences and fluttering American flag. The contrast in wealth and attitudes of the people is very obvious from the housing.

Some of the cheapest homes are found in the Great Plains, from North Dakota to Texas; here average homes sell for less than $75,000. A 2003 study by the National Low Income Housing Coalition found that as housing costs nationally have outstripped wages, those on low incomes have difficulty affording even a modest one- or two-bedroom rented apartment, let alone being able to buy something.

Mobile homes represent the fastest growing form of housing in America. At the time of the 2000 US Census, there were 9 million such homes, accounting for nearly 1 in 10 residences and housing 7.5% of the population. One reason for their popularity is that many people prefer to buy a cheaper home and then spend their money on other things. The following states have the highest numbers of mobile homes: New Mexico and South Carolina (where 1 in 5 families live in one), and Georgia and Idaho (1 in 8). In Long County and Eureka County in Nevada, nearly 70% of units are mobile homes. The next densest concentration (58%) is in Brantley County, Georgia. They are also very popular in North Carolina, West Virginia, Wyoming and Florida.

They are usually grouped together on a park. The home arrives at the park on the back of a lorry and is placed on a platform or blocks; a sewer pipe is connected underneath, electricity and water are plumbed in, the TV arrives, and the family is installed. Owners or renters either pay a space or lot fee to the proprietor of the park or buy their lot (2 in 3 owners do this). If you do not own the land, you cannot get a mortgage, in which case most people buy their mobile home with cash or a property loan. Alternatively, if you can and do take out a mortgage, expect to pay a higher rate than on a conventional home. Furthermore, your 'asset' is apt to depreciate in value, unlike a standard home which should appreciate. New mobile homes typically cost around

$50,000, though in Florida prices have rocketed and such simple homes can sell for millions in select places. Elsewhere, as an alternative to buying, mobile homes may cost around $200/week to rent plus $400/month space fee. Inhabitants do not pay town taxes, yet are allowed full use of all local facilities.

It is no longer politically correct to use the terms 'trailer home' or 'trailer park'; 'manufactured housing' in a 'mobile home community' is preferable. Such parks still have a stigma attached to them. Some have been likened to 'canned labour' as they provide accommodation for the majority of low-wage earners. Families on low income face a real problem finding suitable cheap accommodation, which is in short supply. As an alternative to mobile home living, many low-income families, especially immigrant workers, opt to live in crowded apartments with other, often unrelated people. Some even live in cheap motel rooms, especially if they cannot afford the deposit and first month's rent on something more permanent.

City Living and Towns

As cities evolve and suburbs sprawl, people move to where they think they will be better off. Initially, this usually means a move out to the suburbs, where there is more space and newer buildings. Today there is a growing trend (as in Britain) for Americans to move back into their city centres in order to have easy access to a new dynamic downtown culture. Old areas are being revamped and now serve up an enticing array of entertainment and dining opportunities that were not there before.

Apartment dwelling is becoming more sophisticated. High-rise buildings are often equipped with hotel-style facilities, including delivery services, concierges, guest suites, room service, valet parking, spas, pools and gyms. These services and amenities are especially alluring to working urbanites, who appreciate the convenience and ease they offer, allowing them more quality down-time (rather than spending their free time shopping for groceries or cleaning the car). Added to this is the trend towards Smart House technology, for instance innovative remote-controlled heating and cooking systems and appliances that can be set from outside the home, and green technology, e.g. recycling systems and geothermal heating.

However, city housing is not all as smooth, suave and sophisticated. As John R. Logan (Distinguished Professor of Sociology and Director of the Lewis Mumford Center for Comparative Urban and Regional Research) points out:

> 'The average white person continues to live in a neighborhood that looks very different from those neighborhoods where the average black, Hispanic, and Asian live.'

Researchers at the State University of New York at Albany have been analysing data from the 2000 Census and found that:

- People are still living in largely segregated neighborhoods.
- In metropolitan areas, more than 70% of whites are now living in the suburbs compared with 40% of blacks.
- Metropolitan areas where blacks and whites are most integrated are in the South and in military towns such as San Diego and Norfolk, Virginia.
- More than 60% of blacks live in cities, in neighborhoods with 75.5% minority races.
- Around 30% of whites live in cities, typically in neighbourhoods that are approximately 72% white.

Take a drive through any American city and you will notice very obvious delineations of wealth and quality of housing and the environment. Some areas are ghettos – with homes and businesses boarded up, peeling paint, junk on porches and in front yards, wrecks parked on the road, and usually not a white face in sight. There were certain areas of Dayton, our nearest city, which you just weren't supposed to drive through, for fear of being mugged or worse. Divisions and contrasts in city communities, as in Britain, can be very evident.

Towns vary in style a great deal, as you would expect. In off-beat places, hick towns with one straight high street, dark saloon bars and diners, odd shops and downtrodden or derelict hotels and homes give the impression of having seen better days. With the arrival of out-of-town stores and business districts, many downtowns have lost out and are all but abandoned. High streets, apart from in older towns, student towns or in newer community developments, may be missing; some places do not even have a centre where you can walk about. Instead you may find one main road, often with dual carriageway in both directions, with stores and businesses strung out as far as the eye can see. In these situations parking is free and easy; no one walks between stores. If you're feeling adventurous, you might contemplate crossing the roads between shopping areas, but don't expect necessarily to find pavements, walkways or pedestrian crossing points. You will probably be quizzically stared at by passing motorists as an oddball.

Some cities are trying to develop more of a traditional town centre by providing small shops laid out together, linked by pavements, thus encouraging people to walk around. In student towns you will usually find a thriving downtown area, bustling with restaurants, shops, entertainment venues and historic buildings, much as they were 50 years ago. Housing can also be cheaper in these areas, and they act as a magnet for active retirees, looking for some original community.

Renting

When we first arrived in America, we rented temporary accommodation in an apartment complex for the first 5 weeks. A swimming pool, tennis courts, clubhouse and car wash area comprised the modest facilities on the complex. Our apartment had a sunny veranda, air conditioning (essential in the summer heat), a Laundromat-size washing machine and drier, waste disposal unit in the sink, coffee percolator, large television screen with 78 channels, a dishwasher and loads of room. It felt luxurious, like staying in some quality holiday resort.

American realtors with websites may offer a full listing of properties to rent or buy in the area, from which you can compile a shortlist. If you have the opportunity to visit before the family uproots, all the better. Tim was lucky enough to visit WPAFB a month or so early to meet work colleagues, who filled him in on the local area and took him around to view our shortlist of potential homes. Landlords tend to be ruthless and outsides can be deceptive; inside the fixtures and fittings are often cheap and chipboard is used extensively. If you can, talk to the neighbours of your prospective home and ask about the landlord – does he/she look after things and undertake good maintenance? Locations may not be what they seem from pictures and the internet, so do not take things at face value. Try to get a feel for the area before you commit.

Another tip when you take over a rental is to take photographs and note down *all* marks and anomalies, or you could be billed for them on moving out.

Buying

If you are in the buying market then you need to carefully choose an area that suits you and your family, e.g. depending on school considerations, distance to work, low crime rate, zoning laws, etc. Before starting to look for a house to buy, decide how you will finance the purchase. In America, a seller is more likely to accept an offer if you have a pre-approved loan. This involves contacting a potential lender, who will undertake an in-depth financial analysis of your situation. They will verify your credit rating and work out a realistic loan figure. Bear in mind that you will need to set aside 3–6% of your total loan amount for closing costs. You will usually be asked to put up 20% of the asking price as a down-payment; if you can't, you may have to take out private mortgage insurance (PMI).

Various types of mortgages and loans are available, depending on your circumstances:

- Fixed rate for the term of the mortgage, e.g. 30 years.
- Adjustable rate.
- Balloon mortgage – whereby you pay a low rate for the first 5–7 years, then a big wad to pay off the entire balance (good if you plan to sell your home at that time).
- Federal Housing Administration (FHA) loan – insures home loans, making traditional commercial loans cheaper for those who cannot readily afford them. Requires a lower down-payment of 5% or less.
- Veterans' Administration (VA) loan – for qualifying veterans, offering amounts of

up to $240,000 and no down-payment.

- Rural Housing Service (RHS) loan – low interest loan for those living in small towns or rural areas, for families on a low income.

To qualify for a commercial loan, your debt to income ratio must be around 28:36, i.e. the mortgage lender will lend you the money so long as your interest payments are not more than 28% of your gross income and your other loans and credit card debts are not more than 36% of your income (leaving at least 64% for other living expenses). Lenders offer numerous options to borrowers with less than $50,000 income that require little or no down-payment. This is to allow the young and those less well off to purchase a home. Since 2000, house prices have rocketed, though rents have remained static or even decreased. The average mortgage payment in America is $1600/month; the typical rent payment is half this.

Having worked out the finances, the next step is to search for a suitable house. You can:

- Do it yourself: search online, in newspapers, or drive around locally looking for 'For Sale by Owner' (FSBO) signs – which are common in America. Some realtor websites offer virtual tours of homes for sale. You can look up the Multiple Listing Service for your area by keying in 'multiple listing service' followed by the name of the state you are interested in and inputting your preferences.
- Go to a local real estate agent: but remember, these agents are acting on behalf of the home owner so never reveal the highest price you are willing to pay or disclose other information that might be used against you.
- Use a buyer's agency: these agents work for the buyer, ensuring the property is inspected, undertaking a comparative market analysis to see what other homes in the area are selling for, carrying out a title search, and negotiating the best price for you. Terms are usually negotiable and fees vary, but they can end up saving you money. See the National Association of Exclusive Buyer Agents website for more details (in *Useful Websites*).

Once you have found a suitable home, you will want to make an official offer or bid, contingent on an acceptable inspection report. Employ a professional inspector (someone certified by the American Society of Home Inspectors), even when considering buying a new-built home; the cost (anywhere from $200 to $500) is usually worth it. You will also need to employ an attorney to carry out a title search, or your agent may do this for you. Before transfer of the title takes place, you must have taken out home owner's insurance, to protect the building from hazard. Your local Board of Realtors can be a helpful source of advice and may be able to answer any specific questions you have on buying or selling a house.

Many Americans have huge mortgages, often on an interest only basis. They may end up never owning their own home, though enjoying the privileges of one. Equity loans are big business, whereby homeowners are offered loans for any reason (a new car, holiday, new appliances for the home, etc.) and the house is used as collateral. Yet the family does not actually own the house, they just have a big mortgage on it. The house you live in has become a form of credit card. Needless to say, mortgage foreclosure is becoming rife as people lose sight of the difference between real and perceived wealth. The housing market is a major component of gross domestic product (GDP), and such loose lending standards represent a dangerous foundation to the economy. In 2005, 32.6% of new mortgages and home-equity loans were interest only, and 43% of first-time buyers put no money down on their homes. Lenders have been encouraging people to take out unspecified loans on the basis of the appreciation in value of their house. Of course, when the value of housing falls (as it has been doing since 2005) or if mortgage interest rates rise, these people find themselves in financial difficulties.

As we left America in 2007, the mortgage market was in turmoil. The controversial and risky practice of sub-prime lending was most to blame. Borrowers who do not qualify for usual loans owing to a poor credit history may be granted sub-prime (or B-paper) loans, which command higher interest rate payments than more usual A-paper loans due to the increased risk. (Sub-prime loans also apply to car loans and credit cards, not just mortgages.) However, since late 2006, hundreds of sub-prime lenders have gone bankrupt, while thousands of borrowers have defaulted on their loans and lost their homes. Moreover, the crisis is worsening. This is dire news for the American stock market, and some foresee a crash in the economy based on the 'lending bubble'.

Insurance

The Insurance Services Office (ISO) provides risk information and policies to insurance companies. The basic insurance policies you can take out are listed below:

- HO-3: the most common policy for homeowners, designed to cover buildings and contents.
- HO-4: commonly referred to as renter's insurance (contents only).
- HO-6: for condominium owners.
- HO-7: for mobile home owners.

Premiums can be high, especially in those areas most likely to be hit by floods, earthquakes or hurricanes. The most expensive states are Texas, Louisiana and Oklahoma; Wisconsin is the cheapest. Natural disaster coverage can be a problem in some places, and most basic insurance policies do not provide cover – you will need to purchase riders. Therefore check the details of your policy carefully before committing. AccuCoverage can advise on how much coverage you need to buy.

Household Refuse

The system of collecting household refuse varies from one place to another and is even city specific. We had to set up an account with a local refuse company and pay a monthly charge to have our rubbish removed. You may have the choice of several different garbage collectors offering variously priced packages.

In most places, if you opt to recycle (which may cost you a nominal dollar a month more) you will be supplied with a plastic box, in which to place a mixture of materials – plastic, glass, metal, polystyrene and newspaper/cardboard – it can all be thrown in together. The different materials are separated at the recycling depot. If you want your biodegradable garden refuse collected and taken away by your refuse company, you may have to buy special brown paper bags (available from supermarkets) to put it in. Or you can take it to your local recycling depot. During the autumn fall, some cities offer a leaf collecting service; homeowners simply pile up their dead leaves at the roadside and the city takes care of the rest. Alternatively, compost anything you can, enriching your own soil and saving landfill space in the process.

Conclusion

The town of Seaside in Florida that was used in the film *The Truman Show* was the first planned community of the New Urbanism movement, which is especially associated with America. I am not saying that this is the norm for housing in America, but there are a growing number of other examples of this style of development and living throughout the US. The housing described in this chapter is very much based on personal observations of where we were living in the States – in Greene County, Ohio. Beavercreek is a privileged, relatively young, yet old-fashioned community. It is a suburb of the city of Dayton, which has in contrast some very poor areas, where people live in low-cost housing and there are shootings and other crime-related incidents. My friend Betty, a long-term resident of Beavercreek, likened it to the 1970s' family sitcom *Leave it to Beaver*, which painted an idealised picture of a white family living in a suburban town: 'We don't close our garage door, and no-one takes the rake', as she put it. I will add to that and say no-one takes the rocking chair, wind chimes, flag or garden toys. I found it very surprising how open people left themselves. They also took great pride in their homes and surroundings, to the point of perhaps overtitivating, yet it made for a pleasant and safe environment. However, it is not the case everywhere.

Useful Websites

www.accucoverage.com – for insurance advice.
www.ashi.org – American Society of Home Inspectors.
www.forsalebyowner.com – a real estate website, with no commission charge; it has

lots of useful information under its 'Research & Resources'.
www.naeba.org – National Association of Exclusive Buyer Agents, providing a service for home-buyers (rather than sellers).
www.realtor.com – for information on local realtors, houses for sale, valuations, mortgages and moving quotes. They may also have information about the neighbourhood you are interested in, such as schools, crime rates, etc.
www.realtor.org – National Association of Realtors.
www.salebyowner.com – real estate database of FSBO homes.

Terminology

American term	Equivalent British term	Notes
Bathroom or washroom	Toilet (WC)	
Broker	Estate agent	
Bureau or dresser	Chest of drawers	
Closet	Cupboard	
Comforter	Bedspread, eiderdown, quilt	Not a duvet
Condo	Flats	Usually with communal facilities
Dish pan	Washing up bowl	
Downtown	Town centre	
Drapes	Curtains	
Dump	Tip	
Duplex	Semi-detached or two-floored	
Eminent domain	Compulsory purchase	
Faucet	Tap	
First floor ('1')	Ground floor ('0')	In Britain, '0' is the ground floor in elevators whereas in America it is '1'; their second floor is our first, and so on
Flat ware, silverware	Cutlery	
Furnace	Central heating boiler	
Hideaway	Bed-settee	
Main street	High street	
Moving company	Removal company	

Pavement	Pavement, road	In America, 'pavement' is any area that is paved. So it can be a pavement as we know it or any 'road' for vehicular traffic
Range	Cooker	
Realtor	Estate agent	
Sheers	Net curtains	
Sidewalk	Pavement, footpath	
Stove	Cooker, oven	
Sub-division	Housing estate	
Townhouse	Terraced house	Often upmarket

11 · On the Roads

A car is pretty much a necessity in America and even poor families own at least one. Big vehicles and open roads are part of the American way of life; witness the inordinate number of American road movies. As one friend put it, 'The car is integral to who we are. The automobile directs our country – politically (with our dependence on oil, and the trouble that brings), economically and socially. We have an intimate relationship with our cars'. However, this dependence comes with a price:

- traffic jams in the cities and surrounding metropolitan areas; even six-lane expressways can become gridlocked with fuming cars and drivers at rush hour;
- decay of downtowns, as new roads are built to avoid the towns and take drivers away from town centres;
- environmental pollution;
- destruction of the countryside for road building and more infrastructure;
- poor public health owing to lack of exercise (over-reliance on four wheels as against walking or cycling).

Fortunately, some inner cities have excellent public transportation networks, where the car culture is less extreme and the population resembles other urban Western European ones in the use of buses and trains. New York City is a notable example. According to the US Census (2000), NYC is the only major city where more than 50% of householders are *not* car owners (nationally the rate is only 8%). It has a unique pedestrian-friendly character and very high rate of public transport use. Elsewhere, outside of city downtowns, nearly 90% of Americans drive to work, less than 1% use the train network, other forms of public transport are almost non-existent, and you are lucky if there are even pavements to walk on. One exception to the dearth in public transportation is the school bus – those archetypal yellow buses that seem to be everywhere at certain times of the day.

A Little History

Before automobiles and the great road network came into being, people and goods were moved by rail. The first trans-continental railroad crossed the country in 1869 and opened up a huge swathe of the continent for the movement of goods and passengers. Today railroads carry 35% of the nation's freight, while rivers and the Great Lakes account for 15%. Freight trains seem to stretch on forever when you are waiting at a railroad crossing; at night you can hear their whistles as they speed through the darkness.

At the beginning of the twentieth century, the 'horseless carriage' (or automobile) began life as a rich-man's toy, used for short journeys. Most Americans at this time rarely travelled more than 12 miles from their homes (equivalent to 1 day's horse-drawn carriage ride away). Moreover, automobiles were very unreliable machines and most people never thought they would catch on.

In 1903, Horatio Nelson Jackson undertook the first successful road trip across America, travelling 6000 miles from San Francisco to New York City, a journey that took 63 days. Horatio made an impulsive wager that he could cross the continent coast to coast in less than 3 months – a feat that had taken Lewis and Clark 2½ years to achieve a hundred years previously. He took along a mechanic – Stewart Crocker – and on the way acquired Bud the bulldog, and together they made history. At the time, half of America had only unpaved, dirt tracks and steep rocky trails. These intrepid 'motorneers' frequently lost their way, as there were few direction signs to help them; they got stuck in the mud, creeks and rivers, endured storms in a vehicle without a windscreen or top, lost their possessions off the back of the car while negotiating bumpy tracks, and continually broke down. However, somehow the 20-hp motor 'whiz wagon' as it came to be known and its drivers made it through one difficulty after another, and into the history books as the first cross-American car journey. Horatio's car – the Vermont – is now a revered piece of American history, ensconced in the Smithsonian Institution.

A few years after Horatio's famous journey, the road improvement scheme began. The automobile as an independent mobile status symbol appealed to Americans, who also relished the idea of heading off into the unknown. The automobile became the vehicle of individual freedom and distance. Henry Ford (an American industrialist) embraced the new technology. During those early days, he produced vehicles cheaply for the masses and is quoted as saying, 'The customer can have any color he wants as long as it's black'.

By 1930, the Lincoln Highway (now Interstate 80) reached across the centre of the country, allowing motorists to cross the States in a mere 5 days. Americans have never looked back. The cry went out: 'See the USA in your Chevrolet!'. The 1940s and 1950s were the golden age of the road, when you could make a vacation of travelling a particular route. The roads were different then, with small kitschy hotels, weird truck stops and quirky side attractions along the way.

Interstates came into being following a bill passed in 1956 by President Eisenhower, creating the National System of Interstate and Defense Highways. This committed the government to funding and building hundreds of motorways across the country, laid out according to a grand plan and uniform code of construction. For example, one rule was that there could be no intersections (stop lights or traffic junctions); instead motorists must enter and leave on slip roads. The rules resulted in all the interstates looking pretty much the same, and today you could be forgiven for being unable to tell which state you are driving through. The Interstate Highway System envisioned a network of wide, smooth, fast superhighways across the country. The federal reserve footed 90% of the cost of building the new thoroughfares; individual states put up the rest of the money. Each state was allowed to choose the route across its country and was responsible for maintaining the highways. Today, every state bar Alaska has at least one interstate crossing it, and 250 million registered vehicles use the 46,730 miles of interstate system. Technically, the interstate network has not been completed – there is a gap along I-95 just north of Philadelphia, involving an additional river bridge and new interchange; however, many proclaimed September 1991 as the official completion date of Eisenhower's project.

Finding Your Way

I have to admit that my first driving experience in America was horrible. I got thoroughly lost after taking one wrong turn; I have no sense of direction anyway, and was surrounded by unfamiliar road names, numbers and places. Cloverleaf-shaped junctions take you off, twirl you around and send you off on another route. Verdict: get a compass for the car and, before leaving home, familiarise yourself with the geography (at least the names of major towns and where they are in relation to one another); AAA maps are very useful and free if you join. One British friend couldn't go anywhere even locally without her GPS navigator.

American street atlases can look bizarre, with their chequerboard pattern of straight roads intersecting at 90 degrees; it almost looks unreal the way the roads run so straight and orderly. You can see the way many towns and roads were so obviously planned and deliberately organised. Knowing a little about how American roads are organised may help you find your way about:

- North to south running interstates are numbered oddly, e.g. I-91 goes from the Canadian border south to New Haven, Connecticut, and I-75 goes from Ohio to Florida.
- Those running east to west have even numbers, e.g. I-10, I-80 and I-90 cross the country from coast to coast.
- North to south routes are numbered lowest in the west; east to west routes are numbered lowest in the south. For example, I-5 runs along the West Coast from Canada to Mexico; I-95 runs from Canada to Miami, and is the longest

north–south interstate, at 3082 miles long (approximately three times the length of the UK).

- Interstate numbers divisible by five are supposed to be the major long-distance routes. I-90 is the longest at 4987 km (3099 miles).
- In some states, including Ohio, exits are numbered according to the number of miles since the start of the numbering scheme (for example, the next turnoff after exit 22 may be exit 29, indicating that you have 7 miles to go between exits); this can be confusing at first, but once you are used to the system it makes for a handy mileage guide.
- Local roads are identified by name, e.g. Keowee Street or Indian Ripple Road, and/or number, rather than by directional town, – which doesn't tell you anything about the direction of the road or where it leads to.
- If you stop to ask for directions, bear in mind that 'Turn left on Main' means turn left onto Main Street, not turn left off Main Street.

Half the states of America, mostly in the north and east, have toll roads. If you regularly travel on such roads you might think about buying an RF (radio frequency) tag, which automatically bills your account electronically for tolls. The E-ZPass electronic toll collection system has special lanes which allow cars to pass through without having to slow down too much.

Obtaining a Driver's Licence

Your full UK driving licence should be acceptable when renting a car in America for a period of up to 1 year. If you are buying a vehicle or staying longer, then you need to apply for a US licence. However, different states have different rules, so check with the Bureau of Motor Vehicles (BMV) website applicable to your state.

New residents to a state must surrender their old driver's licence and apply for a new one; they also need new vehicle licence plates and a state title for any vehicle they own. The one saving grace is that the driving test is usually waived if you have a valid out-of-state licence. Non-US citizens also have to provide proof of legal presence, e.g. a letter from a boss confirming where you work, or stating that you are a spouse accompanying your husband/wife on a work contract. A tip is to check with the authorities first regarding what official paperwork you need to present before queuing up in the licencing agency or auto title office; it is all too easy to overlook some vital piece of paper that they need to complete the bureaucratic process.

To obtain a local state driving licence you need to pass a written and practical test. Get hold of a highway code booklet for your state (in our case a *Digest of Ohio Motor Vehicle Laws*). Duly digest it, then make an appointment at your local examination station to take the test. The written test involves selecting the correct answers to a series of computer questions (multiple choice) and is not as scary as it sounds. We had to get 30 of the 40 questions right, but can skip some you are not sure about (make certain you understand how the test works before you take it). The general driving questions are very similar to the UK test; the awkward questions involve US-specific signs and things like alcohol limits and speed restrictions.

The practical test varies according to state. In Ohio, you have to drive through a mini chicane of cones, then reverse back through them, without knocking any over or stopping within the chicane. Then you enjoy a 10-minute drive round the houses, coming to a complete stop at stop signs, using your mirrors correctly, watching out for speed signs, etc. and hopefully doing nothing to ruffle or upset the examiner.

Once you have obtained a US driver's licence, this little card acts as personal identification in all sorts of places, and you should keep it handy in your purse or wallet, ready to show any time you are asked for ID. Opt to leave your social security number off the licence owing to identity theft.

Young Drivers

The rules concerning young drivers differ according to state. Driving age is determined by state; most usually the age is 16, though some states issue learner permits to drivers as young as 14. Young drivers are often restricted from driving at certain times, e.g. between the hours of 11 p.m. and 5 a.m.

In Ohio, you can take a written test at age 15½ to obtain a temporary driving permit. You are then required to complete a mandatory 50 hours of supervised driving with an eligible adult (a parent or guardian who is at least 21 years old and holds a valid driver's licence); 10 of these hours must be at night. You also have to enroll for 24 hours of classroom instruction and 8 hours of actual driving in a licenced driving school. If you pass the driving test, you can apply for a probationary licence. The regular licence is granted at age 17. However, the authorities have to be satisfied that you have 50 hours of driving experience and have completed a driver's education course that meets or exceeds the state's requirements.

Buying a Vehicle

Cars are relatively cheap to buy and you get much more for your money in America compared to Britain, especially with regard to size and standard of equipment. The long, bouncy, classic American car you see in the movies has been usurped by mini vans, SUVs (sports utility vehicles, or sub-urban assault vehicles, depending on how you view them) and pickups. Big is beautiful, and to hell with fuel efficiency. In the late, booming 1990s, half of all new cars bought were light trucks and SUVs (at a cost of $30–40,000 a piece) – mostly as status symbols. Hummer 'tanks' are also fashionable (retailing at close to $100,000) for the power-hungry.

Yet there appears to be a trend towards smaller cars, particularly Japanese makes.

If you read *Consumer Reports* (the US equivalent of *Which?*) you wouldn't buy an American car because of poor reliability, lesser quality, efficiency, fuel economy and low residual value; even though Japanese cars are more expensive to buy they have the edge. Thus, nowadays, there are more Japanese models on America's roads than American-made cars. Americans are complaining that the government has not controlled foreign imports and this is now affecting jobs. Diehards still buy American, as much to support the industry as anything, and many cars sport red, white and blue stickers on their bumpers proclaiming 'Buy American'. Moreover, if you haven't got the money for a foreign import, a US car should be cheap and cheerful.

Most American cars are automatics, so driving your new car should be a doddle. When stopped, it is wise to keep your foot on the brake; otherwise the car will creep forward. You generally drive everywhere in D (drive); use L (low) up steep hills and P (park) when parking. When taking the car out of Park, put your foot on the brake pedal to avoid a jerk forwards. That's pretty much all there is to it. Many of the following features are available in the UK but are far more prevalent in the US, even on 'average' cars:

- a soft alarm sound when you open a door with the key still in the ignition (so there is no way you can forget to take the key out), and likewise an alarm on putting the key in the ignition to remind you to close the door and put your seat belt on;
- a parking brake (separate foot peddle) but not necessarily a hand brake. Almost all cars have an emergency brake;
- cruise control;
- electrically operated seat positioning;
- heated seats (wonderful in winter);
- automatic seat belt sweep.

A word on cruise control: this is especially useful in America, where long-distance and relatively unbroken driving is common. It makes driving on freeways less tiring, avoids the problem of gradually speeding up as the miles clock by, and is better for your fuel economy.

As Americans grow more conscious of their consumption and dependence on foreign oil, some are turning to hybrid cars. Hybrids combine a gasoline engine and battery-powered electric motor which drives the wheels. Computers in hybrids assess the power needs at any given moment, and switch seamlessly between the electric motor and gas engine. Initial purchase costs are about \$2000–-3000 higher than traditional cars, but tax credits are available; the more fuel efficient a particular model, the higher the credit, which is subtracted directly from your US tax bill. Hybrids generally give around 45–65 mpg and give their best mileage in stop–go situations. Some enthusiasts manage over 90 mpg, but through somewhat extreme driving methods. They cost less in routine maintenance, and some US cities, e.g. Portland, Oregon, are actively encouraging the use of electric/hybrid vehicles, with free parking and charging points. Their outstanding fuel economy and lower emissions have created a surge in demand for these cars, and for other small cars.

Yet SUVs and pickups are still very popular. However, studies found that for every fatality SUVs and pickups avoided for their own passengers, they caused four fatalities to passengers in other cars, pedestrians or cyclists, owing to their great mass and high bumpers. New safety features adopted in 2003 involve either building SUVs closer to the ground or equipping them with bars below the bumpers, in an effort to stop them sliding over smaller vehicles in a collision. However, the standards will not be fully in place until 2009. Till then, give big SUVs a wide berth on the roads. Moreover, these muscle cars are prone to roll-overs themselves, are massive gas-guzzlers and air polluters, and require nearly twice the natural resources to manufacture as the average sedan.

Jim comments on how age might dictate what model of vehicle you might own:

> Every American teenager dreams of owning their first car as this will release them from relying on the family taxi service and deliver true independence. This first car is generally small – which in American parlance means something in the order of a 2.5-litre engine in a car the size of an Astra. It is compulsory that this car has something hilarious attached to it, such as a Disney character antenna top or false bullet holes. Add in some DIY paint work and other go-faster accessories and the exterior work is complete. Then it's just a case of installing some friends with the discipline of chimpanzees before driving at breakneck speed while juggling CDs and using a mobile phone to call other friends in different cars. If the teenager survives the extreme risks of these early years, he or she can progress to slightly bigger cars. The current vogue is for Sports Utility Vehicles (SUVs), which are tank-like vehicles with huge engines and battering-ram ballistic qualities. The SUV stretches horizons and allows students to study at colleges a good distance away from parents. The SUV is the size of a small house and it is normally kept as neat as the average college room! This look may not be all-together accidental as the car often has to act as home, either when the driver has the sense not to drive back from a bar or is on a road trip and a motel is too expensive. Your average American may then graduate to the ultimate status symbol – the deceptively diminutive sounding minivan. The irony here is that the arrival of the minivan is precipitated by children and a sudden interest in keeping things clean and tidy – aims that are exactly opposed by those children.

The Process

The terminology of the car salesperson is a whole new language, which can make buying a car far from straightforward to non-Americans (see *Terminology* at the end of this chapter). Typically the best time of year to buy a car is between July and October and the last 2 weeks in December. You might be looking for a loan if you cannot or do not want to buy a car outright. Sourcing a loan yourself, rather than taking the easy option of a dealer's loan, is usually better. Leasing also seems very popular, but make sure you understand the terms. At the time we were looking to buy a car, the interest rate was on a par with UK interest rates on savings, so low by loan standards.

Before committing to a sale, ensure you obtain a copy of the vehicle report in order to protect yourself against fraud. Visit the Carfax website to do a title search to find out information the dealer may be hiding from you. This will also tell you the number of previous owners, whether the vehicle has been in an accident or has been subject to flooding or salvage, and it gives you an accurate mileage check. You will need the Vehicle Identification Number and have to pay a fee for this service. For approximately $75 you can also call out an inspector to check over the car before committing to buying.

If you are happy to proceed, tell the seller how much *you* want to pay and negotiate. The *Kelley Blue Book* (KBB) is an excellent resource; look up the car you are interested in and read the opinions and appraisals on it. It will also give you the retail price range, which Americans stick to pretty rigidly. Check out the trade-in value. There are cars galore in America and a huge number of sellers, so you as a buyer are in a strong position. The KBB website also has a link to Carfax.

Prices in the cities may be lower than in smaller conurbations, so it is worth looking beyond your local town and vicinity; the drive could save you money. The price on the car is a top price, from which you and the car dealer can work. Often dealers discount it immediately. If not, ask them what the 'invoice price' on the car is (this is the price they paid for it); they are legally obliged to tell you. You can then negotiate from there. Alternatively, call the *Consumer Reports* New Car Price Service and, for about $12, they will send a report showing the invoice cost, the sticker price, invoice and sticker prices for all options and packages, and provide good advice on how to use the information in the report to your best advantage when negotiating the selling price. Then bargain up from the invoice price, never down from the sticker price. Unless the car is difficult to come by, expect to agree on approximately $500 over the invoice price.

If you have a trade-in car to dispose of, do not let the dealer know this until you have agreed on the price of the new car. Again, for around $10, the *Consumer Reports New and Used Car Buying Guide* can give you an idea of what your old car is worth.

There is something called the Lemon Law in America, which applies to new vehicles only. This law safeguards you from buying something defective, as it forces manufacturers to buy back faulty vehicles. Every state has a different lemon law – check the warranty in your owner's manual or visit the Better Business Bureau's website (see *Useful Websites*).

The usual procedure for buying a car is as follows. If you are buying from a dealer, they usually handle the process for you.

- The seller shows the buyer the title document, which details the ownership of the vehicle and whether any finance company has a claim on it. The buyer should ensure that the money owed to the finance company has been paid off. Then the seller completes his or her part of the title form, and the buyer completes the other. The seller retains the car's licence plates.
- The new owner takes the title document, application for title transfer and registration to his/her local Department of Motor Vehicles (DMV) auto title office to be processed.
- The new owner can then visit the local licencing agency, to buy new plates.

Registration Plates, Tax and County Decals

When buying a car, you must register it locally with the DMV licencing agency and obtain new registration plates. Thereafter, each year – usually on your birthday – you will receive a reminder in the post that you need to renew the registration. Some states have reduced renewal rates if you are in the military or a veteran, or you may qualify for tax exemption (which saves around $20). If at renewal you forget this (as I did), send the necessary form and a grovelling letter, and they may send you a refund of the tax paid.

Each state has its own plate design. You may decide that you want to pay a little extra for some personalised or special plates. You can also choose from hundreds of novelty plates, with background designs ranging from patriotic, sporting, military, to college, company logos, personalised or special interest. You name it, there's a personalised plate out there for you. Prices start very low at $5 and rise to $35. A portion of this money may go to the charity you are in effect advertising. So you can individualise your car at the same time as supporting a cause.

Instead of road tax, vehicle owners may have to pay an annual motor vehicle property tax in many states and counties (again, each state has its own rules and regulations, so check with your local county whether you are required to pay this). Monies raised often go to fund the fire and rescue services. In Ohio you have to display a county decal (tag) on your registration plates to show that you have paid the tax (other states may have a different ruling). This personal property tax can also be levied on other items such as trucks, motorcycles, boats, planes, campers, trailers, motor homes and mobile homes.

Emissions Check

Driving a car is the single most polluting thing you can do, according to the US Environmental Protection Agency. In the cities of the North-East and Mid-Atlantic states and places like Los Angeles, smog is a serious problem and the incidence of cancer is more prevalent, due mainly to the toxins and pollutants emitted by motor vehicles. Car emissions also contribute to global warming and acid rain. In some counties you are required to have an E check (an emissions inspection) and/or car safety inspection, while in others you are not. Check on your particular county's requirement. Some are stricter than others, e.g. in rundown cities with older cars on the road, the rules may be tighter. Think of it as the equivalent of the car's MOT.

Insurance

Your UK driving licence is barely recognised in the States, and many insurance companies will only insure you if you have a US driving licence. Furthermore, your UK driving record may not count for much, and the cost of your first US car insurance may therefore come as a shock. Shop around. You will probably need to supply the Vehicle Identification Number (VIN) of the car you want to insure. Many American motor insurers quote for cover on a 6-month basis, rather than a full year, so check this before committing. We found the AAA and Sunrise Group gave reasonable quotes.

The AAA (Triple A)

The American Automobile Association (AAA or Triple A) is a useful organisation that gives you breakdown cover and a lot more besides. There are offices all over America where you can sign up for annual membership. After that you can visit local offices and pick up free maps, books and travel information, and get help with route planning (known as triptiks). The AAA also gives its members discounts, e.g. on hotel rooms and entrance tickets, both locally and nationally. So not only do you get peace of mind with breakdown cover, but also the cost of membership can easily be recouped if you plan on doing a fair amount of travelling in the States.

Motorcycles

It is not uncommon to see laid-back motorcyclists riding around on a sunny day without any protective clothing at all (not even a helmet or gloves). Four states – Colorado, Illinois, Iowa and New Hampshire – are totally helmet-free, 20 states have full helmet laws, while the other 19 exempt riders over the age of 18. In Ohio, the law is that helmets are not required so long as the rider is at least 18 years old, has held a motorcycle licence or endorsement for more than a year, and either has a windscreen or wears protective goggles or glasses. Most riders opt for cool shades. Apart from in a handful of states, motorcycle training is not mandatory.

Victory Motorcycles and the Harley-Davidson Motor Company are the only two remaining mass-producers of motorcycles in the US. The latter has been manufacturing motorbikes since 1903. It has a huge, worldwide following and its own culture. Harley Davidson (HD) bikes are one of the most popular products to come out of America, and 150,000 bikes are produced every year, with around 30% sold overseas. Indeed, you might have to wait for a new one from the factory, such is their popularity.

One of the early HD racers had a baby pig called Hog as a mascot, and the name stuck. 'Hogs' were marketed to the United States Postal Service, primarily in rural areas, in place of bicycles. They certainly took the work out of delivering mail. During World War I, HDs were drafted for military use, primarily as dispatch vehicles. By the end of the war, all HD production was for the war effort. During the 1920s, HD was the largest motorcycle manufacturer in the world.

As pursuit vehicles and for highway patrol they were ideal police vehicles, and lent a certain glamour to the American uniformed police force. In 1936, a new-style bike came out of the factory, known as the knucklehead (because of the shape of its cylinder heads), which had double the horsepower of older models. During World War II, motorcycles were a vital part of mechanised warfare. Germany's BMW motorbikes were used very effectively, and HD followed suit. The whole of production was given over to America's contribution to the fight for freedom. Men were trained to ride hard and flat out. This style of riding continued after the war, as returning GIs, eager for more thrills and spills, bought their own bikes. They formed clubs, Hell's Angels of southern California being the most famous. Movies promoted the rebel ethic, and HDs were popularised by Hollywood celebrities and other famous names of the time, e.g. Elvis Presley and James Dean.

During the 1960s, the *Easy Rider*-style chopper bikes became more flamboyant and elaborate. Many riders customised their bikes, and the factory followed their lead, successfully producing factory-customised bikes. There were problems with reliability, and many bikes left the characteristic puddle of oil when parked. Despite this, diehard riders remained loyal to Harley-Davidson. Gradually the company improved quality, so that today they are as good as, if not better than, other manufacturers, even British ones. They have earned the name of the world's most famous motorcycle. More and more women are riding now, not content to be mere pillions. Harley-Davidson motorbikes represent the same pioneering spirit today as they did in 1903.

If you want to catch a rally, head for Daytona Beach, Florida; Myrtle Beach, South Carolina; Sturgis, South Dakota; Laconia, New Hampshire; or Austin, Texas. Washington, DC, also hosts an annual rally, to highlight issues relating to war veterans.

One of the more enduring visions of America is the man proudly astride his Harley Davidson motorbike. While many non-Americans consider the Harley Davidson to be about as close to a modern motorcycle as a tractor cleaved in half, there is no denying that it typifies a unique American style. There are a few other manufacturers, such as Indian and Orange County Choppers, and some Japanese manufacturers that make American-style choppers, some bespoke, but most Americans would never consider anything but a Harley to be their true companion. Another manufacturer is Ironhorse, the name implying that the motorcycle has replaced the horse as the mode of transport for real men; with leather saddle bags, chaps and fringes fluttering in the breeze the evolution is easy to see. It cannot be denied that a leather-clad road warrior reclined on his easy rider chopper is a strong and uniquely American image. However, as with many myths the truth may be less attractive. Harleys are extremely expensive; hence, only really the wealthiest and most enthusiastic can afford to own one. Far from seeing Brad Pitt look-alikes gliding around in bronzed elegance, most Harley riders are middle aged and overweight. Some Harleys have seats that bear an amazing resemblance to lounge recliners and a seating position more suited to watching TV than riding a motorcycle. One highly prized option for the discerning Harley rider is to display a classic biker chick on the rear seat. Tradition dictates that a biker chick should look like Olivia Newton-John in Grease – blond, attractive, with a firm body and clothes that leave nothing to the imagination. Back in the real world, biker chicks often do have the blondness and clothes, but unfortunately not the other two elements, perhaps making the term 'biker chicken' more appropriate.

Cyclists and Pedestrians

In the busy suburbs and towns of America you take your heart in your mouth when you cycle on the road; you are in a tiny minority. Even serious cyclists use the pavements rather than cycling on the busy highways. There is a lack of freedom in respect of just being able to cycle to school or the shops, and very few people commute by bike, apart from in places like college towns. Most cyclists won't go out unless they are fully kitted out. The majority load up the car and head off to the bike paths, which are organised and regulated. In some states, children are required to wear protective helmets by law.

Another strange aspect of cycling in America is that people often cycle on the wrong side of the road. You may be happily driving along a road when you are confronted by a cyclist coming straight towards you on your side. This is not abnormal behaviour in America; just as most people know that when walking along the road you should walk towards oncoming traffic, some Americans on bicycles apply this rule when cycling. However, strictly speaking, it is illegal.

Another user of the roads – pedestrians – can, quite frankly, be a pain in the driver's proverbial. In car parks and shopping areas, they saunter across the road in front of your car, barely acknowledging you are there, taking their time in the full knowledge that you must wait for them. Be cool. Also be cautious – whenever you see a pedestrian intent on crossing the road, slow down and stop if necessary; he or she may presume you are going to stop anyway. Repeat after me: 'Pedestrians are king'. I'm surprised more US tourists in Britain aren't run over.

Trucking

The building of interstates led to a boom in the trucking industry, as goods could be moved faster and more cheaply between businesses. The giant retailer Wal-Mart does not operate many warehouses; instead it uses trucks to deliver goods just in time to its stores (allegedly, the factory is notified within 20 minutes of a sale and new supplies are on their way to replenish stocks). This form of distribution, although efficient for the businesses concerned, means that more lorries are on the roads at any given time.

In 1980 the government deregulated the trucking industry. Before then, most drivers (around 90%) belonged to a union; after 1980, this dropped to 10%, and the shift resulted in tougher working conditions and pay and benefit cuts. The number of interstate trucking companies mushroomed from 20,000 in 1980 to 564,000 in 2005, with 90% of these operating six trucks or less (according to the American Trucking Association), resulting in low profit margins for most in the industry and poor pay for drivers. Average pay is around $35,000 a year, with independent drivers earning a little more (perhaps $40,000), according to the Owner-Operator Independent Drivers Association. However, it has been suggested that to earn this figure, drivers must work up to 120 hours/week; they also tend to suffer from poor health, including obesity and weight problems and early death. A trucker's life is not to be envied.

Of the 3.3 million truckers in America, about 1 in 10 are independent. In 2005, 10.7 billion tons of freight was hauled by truck, representing nearly 70% of total US freight tonnage (rail accounting for most of the rest). The majority of long-haul drivers average 100–110,000 miles/year on the road. Trucks are routinely 53 ft long (compared to 40 ft in Britain). You will not see much in the way of advertising on these vehicles – many are totally plain and white, some have the independent haulier's name on the side, and only a few advertise what they are hauling.

General Rules of the Road

There is so much space in America that main roads can be two or three lanes wide in both directions. Road signs are inconsistent and vary from one state to another, and are often positioned so close to a junction that it is easy to miss them. Also, signs and traffic lights are usually positioned on the far side of an intersection, often high up, so remember when driving to look up and forward.

In America you drive on the right-hand side of the road. Throughout most of the States, roundabouts are a rarity, though you will find more in New England (owing to British influences there). However, most Americans are not used to them and feel intimidated if they come across one. In place of roundabouts, you find the ubiquitous traffic light or four-way stop. On the main road near our house, over a distance of only 2.5 miles in both directions, you pass through seven sets of traffic lights in one direction and an amazing eleven in the other. After a while, you start trying to avoid them by using the back roads. Well, it was an Ohioan who invented the traffic light, so it is perhaps not surprising that Ohio has so many. Most go straight from red to green, with no amber warning. The locals tend to dawdle at lights, especially on green arrows; no-one rushes off. In any case, you will probably get stopped at the next block and speeding fines are hefty, so there's not much point.

In most states, you can turn right at a red light provided there is nothing to say otherwise, i.e. as long as there isn't a sign saying 'No turn on red'. This makes good sense and keeps traffic flowing. However, you are supposed to come to a complete stop and give way to pedestrians and other traffic before making the turn right. New York City is the only major jurisdiction that prohibits turning right on red.

In place of the unpopular traffic light, in America you might find the equally ubiquitous three-way, four-way and all-way stops, where three or more roads intersect. All drivers must stop (regardless of whether there is anyone else at the junction) and then proceed to cross or turn according to order of arrival. Thus the first person to arrive at a junction has the right of way, followed by the second person to arrive, and so on. It is rather like playing a game of solitaire. If two vehicles stop at the same time, the vehicle to the right has priority. Although this means that everyone has the chance to get across the junction (which is a great idea), it also means you again have to stop more often on American roads compared to back home. Flashing red or orange lights at a crossroads with no traffic signs means you should treat it as a four-way stop and proceed accordingly.

A word or two about car lights:

- Americans do not use their indicators as readily as we do, so be careful about making presumptions.
- On some American cars the brake lights double as indicators – there are no separate indicator lights.
- If you have to put your windscreen wipers on in inclement weather, then you are legally obliged to switch your headlights on too.

Take special care around schools. Watch for flashing lights telling you to restrict your speed to 20 miles/hour during school operating hours. A school bus that has its red lights flashing or has stopped means you must also stop and wait for the children to alight and the bus to proceed. This applies to cars in *all* directions, so if you are driving on the opposite side of the road to a flashing or stopped bus, you need to stop too. It is illegal for you to proceed, and the bus driver may book you for it. The only instance when this may not be the case is on roads with two or more lanes, but even then, drivers on the opposite side of the road often stop for a flashing school bus regardless. However, in some states (notably New York, West Virginia, Alabama, Arkansas and Mississippi), if a school bus has stopped and is flashing its lights, all traffic must stop, even on dual-carriageway roads. This courteous behaviour makes it very safe for children getting on and off the bus, but as a car driver you might consider choosing your route carefully at school times.

There are no federal (national) speed restrictions, only state limits, which (like most things) vary from state to state. On a corner you might see a yellow sign with a number; this is an advisory speed. Americans tend to stick close to the speed limits, which are lower than in the UK. On motorways, it is quite common to come across a driver in the middle or outside lane doing the strict legal speed. Other drivers use both the outside and inside lanes to overtake (although, as in England, strictly speaking it is wrong to overtake on the inside). This can be disquieting if you are in the middle lane, doing the requisite speed and someone bombs up the inside. However, you may even catch yourself doing it, following the flow, as sometimes it is the only way to get round some ignoramus doing a fixed, low speed, who shows no inclination to pull over to the middle or inside lane (in their climate-controlled cruise mobiles many drivers seem to be on autopilot). Another area for potential mishap is on slip roads joining a motorway. Other drivers are often disinclined to give way and show you no courtesy of space, so take care as you merge. Lorries have a nasty habit of driving right up behind and trying to intimidate you into going faster or pulling over.

Away from the cities, it is unusual to get stuck in a traffic snarl-up. However, around built-up areas, even with four or five lanes in either direction, major roads can get bunged up. On some freeways, you may see a black diamond-shaped sign in the far left-hand lane. This indicates that the lane is for high-occupancy vehicles (HOVs) only; there will also be a sign telling you the minimum number of passengers you should have in your car (e.g. HOV-2 indicates a minimum of two people) and the times of operation of this lane. Ignore this at your peril. The idea is that HOV lanes encourage people to lift share, and thereby reduce the number of cars on the road. The only snag in using them is that you have to wait for a gap in the solid HOV line before you can exit the lane, and then the road. So it pays to know your road and think ahead, so you can exit without being under pressure.

It's the Law

Policing in America is a serious business. Most police officers carry a gun, so don't be tempted to be facetious. If an officer pulls you over, turn off the engine, switch on the interior light (at night), stay in the car and keep your hands visible on the steering wheel. Be prepared to cooperate and don't make stupid jokes. In the UK, you may smile sweetly at the officer who has pulled you over and apologise for not having your driving licence, car registration or insurance documents on you. 'That's ok', he might say, 'Just make sure you visit your nearest police station and show them there'. In America, you will not receive the same reception and will be asked to produce your licence on the spot, or at least within 24 hours. If you are involved in an accident you must stay at the scene, and, again, you will be asked to produce your documents there and then. Moreover, you will need to send a police accident report to your insurance company if you are making a claim.

Speeding offences and other driving misdemeanours in America are no laughing matter. You could be hit with a hefty fine, court appearance and points on your licence. In particular, take care when you cross state borders as one state often has different road laws to another. Table 11.1 shows the consequences of breaking the law in Ohio. This goes some way to explaining why most motorists seem to take it easy on the roads and are law-abiding. Cameras nab around 4000 red-light runners a day. Sensors embedded in the road detect your speed and determine whether you will run the red light. These sensors signal the overhead camera to begin recording an image of your car as it nears the intersection, recording 6 seconds before and 6 seconds after the car runs the light. The next thing you know, you'll receive a ticket in the mail. Also remember not to park near a fire hydrant or you could be fined.

Table 11.1 Driving offences and fines in the state of Ohio. These vary according to state; however, the table gives an idea of what is considered a serious enough offence to incur a fine or court appearance.

Offence	Fine or action
Speeding 1–15 mph over the limit	$95
Speeding more than 16 mph over the limit	$110
Speeding 25 mph or over in a 55 mph or more limit	Court summons
Speeding 20 mph or over in a 50 mph or less zone	Court summons
Speeding within a school zone	$110–150, or a court summons, depending on your speed
Minor misdemeanours, such as: slow speed improper turn misuse of indicators headlight violations running a red light or stop sign prohibited U-turn driving left of centre passing on the right	$90
Passing a school bus	Automatic court appearance
Following too close behind another vehicle	Automatic court appearance
Failing to yield to a public safety vehicle	Automatic court appearance

Seat Belts, Child Seats and Restraints

Many Americans are lackadaisical about wearing seat belts, and there is a campaign to raise awareness of the importance of belting up. In many states, only the driver and front-seat passenger are required to wear seat belts, unless the driver is under 18, when all passengers must buckle up. Otherwise, it is optional in the back seat. Violation of this law is a secondary offence – if seen, you cannot be stopped for this alone. However, they view the safety of children much more importantly. Violation of the child-restraint law is a primary offence – if seen, you will be stopped.

The District of Columbia and 38 states require the use of booster seats or other appropriate restraining device for children who have outgrown their forward-facing child safety seats. However, there are many gaps and inconsistencies in the regulations. All states have an age limit law, and some have weight and/or height stipulations. Some only enforce the child restraint law up to the age of 4 or for children weighing less than 40 lb. This is despite the fact that it has been proven that booster seats reduce the odds of sustaining significant crash injuries by 59% for children aged older than this (4–7 years old), according to the *Journal of the American Medical Association*. The AAA and other safety experts also recommend using booster seats until the adult lap-and-shoulder belt fits properly – typically when the child is 8 years old and approximately 4 ft 9 inches tall. Rear-facing child seats should not be used in the front where there is a passenger airbag, as in Britain.

There are no rules about dogs being restrained in the car. I have even seen people driving with a lap dog at the wheel.

Driving and Mobile Phones

Three states – New York, New Jersey and Connecticut – and the District of Columbia have banned the use of hand-held mobile phones while driving. Likewise, some cities, such as Chicago, have prohibited drivers from talking on the phone while driving. In the rest of the States there is no law against it (though local laws and state-wide laws can differ and it is a good idea to check what the current situation is). This, together with the often sloppy driving skills, can make driving in America at best unpredictable and frustrating, and at worst downright dangerous. Driver inattention is the leading factor in most accidents, and the most common distraction is the cell phone.

Teenagers are particularly naughty about texting on the move. One said, 'I just do it. I can text without looking at my phone. Everybody texts while driving'. In most states they are not breaking any laws – at least not yet. However, the growing use of cell phones and their increasing role in car crashes is putting pressure on lawmakers. In 2005, Tennessee, Maryland, Delaware and Colorado banned young drivers from using them.

At the Petrol Station

The US MON rating 93 is approximately equivalent to the UK RON rating 97. Prices for petrol are quoted in US gallons; and there are 3.78 litres in a US gallon, compared to 4.54 litres in a British gallon (calculated using www.onlineconversion.com), which represents around 20% less quantity. At $2/gallon, this works out at around 53p/litre (about half the price we pay in the UK). However, before you get carried away, remember that the average American car only does around 25 mpg if you're lucky, so it's not as rosy as it sounds. On the other hand, other motoring costs in America are lower. Tyres are much cheaper and last longer, there is no MOT, and car tax/licence renewal only costs around $54 (local price).

In the US, total state taxes average 23.6 cents per gallon, plus another 18.3 cents goes to federal coffers; the latter rate has not changed since 1993. Inflation since 1993 has eroded the amount the government gleans from fuel, and it has been estimated that of the average 60 cents/mile drivers now pay to operate a car, only 1 cent goes to the state. Compare this with the situation in the UK, where the government maintains a high price at the pump and takes the lion's share.

Unlike in Britain, gas prices change according to fluctuations in oil prices instantaneously. With no warning, prices at the pumps can leap or drop 25 cents a gallon more than once a day. Gas stations base their prices on the wholesale cost of gasoline, which changes daily. They pay upon delivery and this results in daily price fluctuations. Retailers' profit margins range from 5 cents a gallon to zero, with some selling gas at cost and making a profit on other items. Gas stations are the new convenience stores. Most have a coffee and food vending area; some even offer free coffee to motorists (so there are plenty of opportunities for a 'safety break' on a long trip).

On interstates, you may have to drive some distance between gas stations, so it is a good idea not to run the tank too low. This also applies when driving in national parks, along scenic drives, on desert or mountain roads. We know this personally, having had a hairy experience in Sierra Nevada. As we drove up into the hills, tortuously twisting and turning for miles on end through near-deserted country, our petrol indicator began to dip into the red. We began noting the location of passing emergency phones, in case we had to stop and walk back. On cresting the hill, Tim nervously put the car into neutral and coasted most of the way down. It took about half an hour to get to the nearest town, our brakes complaining all the way. As we limped into the nearest petrol station with what felt like deliverance, we vowed to be more heedful in future of signs that say 'No gas for 50 miles'.

The Car Wash

Along with their beloved cars, the car wash is an essential part of most American's lives. You don't see many people washing their vehicles on drives; it's just time-consuming and too much like hard work. What could be easier than driving to the local car wash, feeding $5 into the machine, then sitting back and enjoying the action? With the car in neutral, you are conveyed through a pre-soak, bubble bath, scrub, high-pressure blasters, undercarriage sweepers, rinse and wax, and are finally blow-dried to perfection. You can even have your car interior cleaned and scented. You come out looking squeaky clean and smelling of roses (or wild cherry, French vanilla or 'new car' smell, depending on which button you push). Car wash companies also claim to use less water than homeowners and to dispose of it according to local regulations, not simply down the drains. So a ride through the auto bath may not only be fun for the family (though Jester wasn't keen), it may also be better for the environment. The colder states use a lot of salt in winter, so regular car washing makes sense. Buy multi-wash discount tickets if you can.

Hazards on the Roads

Some states experience very cold winters, with heavy snowfall every year, and are consequently much better equipped to deal with it than we in England. Keeping the roads clear is what they do every season. In winter, whenever you are unsure about driving conditions, the state of the roads, whether the school bus is running, school is open or your evening class is going ahead, switch on the television and find your local channel. The TV is a good medium for broadcasting public information. In severe conditions the TV will run a continuous 'ticker' showing conditions and also which work places, schools, etc. are closed. You can be cited for driving in severe weather, as the authorities want to concentrate on clearing the roads, not helping stranded motorists. Yet walking may not be an option either. If there is a side walk, it will often be unusable in severe snow because the ploughs simply push the snow off the road onto the pavements. Freeze/thaw can also make walking hazardous.

In Britain we are often bemused by mad stockpiling of home provisions prior to warnings of bad weather. In the northern states of America, such a flurry of shopping activity may be very necessary, as you could really be snowed in for days. Snowfall can be substantial and long-lasting, and once schools and/or workplaces are closed, locals will not venture out in their cars more than they have to. It can be fun being holed up for a while – subject to good company, of course, and so long as you have enough milk, bread, dog biscuits, beer, wine, toilet paper, etc. In the suburbs and rural areas, if you cannot drive to the shops – and, let's face it, in America most shops are not exactly handy for walking – you will just have to be inventive.

You can buy road salt from petrol stations and supermarkets. The usual granular salt sold in bags for drives and footpaths can burn dogs' foot pads. So if you have a pet or one that visits, opt instead for the chemical salt version which is supposed to be safe for doggie feet. Many householders own snow blowers, which are great for clearing snow off your drive and footpaths.

Conversely, in summer, it can get seriously hot, especially inside a car. Most Americans drive along with their windows closed and air-conditioning on. They hop from their air-conditioned house, into their equally cool car, to drive to the air-conditioned mall or restaurant, barely raising a sweat. They take it easy; no-one rushes. So follow their example. Invest in a simple windscreen sun deflector; it makes a big difference. Also don't leave home without a bottle or two of water.

As far as natural wildlife hazards go, try to avoid running over a skunk, even a dead one. A pungent odour will follow you around for weeks and pervade your garage. If your car does accidentally pick up a nasty whiff, visit your local car wash for a deskunking. Deer deaths on the road are very common, owing to the large number of wild deer about. If you enjoy a bit of venison, you might be able to add your name to the county road-kill list and pick up a free carcass when your name comes up, though be prepared to accept and deal with the entire animal yourself.

Besides natural hazards on the roads, human ones are noted by Jim:

> Cars are not so much driven as rolled under superficial control. Being almost exclusively automatic, once they've warmed up to warp speed there's very little to do to keep the driver interested. Where we were living in the Midwest, the lack of prominent features, endlessly straight roads, and groundhog-day monotony of identical mile upon mile can lead to a near-comatose state from which it takes a few seconds to recover, sometimes too short of the time actually required to avoid disaster. It is not uncommon to hear of single car accidents where drivers have drifted off (the road and literally). To fill the monotonous hours behind the wheel, drivers can choose from a range of in-car hobbies. In addition to ingesting junk food, it is not uncommon to see books being read, CDs examined and lipstick wielded in a frightening yet impressive fashion. More worrying is the use of laptops, DVD players and even clothes changing. An amateur survey of drivers revealed that around a third use cell phones while driving (or all drivers use cell phones for a third of the time, the survey is not clear). You may have some sympathy for these diversionary activities until the *x*th time you've nearly been flattened by a car with a distracted driver pulling out of a parking space while on the phone. It is often said that the pen is mightier than the sword, but modern communication is proving much deadlier; what makes this statement even less agreeable is the banality of a lot of those conversations.
>
> The car has allowed Americans to spread out and exercise the freedom that is so precious to them. To operate in even a modest-sized US town or city isn't *more* convenient with a car; it's essential. That is why the legal driving age has to be low at 16, why drink-driving (called driving under influence, DUI, which includes drugs as well) is frowned upon but hardly policed, why the driving test is ridiculously easy and why few crimes result in the loss of a licence. The lackadaisical approach to driving and road discipline produces a very dangerous situation, resulting in road deaths being in the order of 50,000 a year, compared with less than 4000 in the UK – that's more than twice the number of road-related deaths in the US versus Britain according to head of population.

Conclusion

Like most things in America, driving is a fairly laid-back affair. Outside of the cities, you do not see many incidences of road rage or furious flashing of headlights, as in Britain. Although there are plenty of bad drivers about, rarely are they chastised by fellow motorists. Tail-gating, mouthing your irritation, gesticulations, horn blaring or any other method of showing the culprit your frustration are not often seen in provincial areas, though it can be a different matter in the cities where stress levels are higher. Generally, there is more space, the cars are automatics and the driving is easy. Our little British cars and roads must indeed seem quaint to most Americans.

The highways and interstates in America are a very efficient means of travel, but it is difficult to enjoy the individuality of a car journey if you simply use them – try playing *I Spy* when all you can see is sky, road, fields and the occasional squashed critter. As Charles Kuralt (CBS newsman) once said, 'Thanks to the Interstate Highway System, it is now possible to travel from coast to coast without seeing anything'. Stores, motels, fast-food chains and other conveniences have sprung up along these super highways, making one exit look very much like another, with its collection of businesses serving the passing motorist. They have expanded suburban sprawl, allowing people to live further away from their workplace, and consequently making people more reliant on their cars and the economy thus more oil-dependent. The car culture of America looks set to continue.

Useful Websites

ww1.aaa.com – the American Automobile Association.
www.bbb.org – Better Business Bureau.
www.carfax.com – to check the title and history of a car against the Vehicle Identification Number (VIN).
www.dmv.org – a commercial site but with useful information; it calls itself the Unofficial Guide to the DMV.
www.fueleconomy.gov – Fuel Economy Guide, published by the US Department of Energy.
www.iihs.org – Insurance Institute for Highway Safety.
www.kbb.com – Kelley Blue Book.
www.leaseguide.com – a guide to vehicle leasing.
www.nhtsa.gov – National Highway Traffic Safety Administration.
www.saferoads.org/issues – Advocates for Highway and Auto Safety.
http://usff.com/flstatutes/50statehls.html – motorcycle helmet laws in the US.

Terminology

American term	Equivalent British term	Notes
Back-up light	Reversing light	
Beltway (loop)	Ring road	
Blinkers	Indicators	
Car	Carriage, truck	Railway
Crosswalk	Pedestrian crossing	
Deductible	Excess	In insurance
Divided highway	Dual carriageway	

American term	Equivalent British term	Notes
Downtown	Town or business centre	
Exit	Junction	
Fender	Wing of a car	Not bumper, as many people think
Fender bender	A minor car accident	
Four way/three way	Crossroads	
Freeway, highway, causeway, expressway, parkway	Main road or motorway	Any busy main street or road. Terminology varies according to region. Beltway and expressway are usually around a city
Grade crossing	Level crossing	
Interstate	Major or trunk road	Roads funded under the legislative act
License plate, license tag	Number plate	
Median strip	Central reservation	
Motorbike	Moped	
Motorcycle	Motorbike	
MSRP	Base price on a vehicle for sale	Manufacturer Suggested Retail Price; excludes optional extras, delivery or destination charges
OBO	Or best offer	In buy/sell adverts
Odometer	Mileometer	
On-ramp/off-ramp, exit ramp	Slip road	
Overpass	Flyover	
Parking garage	Multi-storey car park	
Parking lot	Outdoor car park	
Paved shoulder	Hard shoulder	
Pavement	Road or pavement	Any paved road surface on which vehicles drive
Pull out, pull off	Lay-by	
Rotary, traffic circle	Roundabout	
Sedan (two or four door)	Saloon car	
Semi-trailer	Articulated lorry	
Station wagon	Estate car	
Stick shift	Gear lever	

Sticker price	Intended retail price	Excludes taxes, title fee, registration or tag fees
Sub-compact	Small car	Equivalent to Metro size
Tag	Number plate	
Transit	Public transport	
Truck	Lorry	
Turnpike	Toll road	
Turn signals	Indicators	

12 · Holidaying and Tripping About

Most Americans tend to holiday within the United States. Well, who can really blame them? They have such a wealth of country to enjoy. A survey by the US Tour Operators Association found that Colorado, Alaska and California are the top destinations, and favourite cities are Los Angeles, New York, Las Vegas and Orlando.

- *Colorado* in the Rocky Mountains has approximately 550 mountain peaks and is the only state lying entirely above 1000 m (3281 ft) elevation. With its deserts, rugged mountains, rangelands, alpine meadows and ski resorts (e.g. Aspen, Crested Butte, Steamboat Springs and Vail), it attracts many holiday-makers.
- *Alaska* is the only non-contiguous state in North America, bordered by the Canadian territories of Yukon and British Columbia. Its capital city Juneau is only accessible via air or ship. Approximately 65% of the land is owned and managed by the US federal government as national forests, parks and wildlife refuges; less than 1% is private owned. It offers visitors wonderful scenery in the form of glaciers, lakes and rivers, vast forests, tundra lands and shorelines, the Aleutian Islands and active volcanoes.
- *California* has some of the nation's most agreeable weather and dramatically varied landscape to go with it – two of the features that attracted early movie-makers. Earlier, in the mid-1800s, the gold rush brought an influx of people. You will find more entrepreneurs, radicals and trendsetters here than in any other state. Surfing the big waves off California's flat sandy shores is another lure.
- *Los Angeles* is the home of Hollywood and the largest metropolitan area in America, covering an area of approximately 34,000 sq miles. Disneyland in Anaheim is an escape from the real world for a day. In 1955, Walt Disney hocked his life insurance to finance his dream of creating 'the Happiest Place on Earth'. The Disneyland Resort offers two theme parks – Disneyland and Disney's California Adventure.
- *New York* has the world's largest department store (Macy's) and is a shopper's paradise. Its five boroughs, each unique in character and diversity, are linked by fer-

ries, tunnels and bridges. Fifth Avenue divides Manhattan into the east and west side. See Chapter 6 for more about this great city.

- *Las Vegas* is said to be America's fastest growing city. High rollers get to stay in the top suites, where everything is free of charge. Even for low rollers, food and drink is often complementary while you are gambling. Nevada legalised gambling in 1931 and New Jersey in 1976. Las Vegas boasts nine of the world's largest resort hotels (the MGM Grand has more than 5000 rooms). Players gamble and lose approximately $6 million every year to Las Vegas casinos. Vegas is also famous as a venue for weddings (over 50,000 couples come here to tie the knot each year).
- *Orlando* in Florida has world-class theme parks and championship golf courses. With more than 300 days of sunshine a year, it is the second largest city in America in terms of number of hotel rooms, and one of the busiest for conventions and conferences. Fifty two million tourists a year come here, most to visit Walt Disney World Resort, Sea World and Universal Orlando Resort.

Despite the opportunities for travel within America, it is not unusual to find people who have barely travelled beyond their own or surrounding states. Apparently half of all Americans live within 50 miles of their birthplace and many are ignorant of other places in the States, let alone the world beyond. In our quiet part of Ohio, people appeared to be stay-at-homers, holidaying within their own or neighbouring states, often not having been to half the places we had. Many Americans have never left America's shores (and the fact that 65% of Americans do not have a passport is indicative of this). Some believe it is important not to be corrupted by foreign values, or that other nations are unwelcoming, which in reality is often true. However, if these citizens got out of their comfort zone and saw the world, they might understand other cultures better.

That said, according to travel agents, a new intrepidness is slowly emerging, with more adventurous citizens heading off to emerging countries in eastern Europe and China. They are also venturing beyond the capitals and into the countryside, and being more careful with holiday spending. Rather than splurging out at expensive hotels, they are choosing self-catering apartments, and taking less traditional tours and holiday breaks, such as art, cooking and language classes.

Europe accounts for more than 40% of overseas travel, with Britain (London) one of the most popular destinations, followed by France (Paris) and Italy (Rome) – often in one combined whirlwind tour. Ireland is also a favourite destination. First-timers overseas almost always opt for safety in numbers, with a group coach tour around the British Isles, taking in the main cities and sights such as Bath, Stonehenge, Brighton, Stratford, the Cotswolds, Oxford, Cambridge, York, Leeds Castle and Chester. Edinburgh, Glasgow and Inverness, and perhaps the Scottish Islands may also get a look-in. In Ireland, Dublin, Waterford, Killarney, Connemara and Derry are favourite draws. Most Americans in Britain stay in hotels, or perhaps bed and breakfasts, or they may look for something more historic and unusual such as a castle or manor house.

Going by Air

There are 14,858 airports in the US, and the average number of people airborne over America in any given hour has been estimated at 61,000. Although, per mile, flying is cheap compared to Europe, because distances in America are so huge, fare prices are often, as a consequence, expensive. Fewer small places are served by direct flights; usually you have to fly into one of the main hubs and then jump on a connecting flight. The gateway cities are:

- Atlanta (the world's busiest airport)
- Boston
- Chicago
- Dallas
- Las Vegas
- Los Angeles
- Miami
- Orlando
- San Francisco

Delta is good for non-stop international flights. Apply for the Delta Skymiles American Express credit card, so you can clock up airmiles on all your purchases. It doesn't take long to earn a free flight. Delta states that Tuesdays, Wednesdays and Saturdays and late-evening flights are the lowest-demand travel days (and thus less expensive).

Tripping Back to Britain

Flying out to the UK is generally quicker than flying back (when travelling west to east you are helped along by a tail wind and by following the direction of the earth's spin, which can shave a welcome hour off the journey time). It is sometimes quizzically cheaper to book your flight from the UK, as British operators may have special rates not available to state-side citizens. However, the converse can also be true. Purchasing tickets as far in advance as possible may also save you money.

On returning to the US, you will have to complete a Customs Declaration form, which, among other things, asks you to specify the value of any items you are importing. The limit for non-residents is a paltry $100, above which you may be liable to pay customs duty when you arrive in the US. So it is worth bearing this in mind when you purchase things in Britain to bring back into America. Check with Customs what the current limits are.

Most American airports are modern, spacey and inviting, and airport staff are generally friendly and smiling. Gatwick in comparison has an ugly, old, grey and dirty feel. On one trip back, I noticed a sign that read 'Undergoing refurbishment', and it needs it. In this environment the staff perhaps understandably look rather miserable and unwelcoming. Outside is no better. The infrastructure is messy and looks bad, the roads are clogged with cars, verges are littered and soiled, the roads themselves patched and grubby-looking. I felt let down – welcome back to dreary old England.

Looking at the country through American-tinted spectacles, I can see why Americans think Britain is quaint; everything is so much smaller. The roads are narrow, winding and full of traffic; the cars themselves are small and cute in comparison to the big muscle cars of the States; one-man-band mobile snack bars in laybys serve passing motorists; houses and buildings are squeezed in, like jigsaw pieces, the old and ugly next to the new and modern; and space between commercial buildings is virtually non-existent and certainly leaves little room for attractive landscaping or much greenery.

Receiving Visitors

If family and friends from Britain plan to visit you in America they will not need to apply for a visa so long as their stay is less than 90 days. They will have to complete the green I-94W immigration form in-flight (each individual within a party has to do this) as well as a customs form. It is forbidden to bring into the US foodstuffs such as fresh fruit, vegetables and meat (owing to the risk of disease). On one return trip, I was asked by US airport authorities whether I was bringing anything of this sort into the country (I had a suitcase full of instant porridge, Weetabix, Angel Delight, Hula Hoops and Marmite – much-loved necessities we couldn't get hold of in America – but fortunately none of this was deemed 'hazardous').

It was with some trepidation that I organised a flight out for my father. Although the flight was direct (non-stop, Gatwick to Cincinnati), there was still the opportunity for him to get lost at either airport. It is possible to arrange for a member of staff to accompany someone through Departures and Arrivals, both ends, and to act as an escort. Speak to the airline in advance to confirm the procedure. In order to help my father through arrivals, I went to the airport departures desk, produced ID and explained the situation. I was given a Security Checkpoint Clearance pass. First passing through security with outbound passengers, then through security for inbound, I ended up just outside Customs and Immigration. My father only needed to follow everyone else off the plane, collect his bags from the carousel and go through C&I on his own, where I was waiting to meet him. From there we proceeded to offload the bags again, onto another conveyor belt that took them off to the arrivals lounge. We passed back through security (the third time that day I had had to remove my shoes) and walked the distance of the concourse, following the Baggage Reclaim signs. All that remained was to retrieve his bags from the carousel. Thus the experience went without incident. You may have similar concerns if you have unaccompanied children flying.

Going by Train

America's intercity passenger train network is run by Amtrak, which is semi-nationalised, with government controlling and subsidising its services (the President and Senate elect Amtrak's board of directors). The only states that Amtrak does not cover are Alaska, Hawaii and South Dakota; elsewhere it connects 500 communities. Most of its 22,000 miles of tracks are owned by private freight railroads, which are responsible for maintaining the tracks. Consequently some sections of a track run fast and smooth, while on others the trains crawl through. Passenger rail travel in America is nothing like as efficient and fast as in Europe. In 2004, it served 25 million passengers (by way of comparison, commercial airlines served 712 million) and in 2003 accounted for 0.1% of US intercity passenger miles (private car travel making up the vast majority). It operates 351 diesel and 74 electric locomotives.

Routes are identified by name, e.g. the popular scenic Coast Starlight (Seattle–Portland–Los Angeles), California Zephyr (Chicago–Denver–Emeryville, California; taking 2 days and nights) and Maple Leaf (Toronto–New York), to name just three of the 33 possible routes. The most popular and heavily used routes are in the North-East Corridor, with New York's Penn Station, Philadelphia's 30th Street Station, and Washington and Chicago's Union Street Stations being the busiest. Regular users can apply for guest rewards (a loyalty programme, much like the airline frequent flyer programmes). Amtrak also offers USA Rail Passes and vacation packages. Most long-distance journeys need to be booked and paid for in advance; you can't just turn up at the station and buy a ticket for the next train. It offers discounts to senior citizens, students, disabled travellers, children and members of the armed forces.

Going by Bus

For long-distance travel, Greyhound buses are available in more than 3100 locations across America. Many stations have seen better days, but the buses are clean and efficient, can accommodate more luggage than airlines, and fares are still pretty low. Greyhound's Ameripass allows unlimited travel throughout the States, with passes available from 7 to 60 days.

Trailways offers a more local and personalised service. The privately owned and operated transportation companies that make up Trailways operate primarily along the Eastern Seaboard, in the Midwest and Southeast, but also offer services west of the Mississippi in Texas, Montana, California, Washington and Oregon, and across the border in British Columbia. They also offer various tour packages.

Going by Car, Motorcycle or Bicycle

The cross-country trip is part of American lore and culture, and many families still head off on long trips in the car. Summer just isn't summer unless you've done at least one road trip; however, the current concern over high gas prices means that some of America's citizens are not travelling quite so far, and there are even articles extolling the virtues of taking a vacation at home. To Americans, it is generally more important to get somewhere quickly than to take a scenic route and enjoy the travelling experience. Hence the appeal of the interstates. Cheap and easy accommodation and fast food restaurants along the major roads and at intersections have as a consequence grown up and replaced independents. Many towns and local businesses have suffered as interstate sections become the new commercial centres. It is all to do with expediency and economies of scale.

Alamo, Enterprise and Thrifty are well-known car rental agencies (we had good dealings with Enterprise). If paying by credit card, this may provide you with some basic insurance. Check carefully what the rental agency provides on top. Agents may ask you to purchase theft insurance, and want to see an International Insurance Certificate or green card, to ensure you have liability insurance. Besides car rental agencies and dealers, some travel agents and border crossings may be able to help you acquire a green card.

If you have a hankering for riding a Harley-Davidson across the States, several US companies specialise in fulfilling that part of your American dream. Cruise America, Hemmingways and USA Tailor Made Holidays are three such outfits.

Hitch-hiking is illegal in some parts of America, for instance on the hard shoulder of interstates, and in some states, e.g. Nevada, New Jersey, Pennsylvania, Utah and Wyoming. However, lift sharing is an option, and especially popular with students.

Long-distance cycle paths are now common across many states. *Rails to Trails* is a national scheme, much like Sustran's National Cycle Network in the UK. It makes use of old railroad tracks and provides a recreational facility, linking major hubs of the population (for example, Pittsburgh to Washington). The paved, level, mostly straight paths are a breeze to cycle, rollerblade, power-walk or dog-walk along. They are also very safe places to teach children to ride a bike. After work and at weekends they are popular places to go – with the family or on your own.

Lodging

The AAA describes seven different classes of accommodation, which are précised below:

- *Large-scale hotel*: multistorey, with spacious public areas and a variety of facilities.
- *Small-scale hotel*: multistorey, with limited public areas and facilities.

- *Motel*: one- to three-storey, usually with rooms directly off the parking area, similar in décor and design throughout.
- *Bed and breakfast*: small, personal lodgings, often decked out in antiques; rooms may not have TVs or telephones or even private bathrooms.
- *Country inn*: larger than a B&B, with spacious public areas offering breakfast and usually dinner.
- *Condominium*: apartment-style accommodation for extended stays, usually rented through an agent; basic cleaning, kitchen, bedroom and bathroom supplies are normally included.
- *Cabin* or *cottage*: freestanding units with numerous rooms; again, basic equipment and supplies are usually included.

Hotels and Motels

There are a plethora of inexpensive hotel and motel chains throughout America. At every interstate exit you should find a choice of national chains offering lodging. The most ubiquitous hotel/motel chains (in order) are:

- Best Western
- Holiday Inn
- Days Inn
- Super 8
- Comfort Inn
- Ramada
- Motel 6
- Econo Lodge
- Quality Inn
- Howard Johnson
- Travel Lodge

Super 8 and Motel 6 are good, basic motels. More upmarket are Comfort, Sleep, Quality and Friendship Inns, Econo Lodge and Rodeway – all run by the same company. State welcome centres and chambers of commerce often have free booklets containing discount vouchers (chambers of commerce in America act as local tourist information offices). You can also get AAA, military or government rate discounts. Join the hotel chain's reward scheme (which is free, you just need to fill out a form), so you can accrue points each time you stay, and use these for free nights accommodation or other member benefits.

There is generally no shortage of accommodation, apart from on some peak weekends. For instance, do not try to cuff it accommodation-wise on the weekend of 4th July. I speak from experience. After driving about 7 hours, we found to our dismay that every hotel and motel at every motorway exit was fully booked. However, despite one establishment displaying the 'No vacancies' sign, Tim managed to sweet-talk the receptionist into giving us a room that had been recently vacated. The conversation went something like this:

Hello, I saw the no vacancy sign on the door, but is there any chance a room might be available?

Let me see what I can do. I just love your accent!

(The receptionist taps on the computer)

Would you mind having a make-up room?

Oh, what's that?

One that's got something wrong with it. You can choose between one with no lock on the outside door or one not yet made up. I'm not supposed to offer you this, but I could pop in, change the sheets and have a quick clean round if you like.

That sounds fine, but don't worry about making the room up. We can do that ourselves. How much would it be?

I'll do it for $10 off the standard price.

I was going to ask for a military/government rate.

Ten dollars *is* the usual discount, but as you are making up the room yourself, I'll knock another $5 off.

Well, if I stand here talking long enough, how cheap can this go?

If you stand here talking long enough, you can have the room for free. I just love your accent!

(The receptionist starts to check us in)

Oh, yes. You have a CDL, don't you?

What's a CDL?

A commercial driving licence – you're a truck driver, aren't you? *(winking).*

Well, I've got a mini-van.

That'll do. The rate is $45.

Fantastic!

Gee, I just love that accent!

(Being British in America sometimes has its advantages.)

The definition of room type can be misleading, and it is always best to double-check what sort of room you are getting when you book. As a guide:

- A single room usually has one double bed.
- A double room usually has two double beds.
- A queen-sized room usually has one or two queen-sized beds.
- A king-sized room usually has one king-sized bed.
- An efficiency has kitchen facilities so you can self-cater.

(Note: a queen is a large double bed; a king is a very large double bed.) You are charged by the room, assuming up to four people maximum occupancy (there may be a small extra charge for more than four in a room). Some chains and/or particular hotels/motels allow pets to stay in the room with you. There may be an additional charge for your furry friend, or not, as the case may be. Red Roof Inns were particularly accommodating with Jester.

If you are looking for temporary accommodation while in transit during moving, check out the suites hotels. The Homewood Suites put us up in our last week in America. We had a large bedroom, lounge and kitchen area, everything we needed to live out of. Other chain hotels include Amerisuites, Mainstay Suites, Sierra Suites and Summerfield Suites. Alternatively, some motels have self-catering room facilities (known as 'efficiencies') – also good for families on holiday (as they can save you forking out on breakfast or meals in general).

Most hotel rooms have basic cable television, and some may be equipped with premium stations (such as HBO). Most have air conditioning (though these can be noisy) and a coffee percolator with coffee- and tea-making facilities. Some have a fridge and microwave. All provide towels (usually a good selection) and basic toiletries. If you forget to bring any small essentials, the front desk may provide them free of charge. In most places you will also find vending and ice machines (ice is usually free).

There is commonly a curfew on the use of the swimming pool to curtail noise at night and in the morning. Some motels provide breakfast – either within the motel (self-service) or in next-door breakfast rooms or restaurants. Many provide free coffee and cookies or fruit in the lobby.

Bed and Breakfast

B&Bs in America are not cheap; they cater for the more discerning traveller. Many are historic private homes, with well-kept gardens and character rooms equipped with antique furnishings – fine if you are a couple looking for a romantic getaway, but not really suitable for those with young children or worried about cost. See *Useful Websites* for some B&B listings.

Camping

Camping is cheap, at around $10 per night for a tent. You are charged for the pitch rather than having individual prices imposed for all and sundry, and campground managers do not seem to care how many people you fit into a tent. Some National Forest campgrounds are even free.

There are public sites in provincial, state and National Parks. Private campsites tend to offer more facilities, especially for families. Primitive sites usually have no electricity, and may or may not have toilets, running water or drinking water. Some backcountry sites – known as walk-in or hike-in sites – are geared towards hikers. You must bring everything you need and take your rubbish away. KOA (Kampgrounds of America) is a well-known organisation, offering 450 sites throughout North America and Canada. All are pet friendly and many have the option of hiring a cabin if you prefer not to sleep in a tent or motorhome. Some cabins may be air-conditioned (which may be appealing in summer). Check what facilities and equipment they come with (for instance, whether they provide towels, bed linen, etc.).

Generally, sites are laid out with set numbered pitches, with a personal hard-standing parking place for the car, caravan or RV. It is rare to find an open field where you can pitch wherever you like. American campsites are usually more organised and better equipped than we are used to in Britain. For instance, many individual pitches have a picnic table and fire ring. At night, most people have their camp fires blazing. We wondered how they got such consistently good fires until we saw someone squirting lighter fluid out of a squeezy bottle to fan the flames (what a cheat). Firewood is usually sold at the camp office. In some states, a small beetle called the emerald ash borer has been wreaking havoc, gnawing its way through woodlands in Michigan, Ohio, Indiana, Illinois, Pennsylvania and Ontario, and threatening other surrounding states. Millions of ash trees have died and hundreds of thousands have been destroyed in an effort to contain the mini beast. Camping sites in these states ask that you do not bring in wood from outside the area to burn on your camp fire, for fear of importing this serious problem.

None of the sites we went to had washing-up facilities. At first we couldn't work it out; how are you supposed to wash up after cooking? Then we looked at what other campers were doing – using disposable equipment and eating takeaways or going out. We persisted in cooking over our camp stove, but adapted to using throw-away utensils. Golf carts are a common sight on campsites, used by staff and campers to get about quietly. Statics and RVs tend to be packed in, in straight lines. Most of them are decked out with all manner of adornment – fairy lights, hanging baskets, roll-out lawns, garden ornaments and other home-from-home niceties. Some are obviously fishermen's cabins, the owners coming to use the camp fishing lake or other local waterways.

Dogs may be allowed on the leash in designated places, though well-behaved Mutleys can often get away with the odd moment of freedom if you pitch in a quiet spot. Some sites have dedicated pet exercise areas.

Motorhomes

Wally Byam built his first perfect travel trailer over 70 years ago. Today his Airstream caravan has become an American icon. He employed aircraft construction techniques to improve the strength to weight ratio and reduce wind resistance, resulting in the classic lightweight, curved aluminium caravans of today. Modern designs are as popular now as they were back in the 1920s. They have a strong following, with Airstream-only campgrounds and local and regional rallies.

RVs have enjoyed a resurgence in recent years, with a 15% increase in sales from

2001–2005 and a 58% increase overall since 1980. Nearly 8 million American homeowners have an RV; that's nearly 1 in 12 US vehicle-owning households. RV rentals were also up 36% in 2005. More RVs are now owned by those aged 35–44 than any other age group. The RV clearly does not appeal just to oldies anymore; RVs are cool.

However, you may be surprised to learn that holidaying with an RV will set you back more than if you stayed in motels and ate out. The high cost of hiring, driving and parking these oversized vehicles needs to be weighed up against the pleasures of being able to stay overnight independently in more scenic parts of America. Most only do around 10 mpg and can be a pain driving through small towns, though out on the highways and in mall car parks you will have no problem. The cost of insurance, parking fees, and additional fees charged by the hiring company for going over your agreed mileage all add to the cost. So do your sums before you opt for this very American form of holidaying.

Youth Hostels

Hostelling as a form of accommodation is much less developed in America than it is in the rest of the world, with only about 80 youth hostels in the States (compared to our network of more than 200 across England and Wales). Hostels offer safe, clean, friendly and affordable accommodation at around $15/bed/night. This makes economic sense if you are travelling singly or with a friend, but for families it is often just as cheap to check into a motel. HI-USA (Hostelling International USA) is part of the International Youth Hostel Federation and is responsible for America's network of hostels. We tried out a couple of hostels (our favourite was HI-Marin Headlands, Sausalito, in the lovely setting of Golden Gate National Park, just outside San Francisco). As in England, standards vary considerably.

Parks

Most foreigners have visited or at least heard of America's wonderful National Parks, but even in state parks and local countryside, you can find yourself in another world. A couple of parks and nature areas close to where we were living served me and Jester every day for a walk off the lead, with barely a soul encountered. Apart from the wildlife living there, we had the place to ourselves.

American parks are fantastic public resources. Most of our local ones had picnic tables, shelters, barbecues, drinking fountains and play areas for the children. You can hire the shelters (usually at no cost) for parties or other gatherings, complete with barbecue grills and electric points; or use the volleyball, soccer, softball and baseball pitches, basketball and tennis courts, skateboard parks and minigolf courses, and fish in the lake, all usually free of charge (and often free of other people too). Or check out the information boards to see when the locals are practising, come and park yourself on the bleachers (the tiered seats around the pitches) and enjoy watching a game of baseball or whatever else is going on.

Most parks have a bevy of park rangers, vehicles and equipment looking after them. The parks we encountered (locally and while on holiday) were on the whole free of litter and graffiti, open and inviting. You won't find rows of carefully coordinated annuals or clipped lawns; instead the kids can run free, kick a ball without fear of bulldozing the flowerbeds, fly a kite without losing it in someone's memorialised tree, swing a bat without bumping into something and definitely keep *on* the grass. In place of ambling old-folks and dubious-looking teenagers loitering with intent you find families and sporting enthusiasts. American parks are there for the using – for sport and freedom, not aesthetics.

However, they can have a rather prescriptive feel. More often than not, the trails (what we would call footpaths or tracks) are carefully laid out and maintained, regularly mown or hard-covered, and waymarked. Many of the more popular places do not even allow dogs on leads. I have the impression that, where feasible, America likes to police its countryside. Also much of what looks like great country to explore or walk in is inaccessible to the public because it is privately owned. Jester and I soon started to miss the freedom and enjoyment of roaming the naturally messy and untamed countryside that Britain offers.

State Parks

State parks may offer more freedom. Ohio has an impressive 72 state parks, and this isn't an unusual number for a single state. Most have campsites and other amenities, and offer a great way to commune with nature.

During the Great Depression, President Franklin D. Roosevelt's Civilian Conservation Corps was put to work building roads and bridges, planting trees, improving public access to previously inaccessible places, and building dams, ponds and lakes, community meeting houses and cabins. The government employed jobless people to undertake this work, thus providing job income at a time of national economic crisis and at the same time creating and preserving areas of the countryside for public enjoyment for generations to come.

Today these state parks can be found all over America; wherever you live you won't be far from one. They represent areas of natural beauty, historical importance and/or wildlife havens. Some charge entrance fees. Most have extremely good public facilities such as fishing, boating and swimming lakes, beaches, boardwalks, picnic shelters, barbecues, cafes, nature centres, campsites, horse-riding trails, hiking, and so on. They are well-kept, natural areas designed for R&R. You should be able to find an information point (usually manned), with maps of the park, showing what there is to see and do. There may be schedules of activities for both adults and children. The parks provide seasonal jobs and careers, employing a large number of workers in the form of rangers, campsite administrators, nature guides, etc.

National Parks, Seashores and Forests

Public lands make up more than one-third of America, and most are in Nevada, Utah, Idaho, Alaska, Oregon and Wyoming (in that order). There are 391 officially designated places, including:

- Historic Parks and Sites (122)
- Monuments (74)
- National Parks (58)
- Memorials (28)
- Battlefield and Military Sites (24)
- Recreational Areas (18)
- Preserves (18)
- Rivers (15)
- Seashores (10)
- Lakeshores (4)
- Parkways (4)
- Scenic Trails (3)
- Reserves (2)
- Other Designations (11)

The National Park Service oversees them all (see *Useful Websites*). There are plenty of public land volunteering opportunities – from campground hosting to planting trees. *Take Pride in America* is the organisation to contact if you are interested; you never know, you might bump into Clint Eastwood (national spokesman), cleaning picnic tables in California.

National Parks are one of the great things about America. Most popular are the parks out West. Yellowstone was the world's first National Park, established in 1872. Yosemite, Mount Rainier, Oregon Crater Lake and Mesa Verde followed. Death Valley is the largest National Park in the contiguous United States, with 3.3 million acres of wilderness (about twice the size of the state of Delaware); it also lays claim to both the lowest point (282 ft below sea level) and highest point (Mount Whitney at 14,500 ft). It has the second-highest recorded temperature (134°F) ever recorded in the world, only topped by the Sahara Desert (by 2°). Rainfall averages less than 2 inches/year, and in some years there is no rain at all. Death Valley is a desolate, eerie place, and you really feel for those early pioneering families who undertook crossing it. There are numerous ghost towns left behind after the mines were worked out. The extraordinary geology and changing rock colours attract geologists and anyone with an eye for beauty and a camera. Rippling mirages, salt flats and sand dunes add to the surreal landscape. Fill up with fuel and water before you enter the park area as you will be driving for miles. Radiator water is available along the main routes, and gas is sold at a handful of stopping places in the park.

The gargantuan sequoias in Sequoia and Kings Canyon National Parks are awesome sights. The General Sherman Tree is considered to be the world's largest living tree (with regard to volume). Sequoia bark can be up to 2 ft thick, making the trees virtually impervious to fire and insect invasions. The mighty redwoods have the distinction of standing taller (at up to 367 ft) but are less heavy-set. In comparison with the 3200-year-old sequoias, they are mere babies at 2000 years old. The world's three tallest trees are all redwoods, growing within a mile of each other on Redwood Creek along the north coast of California. I would recommend staying at the cosy John Muir Lodge at Grant Grove Village in Kings Canyon Park if you can. Out of season it costs less than a mediocre motel, and is a great base for seeing the trees and hiking the trails.

National Parks are government-owned and therefore wholly public areas. You will find no private properties in the park and minimal development, besides some accommodation for visitors; in the most popular parks, this is often expensive and hard to book, so you may be better off staying outside the park and travelling in each day. Rather than driving in, you might prefer to make use of the shuttle buses and avoid the traffic jams. Another tip is to plan ahead; with some of the well-known National Parks you need to make an appointment to visit, especially in summer when they are at their most busiest (between 15 May and 15 September) and the number of cars allowed in is restricted. Almost all the parks have camping grounds, which can be booked up a year or more in advance in high season. This crowded aspect rather takes the edge off visiting, and you might do better opting for some of the lesser-known Parks. That said, we visited Yosemite, Sequoia, Kings Canyon and Death Valley during spring break (the children's school holidays in March) and did not encounter any problems.

Parking within the parks is free. You pay an entrance fee (around $20/week for a car), or you can buy an annual pass if you plan to visit more than once – the Interagency Annual Pass (National Parks and Federal Recreational Lands Annual Pass) costs $80 for unlimited admission to federal recreation sites all year. The National Park Foundation publishes very informative free guides (entitled *American Park Network* guides) detailing activities, dining, lodging, trails, history and maps, to help you plan and get the most out of your visit.

In our travels through America's wilderness areas, we were often reminded of the need to be wary of wildlife. In areas frequented by bears and hikers alike, you are asked to bear-bag your food and other delectable-smelling goodies (such as toothpaste, perfumes and deodorants) by hanging them from a tree out of bear-reach or using a special bear-proof canister. You are also warned to remove all such items from your parked car as bears have been known to rip open vehicles in an attempt to steal the contents. In mountainous states, watch out for charging moose. Coral snakes are a hazard in the Southwest, and rattle snakes in desert and marshy areas.

There are ten US *National Seashores*:

- Assateague, Maryland
- Canaveral, Florida
- Cape Cod, Massachusetts
- Cape Hatteras, North Carolina
- Cape Lookout, North Carolina
- Cumberland Island, Georgia
- Fire Island, New York
- Gulf Islands, Florida
- Padre Island, Texas
- Point Reyes, California

We visited several. Point Reyes, near San Francisco, was reminiscent of Scotland, with miles of undisturbed beaches, sand dunes, cliffs, sea lion colonies and whale-spotting vantage points. Cape Hatteras has more than 70 miles of barrier islands, known as the Graveyard of the Atlantic because of its shipwrecks. Cape Lookout National Seashore comprises 56 gorgeous unspoilt miles along the lower Outer Banks. If you get the chance to visit, stay at Calico Jack's Inn and Marina at Harkers Ferry (one of my favourite spots, and convenient for the ferry to Harkers Island and the lighthouse). The 40-mile-long Cape Cod Seashore is another area worth visiting, being easy and fun to drive. It offers cycling and walking trails, historic buildings, marshes and wonderful freshwater swimming lakes.

National Forests are managed by the USDA Forest Service, and encompass 193 million acres. These areas offer something a little less crowded for the purist, and for those who prefer minimal facilities and primitive camping (pit toilets and no piped water). They also provide accommodation in refurbished historic cabins, forest ranger houses, homesteads and lookout towers, in select places. *A Guide to Your National Forests* is available free, along with maps and other information, from the USDA website.

The colour of the *Fall* is renowned in North America and Canada. The flaming colours lure millions of visitors, and foliage tours are particularly popular in northeast America. The peak of the colour explosion in these eastern states is around mid-October. In the Midwest, it is a little earlier (at the beginning of October), and further west, e.g. Colorado and along the Pacific Coast, the display normally starts in mid-September. In the South it is a little later, possibly lasting into November in North Carolina. The USDA Forest Service offers a National Fall Color Update, so you can plan a trip at the right time and see the colour spectacle. Many state websites also keep you informed of their fall foliage conditions.

Scenic Roads and Trails

In 1996 the government devised the National Scenic Byways Program in order to recognise, preserve and enhance selected roads across the country that were considered to have great historic, cultural, natural, scenic and/or recreational qualities. Today there are 126 designated byways recognised as All-American Roads or National Scenic Byways. For example:

- *Route 1*: hugging the California coast, and taking in Portland, Oregon, San Francisco, Monterey, Carmel and Big Sur.
- *Route 66*: this classic route conjures up the golden age of cross-country car travel. Visit the National Route 66 Museum in Elk City, Oklahoma, for a full appreciation of the 2446-mile-long highway, which stretches from Chicago to Los Angeles. Particularly popular with vacationers during the 1950s travelling to California, the route lost out to the interstates and was decommissioned in 1985.
- *Blue Ridge Parkway*: through Virginia and North Carolina, linking Shenandoah and Great Smoky Mountain National Parks, and providing a taste of Appalachia.
- *Skyline Drive*: through beautiful Shenandoah National Park in Virginia.
- *Las Vegas Strip*: a neon sight to behold, representing 75 years of glitz.

Long-distance walking trails, such as the Pacific Crest, Continental Divide and Appalachian Trail (which together are known as the Triple Crown), are popular with hikers. Every year, approximately 2000 people start walking the full Appalachian Trail (the shortest of the three), which crosses 14 states from Maine to Georgia and encompasses approximately 2175 miles (a quarter of which are in Virginia). Covering 15–20 miles/day, this can take 6 months, and only 1 in 20 make it to the end. On the way, camping grounds, shelters and water stops are provided. Bill Bryson gave a very entertaining account of his experience walking the AT in his book *A Walk in the Woods* (see *Suggested Reading and Viewing*). For other long-distance trails see the Wikipedia website cited in *Useful Websites.*

America's World Heritage Sites

A World Heritage Site is classed as being outstanding (mostly as a credit to Mother Nature) and of universal value, and America has her fair share of such sites:

- Chaco Culture, NM: multistorey stone villages with ancient distinctive architecture and Aztec ruins.
- Carlsbad Caverns, NM: more than 80 limestone caves of outstanding beauty, size, diversity and profusion.
- Cahokia Mounds, IL: prehistoric earth constructions, an example of a complex society that lived during about A.D. 700.
- Everglades, FL: a river of grass growing in fresh water, only 6 inches deep in places.
- Glacier Bay, Alaska: between Canada and Alaska, the world's largest non-polar ice field, with spectacular landscapes.

- Great Smoky Mountains, NC/TN: part of the Appalachian Highlands; water vapour and oily residues rising from the land create the effect of smoke.
- Grand Canyon, AZ: a nearly 1500-m-deep gorge with impressive horizontal strata.
- Hawaii Volcanoes National Park: two of the world's most active volcanoes create a constantly changing landscape here.
- Independence Hall, PN: the Pennsylvania State House in Philadelphia, where the Declaration of Independence and Constitution were both drafted and signed.
- La Fortaleza and San Juan Historic Site, Puerto Rico: European military architecture built during the fifteenth and nineteenth centuries.
- Mammoth Cave, KN: the world's largest cave network.
- Mesa Verde, CO: stone houses built on ledges and under huge rock overhangs, dating from the sixth to twelfth centuries.
- Monticello and University of Virginia, VA: Monticello was designed and lived in by Thomas Jefferson; UVA was the first university to separate church and education and to offer alternative courses to the norm.
- Olympic National Park, WA: including Mount Olympus and luxuriant jungle forest.
- Redwood National Park, CA: impressive flora and fauna; the sequoias and redwoods here are the tallest trees in the world.
- Statue of Liberty, NY: see Chapter 5.
- Taos Pueblo, NM: the best preserved traditional architecture of early Indian inhabitants.
- Waterton Glacier International Peace Park, MN: wonderful flora and fauna set in scenic glacial, forested, alpine and prairie landscape; shared with Alberta, Canada.
- Yellowstone, WY/MN/ID: first and oldest National Park in the world; features two-thirds of the world's geysers and half the world's known geothermal features; a 14-million-acre ecosystem.
- Yosemite, CA: rugged granite scenery of the Sierra Nevada Mountains, fashioned by glaciers.

The National Parks Service is chiefly responsible for America's World Heritage Sites. There are proposals for further sites to be added to the impressive list.

Travelling with Your Pet

It is becoming easier these days to take your pet travelling with you – be it the family dog, cat, ferret, rabbit or even fish (apparently not unheard of). A little searching about on the internet can turn up some helpful information (look up the websites listed below, in *Useful Websites*, for example). Some public nature areas and reserves prohibit dogs, even on a leash; this can often take you by surprise, and many was the time we had to change our plans and itinerary because Jester was not allowed to come on a walk with us. *The Dog Lover's Companion* guide books, available from Avalon Publishing, offer the inside scoop on where to take your dog. *Traveling with Your Pet*, produced by the AAA, is another good purchase. It has useful info, together with lists of pet-friendly lodgings and campgrounds, dog parks and veterinary clinics across America.

It is a sensible idea to attach some form of identification to your dog's collar (besides his licence tag), including your mobile phone number, in case he gets lost. It also makes sense to keep a photograph and description of your pet handy when you travel.

Insurance

It is usually cheaper to buy travel insurance (including health insurance and accident liability) for the US from a British insurer before you leave for America, as once you are state-side, UK insurers class you as exotic and will charge a premium to insure you. The other advantage to buying insurance in the UK before you leave, aside from the cost savings, is that you are then fully covered for the trip out. We purchased a family policy through JBI International, which included winter sports and worldwide coverage, for a very reasonable annual sum. Once the initial year was up, we simply renewed it at the same low rate (plus inflation); it made no difference to them that we were long-stay visitors in America.

Conclusion

America has no central office of tourism; instead, each state is responsible for promoting its own tourist attractions. Some counties and cities also have *their* own office of tourism, which supplies travel information.

As a family, we embarked on many exploratory trips across America, and it was interesting wherever we went. The diversity even within one state and the openness of the roads make travelling a good part of the holiday (not boring or frustrating as is often the case in Britain, fraught with snarl-ups and delays). However, in places, the long straight roads, with towns strung out periodically along them, can get a bit monotonous. During numerous trips to Lake Erie, we enjoyed the beaches and quirky seaside towns; the Great Lakes feel more like seas than lakes. Away from the main towns, you can find relief from the chains and franchises, with more independent, individual places to eat and lodge. In close beach-side communities, locals use golf carts (instead of bicycles) to get around.

West Virginia is 80% covered in forest. It has a plethora of gentlemen's clubs. One was situated right next to a motel we stayed in, and the sign on the door said 'No locals may rent a room here'. Appalachia has a strong mountain character, rooted in country music. In North Carolina we saw prisoners collecting rubbish along the road verges, with rifle-toting wardens in attendance – classic movie stuff. Charleston plantations and South Carolina evoke an era long gone, a peculiar southern way of life.

Out West in California, the different culture is very evident; people (boys included) wear their hair long, clothes baggy and live in offbeat communities. Venice Beach is an eye-opener, with its homeless people, promenade street hawkers and wacky vans parked in the car parks. The National Parks are mind-bogglingly vast, and very well maintained and protected. You can drive for miles, soaking up the awesome scenery. The cities of Las Vegas and Los Angeles are unreal.

The West Coast is a popular holiday destination. For one thing, the climate is mild and stable. Moreover, 85% of Nevada is government owned, almost 50% of Oregon and California, and 44% of Arizona; so, for instance, beaches tend to be public property. Out West you have a lot more open public land to enjoy than in the East. Also the geography is very variable, with deserts, mountains, rocky coasts, surf and sand beaches, hunting and fishing country, skiing, vineyards, plains and foothills. On a two-week trip, we were able to take in the scenic coast road (Route 1), one national seashore (Point Reyes), four National Parks (Yosemite, Sequoia, Kings Canyon and Death Valley), and the attractions of the major cities of San Francisco, Las Vegas and Los Angeles, with a day each at Disneyland and Universal Studios. Not bad for one vacation.

Of course, I could go on describing highlights and memorable moments of travelling in America, but really this chapter is meant to inspire you to get out and do it for yourself. It is the only way to see and experience America. Happy travelling.

Useful Websites

www.americanparknetwork.com – National Parks, state parks and public lands of America, including excellent free guides.
www.amtrak.com – Amtrak, the US rail network.
www.bbonline.com – a listing of B&Bs and country inns.
www.byways.org/explore/byways – National Scenic Byways Program; list of designated byways according to state.
www.camping-usa.com – campground information.
www.delta.com/skymiles – Delta Air Lines' Skymiles programme.
www.dogfriendly.com – find out where your dog is welcome in North America and Canada.
www.dogloverscompanion.com – guide books for dog owners.
www.ecampsite.com – camping and RV information.
www.fs.fed.us – National Forest info and maps.
www.fs.fed.us/news/fallcolors – Forest Service National Fall Color Update, detailing fall foliage conditions across the US.
www.gocampingamerica.com – campgrounds and travel tips.

http://gorp.away.com – active travel and lifestyle information.
www.hikewithyourdog.com – best places to go hiking with your dog.
www.hiusa.org – HI-USA or HI-AYH, the US affiliate of Hostelling International (equivalent to our YHA).
www.innfinder.com – for B&B accommodation.
www.innsite.com – for B&Bs, country inns and small luxury hotels.
www.jbionline.com – JBI International Insurance Brokers Ltd.
www.koa.com – Kampgrounds of America.
www.lonelyplanet.com/worldguide/destinations/north-america/usa – fast facts and at-a-glance information on the USA.
www.nps.gov/ – National Parks Service info and booking.
www.nps.gov/history/worldheritage/ – US World Heritage Sites.
www.nps.gov/pub_aff/refdesk/classlst.pdf – National Park designations.
www.railtrails.org – nationwide network of trails along former rail lines.
www.recreation.gov – Federal government recreation-related information.
www.rentalcarguide.com – wide-ranging car rental search.
www.rvamerica.com/ – buying and using RVs.
www.seeamerica.org – travelling, touring and vacationing in the US.
www.store.usgs.gov/pass/annual.html – National Park Foundation; info on buying an annual pass.
www.takepride.gov – nationwide volunteer programme to care for public lands.
www.thebackpacker.com – advice on trails, gear, hiking and backpacking.
www.towd.com – US tourism offices, by state.
www.trekamerica.com – off-the-beaten-path adventure holidays across the Americas.
www.usa-by-rail.com/ – complete guide to US rail travel.
www.usparks.about.com/blparktypes-ns.htm – US National Seashores.
www.visitusa.org.uk/ – vacation and travel planning, and even where to shop.

Wikipedia:
Long-distance trails in the United States – a listing of trails in the US.

Terminology

American term	Equivalent British term	Notes
Back pack	Rucksack	
Caboose	Guard's van	
CDW	Collision damage waiver	In regard to car rental insurance policies
Check room	Cloak room	
Coach	Economy	Inexpensive travel class; tourist class

American term	Equivalent British term	Notes
Comfort station	Roadside toilets	
Desk clerk	Receptionist	In a hotel; a 'receptionist' in AE is someone who greets visitors in a commercial office
Front desk	Reception	
Hideaway	Bed-settee	
LDW	Loss damage waiver	Covers loss of use, theft, vandalism and tyre damage
Legal holiday	Bank holiday	
Lobby	Foyer	
Mass transit	Public transport	
Mobile home, trailer, trailer home	Caravan	Towable behind a car
One-way ticket	Single ticket	
PAI	Personal accident insurance	Car rental insurance policies often try to add this on; your health insurance may already cover this
PLIS	Personal liability insurance	Protects you from being sued by third parties in the event of a car accident
Round trip ticket	Return ticket	
RV	Motorhome	
Schedule	Timetable	
Streetcar, trolley	Tram	
Trailer	Caravan	

13 · Seasons, Festivals and Other Celebrations

Throughout the year, Americans have certain legal holidays (equivalent to our bank holidays), which fall on set weeks or days of the year (see the section below on 'Public Holidays'). These national holidays are celebrated and enjoyed in uniquely different ways. Moreover, the President is allowed to declare other public holidays, calling on people to observe the day 'with appropriate ceremonies and activities'. In addition to national holidays, there is a long list of special days when Americans like to focus on certain groups of people or organisations in their community – for example, Boss's Day, Secretary's Day, Special Person Day, Make a Difference Day (encouraging people to volunteer for community service), National Nursing Home Week, Best Friends Weekend (for pets), National Missing Children's Day, Domestic Violence Awareness Month, and even a month of Romance Awareness. These 'Hallmark' events provide a constant source of revenue for card and gift stores.

Americans love to get together at other times and celebrate publicly with a festival; for example, ice cream, moonshine, maple syrup, tobacco, even twins festivals – you name it, they've probably got a festival for it. The pulling power of parades is very strong, with floats, marching bands, classic cars, veterans and festival queens. Such gatherings are usually free (there is no entrance or parking fee). However, while humans can simply wander round the festival, dogs are usually not so welcome, so check first whether pets are permitted before bringing an animal.

Spring Events

St Patrick's Day on 17 March is a very important event in some cities, especially New York and Boston, which both have a large Irish-American contingent. Thousands march up Fifth Avenue, past St. Patrick's Cathedral to Central Park, and the tradition goes back as far as 1684. In Chicago they famously turn the river green. To achieve this miracle, they employ the help of a dye used to detect leaks in the river, which turns a perfect shade of emerald green. Other cities have tried to emulate this, but without success. Throughout America, folks celebrate the day by dressing up, waving the Irish flag and having a good time – which usually involves consuming vast quantities of beer. Needless to say, Irish pubs do a roaring trade.

Easter has become more of a spring commercial calendar event than a religious one, with shops selling every imaginable Easter thing you can think of. Craft materials are especially popular. Oodles of egg hunts and opportunities for the children to meet the Easter bunny are held.

Daylight saving time starts on the first Sunday in April. Around this time in Ohio, the garden transforms from an unremarkable backdrop into a living, changing scene. Mowers come out in force for the first time since the start of winter and newspapers are suddenly full of adverts and spring promotions, with enticing pictures of patio living and barbecues. In the countryside, birds are calling for mates. Strange belching noises come from the wetlands (the sound of amorous frogs and toads) and snakes are to be found sunbathing on footpaths (so you need to watch where you walk).

Mother's Day falls on a different day to that in England; in America it is the second Sunday in May, a whole two months or so later than the British event. So as a British mum you may be able to wangle two days off a year. According to research data, the average 18- to 24-year-old spent a whopping $122 on Mom in 2006. Like many other special days in the year, Mother's Day is big business in America. Instead of the usual card, I was treated to two special events – Muffins with Mom and Breakfast Tea – at both my children's schools, and better than any card as they involved free nibbles and were wonderfully organised by the children. I could also have enjoyed any number of other special meal experiences, as advertised locally. Whole pages in the local newspaper were devoted to features and pictures of particular mothers who were worthy of public cheers and appreciation. There is no way this date in the calendar can go unnoticed.

Spring flings normally start up around this time of year. They seem to be simply an excuse for a good old knees-up in your local community. Over the course of a weekend, locals and not-so-locals alike can enjoy fairground fun, live bands, street parades, children's competitions, food stalls, arts and crafts, and more. It is a great way to soak up some free local entertainment, get out there and have some fun. Thereafter, festival season begins in earnest. Events in honour of sauerkraut, donuts, pretzels, etc. attract huge gatherings, and you can find some festival or other going on just about every weekend from now until autumn. Americans certainly know how to throw a good public party.

Summer Events

Apart from the *Fourth of July* (see 'Public Holidays', below), summer does not mark any particular celebrations or special days in the American calendar. However, this is not to say there is little going on. On the contrary, a plethora of outdoor activities, summer camps and other organised events keep everyone busy. Local sports events die down, but family fun is hot on the agenda. See Chapter 14 for information about summer activities for the children.

Summer officially kicks off with *Memorial Day* (the last Monday in May) and ends on *Labour Day* (the first Monday in September). *Father's Day* falls on the third Sunday in June, the same as in Britain. There are more collect calls made on this day than on any other day of the year. The 14th of June is *Flag Day*, when the nation issues an annual salute to its flag. Americans are encouraged to fly their flag for the whole week.

Every state and county has its annual summer show or 'fair' (as it is termed in American English). These fairs are often agricultural-based, with showings of animals, crafts and other country entertainment. At our local county fair, church and state vied for equal exposure just inside the gate, with local political party booths alongside Evangelical and Baptist stallholders offering free children's face painting, bangles and bibles.

Autumn Events

In Britain autumn is usually greeted with the depressing thought that summer is over, the days are getting darker and all we can look forward to now is Christmas; for some people the idea of Christmas even adds to their SAD (seasonal affective disorder) attitude. However, in America, autumn is a real cause for celebration – with harvest festivals, hayrides, corn mazes, jack-o-lanterns (carved pumpkins), apple cider and unusual seasonal foods. Apple festivals, fall festivals of leaves, pumpkin and gourd shows offer great excuses to gather together arts and crafts, flea markets and antiques, put on a parade, have a contest and enjoy the season.

You can see why they call this time of year *the Fall.* The decreasing daylight prompts the trees to produce less and less chlorophyll, eventually ceasing altogether. The carotenoid in the leaves (which is always present but usually overshadowed by chlorophyll) then turns them a bright yellow or orange. If anthocyanins are present the leaves will redden. Temperature also plays a part; when a number of warm, sunny autumn days and cool but not freezing nights come one after the other, it will be a good year for reds. Regardless of how the science works, the vivid colours are a magnificent spectacle, and our British leaf changes pale into insignificance. If left to accumulate, gardens are transformed under fiery carpets of colour. Great drifts build up, transforming ordinary places into picture-postcards of soft, moving colour. The colours are best following a warm wet spring, not unduly hot or dry summer and a Fall with plenty of sunny days and cool nights.

Americans celebrate this natural wonder, adding decoration with lights, pumpkins, wreaths, bales of straw and scarecrows, which adorn their porches, front doors and gardens. Probably one-third of the homes in our neighbourhood were decorated, making for interesting slow drives around the area. Even the supermarkets are beautifully decked out, displaying pumpkins of all sizes in a tasteful setting of straw bales, and flowering chrysanthemums in appropriate autumnal colours. Supermarkets are pushing pumpkin pie, pumpkin ice cream, gourds and squashes, apples coated in caramel and nuts, and other seasonal goodies.

Squirrels are everywhere, busily digging holes in your lawn. We missed seeing the chipmunks, as they hole up underground before hibernating and do not appear again until around the end of February. Armed with leaf blowers and rakes, everyone is busy gathering great heaps of crunchy leaves. We left ours as long as we dared; they provided such a natural and beautiful decoration to the garden and house.

Around mid-October, the previous year's classmates return to their old school, college or university for a get-together known as *homecoming*. This involves the obligatory parade, sports matches, parties and entertainment. Bunting in the local school's colours may adorn roadside railings and bridges, welcoming the leavers back.

October is a month of change – from consistently long warm days to cold one minute, hot the next, dark mornings (until the clocks go back around the end of the month) and then darker nights. Sycamore trees lose their bark, revealing their patchy white trunks and branches – giving rise to the Native American name of 'the ghost tree' (aptly in time for Halloween).

Halloween (31 October)

Halloween is almost on a par with Christmas in terms of popularity and dollars spent, and is probably the second biggest holiday for retailers. The shops are marketing Halloween as early as the beginning of September, with a vast array of bulk bags of candy, costumes and spooky goods galore. You can buy glow-in-the-dark ghoul drool, fake vampire blood, talking tombstones, blow-up tarantulas and ghosts in all shapes and sizes (some almost swamping the front yard or roof-top, lashed down to stop them blowing away) – go as mad as you like.

On the run-up to Halloween, events take place virtually every night. For little children, there are 'sweet or treat' nights when they can dress up (not necessarily in scary costumes), get together and have fun. Eerie evenings in the park involve lanterns and story-telling. Fun fests and spooktacular parades of ghosts, goblins and fairy princesses take place, with costume judging, entertainment, food and lights. Even the family pet can get involved, with pet parades and 'best pet costume' competitions.

On Halloween night, sometimes known as Beggars' Night, kids are usually carefully chaperoned and may call at your house between 6 and 8 p.m., not necessarily dressed sinisterly (you may be visited by princesses, cowboys or fairies, whatever their favourite costume). Each suburban community may have an official time frame during which homeowners can expect young visitors. If you do not want to receive little callers, leave your porch light off and you shouldn't be bothered. American children barely consider the 'trick' element and probably will not have a trick to hand if you asked them, so be sure to have plenty of small treats ready for them. These days, with fears of food tampering, only candy or food that is unopened is considered safe. You could also dole out non-food items such as stickers, pencils or erasers (healthier for the children).

Community Halloween festivals have done much to curtail petty vandalism, which used to be customary. Instead, youngsters and grown-ups alike channel their energy into masquerading, parades, contests and games. In some areas, whole streets get involved in the celebration, decorating their homes, dressing up and playing at Halloween, and at the same time fostering community spirit. The house decorations are astounding: porches decked in red lights, giant blowup Frankensteins and ghosts, headless corpses lying around, flashing pumpkin heads and cobweb-covered bushes. People have bonfire parties, without the fireworks. Spooky films are on the television for weeks; it's a great time to catch up on all the horror you've been missing.

Winter Events

Thanksgiving

In 1863 Thanksgiving Day became an official national holiday. It was originally decreed a day to 'express gratitude to a bountiful Creator'. Only half of the original settlers survived their first winter at Plymouth and they gave thanks by hosting a feast and inviting neighbouring Indians to join in their harvest festival – the very first Thanksgiving. People celebrate the Pilgrims coming to North America, and churches hold services to give thanks for the blessings of the past year. Native Americans understandably do not take part in Thanksgiving because it celebrates European domination of their homeland. However, the rest of America comes together and shares the holiday with family. They may show kindness to others, for instance by inviting someone who is on his or her own to come to dinner, or by helping at homeless shelters. Some cities have parades. It is also a last remnant of autumn before the earth takes its winter rest.

More food is consumed on Thanksgiving Day than on any other. The traditional meal consists of turkey, stuffing, cranberry sauce, mashed potatoes, corn or cornbread and yams, among other seasonal things. Pies are a favourite dessert, especially pumpkin. After dinner it is traditional to sit around watching football on the television or there may be a James 'Bondathon' (shades of bank holidays in Britain). Thanksgiving has the same feel as Christmas Day – streets are deserted, and bars, restaurants and shops are closed. Only a small number of places are open for the meal, some starting at 10.30 a.m. and running through until early evening. If you are not eating at home or with the family but instead want a meal out, it is best to ask the locals if they know anywhere open for dinner or you may miss the event entirely. Eating buffet style is very good value, with children often fed for free.

The day after Thanksgiving is a big shopping day, with major sales across all department stores and retailers. It is known as Black Friday, so named because of the sales fever that besets shoppers and propels stores into profitability for the year.

Christmas and Other Religious Festivals in December

On 10 August our local newspaper was telling us it was no time like the present to start thinking about Christmas planning. September sees shops starting their Christmas marketing extravaganza, unseasonably displaying trees with flashing lights and the usual Christmas paraphernalia, when temperatures outside are still in the 70s. There are public events involving caroling, tree decorating, festivals of lights and Santa appearances as early as the beginning of November. Thanksgiving is the real start of Christmas preparations, and many people put their tree up on or around Thanksgiving Day. It is a continuation of the holiday cheer that starts with harvest festivals and the Fall, proceeds through Halloween and Thanksgiving (America's own peculiar celebration), and culminates with Christmas. Some radio stations start playing Christmas tunes from the end of November.

The run-up to Christmas is huge; then one day and it's all over. Americans do not have Boxing Day, so Christmas day is 'It'. The traditional fare is similar to Thanksgiving Day and our British Christmas, with turkey or ham and mince pies. Other nationalities celebrate with their particular ethnic foods. In some households, it is traditional to set an extra place at the table for Christ or someone less fortunate, who may or may not join the family for the meal on Christmas Day. Many people give to charity at this time of year, perhaps adopting a less-fortunate family and buying their gifts, or donating coats and winter woollies to homeless shelters. Americans go to town decorating the outside of their homes, and it is worth going out for an evening drive to see the spectacle. Some neighbourhoods have contests each year to see who will win the holiday decoration award.

American Jews celebrate the *Festival of Lights* or *Hanukkah* in December. In 165 B.C., the Temple of Jerusalem was seized by the Syrians and dedicated to the worship of Zeus. The Jews resisted and eventually claimed back their holy Temple. As part of the rededication, they lit the menorah, but only had oil enough for 1 day, yet it miraculously burned for 8 days. Jewish people celebrate this miracle by lighting candles in a menorah each night during the 8-day-long Hanukkah. African-Americans also have a special holiday called *Kwanzaa*. This coincides with the Christian Christmas season, and reflects the importance of the family, community, environment and African culture.

Other Winter Events

On *New Year's Eve*, 1904, the *New York Times* gave a public party in honour of its new headquarters at One Times Square; a few years later it marked the festivities by lowering a huge light-bulb-studded globe from the flagpole on the top of the building at midnight to mark the final moments of the fading year. The dousing of the light signaled the beginning of the New Year. Every year since, crowds have come to witness the spectacle and welcome in the New Year, and the event is televised around the world. Across the nation, Americans celebrate New Year's Eve and Day pretty much the same as we do.

Once every 4 years, *inauguration* of the new President of the United States and his Vice President takes place in Washington, DC. They are sworn into office at noon on 20 January, following the national election the preceding November. The President then gives an address to the nation. There follows a parade of marching bands and floats, lasting several hours, culminating in official dances.

That all-American date in the calendar, the *National Football Leagues' Super Bowl Sunday*, falls sometime in January/early February following the playoffs. It is as much about the pre-game hype, the half-time show, commercials, celebrities, food and merchandise as football; in short, it is Americans at their best. You've never heard such hollering and high-fiving. About one in seven will be ordering a take-out – pizza being the number-one Super Bowl munchy; indeed, it is pizza makers' busiest day of the year. Super Bowl Sunday comes in second behind Thanksgiving Day for the most food consumed on any one day. The game is also one of the most-watched TV broadcasts of the year.

Groundhog Day (2 February) is a peculiar American tradition. Punxsutawney Phil (the groundhog) awakens from hibernation and has been seen coming out of his hole on this day for the last 120 years or so (so he must be pretty old and crotchety by now). His powers of weather forecasting are apparently second to none. If he sees his shadow, there will be six more weeks of winter weather to endure and you probably won't see him again till then. If he doesn't cast a shadow, he will stay above ground to enjoy an early spring. Groundhog Day is a throwback to Pennsylvania's earliest settlers who celebrated Candlemas Day and chose the ubiquitous groundhog as their symbol. Following release in 1993, the film *Groundhog Day* (starring Bill Murray and Andie MacDowell) became a cult movie, and in 2006 it was deemed to be 'culturally, historically, or aesthetically significant' by the US National Film Registry, which selected it for preservation in the Library of Congress. Following the film, the phrase 'Groundhog Day' has become synonymous with an unpleasant situation that is continually repeated (or seems as if it is).

The buildup to *Valentine's Day* is probably one of the worst times of the year if you are an American man (that and Mother's Day); you certainly won't be able to say you forgot. Shops go into overdrive promoting anything that could conceivably be on your loved one's wish list. My husband and I did our usual thing and didn't bother, though I did succumb to some sparkly, pink-iced, heart-shaped cookies from the local supermarket, which went down well at my little girl's birthday party. Even young children exchange Valentine cards and little presents (typically sweets) with friends and classmates. The school reminded us that, 'When you and your child are purchasing (or making) Valentines, please note that we have 30 Kindergartners and three teachers'. We were asked not to address these Valentines to classmates but instead simply have the child sign his or her name. My two youngsters came home laden with cards and sweet things. Interestingly, there were hardly any homemade cards. The shops must do a roaring trade.

Catholics the world over have celebrated *Mardi Gras* since 1699. However, it owes its origins to much earlier times, when a circus-like orgy was held in Rome in mid-February, and later the Pagans held a festivity. The French brought the idea to New Orleans, where the festival usually lasts for 12 days or so, culminating in Shrove Tuesday. Mardi Gras is always held 47 days before Easter, which is why its exact date varies each year according to when Easter falls. The name literally means 'fat Tuesday', following which 40 days of Lent ensue (traditionally involving abstinence and penitence); so it is a chance to gird yourself before Lent. Mardi Gras festivals are held in many places in America, though New Orleans is still the biggie. It sure brightens up midwinter.

Public Holidays

Public or federal holidays are the equivalent of our bank holidays. This is when most states give employees and children at public schools a day off (though federal law does not compel states to do so). Many private businesses may still open for business, though most close on Thanksgiving Day, Christmas Day, New Year's Day, Memorial Day, Independence Day and Labour Day – the big six.

Christmas Day, New Year's Day, Independence Day and Veterans' Day are always observed on the same calendar date, unless they fall on a weekend. Then the previous Friday or Monday is taken as the day off (depending on whether the official day fell on a Saturday or Sunday respectively). The other public holidays always fall on a particular day of the week, e.g. 'the first Thursday in …'. Below is a brief description of the main holidays of the year.

- *Martin Luther King Day* (third Monday in January)
  The civil rights leader Martin Luther King, Jr. was born in Atlanta on 15 January 1929, and Americans celebrate his life on MLK Day by holding hands, marching in honour and feeling more united – at least once a year.

- *President's Day* (third Monday in February)
  Originally celebrating Washington and Lincoln's birthdays, it has now expanded to honour all who have led the nation.

- *Good Friday* (same date as in Britain)
  However, there is no public holiday on Easter Monday.

- *Memorial Day* (last Monday in May)
  On this day Americans show their respect for those in the military who have given their lives for their country. The President pays his respects at Arlington National Cemetery, Virginia, and/or Gettysburg National Military Park, Pennsylvania. Memorial Day is regarded by the nation's veteran organisations as one of the major patriotic occasions of the year. However, it is now 90% recreation and only 10% recollection, with kids' soccer games and baseball tournaments, picnics and parties in the park dominating the family scene. In an effort to remind folks of why they are enjoying this extra day off work, Congress passed the national Moment of Remembrance Act, asking for a moment of silence at 3 p.m. Memorial Day also traditionally marks the start of summer (hence the happy element).

- *Independence Day* (4 July).
  This important date in the American calendar celebrates the signing of the Declaration of Independence. It is marked by fireworks, parades, speeches, championship sports matches, barbecues, family picnics, parties and other patriotic community displays.

- *Labour Day* (first Monday in September; the rest of the world celebrates on 1 May)
  This can be traced back to the first Central Labour Union parade in 1882 in New York City. It celebrates the labour movement and is regarded simply as a day of rest. Picnics, barbecues, firework displays, river festivals and public events are held throughout America. There is also the all-star show the *Jerry Lewis MDA* (Muscular Dystrophy Association) *Telethon*, which has been held annually since 1966. Labour Day traditionally marks the end of summer.

- *Columbus Day* (second Monday in October)
  This day honours Christopher Columbus, the so-called discoverer of the Americas.

- *Veterans' Day* (11 November)
  The equivalent of our Remembrance Day, Veterans' Day is when Americans hon-

our those who have served their country – past and present (both dead and living) – during times of war. The President usually visits the tombs of the Unknown Soldier in Arlington National Cemetery and lays a wreath at the shrine. The ceremony takes place at 11 a.m., the hour of cease-fire along the European Western Front at the end of World War I.

- *Thanksgiving Day* (fourth Thursday in November)
  A day of giving thanks to God for the past year and the autumn harvest, of feasts and family reunions. See the discussion above.
- *Christmas Day* (25 December)
  The American Christmas Day is very similar to our British (see above). However, Americans do not celebrate Boxing Day and most people go to work as usual.

Conclusion

Many of the seasonal events and other celebrations in America are celebrated excessively and perhaps a bit overdone. Take birthdays for instance. In our time in America, only once were the children invited to a birthday party at home. Public venues varied from bowling alleys and skating rinks to kids' amusement arcades and museums. Being a traditionalist, I often felt a little sad that the emphasis on a special party for the birthday boy or girl was somehow lost, with the kids disappearing off to play or engage in some activity, surrounded by members of the public who happened to be at the same venue; the personal aspect seemed to be missing.

However, at other times the emphasis is much more personal, with family reunions very popular, especially during the summer, when people either throw open their doors at home or borrow a picnic shelter in the local park. They are opportunities for the young and old to get together, enjoy a shared meal and play ball. Alumni (the network of past students who like to keep in touch with their old school or college) are widespread. At times, whole pages in our local newspaper were taken up with area reunions of one sort or another.

Americans clearly love getting together and celebrating in groups. Whatever the time of year, even in the depths of winter, you can lift your spirits and join in the fun at public events and social gatherings; there is never a dull moment. From street parties, community garage sales and bakes, dressing up at festivals, joining the parade and waving the flag, people actively take part and are out to enjoy themselves. Children are an important part of these get-togethers. Alcohol is often completely missing at these events, but there is no shortage of food and fun. Americans also know how to put on a good show, revelling in their marching bands, cheerleaders and parades. If you can look beyond the over-commercialisation, you should have a good time.

Useful Websites

www.chicagostpatsparade.com/river-dye.html – St Patrick's Day in Chicago.
www.festivalsandevents.com – US festivals and events.
www.festivals.com – find festivals and events by state or subject.
www.opm.gov/Operating_Status_Schedules/fedhol/ – list of federal holidays.
www.thanksgiving-day.org/ – information on Thanksgiving Day.
www.usflag.org/history/flagday.html – the history of Flag Day.

14 · Sport and Entertainment

One chapter cannot cover all the innumerable forms of sport and entertainment available in the United States. Instead, it homes in on the main sports played and watched, and talks about their importance in American culture. According to the Travel Industry Association of America, the top five sports that Americans travel most to see are baseball/softball, football, basketball, auto/truck racing and golf. Rodeos, particularly out West, are another popular sporting and social event. The entertainment topics discussed – television and movies, radio, music, reading and home crafts – are hopefully in themselves useful and interesting.

Sport: It's a Big Deal

To say that Americans love sport is an understatement. There are countless opportunities for both watching and participating in sport. Sports-goers and fans are very mixed in so far as age and sex. Whole families regularly trip out to watch a local baseball game, laden with picnics and chairs, swapping hoots and cheers with others. Tailgate parties are popular. Sometimes drunk and disorderly conduct occurs at big games, when emotions run high. Some venues impose rules on congregating before and after a game, and have a strict admissions policy. We saw no evidence of hooliganism or antagonism at the local games we attended; everyone just seemed to be out to have a good time.

Americans expect to be entertained at sporting events. With dance contests, games, silly noises and crowd songs, the time between innings is not wasted. You can eat yourself stupid with popcorn, peanuts, pretzels, hot dogs and funnel cake. The kids are often well-catered for too, with red, white and blue candy floss, big hands and pompoms to wave, even play areas. A roving camera-man transmits pictures of the crowd onto a big screen, so you may see yourself up there, whether you wanted to make a public spectacle of yourself or not.

At baseball matches, *Take Me Out to the Ball Game* is belted out by the standing crowd, and every American knows the words to the song. Crowd participation is keen, with free T-shirts up for grabs, karaoke, tug-of-war, kids and dads water balloon competitions, etc. We watched in awe as two guys from the crowd ran the bases during a baseball game, dressed in flippers, a mask and rubber ring – anything to keep the crowd amused. Well, you've gotta do something – can't sit there watching a game of baseball or American football for 3 hours without some moments of boredom creeping in. Americans don't seem to get frustrated with all the stops in play (it's a bit like their television).

International competitions are not given much place in the American sporting calendar. Major-league professionals do not play teams outside of their organisation, at least not in any meaningful way. There are few cup competitions (except perhaps golf, where these are a fairly new development). Instead, professional sports teams compete in league games that lead to a playoff tournament and thus to a championship game or series. Rather than a system of promotions and relegations, American teams invariably play in the same league each year.

ESPN, the all-sports cable television network, first aired in 1979. Commercial television broadcasts constitute the lion's share of a professional team's revenue. Leagues agree to contracts with TV broadcasters, stipulating how often televised games will be interrupted by commercials. This is why you do not see sponsorship on uniforms and sports fields, as in Britain.

School, College and University Sports

The athletic programmes of many American schools, colleges and universities are very impressive. High-school and college football games are passionate affairs and major events of the school year. Scholarships are given to student-athletes, who are only expected to attain a minimum academic standard, often significantly lower than the norm. Teams practise during the summer, then begin playing games at the start of term. The first football home game of the season is known as *homecoming*, when former graduates revisit their old high school or college and play a special game. In early January, state championships are held. Teams are highly organised and semi-professional, with professional teams drafting (selecting) the top student-athletes. Tickets sold at school/college games are an important source of revenue for the school. Some schools view football very seriously and organise their academic terms around the games. In fact, some universities have been hauled over the coals for putting too much emphasis on the game to the detriment of the educational welfare of the student players.

Baseball and Softball

Baseball is known as America's national past-time. Compared with American football which has only 16 games in a season, baseball has a long season, with 162 games. Major league teams play almost every day from April, culminating with the World

Series in the first week in October. This is a best-of-seven playoff between the winner of the National League and the American League. Little League is a non-profitable organisation of leagues for children aged 5–18 and very popular. Youngest players start off in T-Ball leagues and progress to Big League.

The game is said to have evolved from English rounders and is played throughout America, from city schools to rural backyards, no special equipment being required. The size and shape of the pitch has no limit or strict ruling: the pitch extends theoretically to infinity from a single point – the home plate. There is also no time limit to a game. Games have become progressively longer what with the slower pace of playing, more offences and pitching changes, and extended TV commercials during half-innings. It is not unusual for a game to last 5 hours. As Yogi Berra (former catcher and manager of the New York Yankees) once said, 'It ain't over till it's over'.

Baseball is fanatically supported. Sorry, but I can't see its allure; as alluded to above, there's too much stop/starting, not enough flow, and the players have a nasty habit of spitting every five minutes. You need to understand the rules, the skill, strategy and timing of the players in order to appreciate the game, which, as Yogi put it, '…is 90% mental. The other half is physical'. This probably explains why amateur players are often not the best specimens of physical fitness, unfortunately accentuated by the strange tight-fitting garb they play in.

Baseball has had a strong influence on American English. Below are some examples that even non-baseball aficionados will recognise:

- 'You're in the big leagues now.'
- 'Give me a ballpark figure' (something reasonably accurate).
- 'Cover all the bases.'
- 'I got to first base' (meaning initial success; usually refers to the first kiss on a date, and thereafter 'second' and 'third bases' have sexual connotations in adolescent stages of romance).
- 'You caught me off base' (by surprise).
- 'Do you want to play ball?' (competitive, pushy).
- 'So you want to play hardball? (aggressive).
- 'Let's take a rain check.'
- 'We'll touch base tomorrow.'
- 'He's not a team player' (bad behaviour).
- 'Win one for the gipper' (carry out a selfless act).

Baseball is sometimes referred to as hardball, to distinguish it from softball. Softball is a popular sport with women (both amateur and professional). It was originally an indoor game deriving from baseball and differs in the following respects:

- In softball the bat is shorter and the ball is larger.
- The field is smaller, with a set distance between the home plate and outfield fence.

- The throw is underhand (any method is allowed in baseball).
- Games are shorter, with five to seven innings vs nine innings in baseball.

American Football

With its marching bands, cheerleaders and tailgate parties, American football is a very important part of American culture. Super Bowl Sunday is the biggest day for home parties, and traditionally Thanksgiving and New Year's Day also have important matches. It has become the most popular spectator sport in America. The Super Bowl championship game is watched by nearly half of American households, televised across the world and heavily commercialised, with a 30-second ad slot costing $2.7 million (on Fox's 2008 broadcast).

American football evolved from the game of football played in Britain and is directly descended from rugby football. It was brought to the North American continent by the British Army stationed in Quebec, and Americans then adapted its rules to make their own form of the game. It has a lot to do with coach strategy. There are approximately eight referees and linesmen on the pitch, so games are well policed (compare this with the one ref and two linesmen on a rugby pitch). *Offense* is the American term for forward when describing attacking players in team sports such as football. In scoring, *nil* is not used; instead Americans say 'oh', e.g. 1–0 or one to nothing where we would say 1–nil.

Games between the top university teams in different states can pull a massive crowd. The Ohio vs Michigan State University game in 2006 was played in the Columbus stadium. All 100,000 or so seats were sold out, and the stadium is packed out regularly, even without the hype of a home state versus neighbouring state game. The size of this stadium is not unusual in America, and larger than any soccer stadium in the UK. Out shopping in our local supermarket on the morning of the game, I was amazed to see so many people dressed in their Ohio State University colours, and the store had that 'day before Christmas' feel, with everyone busy buying party food. We were invited round to a friend's house to watch the game on a large projector screen. Everyone chipped in with food and drink, buffet style, and most were wearing their team shirts. The 60-minute game took 3 hours to watch, with all the breaks (as the games are partly funded through TV advertising and patronage, they want to get their money's worth). During the 20-minute half-time, while the crowd at the stadium watches the marching band, TV viewers are treated to commentary and commercials. Professional games also have big stars who entertain during the 20-minute down time. During the proceedings, home-viewers get as excited as if they were there at the game – standing up and roaring at key moments, high-fiving whenever the home team does well, the women as enthusiastic as the men.

The National Football League (NFL) involves 32 teams playing 16 regular-season games each year. Despite the players' extraordinary padding and head gear, injuries are common, especially concussions. Woody Hayes, coach of the Ohio State Football Team, and greatly admired by sports fans, is famed for saying, 'Winning isn't the most important thing; it is the only thing' – a rather shuddering ethic, considering that between 2000 and 2005, 28 players, mostly high-schoolers, suffered fatal injuries.

Basketball

Basketball is perhaps the most played of all American team sports, and a basketball hoop is a standard piece of equipment of most American homes. To play the game all you need is a ball and 'court', two teams and five active players. The NCAA (National Collegiate Athletic Association) national tournament played each spring invokes frenzy among fans and gamblers. During what is termed *March Madness*, 65 college teams compete in a tournament lasting 20 days, with games played at sites across the States.

The game originated in a YMCA gym in Massachusetts in 1892, and the YMCA went on to promote and develop it throughout its network. However, a decade later, the new sport was discouraged as being too rough and attracting rowdy crowds, but its appeal prevailed. Originally players used soccer balls; then in the late 1950s, the more visible orange ball was introduced. Street ball is a form of urban basketball played on a small section of court, one-on-one. Players are fast and flashy; it has as much to do with style and performance as athletic competition.

The National Basketball Association (NBA) is the number-one men's professional league. Eight teams compete in conferences, qualifying for the playoffs in late April. More than 75% of NBA players are African-American, and Chris Rock (anti-politically correct comedian) commented:

> 'Black people dominate sports in the United States; 20% of the population and 90% of the final four. We own this s..t – basketball, baseball, football, golf, tennis, and as soon as they make a heated hockey rink we'll take that s..t too'.

(The 'final four' refers to the last four teams remaining in the NBA playoff.)

Motor Sports

NASCAR stands for the National Association of Stock Car Auto Racing. NASCAR's headquarters is in Daytona Beach, Florida, the premier location for setting land speed records during the early 1900s. NASCAR oversees motor sports in America and sanctions over 1500 races at more than 100 tracks across 38 states, Canada and Mexico. During 2006, the Nextel Cup ran on 22 tracks in 19 states between February and November, so this shows some commitment on the part of fans travelling to see the races.

Americans do not pay much attention to international motor series, preferring to support their home events. Indianapolis 500 (Indy 500) is the biggest race event of the year, so-called because it has always been a 500-mile race. Each speedway lap is 2.5 miles long, so this represents a lot of laps. It was inaugurated in 1911 and takes place at the end of May each year. Motor-racing is the second most popular professional sport (after American football) in terms of TV ratings in America. A single NASCAR race can attract a larger crowd of spectators than a World Series, NBA finals and Super Bowl game combined, and the largest tracks sell out to some 500,000 spectators. People travel miles to attend races (about 25% of fans travel more than 300 miles to watch a race) during the season-long points chase, avidly following their favourite drivers as they compete all over the country. There is strong brand loyalty, with fans shelling out around $2 billion on licensed product sales each year. Demographically, 60% of fans are male, 40% are female.

Golf

Since World War I, the greatest number of leading professional golfers have originated from America. The four big men's tournaments played each year are the US Open and PGA Championships, played at various courses around the States, the Open Championships (referred to as the British Open), played at courses around the UK, and the Masters, played in Augusta, Georgia. The Augusta course was initiated by Bobby Jones, an eminent American golfer, who decided to build an ideal golf course. Since 1934 the 365-acre course has hosted the Masters Tournament each April (barring 3 years during World War II). It is the only golf tournament played at the same course each year.

Away from the professional circuit, private courses, country clubs and some urban courses on prime commercial land command high green fees. However, local authorities try to offer low fees at public golf courses so that it is not prohibitively expensive to play a round (on average, a round costs $36). Michigan has more public golf courses than any other state.

More than 26 million Americans enjoy playing the game. However, golf is still seen as an affluent sport (much like hunting in Britain) and there is a certain status to owning the latest equipment. It is said that the golf course is the unofficial business office, where many decisions are made. 'Business golf' has become so popular that schools and universities now offer courses in it, sponsored by the PGA of America. Classes are popular with women who want to compete in business.

In January 1995, the Golf Channel was launched by an Alabaman media entrepreneur, and now provides (sometimes exclusive) golf coverage 24 hours a day through the American cable TV network. A version of the network is also available in the UK.

Rodeo

If you live in the American West, rodeo may be on TV every day, and your kids will likely be participating in the sport. Every town, every weekend in the summer holds competitions. Travelling rodeo teams are also a highlight attraction at state fairs across the US. Events include bull riding, bareback and saddle bronco riding, roping, steer wrestling, barrel racing and pole bending. The Professional Rodeo Cowboys Association (PRCA) sanctions approximately 700 rodeos each year. Many youth, women, amateur, high-school and college teams compete regularly. Gymkhana, clowns and bull fighters add to the public's amusement. The annual Cowboy Christmas takes place on the run-up to the 4th of July, with cowboys travelling to the mountain West in order to compete in as many rodeo competitions as they can and earn themselves big prize money ('an early Christmas present'), with winnings of more than $100,000 up for grabs.

Hunting

While Britain is a nation of animal lovers, Americans seem to view wild animals rather dispassionately, preferring to treat their wildlife as sport. From their pioneer ancestors, many Americans believe they are natural-born hunters and every autumn set out to prove this. You must have a state licence to hunt or trap in any particular state, but this is cheap to buy if you are a resident; out-of-state hunters pay more. A fur-taker's permit is required to hunt fur-bearing animals and specific permits may also be required for specific game. Excise tax on hunting gear, guns and ammo goes toward wildlife and habitat restoration, land acquisition and wildlife research, and is an important source of revenue.

The state of Ohio is divided into zones with particular deer bag limits. During any one hunting season in Ohio around 200,000 deer are killed by hunters with guns, muzzleloaders and bow and arrow. Deer hunting contributes an estimated annual $266 million to the state's economy and supports thousands of jobs. If you don't want to keep the meat from your kill, you can donate it to organisations such as local food pantries which feed those in the community who can't afford to buy meat.

Hunting seasons vary according to state and what animal you are going after. The range of animals that can be hunted is quite extensive, for example:

- Big game – such as deer, bear, wild boar.
- Small mammals – squirrel, rabbit, armadillo, beaver, coyote, groundhog, skunk, bobcat, fox, mink, muskrat, weasel, river otter, opossum, raccoon, bullfrog.
- Birds – grouse, quail, dove, woodcock, snipe, crow, Canada geese, wood duck/teal, English sparrow, starling.

There are no bag limits in Ohio on crow, groundhog, fox, raccoon, skunk, opossum, weasel, wild boar and coyote. Coyotes, once hunted to the point that they were only found in the mountain West, are now making a comeback. However, their presence is not welcome as they have been known to attack domestic dogs and cats. Raccoon are usually hunted with dogs, which find and force them up trees so that a shooter can dispose of the animal (perhaps Jester has a use after all).

With other animals there may be a daily bag limit, strict opening and closing dates, and even specific times of the day when they can be hunted. There are different seasons for archery (including cross bows), muzzleloaders, guns and young sportsmen. Hunters must verify their kill at check stations and abide by the rules. Wildlife authorities keep a close eye on where animals are in the wild and identify areas with excessive numbers that may need controlling.

Wild turkey hunting is one of the fastest growing outdoor sports in the country. Ohio's spring season for turkey hunting is less than a month long (during the turkey's spring mating period in April/May) and rules are strict; for instance, all turkeys must be shot between 30 minutes before sunrise and noon and taken to an official check point by 2 o'clock on the same day. Hunters can bag one male bird each per season. Hunters imitate female turkeys in an effort to lure amorous males out into the open.

Fishing

If fishing is more your bag, then you can buy an annual fishing licence to take fish, frogs or turtles. Those under 16 years old do not need a licence, but assisting parents do. Fishing is a very popular hobby, in part owing to the huge choice of waterways – from local rivers and small lakes, to wonderful state parks, the Great Lakes and miles of coastline. Fishing options are boundless, and all for the paltry licence sum of $19 a year (in Ohio). Fishing gear is cheap, and bait readily available from shops in popular fishing areas. For information on licences, rules and regulations in your state, look up the website of the Department of Natural Resources for your area.

Soccer

Soccer (football as we know it) is not a popular American sport. The reason that most American adults don't play the game or care to watch it on television is that they find it boring apparently. There are no major well-known American soccer players to cheer on, and the game emphasises defence over attack, which is rather alien to the 'go get 'em' attitude of most Americans. It leaves too much to chance, with no time-outs for coaches to make corrections and only one referee to oversee everyone (unthinkable to most Americans). Cities with a large immigrant population, such as Los Angeles and New York, may field the odd team, and it is a favoured game with women. However, because American football and basketball are so huge, soccer is very much overshadowed.

However, little leagues are a different matter. Youth and school teams start children playing soccer as young as 4 or 5, and the game is especially popular with girls. William joined the local soccer association at age 5 and twice a week played in matches, with practice sessions and special clinics on top. Each team member was given his or her own team jersey, socks and water bottle, and a couple of coaches were assigned to each team. Parents were encouraged to support the young players at games and practices. It was a great introduction to playing team sports.

Cheerleading

Cheerleading is classed as a sport and taken very seriously in America. Cheerleaders lend a certain *Je ne sais quoi* and are an essential component of many American sports events. Some girls make a living out of it, e.g. Paula Abdul was a basketball cheerleader for the LA Lakers before becoming a pop singer. Once a year there is a national cheerleaders competition, when girls try out for the big teams. If your daughter is into cheerleading it may require considerable devotion, commitment and parental support and can become a major pursuit – with practice sessions several times a week, often at far-distant venues, summer camps, and a whole lot of expense in the form of clothing, equipment and transportation. One mum of a competitive cheerleader quoted annual expenses of around $7000. If you are athletic and/or good-looking, you might catch a well-paid husband from the team, so sometimes it pays off.

Other Sports

Other popular team sports are volleyball and ice hockey (abbreviated to just *hockey* in America). The latter is played recreationally throughout the country, especially in city areas, but the Great Lakes region and New England are the main hubs of the sport. Rugby is not well known; interestingly, nearly a quarter of American rugby players are female. Cricket is almost unheard of in the States. Horse racing is centered in Kentucky. Horse shoes and corn holing are peculiar traditional games that have quite a following, and are played on campsites, at family and sporting get-togethers. Corn holing originated in Cincinnati and has now spread beyond the Midwest.

Sporting Opportunities for Youngsters

America offers sports opportunities for children that are second to none, and the array of activities is truly impressive. Even from a very early age (2 and 3 years old), children can partake in gymnastics, tumbling, ballet and dance, mini-fitness, ice skating, martial arts and yoga play. At 4 and 5 they can start basketball, soccer, T-ball (junior baseball) and judo; at 6 and 7, golf and fencing. There seem to be equal opportunities for both girls and boys, and girl's soccer is very popular. The facilities are excellent, with local parks providing baseball, soccer and volleyball pitches. You can drive out on an evening and use the pitches for practising or enjoy an impromptu game of ball with friends. No booking or payment is required.

Many of the team sports are volunteer based, and parents are encouraged to get involved and help with coaching, refreshments, organising games, manning the concession stand, fundraising for equipment and generally cheering on at practices and games. In fact, parents often become a little too involved – there have been cases of parents beating up coaches and other parents – and tensions can transmit to the young players. This is one negative aspect of Americans' love affair with sport. The printed rules of etiquette we received from our little-league coach included something along the lines of please cheer on the little leaguers, but don't shout instructions, rib the players or negatively interfere with the coaching. Only encouragement should be offered. Thus calls of 'Good job!' (pronounced 'jaab') and 'All right!' fill the air, and high-fiving is rife. That parents are even there participating in the games is something to behold. Whole families empty themselves, their chairs, picnic blankets and cool boxes onto the field and take up position ready to spur on the mini teams. It makes for a very positive and enthusiastic atmosphere that is hard not to get caught up in.

Baseball is America's number one sport. However, given the choice, William would always plump for soccer over T-ball. I could see his point. Baseball is a strange game, involving a lot of waiting around while batters get into position, pitchers psyche themselves up, and throws have to be retaken. As little leaguers, they spend a lot of time sitting out, waiting to bat. The most exciting moment according to William was getting dressed up to be catcher.

Fishing equipment is very cheap to buy in America, so it doesn't take much to get the family equipped, ready to enjoy hours of fishing fun and anticipation, at the same time taking pleasure from the natural environment. At weekends, ridiculous numbers of families descend on local lakes and ponds to do a spot of rod dipping. What with all the noise and activity, you may not catch much, but there is a certain amount of camaraderie and the kids seem to be hooked (excuse the pun).

Jim warns about the dangers of over-exerting youngsters with the myriad sporting opportunities available and the competitive element involved:

> Americans don't do anything by halves and most things are overdone. American society is deceptively competitive. This competitiveness seeps into schools where it is not enough just to survive the school day and the considerable homework dished out. On top of that effort comes membership of teams and clubs, including the three main sports plus perhaps swimming, dancing, running, soccer, cheerleading, marching bands and baton twirling. It is necessary for parents to perform domestic back flips to ensure their little Johnnies

and Jessicas attend all the necessary clubs, resplendent in the correct kit and with the proper equipment. Parents can be seen on weekends executing intricate car and child juggling sequences to meet the challenges enforced by parallel but uncoordinated schedules, to ensure that their brood arrives at a sequence of venues on time and suitably attired for a list of absorbing activities. This whirl of endless activity is most impressive but hardly conducive to relaxation. For that, breaks in schooling are required, at least that was the original concept; however, school vacations now give unbroken opportunities for children to be trained even more enthusiastically as if they were entering the Olympics. There is talk that children are getting burned out and that school lessons are quickly forgotten as extra-curricula activities are pursued. Certainly, it is sometimes hard to pair excellently performing and physically healthy children with their hang-dog, often overweight parents, who one can only assume were equally adept performers in their day.

Television

The American TV watershed (known as 'safe harbor') is an hour later than in Britain, beginning at 10 p.m. Despite this, television is surprisingly heavily censored. Terrestrial channels are censored by the Federal Communications Commission (FCC), which does not allow full-frontal nudity or explicit human sex scenes at any time. Often, when watching a film on the box, we noticed a cut where gory scenes or bad language had been taken out, or the swearing had been reworked, e.g. 'You son of a pig!' Scenes of nudity and/or violence (especially blood-thirsty scenes) are simply omitted, which can be disappointing if you are looking forward to watching *all* of *Jaws* or *Predator*, only to find the 'best bits' have been taken out. However, popular shows such as *Oprah*, *Dr Phil* and *Jerry Springer*, on during the day, seem to have few restrictions imposed on them. Many of the topics discussed are not that savoury for adults, let alone for youngsters.

One observation from watching American TV is that presenters like to be noticed, especially women presenters. They are smart, savvy, extremely well groomed, possibly nipped and tucked, and glowing with health and vitality. Take Marilou Henner, for example, as she promotes her diet and fitness regime. Another example is Katie Couric, former host of the *Today Show* for 15 years, and quite possibly the Queen of Perk. She is now a serious network news anchor, chosen perhaps to revitalise the news and make it more popular viewing. Oprah Winfrey no longer looks much like the Oprah of earlier years. And where has Michael Jackson gone? Perhaps he was a woman in disguise after all? It's a job keeping up with them. Even men aren't immune from keeping up appearances, though Mickey Rourke is a testament to why you shouldn't tamper with your sagging yet natural good looks. It's a scary world out there. With regard to the popularity of Oprah, she has become so powerful now that a simple endorsement from her will jettison a book to the best-sellers list. Americans seem to need approval from celebrities.

American Idol was the nation's favourite TV show in 2006, perhaps because it encapsulated the American dream of becoming an instant celebrity. Often the important thing seems to be who you are, not what you're saying – witness news readers and commentators. It is crucial that someone introduces you, that you introduce yourself, read the necessary news, then sign off again with more self-promotion. Who cares? Weather reporters (or chief meteorologists as they are known in America) can be equally image-conscious. Bring back Ian McCaskill and Francis Wilson, who just get on with telling us what we need to know, holding our attention without the gloss.

Children's Viewing

I was becoming depressed at the way William was gluing himself to the couch and remote control at any given moment he was home. Not only that, but when you said something or tried to engage him in conversation he would totally blank you, he was so fixated on the box. We had a basement full of toys and he was spending most of his time watching channel 49 (The Learning Channel). Besides that, the 78-channel cable package we had taken over from our predecessors (pretty standard out there) was a bit much to flick through. So we took the plunge and scaled right back down to the basic package of channels 1 to 26. We lost the cartoon network and I anticipated uproar. Instead I was shocked when the first evening after the household cut, William came home from school and offered to help me clean the fridge and tidy the bedrooms. The next evening he wanted me to sit with him and go through his school work folder, and then went off on his own to play quietly with toys. He didn't even want to put on a kid's video or DVD – and we had borrowed a stack from the library in anticipation of withdrawal symptoms. I was so relieved. No more having to listen to attitudinal heroines, strutting about in short skirts, saying 'Whatever', 'That's *so* not cool' and other 'clever' comments. Kids these days are bombarded with this repetitive, poor language and unrealistic portrayal of human abilities and looks. My advice to anyone with kids is, if possible, don't expose them to it more than necessary. Family communication can be hard enough as it is. Moreover, per annum the average American child watches 10,000 food commercials; 95% of these are for soft drinks, fast-food, sugared cereals and sweets. If you are at all health conscious, this might be another reason to limit TV viewing.

PBS Kids offers a fun, educational channel, which you can let your kids watch without any worries. By way of research for this book, I sat through several Saturday mornings of children's television to see what was on offer. I can report that *Bob the Builder* is alive and well, speaking American and saying things like, 'That looks awesome' and 'Let's go, guys'; Spud and Mr. Pickles have retained their annoying English accents. The music is jazzed up and the scenery is more colourful and detailed.

Thomas the Tank Engine is equally popular in America, shown on PBS and Fox Family Channel. Day Out With Thomas, sponsored by HIT Entertainment, is a US tour involving real trains modelled on Thomas, held at many historic railroads.

Other peculiar American series include:

- *The Berenstain Bears.* Dressed in dungarees and long dresses, their country exploits always end in a good moralistic message. The theme tune is catchy too.
- *Barney*, a purple dinosaur, is popular with pre-school children, both in the US and UK.
- *Dragon Tales*, *Maya and Miguel* and *Dora the Explorer* mix English and Spanish for bilingual education and entertainment. *Dora* is currently the most-watched pre-school show in America, with a huge commercial merchandise spin-off.
- *Clifford the Big Red Dog* is based on the 1963 book series by Norman Bridwell, teaches children life lessons and is very popular.
- *Jakers! The Adventures of Piggley Winks* is the story of a grandfather pig that lives in America and recounts stories to his grandchildren about his childhood in Ireland in the 1950s. As well as showing in the States, it is broadcast on BBC2 and in Ireland, and even translated into Scottish Gaelic for Scottish viewers.
- *Foster's Home for Imaginary Friends* has won four Emmy awards since first showing in 2004. It is broadcast on Cartoon Network and its affiliates worldwide.
- *Sesame Street* began in 1969 and has produced over 4000 episodes, making it one of the longest running TV shows. Broadcast in 120 countries, it is a highly regarded educational show for kids, and has received more Emmy Awards than any other TV series.

Shows that appeal to both kids and adults include the *The Simpsons* (first broadcast in 1989) and *South Park* (1997). *The Simpsons* is a satire of American culture and society, and even television itself. Religion is a staple of many of the episodes, with the Simpsons portraying a typical middle-American family's values. *South Park* parodies pop culture and current events and often relies on shock value and controversy. *Sponge Bob Square Pants* is very funny too, with plenty of adult humour.

The Bane of Commercials

As far as American television viewing is concerned, I'm with Groucho Marx when he says, 'I find TV very educational. Every time someone switches it on I go into another room and read a good book'. It is quite difficult to enjoy watching something on TV when it is continually interrupted by commercials and adverts for what's coming on next. I have even watched people playing a card game before telling us we can continue watching the film after the following commercials. All this may last 4 minutes or so, and the interruptions can average one every 12 minutes during a film. Rod Sterling (American writer, famous for his TV series *The Twilight Zone*) said:

> 'It is difficult to produce a television documentary that is both incisive and probing when every twelve minutes one is interrupted by twelve dancing rabbits singing about toilet paper.'

How true. When flicking through channels it often appears that all that is showing is adverts; you have to wait for them to finish before you can see the actual programme that is on. During one episode of *The Simpsons*, after rolling the introductory credits, the show was stopped while we had 4 minutes of commercials. Then the show really started – at least for 4 minutes – then another load of commercials came on, including a quick weather forecast. We were then allowed a whopping 8 minutes of show, followed by 4 minutes of ads, ending with another 8 minutes of show. That's the sort of programming that really makes my teeth grind, Marge-style.

The first TV commercial aired in 1941 before a baseball game between the New York Brooklyn Dodgers and Philadelphia Phillies. Today, on average, a 1-hour American show will include 18 minutes of commercial time, and, as described above, some half-hour blocks come with a staggering 12 minutes of ads (though 8 minutes is more normal). Television is geared towards the needs of the advertisers. My suggestion is to buy a recorder that fast-forwards through commercial breaks on play-back, so you can sit and watch your favourite shows later without interruption.

Movies

An American, Thomas Edison, invented the movies in 1889. *The Great Train Robbery* (1903) was the first movie that told a story, followed by *The Birth of a Nation* in 1915 (a Civil War epic). Charlie Chaplin, Mary Pickford and Rudolf Valentino were stars of the silent era, which marked the beginning of Hollywood's Golden Age. During the Great Depression, audiences flocked to the silver screen as an escape from every-day life. At the height of popularity of the movies, 400 films a year were produced by Hollywood's studios. They were mostly Westerns, musicals, slapstick comedies, animated cartoons and biographical pictures.

Then came television. Also, in 1948, the federal antitrust act was passed, removing the right of studios to own their own theatres and hold exclusivity rights on which theatres could show their films. This opened up the way for independent producers and studios to produce films free of big studio interference. Thus saw the rise of independent films (low budget, niche films) and blockbusters (which made use of the widescreen to compete successfully with TV). Steven Spielberg, Martin Scorsese, George Lucas, Francis Ford Coppola and Brian de Palma excelled with their spectacular films, as did independent producers Quentin Tarantino, Kevin Smith, Steven Soderbergh and Spike Lee.

Today, home entertainment systems are becoming increasingly lavish, with even the averagely large American home giving over an entire room to sophisticated and expensive equipment. The home theatre craze involves a dedicated room with a projector and movie screen, or a large-screen and/or high-definition TV, and usually a high-fidelity surround-sound system.

Netflix is the world's largest online DVD rental service, with 60,000 titles to choose from (allegedly five times as many as typical video stores). Online you browse and select the movies you want to watch, send in your wish list, and Netflix starts sending out your choices, one or more at a time. It offers various monthly plans; for instance, you can rent one DVD at a time an unlimited number of times each month for $9.99. There are no late fees, due dates or other commitments, and shipping is free. DVDs are delivered to your door within one working day. What could be easier? There are organised subject selections, so you can home-in on the categories you enjoy – be it classics, new releases, children and family, or even gay and lesbian – whatever your inclination. Netflix is only available in the States and on US military bases overseas. Blockbuster in America now offers a similar online service, but you can return media to your local store to save time.

Drive-In Theatres

As multiplex indoor cinemas are becoming increasingly sophisticated and expensive, that classic American icon – the drive-in movie theatre – has enjoyed a resurgence. Their attractions are as follows:

- They often have a larger screen than indoor counterparts.
- Their concession stands charge snack bar prices, which are much better value than the food and drink prices at indoor venues (which are often ridiculously high), or of course you can bring your own refreshments.
- Ticket prices are very reasonable; children are usually charged only a couple of bucks or get in free.
- Some charge by the car load, e.g. $5–10 per car.
- You can often see two or three movies for the price of one.
- Some have children's play areas.
- You can sit in the comfort of your car, enjoying the stereo sound picked up by your car radio.
- They appeal to romantics and nostalgia lovers.

For a list of drive-in movie theatres in your state, see *Useful Websites*. Some are open year round, but many only operate during the summer months, especially in colder states. Another snag is that showings often start quite late in the evening, especially during the summer, as they have to wait for darkness to fall. So if you have young children, the lateness of the hour may deter you from going to a drive-in.

Radio

WKRP in Cincinnati was a popular radio workplace TV sitcom show broadcast between 1978 and 1982, which received Emmy Awards for its comedy. Radio broadcasters are each assigned a three- or four-letter call name: those east of the Mississippi River start with 'W', those west with 'K'. NPR (National Public Radio) provides good debates, classical music and other intellectual listening outlets. You will hear less news and fewer time checks on American music stations than on BBC radio, as they prefer to air more music. Most of the talk shows are on low-frequency AM, most of the music on high-powered FM. For a monthly fee ($12.95 at the time of writing) you can subscribe to one of two satellite radio services – the relatively new Sirius Satellite or XM Radio. They offer music channels free of commercials, as well as BBC World Service broadcasts, and are becoming very popular as people grow tired of regular radio.

American Styles of Music

The blues, jazz and swing, country, and rock and roll are distinctly American forms of music. Country music may be all you can pick up in certain parts of the country (e.g. the South). Christian rock music is also very popular. Weekend music festivals and outdoor concerts in the park are held throughout the summer, usually free. The discussion that follows is an overview of American styles of music, and how they developed and evolved into the popular forms of music listened to in the US today.

The Blues

The blues has its roots in the mournful spiritual music of African slaves (it is music to work to). Hymns, psalms and folk songs were examples of some of the first vernacular music (music we sing and hear naturally) in America. However, because there are no documented collections – it was all handed down by oral tradition – it is hard to say what the music was really like. Spirituals, or religious folk songs, evolved outside of an established church. They represented a source of hope and communication by the slaves in early America, employing coded messages hidden in the text.

Jazz and Swing

The blended pitches and rhythmic/syncopated elements of the blues led to the archetypal American music called jazz. Jazz is a performance style that developed among black musicians during the 1910s to 1920s. It has gone through many developments, but has certain common characteristics:

(1) improvisation – musicians do not play how the music is written, but how they hear it;
(2) embellishments – like the baroque idea of ornamentation;
(3) syncopation – a special rhythmic device that shifts where we feel the accent (the back beat in jazz lingo).

Many people in the early 1900s considered jazz as vulgar music, with its sexual connotations, different energy and feelings strongly influenced by racism. A particular form of New Orleans jazz known as swing developed in the early 1930s as jazz became more popular and adjusted in order to appeal to more people. Today in contemporary jazz or pop music, musicians pull from many sources and it is difficult to categorise the music exactly.

Country Music

If you don't want to listen to country music on a road trip south, have some CDs handy. Country music encompasses a number of styles of music, according to Wikipedia (with the names of some popular artists in parentheses):

- Appalachian.
- Bakersfield sound (Buck Owens and Merle Haggard) – stemming from California.
- Bluegrass (Bill Monroe) – see discussion below.
- Country rock (Linda Ronstadt, Neil Young, the Everly Brothers, the Eagles, the Byrds, Grateful Dead).
- Evangelical gospel.
- Honky tonk (Fats Domino, Hank Williams) – piano playing related to ragtime, melded with rockabilly into rock 'n' roll.
- Nashville pop.
- Outlaw (Willie Nelson, Kris Kristofferson, Hank Williams).
- Western cowboy campfire ballads.
- Western swing dance music (Bob Wills) – music strictly for line and square dancing.

The term country music is used in preference to country and western. Jimmie Rodgers and the Carter Family are said to be the founders of country music back in 1927. Jimmie sang about life and death from a male perspective, while the Carter Family, rural country folk, collected songs and ballads from the hill country of Virginia, and were the precursors of well-known female country singers such as Kitty Wells, Dolly Parton, Tammy Wynette, Faith Hill and Shania Twain. Country music is rooted in old-time, gospel, the blues, Celtic and traditional folk music from the southern states. At least three cable networks are devoted to playing country music, testament to its enduring appeal, and country music bars are popular throughout the US. American folk music (also known as Americana or roots music, because it was the basis of other forms of music which developed in the States) was especially prevalent during the early 1900s, and later made popular by musicians such as John Denver and Peter, Paul and Mary.

Bluegrass

Kentucky bluegrass music has Scots–Irish Appalachian origins. It combines folk, gospel, country and ballads, using guitar, fiddle, banjo and mandolin, sometimes also with the harmonica or autoharp. No drums, no electronics, just harmonisation and a driving rhythm. The skill in playing bluegrass music lies in clever improvisation and speed of playing. The music combines the universal themes of faith, love and honest work. Born in the Bluegrass state of Kentucky and neighbouring areas in the 1930s, today it is popular worldwide and attracts thousands of people to its festivals. People gather at campgrounds, share supper and jam late into the evening. The traditional dance of 'clogging', a mix of Irish step and tap dancing, often accompanies the music. Some retirees spend their whole summer on the festival circuit. The soundtrack entitled *Man of Constant Sorrow* to *O Brother, Where Art Thou?* (a film set in Mississippi during the Depression, which features bluegrass music) became a surprising hit. Well, it does star George Clooney.

Rock and Roll

In the 1950s, rock and roll, a fusion of white and black music, hit America. It was originally a mix of rhythm and blues, gospel and country music. With its boogie woogie blues rhythm and heavy back beat, it quickly became popular, especially among teenagers. In the 1940s' big band era, the piano was the lead instrument; then the saxophone took over, later replaced by the guitar, as the music developed. It is difficult to put a finger on when the music first started up, and it may be that white rock and roll stars have overshadowed black innovators. It occurred at a period in America's history when concern for racial inequality was at the forefront of American culture. The Ku Klux Klan took umbrage against the music and tried to put it down, seeing it as a threat to racial segregation because it brought black and white youths together.

Elvis Presley emerged as king of American rock and roll in the 1950s, though Bill Haley vies for the distinction of being the first rock 'n' roll star. Other well-known early rock stars were Little Richard, Johnny Ray, Carl Perkins, Johnny Cash, Jerry Lee Lewis and Chuck Berry. The music quickly spread to other countries, and in 1964 the British Invasion brought the Beatles, Dave Clark 5, Rolling Stones, The Kinks, Cream and The Who (to name a few) to America's attention.

Hip Hop

In the early 1970s, a particular style of music based on the Jamaican practice of 'toasting' (chatting over a rhythm or beat) became popular. Hip hop music as it came to be known is said to have originated in The Bronx with DJ Kool Herc, as part of the hip hop culture. Many of the lyrics are political, sexual, macho, poetic, slang and/or promoting a criminal or gangster image. Ice-T, Snoop Dogg, Public Enemy and Eminem are some well-known rappers and hip hop musicians. The music employs a repeated beat, over which the emcees (rappers) rap. Scratching is a component of the music, using two turntables simultaneously to produce a distinctive sound, a demonstration of a DJ's skill.

Libraries

I have to include libraries in this chapter because, if not, you might miss out on one of the greatest free sources of entertainment available. Our local library became a favourite family haunt. It acted as a free source of films, music CDs, magazines and newspapers, computers and let's not forget books – all available without cost, as long as you returned things on time. Borrowing movies, documentaries, comedies, concerts, self-help, travel and other videos/DVDs is a real boon if you're fed up watching television with commercial interruptions.

Throughout the year, particular themes were used to promote reading and thinking. For example, on St Patrick's Day a plethora of Irish books would appear in the theme part of the library; at Halloween, a selection of spooky reads and viewings were on display. At odd times of the year, the kids could sit down at a little picnic table with resident teddy bears and enjoy a teddy bears' picnic while reading bear books, or sit in the wigwam and read books about Indians – how those bears and picnic toys never went missing, I don't know. A large room was devoted to children, with bean bags, cuddly toys and fish tanks. Youngsters casually sat around with their shoes off, books spread out, or were (more usually) engrossed in interactive games on the computers. There were story readings for different ages, quizzes and competitions, give-aways such as meal vouchers at local restaurants, arts and crafts and other activities throughout the year, all at no charge and designed to encourage children to use the library and instill a love of reading and learning. A permanent table and chairs with a different activity each week, usually based on a particular book or subject, meant you and the children could spend a good hour just sitting in the library playing and learning. Around Father's Day, they even supplied cards for the children to colour in and personalise (what a god-send for mums).

During the long summer holiday, all the libraries in our state agreed on a theme designed to encourage the children to visit the library. They provided cards with a list of fun activities and projects for you and the children, involving books, music, drawing, the internet, imagination and learning new skills. Once completed, children could choose a free book and/or be entered in a prize draw. At the end of the summer reading programme, there was a party with cake, party bags and lucky dips. I couldn't believe we didn't have to pay for any of it.

Grown-up visitors to the library are well catered for too. There were computer courses, book searches and free reservations, 'Friends of the Library' special events and regular book sales. You can access your membership details online, renewing borrowed media yourself and requesting the library to reserve any item from the catalogue or library system. I couldn't help thinking how much more used our libraries back in Britain would be if they could only offer some of this atmosphere, accessibility and free resources. Compared with our local library back home in Dorset (which had nothing going on for the children and where you have to pay for everything), American libraries are far superior.

Books and Magazines

Aside from the great free selection of magazines and newspapers available in American libraries, personal subscriptions to magazines are a fraction of the cost compared to back home. We took advantage of some amazing deals – offered through our credit card, on the internet and others that landed in the mailbox. If you are thinking of subscribing, shop around for the best deal. We had about six magazine subscriptions on the go in the States for about the same price of one in the UK. When you want to renew a subscription, a tip is to hold out; if you sound reluctant, you will often be offered a 'special' price or 'super discount' in a bid to keep your custom. A plethora of interesting (and, to a Brit, unusual) magazines are published in America. One word of caution though: some familiar British titles are not the same in American format. For instance, I was disappointed with the American version of *Country Living* – which is full of advertisements and superficial articles (in comparison with the British version, which has better depth to its features); it was more of a coffee-table magazine than one containing useful information.

Americans also get a better deal when buying books, the dollar price on the cover often being 25% cheaper than the price in pounds sterling. If you have a literary appetite, you may find a book discussion group that meets locally. Subjects include the classics, spiritual awareness, gardening, self-help, mystery (for instance, our local bookshop had an Agatha Christie club), romance, teen and science fiction. I joined a Great Books Foundation discussion group which met every 3 weeks in the library to discuss short stories, extracts from longer books and poetry. It challenged me to read and talk about some things I would never have thought to tackle on my own. Book clubs are very popular and held at different venues, including libraries, churches, bookstores and in people's homes. Once a year a book is chosen as the national 'Big Read', with public discussions aimed at promoting reading and community.

American book shops are popular places to arrange a meeting (social or otherwise). Some open late into the evening (11 p.m. or so) and are a great place to hang out, enjoy a cuppa, browse magazines or books without having to buy, surf the internet, even listen to some live music; all in all, a very civilised way of passing the time. Sign up as a book store member and receive discounts on all purchases, including coffee. Many also offer writers groups, readers groups and literary talks.

Newspapers

It is difficult to find a quality national newspaper in America (I speak from personal experience and also this is the opinion of many American friends). The most popular newspapers read nationally are *USA Today*, the *New York Times* and *Washington Post*. The sensational tabloids – *The Star*, *National Enquirer* and *Weekly World News* – are routinely sued for slander and libel by celebrities. However, unlike their British counterparts, you won't find any swear words (or asterisks) printed, and no nudity or Page Three girls. *The Wall Street Journal* is available Monday to Friday, primarily catering for business readers. It carries business and economic news, and political commentary as it affects the financial world. *USA Today* is probably the most popular read of the general population, but it is not much above the standard of *The National Enquirer*. The *Christian Science Monitor* is a well-respected publication. *The Wall Street Journal* and *New York Times* are famous for their crossword puzzles, and regularly produce Pulitzer-Prize-winning media writers.

It is also possible to subscribe to the US edition of *The Times*, which offers readers the best of international news, business, arts and sports, and good commentary on world and British politics. *The Week* also gives good US and international media coverage for the past week. It has the same format as the British version of the same name, but is geared towards the US market. If you miss the UK/European angles, subscribe to the British version. *The Weekly Telegraph* is also worth considering.

Home Crafts

Arts and crafts, stamping, scrapbooking, quilting and other handicraft projects are very popular in the States. Americans like to make things. They have fantastically big, all-encompassing craft stores, which are a real inspiration, with every imaginable crafty thing you can think of – and more. Some even offer summer school programmes for the children, or a room and craft project for birthday parties. Home crafts are especially popular with stay-at-home mums and retired people; working women and those living in more rural areas may not have the time luxury. Sewing and knitting are making a comeback, perhaps because today people are so busy and information overloaded, they are looking for quieter pursuits. It is common to see women knitting on the train or when waiting in a queue.

Scrapbooking

Allegedly, there are now more scrapbookers than golfers in America, such is the popularity of the hobby. Although scrapbooking has been around since the time of photographs, in America it has grown to be a multi-billion dollar money-making business (Americans are good at creating businesses). People meet together to scrapbook; they have house parties, go on courses and retreats, to conventions, even on special scrapbooking cruises. Scrapbooking is a way to preserve a personal history, hand-make a gift for someone, or simply to meet and socialise. You can buy materials from many large general stores, most craft suppliers, specialist scrapbooking outlets and over the internet (see *Useful Websites*).

Quilting

The art and skill of quilting is still thriving in America. In the early days, fabric was a premium material, which only arrived by boat after a long wait. In the meantime, and if you couldn't afford the high prices for cloth, women would cut worn-out clothing into little patchwork pieces and sew them together. Quilting was a domestic necessity for these frugal pioneers, but it also acted as a social outlet. Groups of women would gather together to work on communal pieces, often as a gift for a new bride. This was known as a quilting bee. Someone might read to the group while they were stitching, or they would discuss some topic of interest. With great variety and skill, they produced blankets, bedspreads, wall-hangings (in the old days these were of practical use, to keep the homes warm) and other useful household items. The Amish still do this today.

Quilters these days continue to use their skills and imagination to make house-warming gifts. Most of the blocks are traditional, originating from American folk law. The back of the quilt should be as pretty as the front. Some ladies hand stitch the whole thing, others machine stitch, while some employ a half and half method. Quilting guilds meet regularly. There are quilting shows – especially throughout Ohio, Kentucky and Illinois – where spectacular pieces of craft are shown. Some quilters become famous and go on to sell books, lessons, etc. Others do it simply for fun and the social aspect. Still others are compulsive collectors, with whole rooms turned over to their craft – shelves stuffed with fats (the small pieces of cloth used in quilting or appliqué), sewing machines, patterns and books. It can become a bit of an obsession.

Conclusion

Sport in America is more popular and heavily funded than the arts, and is inseparably mixed up with commercialism. Museums, theatres and other venues for the arts are always begging for money, and often have to charge high admission prices to make ends meet, thus pricing themselves out of the general market (and so the funding problem becomes self-perpetuating). In contrast, the quality, availability and free use of public sporting facilities are impressive and astounding.

The American love of sport is testament to their upbeat psyche:

> 'I always turn to the sports page first, which records people's accomplishments. The front page has nothing but man's failures.' (Chief Justice Earl Warren, 1953–1969)

They have halls of fame for just about everything. They know how to enjoy themselves, and have a great recreational and sporting culture, even in the colder states. Events and activities go on year-round, and there is no excuse for staying home.

On the subject of home entertainment, Jim provides a good summation on American television:

> America is awash with TV, both with the quantity of screens and number of channels. To test your resilience to sensory overload just spend time in a sports bar, where a multitude of screens show matches of different sports – well, normally just the 'big 3': basketball, baseball and American football – all with the sound turned up. Satellite and cable channels now number in the hundreds, but sadly quantity has come at the expense of quality, which has been stretched to fit. A large number of channels offer reality TV, where any sort of banality can be wrapped up and delivered to a niche audience. One of our local channels covered meetings of the Beavercreek City Council, such a hit that repeats are unhappily easy to find. Another of more mainstream appeal is the Weather Channel which has expanded the 30-second weather report, so often the stalwart of quality news programmes, to fill an entire 24 hours. While this might test the ability of the presenting meteorologists to find different and interesting words to describe the weather, it is also distressingly fascinating. While many programmes have the intellectual content of a tin of peas, most are designed with a strong hook so they are startlingly addictive. Once a programme starts, you must tear yourself away within the first few minutes; otherwise you're hooked until it ends. Sadly, this means enduring endless repeats of even the simplest information and commercials, which, of course, is the reason why many channels exist.

Useful Websites

www.answers.com/topic/list-of-halls-and-walks-of-fame – list of halls and walks of fame.
www.driveinmovie.com – list of drive-in movie theatres according to state.
www.greatbooks.org – the Great Books Foundation.
www.huntingtripsrus.com – hunting information.
www.neabigread.org – the Big Read initiative.
www.netflix.com – rent movies by post or watch online.
www.news.bbc.co.uk – key in 'NFL in a nutshell' for a simple guide to the basics of American football.
www.quiltguilds.com – find your local quilt guild.
www.radio-locator.com – find your local radio station.

www.scrapbooks.com – ideas and materials for scrapbooking.
www.telegraph.co.uk/global – *The Weekly Telegraph* for expats.
www.theweekdaily.com – overview of and subscription to *The Week.*
www.timesonline.co.uk – global edition of *The Times* online.

15 · Religion

According to Pew Global Attitudes Research, 59% of Americans feel that religion is 'very important' in their lives (compared to 33% of people in Britain); moreover, Gallup International reported that 41% of Americans said they regularly attend church (compared with just 7% of British citizens). Indeed, more Americans believe in God and regularly attend church services than in any other developed country. The Barna Group conducts surveys each year in order to report on faith issues and cultural trends. In their 2005 random survey of 1003 adults, spread evenly over the 48 contiguous states, they found that more than 9 out of 10 American adults engaged in some form of faith-related practice each week, and that 45% read the Bible outside of church (up from 31% in 1995). The increase was mostly seen in the baby-boomer generation and those living in western states, especially Evangelical and born-again Christians.

The prominence of religion does vary according to where you live. In the South, it is a very dominant influence, and if you do not go to church, you may suffer prejudice. Religion there is instrumental in local politics, which is why many places in the South are 'dry'. The Bible Belt (which extends up into the states of the Midwest) is an area known for its fundamentalist Protestantism (where people interpret the Bible literally). The majority of people are Evangelical, especially Southern Baptist. Also, in the Midwest, people are openly religious and belong to church groups. Everywhere you go you see car stickers proclaiming 'Jesus lives', quotations from the Bible plastered on boards in people's gardens, or three bare crosses rising up out of front lawns. In the North, religion is much less pervasive, though most people adhere to one faith or another. They tend to be members of more liberal Christian denominations. On the East and West Coasts, people may be more earthy and spiritual, with alternative beliefs and 'religions'. Indeed, the West Coast is said to be relatively agnostic.

The Allure of the Church

Why then is religion such an important element in American society? Below I suggest several reasons for the appeal of the church:

- Most Americans have grown up with religion, attending church as children with their families. Therefore they are comfortable with it.
- Many of those first settlers came to the New World in order to practise religious freedom; from those early people, the basis of American society was formed.
- Many people today feel an emptiness in their lives. Americans like to have 'carrots' – get good grades in school so you can progress to the right university; earn good grades at university so you can get a good job; get the right job so you can afford to live in the right place; live in the right place so you can meet and marry the right person; work hard so you can afford to buy that big house and have everything that goes with it. This constant striving for the American Dream can lead to a void, which they look to fill through religion and their church.
- Aside from fulfilling a spiritual need, many churches offer recreational facilities and social activities far beyond any that we encounter in Britain. For example, children's classes during services, men and women's ministries, singles groups, exciting youth programmes and senior activities, community centres, cafés, bookstores, discipleship classes and mission work, counseling and support groups, even online sermons – they've really got it nailed down. Many view their church as a social outlet, a kind of religious country club.

Members of a church happily pay a tithe of 10% of their earnings to their particular house of worship. This money goes to charities at home (for instance, to people in the church community who may be in trouble physically and/or financially) and abroad (e.g. aiding disaster victims). A large part is also spent on church facilities, amenities and salaries. Some churches offer children's centres and day care facilities. My little girl joined a pre-school connected with a church, with better facilities than some of the franchised nurseries in the area. We did not have to be members of the church to use the school, or even profess to believe in God. We chose the school because we admired the messages of love and discipline the school was instilling in its children; many other facilities not connected to a church were big on love, encouragement and freedom (as Americans generally are) but lacked discipline, for example in making the children join in with lessons.

The rather derogatory term *McChurches* has been coined when describing some houses of worship that seem to be more entertainment orientated than spiritual. Protestant Christian, Southern Baptist, Evangelical and Pentecostal faiths in particular tend to go in for mega-churches. Their huge auditoriums look more like entertainment palaces than church halls. They often use stage lighting, video projections, a sophisticated audio system and professional musicians, who play a popular-style of praise music. Well, if you typically cater for 2000 or so worshipers per weekly service, you probably need some gizmos. They employ individual seating facilities (no pews) and choreograph services, where worshipers are more audience than participants. Many have cafés, stores, gyms and McDonald's-style play areas for the kids. They may also offer extra-curricular activities, including support groups and mission groups, and other facilities not directly linked to worship, such as foreign language classes, sports, music and dance classes. How can small, traditional churches compete with all this? It's no wonder that the latter have trouble attracting 'customers'. As one church member put it, 'People today, they have to be entertained'.

Critics refer to mega-churches as 'fast-food Christianity', having succumbed to commercialisation and consumerism – representing the recent move towards the population being more self-centred. Others see them as too middle of the road. Yet many people do not formally align themselves to an established denomination, and there may not even be a cross in their church rooms. Such churches welcome people from different faiths and with different political views. They appeal especially to the baby-boomers, who favour the movement away from authority. Moreover, anonymity has its appeal; in a large crowd nobody knows your business.

Large plots of prime urban land are often given over to churches, of all denominations; and with their huge car parks and buildings, they seem to reflect the US trend for urban sprawl. Most of these churches provide an impressive number of daily services, and many of these services are packed, with standing room only. Thus the size of church buildings and car parks often looks astounding, until you realise that they are regularly filled with cars and people at peak times.

Different Faiths

Our local Dayton *Yellow Book* (the equivalent of the UK's *Yellow Pages*) had a huge section devoted to churches (18 pages in fact). Compare this with little over one page in our local British *Yellow Pages* (for Bournemouth) and you can perhaps appreciate the difference in the importance placed on religion in America versus Britain. Indeed, the United States has more religious groups than any other country. National figures (taken from the CIA *The World Factbook*, 2002 Census data) reveal that:

- 52% of Americans are Protestant (including Presbyterian, Lutheran, Baptist, Methodist, Episcopalian, Pentecostal and Evangelical)
- 24% are Roman Catholic
- 2% are Mormon
- 1% are Jewish
- 1% are Muslim
- 10% are other
- 10% are none.

Compare this with UK figures (from the 2001 UK Census) of around the same number (71.6%) Christian (Anglican, Roman Catholic, Presbyterian, Methodist), 2.7% Muslim, 1% Hindu, only 1.6% other, and 23.1% unspecified or none – more than twice the number of Americans.

The Predominant Bible-Based Faiths in America

Presbyterians

The North American Presbyterian church is rooted in the 1560 Scottish Reformation, led by John Knox and based on Calvinism. The church is governed by representatives of the local congregation – presbyters, made up of elders and ministers. Presbyterianism emphasises the authority of the Bible, sovereignty of God, and importance of grace through faith in Jesus Christ. There are many Presbyterian colleges and seminaries in the States. Ronald Reagan, Mark Twain and John Wayne were all Presbyterians. In England and Wales, the Presbyterian church is now known as the United Reform Church.

Lutherans

In 1517, a German monk, Martin Luther, broke from the Roman Catholic church and launched the Protestant Reformation. His followers believe that we are all sinners (having descended from Adam and Eve and original sin), and that the only way to achieve salvation is by grace alone. They believe the Bible is the word of God and the final authority on all things. They practise infant baptism, and nearly all have Sunday schools. In America, many Lutheran churches also have private nursery schools, and operate schools for older children – from primary right up to university. Services are usually very musical. Lee Harvey Oswald, Karl Marx and Immanuel Kant were Lutherans. The faith is especially dominant in North and South Dakota.

Baptists

Baptists openly and vociferously praise God, with affirmations of 'Amen' and 'Hallelujah'. They practise religious liberty, believing that each person is free to choose what his or her soul or conscience dictates is right. They also believe that any Christian can directly access God – it doesn't need to be through a priest. Each Baptist church is governed democratically by its congregation, not by any national council; this accounts for the often varied beliefs and doctrines. Believers have to publically profess their faith before they can be baptised; hence, young children are not counted as members of the church or baptised until such time as they fully understand what they are entering into.

There are an estimated 47 million Baptists in America, and the Southern Baptist Convention is the largest Baptist association in the world. The Baptist church is said to be the second fastest growing Christian denomination in the world, after Pentecostals. Bill Clinton, Aretha Franklin and Eddie Murphy are Baptists.

Methodists

The Methodist movement began in 1729 with John Wesley and a group of Oxford friends meeting to discuss the perceived apathy in the Church of England and to find ways for mutual improvement. They focused on Bible study and Christian living. Methodists believe that all people can be saved, through loving your neighbour. Thus social services, education and missionary work are important components of their faith. The Salvation Army was founded by a Methodist. The church is run on an organised basis, with bishops, ministers and pastors, and services are characterised by enthusiastic sermons and singing. There are approximately 20 universities and colleges in America that call themselves Methodist or Wesleyan. Delaware has the highest number of Methodists. Hillary Clinton, Stephen King and George Lucas are Methodists.

Episcopalians

The Episcopalian faith is an American branch of the Church of England, which follows 'the middle way' between Roman Catholic and Protestant. Robin Williams, as an Episcopalian, describes his faith as 'Catholic Lite' or 'same religion, half the guilt'. The Episcopalian Church (TEC), often abbreviated to ECUSA (for the Episcopalian Church in the USA), has a democratic structure, being both liberal and conservative. It uses real wine (not grape juice) in the Eucharist, which is open to all baptised Christians.

There are around 2.5 million Episcopalians throughout America, but only 800,000 or so attend Sunday services. With more than 7000 congregations and 111 dioceses in the US, Episcopalians are pretty well spread, though the North-East has more than its share, and there is a WASP connection. Despite this, most Episcopalians see racism as a sin, and are both progressive and liberal, for instance allowing the ordination of women and homosexuals, non-celibate priests and same-sex unions. TEC believes homosexuals are children of God and entitled to full civil rights, yet it is divided over the issue of abortion. They are quietly religious, believing religion to be a private matter. More than a quarter of America's presidents were Episcopalian, including George H.W. Bush; the current president, George W. Bush, originally followed his father's faith but is now Methodist.

Pentecostals

The Pentecostal church has its origins in North Carolina at the end of the nineteenth century. Pentecostals believe in a personal experience with God through baptism and in physical evidence that the Holy Spirit has entered a person. (According to the Bible, the Apostles received the Holy Spirit, and this is celebrated on the Day of Pentecost.) The religion received greater attention in 1901 when a woman at a prayer meeting at bible college in Kansas apparently received the gift of tongues (falling on the ground in a convulsion and babbling). 'Speaking in tongues' may also take the form of miraculous signs, healing, prophesying, a person falling on the ground as if asleep, and so on. The church in America has now grown to an estimated 20 million members, including a large number of Hispanics and African-Americans. It is said by *Christianity Today* to be a 'vibrant faith among the poor'.

Evangelical Christians

Evangelical Christians believe that the Bible is the word of God without error. They practise evangelism or the spreading of the gospel. Evangelism emphasises individual conversion – being saved or born again (hence the term 'born-again Christians'). They have strong alliance with the Methodist and Anglican faiths, the Quakers and Congregationalists. Most Evangelicals live in the South, and the least number in the North-East.

The origin of Evangelism is said to be London, when, in 1846, the Evangelical Alliance was formed. The movement has always been politically active and right wing; for example, it was involved in women's rights and suffrage, in advocating prohibition and the temperance society, and in anti-immigration. Yet surprisingly it was basically the only religious group that did not join in the civil rights movement. Today, Evangelists devote much time and effort to welfare and social issues, providing help groups, study centres, marriage counselling, and so on. Billy Graham (a Southern Baptist) leads large meetings and is a very public crusader of Evangelism.

Roman Catholics

Catholicism was brought to North America by Spanish explorers in 1513, and by English settlers coming to Maryland in 1634. European immigrants arriving in great numbers during the nineteenth and early twentieth centuries swelled the ranks. Today there are an estimated 77 million Catholics in America, which represents the third largest Catholic population in the world, after Brazil and Mexico. The states with the highest proportion of Catholic citizens are Rhode Island, Massachusetts, New Mexico, New Jersey, Vermont and New York. Almost 20,000 churches provide Catholic services, with masses often held all weekend, and 'last chance mass' on Sundays as late as 10 p.m. Only one US president has been Catholic – J.F.K. According to a 2004 poll by the Barna Group, 60% of Catholics are Caucasian (a high proportion Irish), 31% Hispanic, only 4% black and 5% of other ethnicity. Catholics, along with Lutherans and Methodists, have a disproportionately high number of older members.

Mormons

Mormonism is a home-grown religion, established in 1820 in Upper New York State. Local suspicion based on the Mormon practice of secrecy and polygamy resulted in persecution and warring with locals, forcing the Mormons to begin their exodus west – one of the largest mass migrations of people in the history of America. (Although the church renounced polygamy in 1890, the practice still lives on among some fundamentalist followers, and this has been an enduring stain on the Mormon's reputation.) Headed by various dictators, the Mormons (aka Latter Day Saints) eventually found refuge in the Great Salt Lake Valley, Utah, which they proclaimed as the Garden of Eden. Today, Salt Lake City is their headquarters, centred in what is known as the Jello Belt, a term coined from the fact that Mormons love Jell-O (in fact, Jell-O is Utah's official state snack food). Parts of Nevada, Arizona, Wyoming and Idaho also lie in this Belt. As a rite of passage, young men give up 2 years of their lives to missionary work (at home and/or overseas), and today the Mormon religion has over 12 million members worldwide (though the conversion rate is dropping); in fact, there are now more Mormons overseas than in America.

Some of their doctrines and ideals are as follows:

- The Mormon religion is intent on establishing a New Jerusalem and spreading the word to others.
- Mormons are asked to contribute 10% of their wealth and a great deal of time to their church.
- They live under strict rules, with conversion involving radical transformation of their lives.
- Mormons are very preoccupied with the family. Women try to be perfect wives and mothers, bearing heavy responsibility for the eternal salvation of the family; they nurture the children and are always subordinate to the men. They are hard on people who are divorced, gay or without children, as the family is the spiritual core.
- They believe in a collective moral responsibility, not individualism.
- Questioning authority is taboo. So is feminism and intellectualism, as elders see it as a danger to the church, and you risk being excommunicated. Trouble-makers and dissenters are logged and have a file kept on them (of all the religions in the world, Mormonism is unique in this respect).
- Many Mormons still crave distinction and separateness from mainstream society.

In 2004, Steven Greenstreet produced a documentary called *This Divided State*. It centred on the visit by speaker Michael Moore to Utah Valley State College, and the huge ruckus the decision to allow him to come to Utah caused. Seventy five percent of Utah's population is Mormon and wholly Republican, so Michael Moore's anti-American speeches did not go down well. Utah is one of the most conservative states in the union, protecting its citizens from evil incomers (such as M.M.) intent on rocking the boat. TV personality and host Sean Hannity is seen on the documentary ridiculing those in the Mormon community brave enough to speak out against the attempted ban on free speech. In my opinion, he came across as a slimy, egotistical bully. The scary thing was the reaction of the crowd at UVSC in support of him. Watch the documentary and make up your own mind.

Amish

Living where we were, I couldn't fail to mention the Amish religion, which is very much a part of Ohio. According to the US Census 2000, nearly 200,000 Amish live in the US – 55,000 in Ohio, 47,000 in Pennsylvania and 37,000 in Indiana, the remainder being scattered throughout 24 other states in America. The religion was founded in Europe in 1693. The Amish (also known as Anabaptists) believe that a person cannot freely choose to follow Christ until he or she is mature enough to make that decision; hence they do not believe in the baptism of children, and it was this belief that resulted in harsh persecution by the church in Europe. In the New World they found religious freedom, and by the year 1860 virtually all European Anabaptists had migrated there.

Their doctrine is based on the following verse from the Bible:

> 'Love not the world, neither the things that are in the world. If any man love the world, the love of the Father is not in him. For all that is in the world, the lust of the flesh, and the lust of the eyes, and the pride of life, is not of the Father, but is of the world. And the world passeth away, and the lust thereof. But he that doeth the will of God abideth for ever.' (1 John 2:15–17)

Consequently, they cherish many values and ways of living that modern society has discarded, and their abiding principles are a high regard for the family, community and God. The New Testament teaches them to live in love, simplicity, humility and service. The Amish Articles of Faith (1633) read as follows:

> 'We do not care for fellowship with any churches that allow or uphold any unfruitful works such as worldliness, fashionable attire, bed courtship, habitual smoking or drinking, non-assurance of salvation or anything contrary to sound doctrine.'

Their whole lifestyle is tied to being Christian, not (as some people believe) merely eccentric living as a folk group without modern 'necessities'. The Amish distinguish themselves by the following:

- Their outward appearance: they are plainly dressed, with no makeup or jewellery, not even a wedding ring. Married men instead grow beards.
- Their homes: neat and simple; bare of curtains and other worldly luxuries such as public electricity.
- Vocation: they consider farming as the best and most respected work. They farm without modern equipment, preferring to labour hard with horses and manpower. They believe in not making life too easy for yourself and idleness is shunned. These days they also engage in craftsmanship and sell their products and produce to the world at large.
- Living outside general society: they are not reliant on outside energy sources; they have no telephones or cars but instead visit their neighbours rather than driving all over the country. The outside world is considered to be the devil's playground,

yet they do not contrive to be cut off from their non-Amish neighbours.

- Leisure: singing, auctions and visiting others are their main leisure pursuits. Young people enjoy softball, fishing, skating and hunting. The women are skilled in quilting, the men as artisans. They have no televisions or radios as these are considered distractions.
- Language: Pennsylvanian German is spoken at home and within the community. Standard German is used in worship and ceremonies (hymns are sung in German); the Bible is predominantly read in German. They learn English at school and from their non-Amish neighbours.
- Education: they use state schools where possible but also have their own schools and rely on the community and home teaching. They receive lessons in the Christian religion and all its teachings, as well as German and the three Rs (reading, writing and arithmetic). They leave school at age 13 in order to start work in the family business or within their community.
- Community: they have their own insurance programmes to help the needy within their community. The benefits of such a close-knit 'family' mean they have to give up some degree of individuality and simply accept things. Generally, they have few worries and none that cannot be solved by the community.
- They worship in a house or barn, while Mennonites (a close religion; see below) use churches.
- Family: they usually have large families, ten children being quite common. However, babies are not revered as they are in normal society. Early on they are taught love and discipline and given chores to do to help the family, including caring for younger siblings. Men are the heads of the house, while women must be content with being homemakers and mothers. The old carry on living on the family farm and are cared for by the family.

The Amish do not recruit people to their faith and style of living, but rather respect others' differences. They follow an ethic of love and sharing among each other. If one of their people sins, he or she is helped to repent. However, if the sinner has been baptised into the church and still does not repent, then he/she is excommunicated and shunned socially, even by the family. This applies also to those who decide to join the church but then change their minds and leave. They lose the support of their family and community. Between 16 and 22 years of age, and before marriage, a young person is allowed time to experiment and leave the community. Marriage is for life and Amish people usually marry within their own people. It is testament to their strong way of life that almost 90% of young people return to their community and join the church, despite having experienced the temptations of outside life.

The commandment 'Blessed are the meek' is observed strongly – to be plain is to be humble and pride is a sin (for instance they avoid photographs and sing in unison). This humility is in contrast to the merits of success and power instilled into the average (non-Amish) American.

Mennonites

Mennonites are very closely associated with the Amish and follow the same beliefs, but not as strictly. For example:

- Vocation: Mennonites care deeply about food resources and the world's hungry, but farming is not the only or main employment followed; they engage in most other normal work, except the military.
- Helping others: they travel to poor countries to work as missionaries, to actively help and publicly highlight where help is needed.
- Leisure: they enjoy more commonplace and varied entertainment and sports.
- They drive energy-efficient cars, while the Amish travel by buggy.
- Family: they may marry outside their faith, as they have much wider contact with the community at large.
- Dress: their religion dictates that they should dress modestly and simply. Traditionally conservative women wear cape dresses and large bonnet-style head coverings; more contemporary Mennonites may wear denim trousers and even shorts.

They value their Protestant and Catholic origins and are a multi-cultural church. They account for more than 1.3 million of the world's population, living in 65 different countries. Around 323,000 live in the US, mostly in the East and Midwest, and nearly 20% are African-American, Asian or Hispanic. They place great emphasis on faith, words and action. Mennonites have acted as skilled leaders in conflict resolution and as important helpers in natural disasters and other aid programmes.

Non-Traditional Christianity

Betty, an American friend, stated that, 'God is everything to me, but religion is nothing. I participate in no formal rituals, services or organisations'. I take her point. Perhaps, as in many other things, Americans have taken it a little too far and are overly 'religious' and showy. Buildings, formula and hierarchy are not necessarily what it should all be about. There is a movement now for more private, personal faith, not necessarily involving church membership or attendance. This is variously referred to as home/house/simple/para-church or 'unchurching'. It represents a significant proportion of practising Christians and is growing in popularity.

Such people meet together in small groups, informally, in each other's homes or at simple meeting houses, to discuss the Bible and their beliefs. Bible-based churches with no denomination (free of institutional obligations) are springing up. They practise their faith without any formal structure and are deliberately unspectacular in worldly terms. They view 'churchianity' (as Betty puts it) as basically unbiblical and frequently involving bizarre behaviour. They stress the importance of community, Bible study and prayer. As one such local church stated, 'Our goal is not to "feed" people, but to make them hungry to know more, because that's the way Jesus taught'.

Upholding the Christian Religion

America was founded on the Christian religion and her Christian heritage is still very strong. The Pilgrims came to the New World for 'The great hope, and for the propagating and advancing the gospel of the kingdom of Christ in those remote parts of the world' (according to William Bradford, leader of the separatist settlers and Governor of the first Plymouth Colony). In 1765, Patrick Henry (orator and prominent figure in the American Revolution) is reputed to have said (though this may be disputed):

> 'It cannot be emphasised too clearly and too often that this nation was founded, not by religionists, but by Christians; not on religion, but on the gospel of Jesus Christ. For this very reason, peoples of other faiths have been afforded asylum, prosperity, and freedom of worship here'.

Whether or not Henry did say this, it is a strong sentiment on which America is based. Noah Webster (America's greatest lexicographer and spelling reformer) stated that, 'The Bible was America's basic textbook in all fields'. The Bible is used to swear in her Presidents and in courts of law. The Liberty Bell is inscribed with a verse from the Old Testament: 'Proclaim liberty throughout the land and to all the inhabitants thereof' (Leviticus 25:10). The National Motto is still 'In God We Trust'.

America has even decreed an annual National Day of Prayer (designated by Congress) – a day on which all Americans (regardless of faith or ethnicity) are asked to come together and pray. Universities and schools across the nation are finding that religious studies and Bible courses are more popular than ever before, with students living in dormitories 'where...faith and spirituality are a part of daily conversation' (according to *The New York Times*).

Politics and Religion

Founding Ideals

The majority of American Presidents have been open Christians. In 1798, John Adams (second President of the United States and one of the Founding Fathers) wrote that

> 'Our Constitution was made only for a moral and religious people. It is wholly inadequate to the government of any other'.

As John Jay (one of the Founding Fathers) stated in 1816:

> 'Providence has given to our people the choice of their rulers, and it is the duty, as well as the privilege and interest of our Christian nation to select and prefer Christians for our rulers'.

However, despite their personal religious leanings, the rulers of America have always upheld *freedom* of religion for America's citizens. Thomas Jefferson stated that 'Erecting the "wall of separation between church and state"...is absolutely essential in a free society'. It was believed that keeping religion and government separate was essential to the purity of both. (Note: the distinction is between church and state, not faith and state.) His Virginia Statute for Religious Freedom was made law in 1786. It states that:

> '...no man shall be compelled to frequent or support any religious worship, place, or ministry whatsoever, nor shall be enforced, restrained, molested, or burthened in his body or goods, nor shall otherwise suffer on account of his religious opinions or belief; but that all men shall be free to profess, and by argument to maintain, their opinion in matters of religion, and that the same shall in no wise diminish, enlarge, or affect their civil capacities.'

The Bill of Rights goes on to say, 'Congress shall make no law respecting the establishment of religion, or prohibiting the free exercise thereof' and that 'All men are equally entitled to the free exercise of religion'. Even the division of government into three branches – Judicial, Legislative and Executive – was based on the Bible. James Madison (fourth President and one of the most influential Founding Fathers) decreed at the Constitutional Convention in 1787 that the new United States should be governed on the basis of Isaiah 33:22: 'For the Lord is our judge, the Lord is our lawgiver, the Lord is our king; He will save us'.

In Practice

Since the first colonists, American leaders have upheld this religious freedom, and, on the whole, Americans are deeply reverent towards these founding rules and sentiments. Among other things, they have decreed that:

- It is unlawful to erect a religious monument on government property.
- Since 1962, prayers and readings for religious purposes have been banned from public schools.
- Religious songs are allowed at public performances so long as they are accompanied by secular ones; this is why, in school concerts, *Hark the Herald Angels Sing* and *Rudolph the Red Nosed Reindeer*, for instance, might be sung one after the other.
- Nativity plays are not allowed in primary schools.
- There is no official celebration of the religious aspects of Christmas or any other Christian events in the year.

However, this dedication to the ethos of the wording of the Constitution is only taken so far. As America is predominantly Protestant, the Christian-based celebrations of Christmas and Thanksgiving are federal holidays, judges can still order a court to open with prayer, and churches are granted special privileges such as relaxed zoning rules and tax-free status.

In 1925 in Dayton, Tennessee, the first American trial to be nationally broadcast on radio occurred – a trial involving a debate over whether the theory of evolution could be taught in state-funded schools. The State of Tennessee had decreed that:

> 'It shall be unlawful for any teacher in any of the universities, normals and all other public schools of the State...to teach any theory that denies the story of the Divine Creation of man as taught in the Bible, and to teach instead that man has descended from a lower order of animals'.

The American Civil Liberties Union (ACLU) contested the statute in court, in what became known as the Monkey Trial. It received as much media attention as the O.J. Simpson trial, causing profound religious argument. However, in the end, the State of Tennessee won. In 1927, 12 other states also had some form of anti-evolutionary law. It wasn't until another case in 1968 that the US Supreme Court ruled that such state laws contravened the Establishment Clause of the First Amendment (i.e. that 'Congress shall make no law respecting an establishment of religion').

Thus, in reality, the issue of faith and politics is an old one, one that has proved difficult to untangle and is full of contradictions. Separation of church and state is one thing; separation of church and politics is a completely different other. Today there is a strong link between frequency of church attendance and which presidential candidate an American voter supports. In some states, religious conservatives have shifted politics to the right and contributed to a polarised electorate. Some are worried that democracy is hindered by this and by candidates who promote a particular faith. It doesn't seem like the current President and his Republican Party are doing much to alleviate this problem. President George W. Bush has often been criticised for his religious right-wing stance and controversial conservative policies. Brian Reade, writing in *The Mirror*, is particularly scathing in his article entitled *God Help America* (5 November 2004; see *Useful Websites*). Moreover, America's foreign policy is often at odds with the rest of the Western world with regard to the language and style employed by her current leaders.

The recent trend is for Americans to be concerned with social injustice, intolerance and oppression worldwide, yet tolerance of fundamentalists (those who proclaim exclusive truths) is a no-no; they view these people as dangerous and a threat. Following 9/11, President Bush stated that fundamentalists are evil people. In most other cases, mainstream Americans strive to be politically correct and sensitive to different cultures and religions.

Conclusion

Since 1980, church attendance has dwindled in Britain by more than 30%, and membership of a religious denomination has fallen by more than 20% in Belgium, 18% in the Netherlands and 16% in France. The Catholic faith – with its harsh doctrine and often scandalous accounts of clergy paedophilia – has seen a loss of more than a third of its followers since 1978. Religion is unimportant to more than half the population of Britain, France, Germany, Spain and the Netherlands (according to data collected by the European Values Study 1999/2000 – Third Wave). Most European countries have abandoned an 'official' state religion, Britain and Norway excepted, and done away with the church's legal and tax advantages. Even the Archbishop of Canterbury supports the disestablishment of the Anglican Church of England.

As church attendance shrinks and churches are sold off and converted into homes or used for other alternative uses, Europe is seeing a reduction in the number of its houses of worship, and a more private belief system. This is in contrast to the general situation in America, where church attendance is active and growing. Perhaps this has something to do with the following:

- The basis of the American nation – in the form of the Constitution and religious freedom. Religion has always been a part of the national character.
- The obvious faith exhibited by the nation's leaders.
- The less traditional nature, doctrines and greater freedom and accessibility exhibited by churches in America compared with their counterparts in Europe. This allows people greater scope to practise their religion how and when it is convenient to them.
- The clever marketing and promotion of the church's role in other aspects of society (better packaging).
- The huge number of immigrants who have made their home in America, many of whom join a church in order to find solidarity among kinsmen.

Some believe that religion keeps society in check and under control. Americans openly speak of their church and their church friends, without embarrassment, and the church obviously provides a wide social outlet for its members and a safety net in times of trouble. You have to admire this and compare the situation we have back home – of dwindling numbers of church-goers; lack of respect for parents, the elderly and other people in general, which is becoming more prevalent in young people; an unsupportive and disinterested community; and the loneliness of individuals, especially elderly people living on their own.

While Europe seems to be growing less religious, religion in America is thriving. Alexander Hamilton, politician and lawyer (pictured on the current US $10 bill), declared that the two things that made America great were (1) Christianity and (2) a Constitution formed under Christianity. George Washington said, 'To the distinguished character of patriot, it should be our highest glory to add the more distinguished character of Christian' (1778). This sentiment still appears to prevail today. God Bless America.

 Useful Websites

www.abcnews.com – search for article '*Mega-Churches Offer Prayer*'.
www.barna.org – the Barna Group has interesting 'updates' on religious beliefs and practices.
www.europeanvalues.nl – the European Values Study.
www.lifeintheusa.com/religion – religion in America.
www.mirror.co.uk – search for article '*God Help America*' (use quotation marks when typing in or you'll never find it!)
www.pewglobal.org – Pew Global Attitudes Project.

Google:
USA Mega-Churches

16 · The Shopping Experience

Beside America's pious leanings (as discussed in the previous chapter), her other religion is perhaps shopping. Napoleon disparagingly referred to Britain 'as a nation of shopkeepers', as did Samuel Adams (eighteenth century American patriot and politician) and Adam Smith (Scottish moral philosopher and author of *The Wealth of Nations*), though the latter's emphasis was somewhat more positive. In contrast, America is a nation of stores – and big ones at that.

In order to go shopping in America, a car is pretty much a necessity. Unlike in Britain, where it is usual to go to town, park and walk to various shops, in America most shopping areas are laid out along one or two main roads. Idaho has the longest main street in America, stretching 33 miles. Thus you have to decide which store you need and then drive to it, then on to the next one, and so on. Alternatively, you find your nearest mall, park and walk indoors. However, as most malls are heavy on department stores, gifts and specialty shops, and light on practical stores such as DIY, pharmacy, stationery and the like, you may not find what you are looking for, and end up having to drive around anyway. Most stores don't open till fairly late in the morning (perhaps not until 10 a.m.), but then stay open till late at night (10 or 11 o'clock); many supermarkets are open 24/7.

The All-American Mall

Fifty years ago, the first fully enclosed, climate-controlled shopping mall was opened in Edina, Minnesota. Shoppers took to it so much that the Edina prototype became the basis of virtually every new regional shopping centre in America thereafter. Now there are 1104 enclosed malls in the US (reference *USA Today*, 15 March 2007).

The largest is the Mall of America in Bloomington, Minneapolis. It has 520 stores, 50 restaurants, and numerous cinemas and other entertainment outlets spread over 4.2 million sq ft, employing 10,000 people. It is one of the top tourist attractions in the country, attracting up to 40 million visitors a year. It incorporates a 7-acre amusement park in the middle of the mall, complete with the world's largest collection of life-size dinosaurs, and has itineraries for families and groups. It offers romantic packages: starting with coffee, then a visit to one of the many jewelers or gift shops, followed by a ride on the Ferris wheel, ticket to the aquarium, a movie, and ending up with dinner. You can even get married in the mall at the Chapel of Love Wedding Chapel.

Las Vegas malls offer similar entertainment possibilities. Enjoy a gondola ride along the Grand Canal Shoppes (a Venetian-style shopping area), a live rainstorm at Merchants' Harbor, animatronic statues, light shows and more. Many of the malls are part of large hotel and casino complexes. Other great shopping cities, according to *Travel & Leisure*, are New York, San Francisco and Chicago. Potomac Mills in Virginia attracts more visitors each year than nearby Shenandoah National Park, the most visited National Park in America. Airlines offer package flights to this huge discount mall, which is organised into neighbourhoods, and has tour buses and regular special events to attract shoppers.

Elsewhere in America, regional malls do their best to entice people in. New ones are constantly appearing, and old ones are revamped and updated, or simply close. 'It's the retail world's response to customers – to keeping them curious and always coming back', said our local mall manager. New malls attract a lot of publicity and people flock to them, to the detriment of the old mall down the road. The emphasis is always on more glitz, more style. New seems to be better, in most people's eyes; people get bored with shopping at the same old mall and crave a different experience. Unfortunately, this results in older stores closing and often becoming eyesores.

Malls are often social places, where families spend the day. They may simply come to window shop, socialise with friends, enjoy the food outlets and soak up the ambiance, with hardly a thought for actually shopping. Free events and seasonal festivities often draw people in. Youngsters can be entertained in the cinema within the mall while parents go off to shop or for a meal. Teenagers hang out in their own groups. In our well-behaved suburban-Ohioan neighbourhood, antisocial behaviour appeared to be taboo – there was very little vandalism, rowdiness or public displays of affection; nothing to upset the relaxed, elegant, family atmosphere. Things can be different in other towns and cities, where mall managers have to contend with gangs and vandals, and adopt rules to limit who is allowed into the shopping area. A growing number have banned unescorted teenagers from being in the mall after a certain time of day.

Malls are certainly America's answer to shopping (or at least good, clean, family entertainment) and seem to be catching on in the UK too. However, unlike in Britain where you have to wrestle with crowds of shoppers, a visit to a mall in America is quite a different experience. In my experience, no-one seems to be in a rush, the temperature is comfortable (not too warm), there is no mindless elevator music; strangely quiet and spacious, I found it a refreshingly relaxed and enjoyable experience to visit the mall. There were plenty of drinking water fountains and a good choice of food and drink stands, as well as comfy seating areas; you could even plonk yourself down in a massage chair and, for a couple of dollars, let the world go by while you had an all-over body rub-down.

However, indoor malls do have a rather unreal feeling, being under one roof, with one lighting and heating system, the whole interlinked by marble floors and glass. I missed being out in the fresh air, my feet on the pavement, a view of where I was going and some bearing on my geography, because – having been lulled into a relaxed and happy state – you then have to navigate your way out of the mall. I think malls are designed to confuse you, with their many entrances and exits, often on different levels. Not only did I have trouble finding my way out and deciding which parking lot I had left my car in, but also I had the uncanny knack of losing my vehicle once out there. This was partly due to my car, a sub-compact hatchback, being swamped by all the large SUVs, pick-up trucks and minivans; and partly due to my over-charged brain trying to take in all the different inputs involved in shopping in a strange, unfamiliar environment. The ability to lose myself in malls, car parks, even in shops themselves became infuriating. One episode was particularly embarrassing; having food-shopped in a local supermarket with Rosie in tow, the young man who had bagged our shopping at the checkout proceeded to push the trolley out to the car. After we had walked up and down several rows of parked cars, with me apologising profusely, I eventually located the car. After this episode I vowed to park under a numbered pole or some other distinguishable place in future, even if it meant having to walk a little further.

Another area for potential mishap was at the junction off the main road onto the mall 'ring road'. At our local mall, priority was given to drivers coming into the mall; if you were leaving the shopping area you had to stop and give way to cars turning across you. It was a little disconcerting, and made me wonder again whether they are really trying to prevent you from leaving.

Some new malls are taking a different approach to the traditional all-under-one-roof style of development. They seem to be going back to the more traditional, open-air, high street/shopping area principle, with pavements, pedestrian crossings, outdoor seating, and individual buildings and shops fronting the pavements. Streets are named and laid out on a grid pattern, with grass, plants and trees to break up the concrete. There is some street parking at meters; otherwise you use the free car parks. You are outside, walking on pavements, not cocooned inside an unnatural environment – something akin to what we are used to back home.

Shopping Elsewhere

Warehouse and discount stores which sell everything (e.g. K-Mart and Meijer) and wholesale buying clubs such as Costco and Sam's Club are the fastest growing and most formidable threat to smaller retailers. Costco merged with Price Club in 1993 and is the largest membership warehouse chain in the world, according to sales volume, with 377 outlets across America. Though Sam's Club is part of the Wal-Mart empire and has more warehouses (551 in the US), Costco has a higher total sales volume. Members pay an annual fee to join and shop at these warehouses (the fee ranges from $35 at Sam's Club to $50 at Costco; prices correct at 2007). Entering and leaving a Sam's Club feels a bit like going through airport Customs. You are asked to show your membership card several times on a shopping trip – once to get into the store, again at the checkout and finally on exiting. Items are sold in bulk, directly off pallets on the retail floor, and at a discount, though not always – watch the prices and don't assume everything is cheap.

Big box stores specialise in selling one type of commodity; some examples are Office Depot (office goods and equipment), Best Buy (electronics) and Lowes (DIY). They are franchises of chain stores, the same wherever you go. The stores look a little like big boxes (hence the name perhaps). If you are a store employee you may get an associate discount, even on sales prices. This is a big incentive for people to work there, though the temptation is to go crazy buying things because they are such a bargain. Otherwise, it becomes a self-perpetuating mechanism, and basically you end up working for the company for free.

If you are looking for a bargain, factory outlets are the place to go. You will usually find a collection of named stores selling overstocked items and damaged goods in one shopping area. They represent one of the fastest growing retail outlets today and there are more than 300 throughout America. Some operate along similar lines to the malls, offering entertainment alongside the shopping experience.

TV shopping channels such as QVC and Shop NBC are also very popular. There is something mesmerising about them – the presenters are so enthusiastic in extolling the virtues and advantages of owning that glittering, 'must-have' trinket, which is so easy to afford. Of course, you must phone in the next few minutes to secure the special price, or you will miss the amazing bargain of a lifetime. It is simple and easy, just pick up the phone, and your satisfaction will be guaranteed. How can you resist?

Prices, Discounts and Savings

Shopping in America is a bit of a bargain as prices for most things are cheaper than in Britain. Also, 'Don't buy anything unless it's in a sale', one friend told me, and I found this to be good advice. Shops are always having discount days and sales in particular departments. In England I had been shopping averse; in America it was fun to see just how cheaply I could buy something. Unlike in Britain where usually only one discount is allowed on a purchase, in America they double and even triple discount, so that by the time you hand over your dollars the price has dropped so dramatically from the ticket price that you can't help smiling like a Cheshire cat.

Free sales brochures arrive in the post or you can pick them up in store; they are often full of money-saving offers. Even the *Yellow Book* (the *Yellow Pages*) has a whole section of coupons. So it is worth 'clipping the coupons' and leaving them in your car in case you are out and decide to drop into a shop for something. Also, stores sometimes accept vouchers even days after you have bought something; so if you forget to bring your coupon at the time of purchase, you can still use it. Mail-in rebate offers are also very common, working on the principle that in reality only a third or so consumers actually bother to send off for the rebate.

One of my American friends recommended shoppers' surveys as a means to save money. Companies need to collect demographic details for marketing purposes, so they can target someone who fits a particular demographic character. If you have the time, these surveys can be entertaining to fill in, and your reward may be free shopping coupons.

Food supermarkets often employ dual pricing, offering customers who have a loyalty card a lower price. As these are freely obtainable, it is worth getting a card for the places you use regularly. If you forget to bring the card with you, the cashier can usually look you up by phone number. Alternatively, you can always return later and present the shopping receipt to Customer Services, who will credit the savings you would have made. If you sign up for a store card, you will be sent special member discounts. It is worth applying for these cards if only to build up your credit rating and enjoy the opening offer, which ranges from $10 off your first purchase to 10% off everything you buy thereafter using the card, plus other special member privileges.

Practical Considerations and Thrifty Tips

In supermarkets, it is usual for the cashier or another member of staff to bag your shopping; it is rare that you are expected to do it yourself. In some places, baggers are not paid; they work for tips only. It might be prudent to quietly ask the cashier what the supermarket's policy is regarding this. Also ask about plastic bag recycling. Some give you the option of using brown paper bags over plastic, which is eco-friendly. Others give money off for every plastic bag you bring with you and use at the checkout, though this policy is not advertised. I would always try to use my own bags to avoid filling up landfill sites with plastic, and save a couple of nickels myself at the same time.

Do be careful of the ringing up at the checkout – take advantage of the free packing service to watch the computer. In particular, check that any reduced-sticker items have gone through correctly; often cashiers ring them up at full price. I used to kick myself every time I had to return to Customer Services and ask for a refund on the overcharge.

Below are a few more tips that might save you money on your shopping:

- Most coupons are distributed in free-standing inserts (FSIs) in local Sunday papers, so purchasing a Sunday paper could give you savings.

- Special discounts advertised in newspapers, brochures and in-store can be used in conjunction with other coupons – you can double them up to make big savings.
- Combine manufacturers' money-off coupons with store cards to get double discounts.
- If the item on sale is out of stock when you go to buy it, ask for a rain check (i.e. for the store to honour the discounted price after they have restocked and when you return to buy it).
- It is often better to buy the smallest size you can with a brand coupon in order to get the maximum saving per unit of product.
- Take advantage of any rebate (refund) offers – all you have to do is send in the UPC (universal product code) and your till receipt, then wait for a cheque refund (though it might take 8 weeks or more to come).
- Prices on US websites can work out cheaper than those on UK websites for the same product.

Garage or Yard Sales, and Estate Sales

I once saw a sign on the back of someone's car that read, 'Warning. I break for all garage sales'. I could identify with this sentiment. Apart from during the dead of winter, signs for yard or garage sales are a common sight – taped to signposts, on street corners, waving in the breeze or flashing fluorescently. Follow the mysterious trail until you come to a house with a big sign and perhaps balloons outside. With household paraphernalia spilling out onto the drive, the garage is often piled high, and the lady or man of the house is seated at a little table with cash tin at the ready. A friendly hello gains you entrance to this Aladdin's cave, where treasure galore is possible – all clothing 25 cents, toys and games anything from 10 cents to $1, sporting equipment, any manner of household goods and quirky items. Sometimes there is even lemonade and cookies, and a box of free goodies, people are so desperate to get rid of things. I was hooked. Some garage sales looked as if they were semi-permanent and I think one old boy just wanted to get people to call round, so he could have a chat.

The mother of all garage sales is an annual event lasting 4 days (starting on the first Thursday of August) and crossing four states. It began in 1987, originally as a way to bring travellers away from the busy interstate system to the less-travelled highways of Kentucky and Tennessee. It has grown every year and now stretches 450 miles or so from Covington, Kentucky, through Chattanooga, then on to Gadsden, Alabama. It follows Route 127 and thus has come to be known as the US 127 Corridor Sale. Homeowners, professional dealers and vendors line the route, vying for bargain-spotters' attention with their antiques and bric-a-brac.

Elsewhere, these private sales are as popular as our car boots. In our local area they ran Thursday to Saturday, May to September, beginning as soon as the weather chivied up after winter. Besides buying what we personally wanted, because of the ridiculously low prices we could have made a good trade buying up stuff that would sell well at a car boot back home. In any case, they are good fun, and you get to explore your neighbourhood at the same time. Estate sales and auctions are also worth a look. When someone moves or passes away, the family organises a private sale of goods and furniture, along the same lines as a garage sale except you can usually wander throughout the house, viewing the contents for sale. Alternatively there will be a public auction at the premises. Your local paper should have a section on the week's sales.

Charity Stores

Goodwill and Salvation Army stores are the American equivalent of our charity shops, and are on a typically large American scale. If you are not opposed to buying secondhand items, then this form of shopping may be for you. Because new goods are fairly cheap to buy in the first place, what with all the sales and discounts, you can see why prices of second-hand goods are so low. It is an interesting experience to be in the store when they bring out the crates of new, unsorted goods; it's rather like the frenzy at our jumble sales, with people jostling and rummaging through the crates.

Goodwill Industries (GI) is a non-profit organisation. It offers a civil service by employing people who are working their way out of poverty, often giving them job training. It offers 'a hand up, not a hand out', and maintains that work should be within the reach of anyone who wants to hold a job. Thousands of people with disabilities, on welfare, homeless, with criminal convictions, lacking education or work experience are provided with work at GI's 2000 or more retail stores and donation centres. It also supplies workers to businesses needing extra staff in times of labour shortage. GI is a worldwide organisation, extending to 24 countries. In England the GI network is associated with the Queen Elizabeth's Foundation and The Shaw Trust, and in Scotland, with Momentum. It collects clothing, household goods and electronic items, and promotes electronic recycling. Besides retail outlets, it sells secondhand goods through its internet auction site.

If you donate something to Goodwill, you can write off the value against your US income tax. In exchange for your donation of goods or clothing, you are given a receipt that acts as your tax break. The Salvation Army and Vietnam Veterans of America also offer similar outlets for your secondhand items. VVA sells your donated goods to private companies by annual bid. Again, your support is tax deductible at the present 'fair market value', and the responsibility for estimating this rests upon the donor rather than the agency receiving the gift. They can arrange regular pick-ups of items from your door.

America's Love/Hate Relationship with Wal-Mart

America's number-one retailer, Wal-Mart, is also the largest private employer in the States. It has almost as many employees as the US military has uniformed personnel. Wal-Mart attracts around 20% of the nation's grocery business, with shoppers saving an estimated 17% or more on their grocery bills versus shopping at other grocery stores.

In 1962, Sam Walton opened his first Wal-Mart store in Arkansas, specialising in named brands at low prices. The store was a success and he expanded his rural base, going public in 1970. The company owed much of its retailing edge to Walton's (then unique) profit-sharing ethos and decentralised distribution system. He remained on the board until 1988 and died in 1992, the world's second richest man (after Bill Gates). By then, Wal-Mart had become the largest retailer in America, with 1700 stores across the country. In 1991, the company went international and now has 2700 retail units in 14 countries outside America.

However, although Wal-Mart may be good for shoppers, it has received much bad press regarding various aspects of its operating methods. Seventy percent of the products on its shelves come from China, yet Chinese plant workers are paid as little as 25 cents an hour. The pressure it places on its vendors to outsource manufacturing to China and other underdeveloped countries in order to cut costs and meet its low-price demands is well known. This severely undermines American jobs and transfers whole industries overseas. Furthermore, it wields its market power on producers, forcing them to sell their produce to Wal-Mart at cripplingly low prices. It has also wiped out many domestic retailers, who cannot compete with its low retail prices. An Ohio State University study based on small and rural towns in Iowa revealed that between 17% and 60% of local businesses fold when a Wal-Mart store is built nearby. Furthermore, despite community opposition to Wal-Mart's building of new supercentres, it is often granted land solely because it can throw its financial and political weight behind the proposed project. This can contribute to suburban sprawl and poor land-use planning.

It is also a notoriously poor payer of its American workers. However, this is somewhat offset by its profit-sharing plan, whereby employees are offered stock options and store discounts. Yet, when the company attempted to expand into the German market in 1998, its American-style management practices went down like a lead balloon. German employees resisted the company's attempts to make them work longer hours than laid out in their contracts, to introduce video surveillance of their work and a telephone hot line for employees to inform on colleagues. Restrictive rules such as no flirting with other employees or dating colleagues in positions of influence were also unpopular. After several run-ins with German trade unions, and, on top of these problems, poor retail sales, the company said *Auf Wiedersen* and pulled out of Germany in 2006.

Wal-Mart's winning low-margin, high-volume formula will endure as long as consumers demand low prices, wide selections and big stores – despite the hidden social costs. It and other large out-of-town stores feed the high-consumption culture. Some see Wal-Mart as symbolic of one of the things that is wrong with America.

Conclusion

Perhaps by now you have cottoned on to the fact that I am a thrifty and prudent shopper (yes, I boil bones for soup.) However, with a little thought and organisation, it isn't difficult to save money. Shopping is a skill and an art. For some, it is also a hobby and source of entertainment. In one poll, 93% of teenage American girls said that shopping was their favourite pastime. The shopping culture is very strong in America, as it is in Britain. Americans strive for progress, and manufacturers try to accommodate this by creating 'new and improved' products. Roughly 12,000 new or different products come onto the market every year, and the average supermarket now stocks two-and-a-half times more items than it did 20 years ago. The result is more and bigger stores to accommodate these new products.

Although choice is good, personally I think we have too much of it. It can make a trip to the shops exhausting and unnecessarily time consuming. This is especially true for foreigners, unfamiliar with American stores and products. Even something as simple as a cucumber comes in four varieties – plain green, hothouse, organic and baby seedless. By the time you have weighed up the pros and cons, and converted into relative prices, perhaps after any two-for-one offers or other discounts, *and* compared prices between stores, you'll be forgiven if your head explodes. If you are in the right mood, it can be satisfying, even a little fun, to invest the time and effort in shopping prudently; if not, the pressure to make decisions between the countless products and sales outlets can be humour-threatening. Professor Barry Schwartz (social scientist) sums it up in his book *The Paradox of Choice: Why More is Less*: 'Unlimited choice…can produce genuine suffering'.

With all these shopping options and emphasis on shopping, America is experiencing retail overload. Americans are constantly bombarded with advertising, trying to persuade them to buy something. You only have to turn on the television to see what I mean. There are five basic shopping channels, continually broadcasting. On other channels, commercial breaks occur with irritating frequency, even interjecting within the last 30 seconds of a programme. However, the effectiveness of TV advertising has diminished as the number of channels has increased. There is now a huge amount of mail devoted to sales promotions – store brochures, catalogues, coupons and festive marketing. At 'special' and/or seasonal times of the year, such as between Thanksgiving and Christmas, around Valentine's Day or Mother's Day, our local newspaper was stuffed with as much sales literature as news. It goes without saying that paper recycling is big out here.

However, don't let my grumbles concerning materialism and overcommercialism put you off enjoying the shopping opportunities in America; prices there are so good that you would be foolish to overlook them. Just make any big purchases at least 6 months before moving back to Britain; otherwise you may have to pay tax on them (see Chapter 22, *The Move Back*).

Useful Websites

www.127sale.com – the official website of the world's longest yard sale.
www.abc.net.au/news – search for article '*In America, plastic shopping bag still rules*' (24 January 2008).
www.mallofamerica.com – billed as the nation's largest retail and entertainment complex.
www.officialusa.com/state/malls – a list of malls according to state.
www.shopgoodwill.com – Goodwill Industries online shop.

Terminology

American term	Equivalent British term	Notes
Close out	End-of-range sale	
Goodwill store	Charity shop	
Mall	Shopping centre	In America, a 'mall' usually refers to covered shopping
Sales clerk, sales associate	Shop assistant	
Sales tax	VAT	Varies according to state and even county
Shopping centre	High street	Usually refers to non-covered shopping
Store	Shop	
Strip mall	Parade of shops	
Twofer	Two for the price of one offer	
UPC	Barcode	

17 · Food, Glorious Food, and Drink

The International Federation of Competitive Eating sanctions dozens of fast-food-eating contests in America. On Coney Island, New York, the famous Fourth of July annual hot-dog-eating competition draws thousands of onlookers. Following months of training, competitors vie to see how many hot-dogs and buns they can down in 12 minutes. The record is 53.3 franks. There are also bratwurst- and hamburger-eating championships, both popular enough with viewers to be broadcast on the TV sports channel ESPN. Top scoffers are surprisingly skinny, weighing in at a mere 100 pounds, and of Japanese origin, or contrastingly super-heavy at 420 pounds or so. Many view their abilities as athletic and take their training very seriously. The rest of us are aghast yet compelled to watch and revel in their obvious misery as they reach capacity.

According to nutritionists, a 3 oz serving of meat as a main course (about the size of a pack of cards) is a sensible portion. You are unlikely to get this in American restaurants, where big is considered beautiful. In the past, fast-food restaurants offered one size of French fries – 2.4 oz. Today this is classed as a small portion and rarely sold. The usual medium-sized portion is now more than twice that amount. Likewise, servings of soda vary from a standard 12 oz cup up to 42 oz (which is half a gallon of pop, containing on average a staggering 48 teaspoons of sugar). High-fructose corn syrup is the major sweetener in most foods, from soda to ketchup to hot dog buns. It began to be widely used in the 1970s, the same time that American bellies started expanding. Moreover, there are now so many preservatives in our food that it is apparently affecting how our bodies decompose. Just look at the expiration dates on some of the food you buy. In America, the average carton of milk has a best-before date days later than milk sold in Britain. What have they done to make it last that long? Moreover, issues concerning animal welfare are rarely voiced (to quote a friend: 'We tend to look the other way'). They expect and demand cheap food, apparently without much concern for the conditions animals are kept in or how they are raised and killed.

Jim observes the problem with the insatiable human desire for food thus:

> Food in the US is a national fixation, perhaps rooted in the original push West when the supply of food was uncertain and difficult. While times have changed, the national psyche has not. Many places are now over-supported by family restaurants and fast-food outlets. This competition keeps quality high and prices low and so it's a common event to eat out. For some, there is no alternative. Workers even 'catch' breakfast on the way to work, this routinely being cooked fare complete with a stack of pancakes lubricated with maple syrup. It's easy to sneer at the over-provision of such meals until sampled and the source of the addiction becomes clear. It's easy to overindulge and the increasing number of Xs in front of L on the labels of parachute-proportioned clothing is evidence of this. The provision of food to people with low abstinence thresholds is huge business in the US, but the tide is turning and like many other aspects of American life the change is not being made passively. Now that the shocking truth linking consuming too many calories and weight gain has emerged, the US is quickly turning from an obsession with unhealthy food to an equally fervent craze over healthy food. This is very commendable, but notice that the fixation remains, only the subject has changed. Certainly, you can eat well in the US and it is recommended that any visitors take full advantage, as the quality, range and prices are fantastic.

Eating Out

Dining out in America is often fun and family-orientated. Our local ice cream parlour (which was open all year round, even when it was minus degrees out there) had regular kids' evenings, offering a special menu, free bouncy castle, face painting and pavement chalking, all for the price of an ice cream. There were even 'dog days', when you could bring your Mutley along for a cone.

One question taken from my survey (see Chapter 4) was *On average, how often do you eat out each week?* Virtually every American answered at least once, and about a third of respondents reckoned on 3–5 times a week. This may seem a little extravagant to the average British person. After all, how many of us can afford to go out to a pub or restaurant once a week, let alone more often than this? What the answer reveals is that Americans think nothing of eating out regularly – whether this entails a sit-down meal in a restaurant or fast food. Also they do not regard it as a particularly special event, one that should take up the whole evening. Convenience is usually the name of the game. Most people eat out to save having to shop, cook and wash-up at home. They are there to eat and then leave, and you may feel overdressed if you put on a skirt and jewellery. Men rarely wear a tie (unless they have just come from the office). Along with their casual attire, Americans also like to eat rather informally, cutting up their food, then ditching the knife and eating simply with a fork. Tablecloths and cloth napkins are a rarity.

Perhaps one reason for their rather mundane view of eating out is that most chain restaurants in America lack individuality and the atmosphere can be pretty dire. They are geared to family and group catering, fast service, and informal, often buffet-style eating. You won't find much candlelight, flowers and music. Even in many ethnic restaurants and those specialising in foreign food, you could be anywhere; there is often no attempt to create an ambience. It wouldn't take much – just a few empty bottles of Chianti strung up round the room, some plastic grapes and vines, checked tablecloths and candles, and Pavarotti singing in the background might be enough to transport you to Italy. Instead, you are more likely to be sitting at a table surrounded by other families, in bright light and surroundings, with barely the hint of Italian ambiance. The focus is on food, not on the culture of a place.

Americans tend to go out to eat early and finish promptly. Do not be surprised if you are the last ones in a restaurant at 10 o'clock at night, with the staff hovering around, eager to dismiss you with 'Have a nice night'. Perhaps for the same reason, if you invite Americans to your home for a party or dinner they will expect to eat almost as soon as they arrive. Pot luck dinners are very popular. This makes party-throwing a doddle, as pretty much all the catering is done for you; all you have to supply are the drinks and eating irons.

There is a huge choice of inexpensive places to eat out, from drive-throughs to buffet-style eateries and all-day breakfast bars. A constant stream of coupons and special offers for eateries arrive in the mail and local newspapers. Leave these valuable clippings in a wallet in the car, and you will always have them whenever you feel like a pit stop. Sometimes it's hard to believe how cheap the prices are (whether discounted or not). It may be false economy to shop for ingredients, prepare, cook, serve and wash-up a meal at home, when the whole family can go out and eat like kings for the equivalent cost of one person eating one main course in Britain.

In traditional restaurants, don't be shy requesting a doggy bag or box; in fact, you will probably be offered one. Also, if you are not sure about portions, ask your server about the size of a particular starter and how many people it might stretch to, as it is often the case that one starter is large enough to share. They are also very amenable to varying the order to suit personal tastes; for instance, you might prefer your salad dressing on the side, vegetables instead of fries, no ice in your drink, etc. America is very customer focused, and staff are usually pleasant and helpful. Service is infinitely better than the grouchy 'diservice' you receive in Britain, where you get the feeling they can't be bothered. But then in America it is normal (if not expected) for customers to tip servers 15–20% (in order to supplement the low wages restaurant staff receive). Perhaps this is why grumpy service is the norm in Britain because waiting staff have no real incentive to be attentive. The British put up with such poor service and rarely complain – probably because we half-expect it – whereas Americans will voice their displeasure if they receive shoddy service.

Standard Fare and Outlets

A typical American menu comprises soups (chilli and clam chowder being favourites), sandwiches, steaks, chicken, battered fish and shrimp, salads, sides, ice cream sundaes, pies, cheesecakes and other sweet puddings. Desserts are often a work of art, and ice cream is usually dressed up with any number of toppings and ingredients (truly wicked). Apart from salads, you'll be hard pushed to find many vegetarian dishes. George Bush is repudiated to have said, 'I do not like broccoli. And I haven't liked it since I was a little kid and my mother made me eat it. I am President of the United States, and I'm not going to eat any more broccoli'. I guess if you *are* the President, you can refuse to eat your greens. Perhaps that goes some way to explaining the lack of veggies on the American menu.

American fare is a bit heavy on the sugar and salt, and I kicked myself many times at forgetting to ask them to hold the salt on the children's French fries. Battering and deep frying is the usual method of cooking; you often pay extra for plain broiled (naked grilled) food. There is always a children's menu, generally offering the usual rather unnutritious fare – hot dogs, burgers, grilled cheese, macaroni cheese, pasta in tomato sauce (marinara), pizza, fish sticks or chicken tenders, served with fries, washed down with a soda, and followed by ice cream and sprinkles. Don't be afraid to ask if it is possible to substitute some part of the meal with a healthier alternative, for instance grilled chicken instead of fried, veggies instead of potatoes. Children's food should be fun and appealing, but it is usually heavily processed, and I soon yearned to order some unadulterated, wholesome food for them. Kids' meals range in price from a mere $1.95 to $4.99 – whichever way you look at it, pretty reasonable. A small bowl of apple sauce sometimes strangely appears with the main course (especially with children's meals). We were never sure what to do with it, but I usually enjoyed it as a free dessert if no-one else claimed it.

Most restaurants are franchises of a large chain. Examples include TGI Friday's, Bob Evans, Steak 'n Shake, Taco Bell, Captain D's, the Olive Garden and Red Lobster, to name a few. They have a set, standard menu and décor, so whichever one you go to, you know what to expect. The independent, privately owned/run restaurants (also called mom and pop's) usually try to compete with 'the big boys' by offering better service or food, and ambiance in the form of original style. So if you want something a little out of the ordinary, opt for a locally owned place rather than a franchised one.

Buffet restaurants are usually very good value. *Big Boy*, *CiCi-s Pizza*, *Luby's* and the *Golden Corral* are all great places for cheap, plentiful family nosh, if you can turn a blind eye to the environment, crowd and noise. Family-orientated eateries are usually open-plan with stark lighting, sticky floors and plastic-covered everything, with the hustle and bustle of families traipsing back and forth to graze at the self-service bar. Some offer an astounding choice of different foods, so much so that you probably won't need to eat for the next 24 hours.

Chinese restaurants offering buffets are especially good value. We regularly feasted at a couple of local places for a paltry $5.99 per adult and $2.99 per child – amazing value. They provided a huge variety of freshly cooked and delicious Chinese dishes (plus pizza and chips for the kids), followed by an extensive fruit and dessert bar, and there is no limit to the number of times you can fill your plate. However, as Miss Piggy once said, you should never eat more than you can lift. You wonder how they can afford to offer this style of eating.

Take-Outs, Diners, Coffee Shops and Drive-Throughs

Take-aways (*take-outs* in American English) are hugely popular. They are very good value, especially when combined with a coupon or other special offer. Pizza is said to be America's number-one favourite fast food. Jeff Arder commented that, 'We live in an age when pizza gets to your home before the police'. You won't find good old British-style fish and chips in America. The closest we could get to was the fish and chips at *Long John Silver's*, though their fish is heavily salted and they only offer crunchy, American-style 'stick' chips. There is a huge choice of burger and steak outlets. In my humble opinion, *Hardee's* does one of the meatiest-tasting burgers, and their milkshakes are also first-rate.

The quintessential American *diner* is the equivalent to our café. Traditionally they were narrow, mobile lunch wagons, which set up in busy downtown locations and near factories to catch night-shift workers. They started out in the North-East, and today the greatest concentration of diners is in New Jersey, where approximately 600 still operate. They are independently owned, offering cheap American food, much of it fried, including all-day breakfasts, and are often open 24 hours. Despite being usurped in the 1970s by the new fast-food restaurants, traditional prefab, chrome and stainless-steel diners with Art Deco furnishings, long counters and individual booths have endured, and they are now part of popular culture. Nowadays, many local non-franchised restaurants call themselves diners.

Of the nationwide coffee shops, *Starbucks* is now found everywhere, selling under licence, especially in select areas such as airport lounges, book stores and in ski resorts, around colleges and universities and in higher-income areas. *Tim Hortons* is popular in the East and Midwest, having migrated from Canada where it is more ubiquitous than Starbucks. It has its roots in coffee and doughnuts and is open 24/7 (apart from Christmas and Thanksgiving Day). They bake on the premises and their mission statement is 'Always fresh', to which they are fanatically dedicated. Other doughnut shops include *Dunkin' Donuts*, *Krispy Kreme* and *Mister Donut*.

For more sophistication, *Panera Bread* is hard to beat (apart from the slightly annoying classical music). Its mission statement is 'Getting people back together' and it does this by offering outside catering (for example to offices, for special occasions, and groups), providing a meeting place in comfortable surroundings, taking pre-orders for its bakery products and just encouraging you to sit awhile. Once you have bought a cup of standard coffee, tea or soda, you can help yourself to refills, while reading one of their free newspapers. Along the lines of European bakeries, Panera offers 'proper' bread made with no preservatives, minimal sugar and higher quality ingredients such as rice flour, all freshly baked on the premises. At the end of the day, all leftover food goes to local soup kitchens.

Another classic American eating experience is the *drive-through*. Only cars are allowed to use them, not pedestrians or cyclists (for insurance reasons). Some restaurants promise to give a free meal if you do not receive prompt service. The popularity of the drive-through is such that often times, at busy moments of the day, a line of queuing cars forms and slowly inches its way through the system. If you park your car and walk in, you can often be in and out with your order before the line has moved. So do not assume that the drive-through is always the quickest way to pick up a take-out. It simply allows Americans to stay in their hallowed vehicles. America also has drive-through liquor stores, coffee shops, dairy stores, pharmacies and even marriage chapels, e.g. in Las Vegas.

Shopping for Food

Kroger is the nation's largest grocery retailer, and Safeway comes second (Table 17.1 lists other national chains). However, each region of America also has its particular local supermarket chains. When you first arrive in the States and go grocery shopping it can be bewildering – negotiating the aisles, trying to find familiar things, making a stab at translating labels, and converting prices from dollars to pounds. I used to leave the shop feeling exhausted. I had been told that everything was much cheaper in America, but this is not necessarily true in the case of food purchased in the supermarket. However, some groceries *are* definitely better value: for instance, ice cream (which is good quality and comes in an astounding number of different flavours), nuts and seeds, wine, big bunches of fresh herbs and watercress, eggs and meat. The beef sold in supermarkets is good quality, the burgers generally continental-style, with the taste and texture of real meat (unlike our dubious-looking flat British burgers). Other fresh meat is often water injected and loses weight after cooking, so allow an extra 3 or 4 oz to each pound of meat when using specific quantities. Staples such as bread and dairy products are about the same price as in the UK. Anything other than rubbery, tasteless American cheese is more costly. I hadn't fully appreciated before how good English cheddar was and the variety of British and French cheeses we enjoy back home. Mushrooms are strangely expensive.

Table 17.1 National grocery stores in America (in alphabetical order). Those marked with an asterisk are deep-discount and limited assortment chains.

AA&P	Kroger
Ahold	Piggly Wiggly
Albertsons LLC	Safeway
Aldi *	Sears Grand
Costco	SuperValu *
County Market	Target Stores
Delhaize Group	Wal-Mart
Harris Teeter	Whole Foods
Henhouse	WinCo Foods *
Kmart	

Americans are used to bulk buying and think nothing of buying eggs in boxes of 18, milk and orange juice by the half gallon, etc. It doesn't take long to fill a trolley and American pushcarts are consequently on the large side. As if heaving one around wasn't hard enough, some supermarkets offer trolleys disguised as cars for the kids – fun for them, as they pretend to drive round the aisles, but a nightmare for mum on the steering end.

Get into the habit of reading the ingredient labels, especially on convenience foods, as these give a good indication of how heavily processed and refined the food is. Make decisions based on that information, not on packaging and child pressure. Sometimes the number of ingredients in even a loaf of bread is staggering, and the sodium and sugar levels can be high; you pay a premium for simple, untampered-with bread. If you like your food unadulterated, without an excessive amount of artificial flavourings and preservatives, make a point of reading the labels.

If you hate standing in queues, look to see if there are any self-service computerised tills where you can checkout your own shopping. If you opt for a cashier, then do watch the ringing up and check your bill afterwards; they often overlook reduced price stickers. Many shops do not have reduced sections where they display food that is near its sell-by date or slightly damaged; instead, they may give to local food pantries.

American Equivalents and Substitutes

It is possible to find familiar British products in specialist outlets, but you will pay considerably more for them. Some familiar things are completely missing and/or difficult to find, though, over time, I discovered some good substitutes. Here are some suggestions and findings:

- A tin of pinto or vegetarian beans served up with a dash of tomato ketchup is a reasonable substitute for British-style baked beans, without the overpowering sweet, salty or smoky taste of American 'pork and beans'. Moreover, tins of pork and beans often contain offputting lumps of white stuff, which looks suspiciously like lard to me.

- As American writer Henry Miller observed, 'You can travel 50,000 miles in America without once tasting a piece of good bread'. If you do not like American-style bread (which is light and sweet) opt for French or Italian breads, which are somewhat akin to British bread. You may also be able to find unbleached, unbromated bread with no added sugar in the fresh bakery section of your local supermarket. Failing that, Panera Bread does delicious loaves; though you pay about twice as much, you feel you are eating 'real' bread rather than something processed. The cheap supermarket chain Aldi also does surprisingly good bread.
- American supermarkets don't sell what we call muesli – granola-based cereals are their equivalent. Try looking in your local health food store.
- Most American breakfast cereals are sugar-coated and flavoured. However, you can still buy plain cornflakes, bran-based cereals, Rice Krispies and porridge oats as healthy alternatives.
- It is difficult to find fruit squashes (orange, lemon, etc.) that you add water to. Instead they sell bottled juices that have water already added, though I found them rather strong and usually a cocktail of flavours (no plain orange or lemon).
- Vegemite or yeast extract (Marmite) is unheard of and virtually non-existent.
- Orange marmalade is hard to find. You can buy orange jam, but this isn't the same thing. I brought over from England a tin or two of Marmade marmalade mix and made my own supply (one tin makes 6 lb of good marmalade).
- You have to seek out low-sugar and low-salt alternatives; tinned, convenience food in particular is often heavily sugared, salted and coloured.
- The chain CVS Pharmacy is a good outlet for Cadbury chocolate, regularly offering it at a 'Two for One' price, but it's made in America under licence and the taste isn't quite the same as the Cadbury's you get back home.

You could try sourcing items over the internet (see *Useful Websites* for some suggested outlets). If all else fails, ask the family to send you a Red Cross parcel.

In the Kitchen

In the UK, we are encouraged to compost biodegradable kitchen waste, whereas Americans prefer to macerate and wash it down the 'insinkerator' or garbage disposal unit. This is a standard piece of equipment in many American homes. In hot summers, disposing of biodegradable food this way is preferable to putting it out in the dustbin, though not as good as composting it. You can drop teabags, coffee grounds, plate scrapings and all soft vegetable matter down the hole in the sink. Just make sure you run the tap at the same time as operating the macerator. Sweet corn, potato peelings, bones and anything stringy do not go down well and will have dire effects on the grinding machine. Be careful also about dumping globs of food, such as pasta, down the sink. Grind up a lemon every so often to freshen the beast, and keep its teeth sharp with ice cubes.

In order to assess differences in American and British eating habits, I asked American friends to report on the basic contents of their fridges, freezers and kitchen cupboards. Below are some of the staple items they listed which you wouldn't necessarily find in a kitchen back home:

- peanut butter and jelly;
- several litres of fizzy drink and bottled water;
- a huge variety of condiments (ketchups, mustards, sauces, dips, salad dressings, etc.);
- one-gallon cartons of milk;
- half-gallon cartons of orange juice and/or frozen concentrate;
- frozen corn on the cob;
- frozen waffles;
- boxed macaroni cheese;
- Bisquick (pre-made flour mixture for making pancakes, biscuits, casserole toppings, etc.);
- cake, brownie and/or cookie mixes;
- pizza and pasta sauces;
- hot dogs;
- apple sauce;
- real coffee, for use in the coffee percolator (an essential American kitchen item).

Most American home-owners do not have an electric kettle, tea not being one of their daily necessities. Instead they have coffee percolators and smoothie makers, and huge fridge freezers to keep everything cool. Many also have an ice and water dispenser on the freezer door, so you can dispense cool water and as much ice as you could possibly want, whenever you want.

Below are a few tips for the chef:

- Invest in a set of American measuring cups.

- In recipes, US liquid measures (e.g. a pint) are not the same as UK. Check your ready reckoner.
- When making pastry, use a mixture of 5 oz all-purpose (plain) flour to 1 oz corn starch, sieved well, and add an extra 1–1.5 oz of fat for best results.

Drink

Americans drink vast amounts of coffee and cola, and smaller quantities of tea, milk, wine, beer and juices. Approximately 87% of all beverages consumed by Americans are non-alcoholic, carbonated soft drinks making up the lion's share (approximately 28%) of this consumption. Smoothies (a mixture of blended fruit and ice) are popular. Chocolate milk and fruit juices are good healthy options for the children.

In 1975, consumption of soda (fizzy pop) surpassed coffee and milk and it is now the nation's single biggest 'food'. One in every five calories consumed is in the form of a sugary drink, and every year the average American consumes 56 gallons of the stuff. This makes for a lot of extra, sneaky calories. There are 3 million soda machines in America alone, one for every 97 members of the population. With one-third of children now overweight or on the brink of becoming so (according to a national nutritional survey), government and public pressure has persuaded companies to stop stocking soda in vending machines in elementary and middle schools nationwide. They have agreed to only sell water, unsweetened juice and low-fat milk in these schools and in addition only diet soda in high schools.

Coca-Cola has been around since 1886. It was first advertised as medicinal 'for headache and tired feeling', probably with some basis as it originally contained a small amount of cocaine. During World War II and sugar rationing, the government gave dispensation to the Coca-Cola Company to supply free Coke to the US Army. Today Coca-Cola is one of the most widely distributed products in the world and the world's most popular soft drink. Pepsi-Cola comes second in the popularity stakes. Formulated by a pharmacist, Caleb Bradham, in North Carolina in 1898 and advertised as 'Exhilarating, Invigorating, Aids Digestion', it has an equally long history. In 1964, the company introduced Diet Pepsi, America's first diet soft drink. Some sodas are marketed as zero calorie, but they still have a high sugar content.

Drinks, especially alcoholic ones, tend to be disproportionately expensive to food and considerably bump up the bill when you eat out. Check the price before ordering so you don't have a nasty surprise. Also, I could kick myself the number of times I forgot to say hold the ice. Even in the depths of winter, drinks come iced to the teeth. If you do not say otherwise, you will end up with a glass full of ice and a watered-down drink. Don't be afraid to ask for a (free) glass of water; servers will not be put out, and indeed often bring you a large glass of iced water without prompting. When you order a soft drink, check what the policy is regarding refills. Many casual restaurants allow you unlimited refills and sometimes you may even leave the restaurant with a full cup.

Coffee represents approximately 71% of total US caffeine consumption, followed by soft drinks and tea. Americans walk about, glued to their insulated mugs of coffee; they can't seem to operate without their caffeine fix. The purchase of a cup can be an experience in itself. First you have the difficulty of selecting from the huge choice (Starbucks offers an alleged 55,000 different combinations of coffee). I once spent 10 minutes in a queue while somebody ahead of me ordered something exotic (the restaurant scene in the film *L.A. Story* with Steve Martin came to mind). The counter girl then proceeded to brew, pump, blend, whip, steam and swirl, before presenting the incredible mixture to the nonplussed customer. I felt like shouting 'Hooray' or 'Bravo', but knew all eyes would turn questioningly to me without seeing the funny side. You can order something so far removed from coffee that it is hard to believe any of those dark little grains are in it. Ordering a cup of coffee has become an art.

If this sort of excitement is not your cup of tea, then just try ordering a simple cuppa – you may end up with a glass of iced tea or, failing that, hot tea with creamer (equally horrible in my opinion). If you like English tea with milk, you should ask for hot tea with plain milk (not half and half, dried sachet milk or tiny cartons of long-life milk) and hope for the best. As most Americans do not drink tea at home, when you are offered a drink, don't be surprised if they do not have any tea, or can only produce something herbal or fruity. They may then proceed to take a mug of cold water, put it in the microwave for a couple of minutes, and dunk a teabag in the resulting hot water. As in Europe, Lipton seems to have cornered the market with black, herbal and fruit teas. A good, strong British tea is hard to come by, and most British families in America rely on home-sourced tea (add it to your Red Cross parcel list).

Alcohol

Many Americans appear to be rather conservative where alcohol is concerned. Perhaps this is a hangover (excuse the pun) from the era of Prohibition. In 1917 a coalition of Protestants, temperance societies, businesses and women's groups spurned the 18th Amendment, which, from January 1920, banned 'the manufacture, sale, or transportation of intoxicating liquors' across the United States. A thriving bootleg market resulted, with Al Capone's mob in Chicago servicing the 'speakeasies' (bars where alcohol was sold illicitly). Whisky was available by prescription for 'medicinal purposes' and doctors didn't seem to have any qualms dispensing it; unsurprisingly, the number of 'patients' requiring their 'medication' increased noticeably. There were some social advantages to Prohibition, as drink-related crime and diseases declined, but the social and economic costs of the criminal activity brought about repeal of the unpopular law in 1933 under the 21st Amendment; however, individual states were still allowed to ban the purchase and sale of alcohol.

Today, there are considerable variations across states and counties in alcohol laws, with more than 500 counties throughout the nation still 'dry', particularly in the southern Bible Belt.

- Mississippi prohibited alcohol in 1902, 12 years before the rest of the country. Following nationwide rejection of the unpopular federal law, the state continued to ban it for another 33 years. Thereafter it allowed local counties the option to remain dry, and today almost half of them exercise that option.
- Utah (Mormon country) is the second most severe in its temperance laws. The only bona fide drinking that goes on is in private social clubs where drinking is permitted by members, and at a limited number of restaurants, which cannot advertise or display the fact that they sell alcohol. It is even illegal to swallow at wine tastings.
- Texas has 254 counties, 79 of which are dry and some of the others are 'moist' or partially dry. Taking more than three sips of beer in one go while standing is a prohibited act in Texas.
- Kansas is totally dry. The rule of not drinking alcohol is allegedly even enforced on airline passengers flying over the state.
- Approximately two out of every three counties in Alabama are dry (though the state allows tobacco, firearms and fireworks to be sold without restrictions).
- Alaska has 83 dry towns and villages.
- In South Carolina, a law requiring bars and restaurants to serve liquor from mini bottles was only repealed as recently as 2006. The mini-bottle law was one of the last vestiges of Prohibition in this state.
- In Colorado you won't find any alcohol in hotel minibars.
- In Iowa, 'tabs' are illegal.
- In Kentucky, supposedly you can be thrown in jail for merely giving a friend there a bottle of alcohol as a gift.
- Public intoxication is considered a crime in Pennsylvania. Giving your under-18-year-old children even a sip of alcohol means you are breaking the law.

Despite these inconsistent and often rather odd rules, many people still quietly enjoy their drink. In fact, Ohio enjoyed a record year in 2006 with regard to sales of liquor (with vodka, whisky and rum topping the popularity stakes). Yet the temperance mentality is still very much alive. If you are lucky enough to be in a state with lenient laws, then bottles of alcohol are usually sold in brown paper bags to disguise them. Unlike in much of Europe, alcohol is not consumed routinely with meals. Many restaurants do not even offer it, or only after a certain time of day, for example after 5 p.m. Sixteen states still ban Sunday sales of alcohol and alcoholic beverages. In state parks, signs remind you that consuming alcohol openly in public is an offence. Some American parents are strict about letting their kids see them drink. When asked, 'What would you like to drink?' at get-togethers at our house, most American friends opted for iced water or something fizzy and non-alcoholic. This seemed strange to us, used to the British norm of openly having a beer or glass of wine. Dave, an American friend, suggested that his countrymen's rather prudish attitude to drinking arose from people worrying what others might think of them. Another reason for abstinence might be religious beliefs. So never press an American to drink alcohol. Paradoxically, many major sports events are sponsored by alcohol companies, who spend billions on promoting drinking. So Americans receive mixed messages about consuming alcohol.

In a Gallup pole (conducted in July 2006) of 1007 Americans aged over 18, 64% said they drink alcohol, with beer being their favourite choice. Most American beer is light and gassy, of the lager variety. Budweiser is the most popular American beer, accounting for 50% of all beers sold. Sam Adams does a good range. Montana produces something called Moose Drool, Louisiana has Funky Butt Juice. Worth a try perhaps? Americans do not distinguish between what we call beer and lager, so when asking for a beer you will usually be served a chilled lager. If you want something resembling a British beer, ask for a dark beer or ale. You will still probably end up with something on the chilly side. They have mostly bottled beers, which are usually better tasting than something on draft. If cocktails are more your thing and you are willing to pay around the same price for your drink as your entrée, Americans can whip up a good cocktail, but ask them to go easy on the ice. Margaritas are very popular.

Some sources say that around 40 states in the US commercially produce wine; others say that all 50 are producers. The best known region for grape growing is California, which produces 90% of the nation's wine and is home to 1800 wineries; New York comes second. The Hudson Valley is the oldest wine-producing region in America, thanks to French settlers. Oregon and Washington State are also major producers. Wine is a relatively new, sophisticated drink for the average American. A fun movie to watch is *Sideways* (starring Paul Giamatti), which highlights the snobbery of some would-be wine connoisseurs.

The minimum age for drinking and purchasing alcohol in the States is 21 years. The Wikipedia website (see *Useful Websites*) describes what this actually means in practice.

Regional Cuisine

As America is a mixed and diverse nation, so is her cuisine, with every ethnic group bringing its own style of cooking and ingredients. Overall, American dishes tend to be rustic rather than gourmet. Annual food festivals and other celebrations are very popular; there is even a National Bread Month. Certain foods are associated with particular regions or states, and below is a brief résumé. Although borrowing extensively from other cultures, where American cuisine comes into its own is in the diversity of its food flavours, e.g. in the huge variety of pizza types and ice cream flavours.

Native Americans were eating sweet potatoes, quinoa, fried green tomatoes, pumpkin and turkey (to name a few) long before the white man arrived. They were also into pit-barbecuing. Their 'Three Sisters' were squash, beans and corn (maize). These foods were passed down over the centuries and are now very much associated with American cuisine. Native Americans also enjoyed grilled guinea pig, squirrel and horse, though these don't seem to have made it onto today's menus. Foods hailing originally from Europe, such as burgers, pizzas, apple pie and chowder, are now typical American fare. Mexican dishes such as salsa, burritos, tacos, fajitas and chilli con carne are also very popular.

The South really knows how to cook decadently. Just take a look at the recipes in the popular magazine *Southern Living*. This region of America has close associations with African-based cuisine, favouring fried chicken, black-eyed beans, grits and biscuits (especially with gravy), catfish, butter and pinto beans, sweet tea and mint juleps. This is 'soul food'. Gumbo stews, peaches and peanuts, and key lime pie from Florida are also well known. The big cooked breakfast is a mainstay in the South, originating from English settlers. The Cracker Barrel chain serves up hearty, southern, comfort food. Some fast-food outlets have their roots in the states of the South (Krispy Kreme, Waffle House and KFC), along with the drinks Pepsi Cola hailing from New Bern, North Carolina, Coca Cola from Atlanta, Georgia, and Dr Pepper from Texas. Tex-Mex cuisine from Texas, Creole and barbecue are also typical southern food styles.

New England excels in seafood (e.g. Maine lobsters and clam chowder) and dairy produce, as well as cranberries and maple syrup. Boston has baked beans and Samuel Adams beers to add to its fame.

The Midwest is known for its hearty, simple dishes, e.g. meatloaf, mashed potatoes, green beans and sauerkraut. German immigrants also brought bratwursts and beer. Frozen custard (thick ice cream, made with egg yolk) is another Midwest speciality. Kansas City and Chicago are centres of the beef trade, Iowa of the pork market. Kansas City and St Louis, Missouri, are also barbecue lovers. Wisconsin is America's dairy capital, known for its cheese.

Some Peculiarly American Food and Drink

Staples

Corn is grown and eaten extensively in America; for instance, in the form of grits, hominy, chowder, bread, mush, popcorn and tortillas, and of course as corn on the cob. When Americans refer to corn they mean specifically sweet corn or maize, not wheat or any other cereal (the usual British connotation). At the dawn of American civilisation, the colonists at Jamestown traded with the Indians for corn. The Indians also shared their corn with the Pilgrims during that first hard winter and then instructed them on how to grow it successfully themselves. Corn was a staple food and, as such, was important to their survival.

Grits is coarsely ground corn, boiled up for breakfast, and very popular, especially in the South. Indeed, it is the official state food of Georgia. Maize is ground into fine particles known as cornmeal and coarser grits. These are cooked with a variety of added flavourings, such as butter, sugar, gravy, cheese, tomatoes, shrimp, fried fish or peanut butter. When served sweet it is rather like eating a bowl of semolina and is better than it sounds. Grits makes a simple breakfast dish or can be the basis of a gourmet recipe.

Indiana produces the most *popcorn*, and Illinois has claimed it as its official state snack. It has been around since the time of the Pilgrims and is America's favourite nibble. With the first steam-powered popping machines invented in 1885, which could be set up at social events, popcorn went public. Today supermarkets sell corn for popping in the microwave at home or at work. Sweetened puffed breakfast cereals originated from classic popcorn. Popcorn at the movies has always been popular, but in the early days it came to be viewed as antisocial (too noisy and messy) and was therefore banned inside theatres. This ban was later conceded during the 1930's Depression era when 'concession stands' were allowed to set up in the lobbies (hence the name).

Sweet potatoes are indigenous to America and a long-time traditional American food. They were a very important staple during the Civil War, but recently have declined in popularity with increasing affluence – they are now viewed as a poor man's food. They are almost twice as nutritious as the common potato, with dark-orange varieties highest in vitamin A. North Carolina produces 40% of the nation's sweet potato crop, and it is a popular component of southern cuisine. Sometimes incorrectly called yams, sweet potatoes are a common side dish to the main course, often served with brown sugar (strictly for those with a sweet tooth).

American *mac 'n cheese* is a popular choice on children's menus. The boxed variety contains powdered cheese sauce rather than real cheese, and is a strange orange-yellow colour; in fact, Crayola named one of its crayon colours after it. The first time I tasted this doubtful-looking, rubbery, barely cheesy form of macaroni, I vowed never to let my children order it again, yet somehow you get used to it and come to view it as normal and okay. Perhaps I am too suspicious, but it doesn't taste or look like real food somehow, though the kids enjoyed it.

Peanut butter was originally sold as a medicinal nutritional supplement at the beginning of the twentieth century. It was given to the US Army in their rations during World War II, along with *jelly* (jam as we know it), as both have a long shelf-life. It is a classic children's pack lunch sandwich filler.

Sweet Tooth and Bakery Goodies

If you have a sweet tooth, America will be heaven (or perhaps hell) for you. Their *doughnuts* are much less stodgy than ours and a real treat. They come with a huge choice of toppings and fillings. The small, rich chocolate cakes known as *brownies* are quintessentially American. *Blondies* are a variation, made without cocoa and sometimes containing white chocolate or nuts.

American *biscuits* – which are soft, look like scones, salty rather than sweet and eaten with savoury meals – are delicious. Look for them in the freezer compartment and bake them at home for that fresh, restaurant-style taste.

Girl and boy scouts love to sell *cookies*. They make a killing on their sales of specially boxed biscuits; there are even competitions and prizes for the scout who can sell the greatest number of boxes. Proceeds help fund the scout group, so you can feel good about buying them.

Pretzels are made with wheat and yeast, baked and usually salted. Cities like Philadelphia and New York are famous for their soft pretzels, but hard varieties are more common. The US pretzel industry is worth $550 million a year.

American *muffins* are different to our English muffins. They resemble small domed cakes, with any number of flavourings, e.g. classic blueberry, chocolate chip or apple. Some states have adopted their own flavour 'state muffins'. The trend is for ever-increasing size and, conversely, bite-sized muffins. Don't confuse them with our bread-style muffins, which are called English muffins in America, popularly toasted at breakfast time.

There is a strong *bagel* culture, especially in cities with an ethnic Jewish population. Real bagels (not the supermarket type) are tough and chewy, not bready. Bagels are part steamed, part baked and often flavoured – either sweet or savoury. Panera Bread does good bagels. Nutritionally, a bagel can be the equivalent of several slices of bread, so take it easy how many you eat if you are worried about calories.

Sourdough bread is made with a starter of flour, water, salt and yeast that has sat for 3 days in a controlled temperature to bring out the flavour. Traditionally, each time bread is made, a small piece of starter is kept back for the next loaf. This gives the dough its distinctive, slightly sour taste. Some bakers/housewives have been using the same starter for 20 years or more. It is traditionally given as a wedding gift.

Pumpkin pie (consisting of pureed pumpkin, seasoned with ginger, cloves and nutmeg and sweetened with brown sugar, then put in a pie crust) is another popular creation that dates back to Pilgrim times. In the autumn, pumpkins festoon every other porch or front yard it seems, so they are very much a feature in the American calendar. However, the classic jack-o-lantern pumpkin has a rather coarse texture, so tinned squash is often used by home-cooks.

Pecan pie is made with corn syrup or more correctly with sugar and eggs (a classic custard base) and of course pecan nuts. It is associated with Christmas and other special occasions. Pecans are also used to flavour other desserts and ice creams.

Shoofly pie came from the Pennsylvania Dutch and is traditionally found in the South. It consists of molasses. Order a 'wet bottom' and you'll get a crumb topping above a layer of gooey molasses; a 'dry bottom' will give you something more cake-like – the choice is yours.

'As American as apple pie' is commonly used to mean something typically American (as the title of this book suggests) – something wholesome. During World War II, American soldiers were often quoted as saying they had gone to war 'for Mom and apple pie'. Though *apple pie* is not peculiar to America, it is a favourite dessert. Some people put a slice of melted cheese on the top.

Kellogg's *Pop-Tarts* are so popular that they now come in around 32 different flavours. These rectangular pastry sandwiches with a sugary filling caused controversy in 1992 when a toaster caught fire and the owner sued Kellogg for damages. Since then, they have carried a warning: 'Do not leave toasting appliances unattended due to possible risk of fire'. In one episode of *The Simpsons*, Dr Nick advises Homer to use Pop-Tarts instead of bread when making sandwiches in order to put on weight quickly.

The first recipe for *s'mores* was found in the 1927 *Girl Scout Handbook*. They consist of roasted marshmallow and a slab of melted chocolate sandwiched between two graham crackers. They are traditionally eaten round the campfire. First the marshmallow is melted on a skewer over the fire, removed and laid on top of soft chocolate and a cracker, sandwiched together, and the whole molten mess is consumed. With a mouthful of goo, all the eater may manage to say is 's'more' – hence the name. *Fluffermutters* are something similar, made with Marshmallow Fluff and peanut butter or groundnut paste in a bread sandwich.

Maple syrup is another popular American sweetie. Maple sugaring involves extracting sap from the sugar maple tree. It was developed by Native Americans, who passed the skill on to the pioneers. Vermont produces more maple syrup than any other state. Ohio is the third largest producer in terms of syrup volume, with an industry worth $2.3 million a year; the extracting season lasts from Valentine's Day to 1 April. Maple syrup festivals are popular in April, with pancakes drowned in syrup, often teamed rather inexplicably with sausages.

For the Meat Eater

Coney Island, New York, is the birthplace of the *hot dog*; which is why sometimes they are simply called *coneys*. They are often topped off with a weak chilli sauce and tasteless grated cheese. *Corn dogs* are hot dogs coated in sweet cornbread batter and deep fried, then stuck on a stick. They are a popular street fair food, but rather sweet and artificial tasting.

Jerky comprises strips of meat with the fat removed, marinated and dried, to produce a long-life product that does not require refrigeration. The result is a chewy, salty/sweet snack that is low in fat and high in protein. Some cheaper varieties use highly processed meat rather than traditional whole muscle meat and can be heavily salted, so buy high-quality jerky if you can. Beef jerky is the most popular.

A *sloppy joe* is a loose meat sandwich, allegedly first put together by a chef called Joe in Iowa, which tends to slop out of its bun, hence the name. It comprises ground beef cooked in a frying pan, with highly seasoned tomato sauce spread on the bun. If it is made from ground turkey it is known as a *sloppy tom.*

Contrary to first thoughts, *buffalo wings* have nothing to do with the mighty beast the buffalo, though some advertisements have hammed up this image. Buffalo wings originated in Buffalo, New York, and are deep-fried chicken wings, coated in a cayenne pepper sauce.

Peculiar Drinks

Root beer is similar in taste to sarsaparilla, and contains a variety of fermented ingredients (for instance, liquorice, cherry, vanilla, spices, anise and/or molasses). The taste of home-made and local brands can thus vary considerably. In Britain, dandelion and burdock and ginger beer are root beers. Root beer is popular with youngsters and as an alternative to alcoholic beer.

Malt liquor is a lager with an artificially produced high alcohol content (6–9% alcohol by volume; known as super-strength lager in Britain). In place of hops, dextrose, barley or rice, which is sprouted (malted) slightly before being fermented, gives the drink its taste. *Malted milk drinks* (like a shake) are also popular at places like Dairy Queen.

Iced tea is traditionally served with a slice of lemon or lime, or it may be flavoured with other fruits. It is a popular alternative to soda and more refreshing, especially in the hot southern states. It is usually sweetened with corn syrup.

Conclusion

Table 17.2 lists some personal great and not-so-great experiences concerning food and eating out in America. Americans are renowned for their cheap, plentiful, good quality food and great service. Portions are famously generous – sometimes obscenely so – and have been getting larger over the past decades. It has been said that Americans have more food to eat than any other people, and more diets to keep them from eating it. Politician and economist John K. Galbraith observed that, 'More die in the United States from too much food than from too little', and Thomas Jefferson once said, 'We seldom report of having eaten too little'. The biggest concern we had on coming to America was that before long we would adopt the physique of many of her citizens. In reality, this didn't happen; you learn to curb your appetite and choose a single course (not the usual two or three you might order in Britain). You also learn to doggie bag a lot.

One of the downsides to the American culture of cheap, plentiful food is that you are constantly tempted to eat things you shouldn't. You can't even walk into a petrol station without being lured by the smell of hot dogs or pizza and fresh vending machine coffee, with enticing doughnuts or bagels conveniently near the cash till. Children are particularly easy prey. You can slip into the habit of eating too much processed convenience food, with adverse effects on your wallet, waistline and possibly health. So I end this chapter with a few words of advice:

> 'A good meal ought to begin with hunger.' (French proverb)
> 'You are what you eat.' (Anonymous)

It's common sense, but bear these two points in mind and you shouldn't go far wrong in America.

Table 17.2 Personal experiences of eating out and shopping for food in America: pros and cons.

Pros	Cons
Eating out	
Cheap prices, special offers and discounts	Not necessarily good value in terms of food quality or taste; can be mediocre in taste; tax added at end often bumps up the bill unexpectedly
Large portions; you never leave hungry	Wasteful; encourages you to consume more than you need or should
Emphasis on convenient, fast delivery of food to your table	Servers barely give you time to sit down, let alone read the menu
Very family orientated; kids welcome virtually everywhere	Ambience is lacking; not much effort given to making the atmosphere cosy or romantic
Kids menu always available, at a good price	Often nutritionally and choice poor
Buffet-style eating	Leads to overgrazing and consequent guilt
Free refills on drinks	Often watered down with too much ice; alcoholic drinks are expensive
If you choose one of the many chain or franchise restaurants, you know what you are going to get	Lack of originality – most places offer very similar, standard American fare; even the food in many ethnic restaurants lacks 'spice' and authenticity
Choice of dips, dressings, condiments	Overseasoning, e.g. French fries, salad dressings, over-sweet sauces

Pros	Cons
Shopping for food	
Huge range of convenience foods and ready-made items	These contain a scary number of ingredients with an inordinately long shelf-life, which raises health questions
Huge choice of any one particular food item	Pressure of too much choice and decision making
Convenience of all-under-one-roof outlets	Crowded, overlarge supermarkets, lacking in individuality; it takes you a long time to get round and you are easily seduced into buying more than you need; takes the joy out of shopping at small places, where you can concentrate on buying one or two quality things, e.g. compare with individual British butchers and bakeries
Discounts/special prices advertised on shelves, e.g. 10 for $10	Often not clear how the discounting works, e.g. do you have to buy 10 to get the discount? Usually not – which misleads you into buying more than you needed (a good marketing ploy)

Useful Websites

www.englishteastore.com – the English Tea Store, based in Pennsylvania, which sells British food products and tea.
www.lifeintheusa.com – look up what 'America Eats'.
www.xpatshop.co.uk – a shopping service for expats, offering basic products at affordable prices (food and non-food).

Wikipedia:
Legal drinking age – select Americas and scroll down for the United States.

Terminology

American term	Equivalent British term	Notes
2% milk	Semi-skimmed milk	
All-purpose flour	Plain flour	Contains raising agents and salt, so is best used in savoury dishes only
Appetiser	Starter	
Beer	Lager	
Bird's dessert powder	Custard powder	
Biscuit	Scone or bread roll	
Blush	Rosé wine	
Broil	Grill or bake	To cook food with high heat, usually applied directly to the food
Cake flour	Plain flour	Extra light in texture
Candy	Sweets	
Canola	Rapeseed oil	
Check	Restaurant bill	
Chips	Crisps	
Cider	Apple juice	Alcoholic cider is hard cider
Cilantro	Coriander	
Confectioner's sugar	Icing sugar	
Cookie	Biscuit (sweet)	
Cook out	Barbecue	
Corn starch	Cornflour	
Cotton candy	Candy floss	
Diner	Café	
Easy over	Fried egg cooked on both sides	
Eggplant	Aubergine	
Entrée	Main course	
Fries, French fries	Chips	
Funnel cake	Doughnut ring	Common at fairgrounds, festivals and ball parks; consists of piped doughnut dough, deep fried, with icing sugar sprinkled on top. Heavenly!
Golden raisins	Sultanas	
Graham crackers	Similar to Digestive cross Rich Tea biscuits	Made from wholewheat flour

American term	Equivalent British term	Notes
Heavy cream	Double cream	
Hush puppy		Small, savoury cornmeal bread, deep fried
Jello	Jelly	
Jelly	Jam	
Ice cream soda	Milk shake	
Lady fingers	Trifle sponges	
Lifesavers	Similar to Polos	
Make a reservation	Book	
Mimosa	Buck's Fizz	
Picnic pork	Pork leg	The only pork joint that has crackling on it
Plastic wrap	Clingfilm	
Popsicle	Ice lolly	
Porterhouse or club steak		Sirloin steak
Rutabaga	Swede	
Server	Waiter/waitress	
Shrimp	Prawn	
Sirloin steak	Rump steak	
Soda, pop	Soft drink, fizzy drink	
Sub, submarine, hoagie, hero, poor boy	Bread roll	Regional variations in terminology
Sunny side up	Fried egg cooked on one side	
Take-out, food to go	Take-away	
Vitamin D milk	Full fat milk	Enriched with vitamin D (for supposed health benefits)
Wheat bread	Brown bread	
Zucchini	Courgette	

18 · Health Matters

A study reported in the *Journal of the American Medical Association* (2006) found that while the United States spends more on health care than any other industrialised country (on average $5700 per person per year, which represents 15% of Gross Domestic Product), the life expectancy of the nation lags behind 24 other countries. Forty-three countries (including Lebanon and Mongolia) have more doctors per head of population and 49 have more hospital beds. The US government spends double what England spends on the health care of its citizens, yet, despite such high spending, it looks like American citizens are getting a raw deal. According to research conducted in 2002 across America and England, the health of richer Americans is on a par with that of low-income earners in England. Compared with your average white, middle-aged Englishman or woman, American counterparts have higher rates of sickness in every health category, including hypertension, heart disease, cancer, lung disease, heart attack and stroke. Reports of diabetes are twice as high in America. England has more heavy drinkers, but the number of smokers is about the same on both sides.

Economics plays a large part in the differing health status of America's citizens. There is a distinction between the health care experiences of the rich and/or well-insured and the poor with minimal or no health insurance. There are disparities among racial and ethnic groups, with African-Americans, Hispanics and Asians generally having poorer health than whites. For instance, the cancer rate is 10% higher for African-Americans than whites, and the incidence of diabetes is twice as high. Minority groups tend to rely on emergency-room treatment and clinics rather than a regular source of care, and are often uninsured. There is a scarcity of medical facilities and personnel in inner cities, rural areas and communities with high concentrations of minority populations. Only 5% of American physicians are Hispanic and 4% are African-American.

The Fat Problem

It is estimated that:

- 65% of American adults aged 20 years and older are overweight; that is, their body mass index (BMI) is 25 or more.
- 30% of Hispanics born in America are obese.
- 24.3% of Americans have high blood pressure.
- 7.6% have heart disease.
- 6.1% are diabetic.

Since 1980, the total number of overweight or obese adults has doubled and America is now regarded as the fattest nation in the world. An unwieldy body generally represents a lack of self-control, and it is very sad to see whole families with the same problem, including young children following in the same unhealthy footsteps as their parents. More than 400,000 deaths per annum are associated with eating-related illnesses, and obesity is second only to smoking as a major preventable cause of death.

Rates of childhood obesity began escalating in the 1980s, at the same time that adult weight began to increase. Today, according to the National Center for Health Statistics, 34% of American children aged 6–19 are overweight, and about half of those are considered to be obese (up 11% from 1994 figures). One paediatrician has estimated that 11.6% of American children between the tender ages of 6 months and 2 years are carrying too much weight. Moreover, today's children are showing medical conditions that are more common in middle-aged adults, for example cirrhosis (liver failure). Childhood obesity is not just a cosmetic problem, but a serious health problem facing American society.

This is partly the fault of the food industry, which promotes junk food on children's television. A 2004 study by the American Psychological Association found that the average child sits through 40,000 TV commercials a year, most of them for sweets, fizzy drinks, sugary cereals and high-fat snack foods. Research has shown that many kids spend more time watching TV than in school, and that children under the age of 8 cannot distinguish between truth and persuasive advertising. They are thus highly susceptible to such ads. Americans pride themselves on protecting their young, yet they are ignoring this simple aspect of their children's health.

Some people's attitudes in the States are shifting from rejection of being overweight towards acceptance. Witness T-shirts that proclaim *I'm not fat, I'm an American.* According to the research firm NPD Group, today only 24% of Americans find overweight people less attractive than normal-weight people. There is even a National Association to Advance Fat Acceptance for those feeling prejudiced or lacking 'empowerment'. The Association offers meetings, events and holidays for BBWs (big beautiful women) and BHMs (big handsome men).

However, the majority of Americans are beginning to recognise that overeating has become an epidemic of huge proportions. In February 2007, the two top-selling non-fiction books, according to the *Washington Post*, were *The Best Life Diet* and *You: On a Diet: The Owner's Manual for Waist Management.* Some people take their health very seriously, and this has spurned a vast fitness industry. Even some employers now offer wellness programmes at work. Personal fitness trainers are highly employable, charging between $60 and $150/hour for their services. Come the New Year, the gyms are heaving and every other TV commercial is for *Thinzymes* or some other amazing aid that is supposed to reduce the size of your midriff. Americans appear to be especially vulnerable to wonder drugs and diets claiming to transform you into a svelte body in just a few easy weeks. You can apparently now lose weight without exercising, by simply popping a pill. New skinny pills claim you can lose up to a pound every 8–12 hours without changing your diet or exercise regime (though if you read the small print it says that results are not typical). With claims of fat-burning chain reactions, caloric abatement formulas, dissolving lard and slowing down the effects of calories by simply ingesting a pill, what could be easier?

A more drastic solution to the truly obese is to reduce the size of your stomach. The incidence of stomach surgery has increased over the last 5 years and the procedure has gone overboard. Adverts for bariatric, laparoscopic or lap band surgery are common, despite the fact that 1 in 10 patients who undergo the surgery experience complications, often requiring further treatment. Bariatric surgery leads to vitamin deficiency (because if you take away half the stomach, you can't absorb all the necessary vitamins), and the long-term consequences are not known. Moreover, as the stomach can stretch again, it is possible that many will regain their girths.

The Nation's Diet

Since 1955, McDonald's has grown to become the number-one fast-food chain, commanding 43% of the total market. It has 30,000 restaurants globally in over 100 countries and feeds 46 million people every day. Most Americans live less than 3 miles from a McDonald's (and where there's a McDonald's there is usually a Wendy's, Burger King, Taco Bell and/or Kentucky Fried Chicken competing for your taste buds). You will even find them in hospitals. Burger King was started in 1954 and struggled until the launch of the Whopper sandwich. For a long time it was the second-largest hamburger chain behind McDonald's, but recently tied for second place with Wendy's. These companies have an advertising budget of billions, ensuring that their products are ever on people's minds and in their mouths. McDonald's in particular appeals to children, offering restaurants with indoor play areas, birthday parties, Happy Meals with got-to-have free toys and Ronald McDonald, the clown.

One in four Americans visits a fast-food restaurant every day. However, it is not just the frequency of visits that is concerning. The food is also fattier in the States.

According to the *New England Journal of Medicine*, French fries served up in McDonald's and KFC restaurants in New York contain a trans fat content that is, respectively, 1.5 times and 16 times higher than the same fries served up in Scotland, while KFC chicken contains 1.66 times more trans fat. The amount of trans fat content varies even from city to city and restaurant to restaurant in the same country. The reason appears to be the choice of frying oil (oil high in trans fats is cheaper).

Some fast-food outlets are undergoing a process known as 'premiumisation'. Eateries such as Panera Bread, Chipotle and Baja Fresh are going upmarket, with improved ambiance, high-quality ingredients and higher prices. These fast-casual restaurants are part of a growing trend, as people demand more healthy options. However, they cater for only a minority of discerning consumers.

As supermarkets have increased in size, so has the range of foods on offer. As a mum shopping with kids, it can be a real headache battling your way round the shelves, trying to make healthy choices. For instance, in the cereal aisle, all the sugary cereals are placed strategically at children's eye level, in popular packaging, while all the healthy cereals are on the top shelf, and may even require steps to reach them. Opposite the cereals, on the other side of the aisle, you may have a sweet battle on your hands as the candy bars are often placed there. Once at the checkout, cool fridges of soda are temptingly at hand, as are more sweets. Apparently, a few supermarkets now offer 'candy-free' checkouts for hassled mums (though I never encountered one).

Food these days is transported huge distances, another factor in the general decrease in its goodness. In American supermarkets you do not see signs for 'local' produce, as you do in British supermarkets, and I never once came across a farmers market. The last 50 years have seen a huge rise in food processing, with ready meals providing convenience, enhanced flavour and pleasure, often at the expense of good health. Processed food is often highly sugared and/or highly salted, and the average American now consumes more than twice the recommended amount of salt daily.

Aside from the quality of the food, quantity is an issue. As mentioned in Chapter 17, American servings really are large. Servers in some fast-food restaurants are even trained to encourage customers to order larger portion sizes. Moreover, many Americans have poor eating habits. They tend to have a small breakfast, grab lunch (often on the go) and get home late, feeling tired and overhungry: as my friend Dave put it, his priority on walking through the door after work is, 'Give me the fridge!' After fulfilling your appetite, all that is left is to sit and digest dinner in front of the TV, then go to bed. Any thought of exercising is blown out the window. If you are inclined, you might just manage to strap on a belly buster – a vibrating machine, which is supposed to make the fat simply drop off as you put your feet up. Way to go!

Eating Disorders

Guilt is often the result of all this emphasis on food and body image, which pushes some people to go to opposite extremes. According to the Academy for Eating Disorders:

- 0.3–1% of young women have anorexia nervosa;
- 1–3% have bulimia nervosa;
- approximately 3% of the population has binge-eating disorder;
- 4–20% of young women practise unhealthy patterns of eating (dieting, purging and/or binge-eating);
- even men are not immune to eating disorders, especially binge-eating.

In a poll of 1500 American adults conducted by the National Eating Disorders Association in March 2005, 43% had suffered or known someone who had suffered from an eating disorder. Anorexia nervosa and bulimia are particularly prevalent among young girls between the ages of 10 and 25, obsessed with the Hollywood-perpetuated image of a size 0 figure – thin is in. Whereas in real life, the average or standard size of women has gone up a size, on TV a thin image is still the beautiful norm, and it is frightening how far some go to emulate this. Athletes such as gymnasts, dancers, ice skaters and cheerleaders are most susceptible to this image.

Binge-eating disorder affects many individuals, especially those who are significantly obese. It is considered to be a psychiatric disorder rather than simple overindulgence. Bulimia is characterised by recurring episodes of binge eating, followed by compensating behaviour; the disorder is often associated with depression, phobias and substance abuse. A survey conducted between 2001 and 2003 by Harvard researchers found that 94% of people with bulimia, 79% of those with binge-eating disorder and 56% of those suffering from anorexia had at least one other psychiatric diagnosis.

Smoking

Around 1 in 4 Americans smokes. While there is no federal legislation banning smoking, some state and local laws exist. Many American cities are on a big anti-smoking kick, and some have banned smoking in public places and workplaces. In the state of Ohio, legislation came in at the end of 2006 making it illegal to light up in restaurants, bars, bingo halls and bowling alleys, unless privately owned and operated. Even lorry drivers are restricted from smoking in their cabs if the lorry might be driven by other operators. In Ohio, the only places you can now legally smoke are in your own home, on your outdoor patio, in private clubs, family-owned businesses, tobacco stores and designated smoking rooms in nursing homes, hotels and motels. Forty six states prohibit the sale of tobacco products to people under the age of 18 (in the UK the minimum age is 16).

Tobacco is indigenous to North and South America. There are thousands of tobacco farmers in America, all contributing to the 408,000 tonnes or so of tobacco produced annually (according to the United Nations Foreign Agricultural Office, 2000); this ranks the USA as fourth in the world in terms of tobacco production, after China, India and Brazil. Tobacco is a vital part of America's economy, contributing billions of dollars to the federal government's coffers. Virginia is the home of tobacco, and in 2002 the gross income from tobacco production in this state alone was around $132 million.

Owing to the American legal system, which allows lawsuits to be brought against the tobacco industry, many tobacco businesses have seen their high revenues stripped by successful and continuing lawsuits brought against them since the 1990s. However, they are making so much profit that they can continue trading successfully.

Cigarette taxes vary from state to state. According to the FTA (Federation of Tax Administrators, January 2006), Rhode Island imposes the highest tax on a packet of cigarettes at $2.46 per pack, while South Carolina only takes 7 cents. Some counties and cities add their own taxes. The average price of a pack of cigarettes in New York City is $7, a fairly high rate by US standards. Compare this with the average price in the UK of £5.50 (equivalent to around $13), and you can see why smoking is more prevalent in the US than back home.

The American Health Care System

Dave Barry (American writer and humorist) joked:

> 'We Americans live in a nation where the medical-care system is second to none in the world, unless you count maybe 25 or 30 little scuzzball countries like Scotland that we could vaporize in seconds if we felt like it.'

According to the World Health Organization, 28 other countries have a lower maternal death rate and 33 have a lower infant mortality rate than the US; in fact, infant mortality is higher in the States than in any European Union country, and African-Americans fare the worst.

A little history lesson may be useful at this adjunct. Britain's National Health Service came into being during the post-war years, overseen by the Labour Party. The benefits of a free medical and hospital care system for all, without regard to income, was hailed by Britain's citizens, virtually unanimously, as a good thing. Around the same time, Congress was debating President Truman's proposal for a national health insurance system in America. However, the physicians' lobby on that side of the Atlantic was very strong and the idea of 'socialised medicine' was denigrated. While Europe adopted universal health insurance for its citizens, guaranteeing health care for everyone, America held sway. A government-provided health care service was perceived as just too much of a threat to the state of affairs in America. Over the years, various brave souls have tried to upset the apple cart, but their efforts to reform the

US system have usually fallen on deaf ears. Despite the general electorate's desire for change, the American Medical Association and insurance companies simply have too much financial clout.

The federal government went some way to addressing this problem in 1965 by creating various programmes such as Medicaid and Medicare, though these heavily bureaucratic systems are now in dire straits. In 1993, Hilary Clinton decided to take on reform of the health system, by heading up the Clinton administration's Task Force on National Health Care Reform. She was drummed out, humiliated and scorned by all and sundry. This indicates how deeply vested interests run. There is simply too much profit involved in the business of insurance and providing health care for the status quo to be upset. No real efforts at reform have been attempted since. Another reason for the lack of reform is fear of the rationing that would occur with socialised medicine (i.e. fear of the downsides). Americans want what they need right now, and are averse to waiting lists.

The American health care system is extremely bureaucratic, fails to provide an adequate service for many of its citizens and is expensive. Each year an estimated 18,000 people die because they lack insurance (according to an Institute of Medicine report, 2004). America has no free nationwide system of health care, as we do; instead each individual is expected to buy private health insurance. Some poorer families and individuals who cannot pay the high monthly premiums simply cannot afford to get sick. Without health insurance, you have no real access to health care. If you are a worker, however lowly paid, your family may not qualify for Medicaid. Furthermore, finding physicians who accept Medicaid patients may be problematic.

Thus, the seasonal worker, minimum-wage earner or part-timer who cannot afford the often exorbitant fees for health insurance find themselves out of the system. But even those earning a decent wage often find insurance too costly. A premium of $500/month is not unusual for private insurance. If you work for a company, you may be able to get cheaper health insurance under a group policy. However, if you suffer from past health problems you will pay far more, or even be turned down for coverage completely.

Even if you can afford some form of limited insurance, hefty deductibles and policy exclusions can catch you out, making people reluctant to seek medical care until they are so sick they don't have any other option. An American friend, Alison, said that, over the last few years, she had experienced a hike in premiums and the deductible (excess) on her health insurance plan. As a self-employed person, she was paying just over $200/month in premiums but still had a massive $5000 deductible. Despite the premiums being 100% deductible from her federal tax bill, she felt that the figures were probably too high to be workable for the long term.

There are approximately 46 million uninsured people in America, which represents around 16% of the population. If you don't buy insurance, you run the risk of going bankrupt. A heart attack could set you back $92,000 (and give you another one), and if you can't pay the hospital's fees, you are liable to go under. There are moves afoot (beginning in Massachusetts) to require that all but the very poorest people buy health insurance, much like car insurance. The governor of MA is proposing to subsidise or offer it free to those who can't afford it, and penalise those who can afford it but refuse to pay for it. Massachusetts and Vermont have recently passed laws to cover the uninsured, and other states are debating similar action.

Medicare

In 2003, Medicare accounted for nearly 13% of the federal budget. It is a federal health insurance programme for the elderly and disabled, financed by taxes paid through the national Social Security fund by the working population. All working Americans have to contribute. In 2006, 1.45% of an employee's earnings went towards this funding, along with 1.45% from the employer. The self-employed have to pay the full whack of 2.9% of their net earnings. Medicare is only available to citizens or permanent US residents aged 65 years or over who have worked at least 10 years in Medicare-covered employment, plus all those receiving disability benefits. In 2005, 42.5 million Americans were eligible, and this figure is expected to double over the next three decades as the baby boomers mature. The current fund is expected to run out of money by 2018. Fraud costs are contributing to the crisis.

Medicare covers the following:

- Part A provides insurance for hospital and nursing-home stays. If you have not paid enough Federal Insurance Contributions, you can purchase Part A cover at a cost of between $226 and $410/month (at 2007 prices).
- Part B provides insurance for out-patient expenses, including (among other things) X-rays, flu and pneumonia vaccinations, medical equipment such as wheelchairs, scooters and walking canes, and limited ambulance transportation. You pay an insurance premium for this cover ($93.50/month in 2007), which is usually deducted automatically from your Social Security cheque.
- Part C allows Medicare benefits through private health insurance plans instead of through Parts A and B. It is known as the Medicare Advantage Plan.
- Part D is the Prescription Drug Plan. In 2006, this was extended to include greater drug coverage than before. Anyone eligible for Parts A or B is also eligible for Part D. However, it is expensive, apparently inconsistent and confusing, especially for the people it is designed to help. There are quite specific eligibility criteria, and you have to figure out whether you qualify for help with your prescription on a drug by drug basis.

The whole Medicare system is complex and ever-changing. Not all medical costs are covered – there are deductibles and co-payments (see *Terminology* at end of chapter), and restrictions on the number of days you can claim. Ask most Americans to explain how it works, and they'll throw up their hands in hopeless ignorance.

Medicaid

Medicaid is a social welfare programme, funded jointly from federal and state coffers (approximately half each). The programme funds approximately a third of all childbirths in the US. About a quarter of each state's budget is spent on this single health scheme, and each state is responsible for administering its own variation of the programme. Thus eligibility criteria vary from state to state. The scheme is designed to help low-income earners, children, the elderly and people with disabilities. Each person is assessed according to his or her age, income, assets and resources, and may be asked to pay a small part of the medical costs (co-payment). You have to be a US citizen or resident alien to qualify for Medicaid; immigrants who have been in the country less than 5 years are not eligible.

Footing the Bill

Deciphering your hospital, doctor's or dental bill can be a major challenge, with the use of jargon, abbreviations and symbols designed, it seems, to confuse you. If you are well insured, it is hardly worth your while to read, let alone challenge, your bill – leave that particular headache to the insurance company. However, the outlandish prices and mark-ups charged by many hospitals and doctors are often simply swallowed by the insurance providers (and thence the faceless taxpayer). Moreover, most insurance companies have agreements with medical providers to pay only a portion of the bill. If you are a private individual you have to pay the full amount.

In response to criticisms of the charges for patient supplies, many hospitals counteract with the argument that they have to reflect the total cost of the care service they provide. That container of saline solution which is billed at $50 (when it actually costs around $1) is justified in the context of overheads and the overall service provided by the hospital or establishment. As the chairman of Humana (a health insurance company) put it, 'We are not a drugstore. We provide these items as part of the entirety of our patient care…'. Moreover, the hundreds of different insurance payment plans involve an army of personnel to deal with them, each insurer having its own rules of coverage and paperwork. It is estimated that approximately 25% of patient charges goes on administration costs.

Feeling rather bemused by the whole American insurance system, I asked another American friend to explain how her insurance policy worked (for a family of four). Her husband was self-employed and therefore had the unlucky task of having to pay the entire bill for the family's health insurance (with no employer help). His coverage alone cost $400/month. Maternity and family cover were an extra $100–150/month. The policy had a deductible of $500 per person, subject to a calendar year. Once each person in the family had incurred 500 dollars' worth of treatment, they paid only a percentage of the doctor's fees, e.g. 20% (but note, they still had to pay). Each time my friend took her children to the doctor for an office visit, e.g. for a check-up, ear infection or other minor hiccup, she had to co-pay an additional $25 per child.

In the past, there were no co-pays, so people would go to see their doctor for a stubbed toe. Some policies today still have no co-pays, but most do. Deductibles and co-pays vary considerable, according to which health care plan you opt for. The amount of co-pay also varies according to why you are seeing the doctor (there are a list of conditions and associated fees). Everything else that can possibly be charged for is, on top of the co-pay, e.g. vaccines. It certainly makes you think twice about taking the family to visit the doctor unless it is absolutely necessary.

My friend commented that choosing a health insurance plan from the myriad available and following the terms of the policy was very complicated. Her family's case also highlighted the big difference between the employed (who get about half their health insurance premiums paid for by the luckless employer) and the self-employed (who have to foot the whole bill themselves). She could have opted for a 'catastrophic plan', to cover certain events only, such as car accidents or having to go into hospital for an operation. However, every-day health issues would not be covered. This sort of plan may be fine for a healthy single person or young couple who are only responsible for themselves, but for families with children it is something of a gamble.

Some of the biggest names in the health insurance business are Blue Cross, Anthem, Aetna and Kaiser Permanente. If you are contemplating buying health insurance you should shop around and compare the policies offered very carefully. There are lots of exclusions and rules, and a huge industry of lawyers getting fat deciphering them. Nothing is free in the American health system. If you are poor, you may be able to claim Medicaid and other benefits; if you are rich, you can afford to pay. It is those in the middle who have the problem of affording the high premiums. People are crying out that the system needs changing, and, at last, health reform seems to be back on the political agenda.

Coming to America: Taking Care of Your Health

There is no reciprocal health care agreement between Britain and the United States, so, unless it is a fringe benefit of the job offer, you will need to take out your own health insurance. Job-related insurance usually only covers you, not your family. Dentistry and optometry charges are also normally excluded. Pregnancy tends to be covered on family policies only. American veterans are entitled to use the facilities on their nearest military base, and many make a decision to live close to a base for just this reason. Being in the British RAF on a US posting, the Tricare company looked after our health care arrangements.

If you are applying for permanent residence in the States, check with the Centers for Disease Control and Prevention (CDC) concerning what vaccinations you need.

If you are not applying for permanent residence, then there are no special immunisations required for adults, but children attending school or daycare facilities will need to have certain statutory vaccinations. All state schools and many private schools require children to be vaccinated against rubella, hepatitis B, DPT (diphtheria, pertussis and tetanus), varicella (chicken pox) and rubella (measles) before starting school. However, as rules vary from one state to the next, check exactly what is required with your chosen school or daycare provider. The National Network for Immunization Information (NNII)'s website allows you to search for school entry requirements state by state. The CDC is another useful port of call for information on immunisations. Also visit Dr. Paul's website for up-to-date information (see *Useful Websites*).

Your child cannot attend school until the school authorities have seen documented evidence that your child has been vaccinated and/or has immunity, so bring all UK immunisation records with you. They will probably also insist on tuberculosis testing and a medical before starting school. One important point to note is that although immunisation requirements in America and Britain are similar, re-immunisation may be necessary if the dates your children were immunised in the UK do not tally with those required by the state. My two children both needed extra shots, even though their UK records were fully up to date. It is quite a complicated scenario to go through, but go through it you must.

You often need a doctor's prescription for fairly ordinary drugs that are freely bought over the counter in Britain. Some medicines commonplace in the UK simply aren't available; for instance, paracetamol is considered too strong a painkiller to be sold to the public. Furthermore, some of the newer medications available on prescription in the UK are not available in the US. Children's medicines are often pink and sweet. So if you have any particular favourite medicine-cabinet staples, it may be an idea to ask someone back home to post them to you.

Some Particular Health Hazards

A great example of American informality and efficiency is in the administration of *flu* immunisations to those at risk (e.g. the elderly and pregnant women). In true American fashion, drive-throughs are available in many health districts. You simply head for the nearest clinic (a temporary jab station, perhaps in a church car park or at the county fairground), join the queue of cars, stick your arm and some money out the window (if you have to pay), and receive a passing shot. Americans sure are expert in making things easy and convenient.

Lyme disease (see also the discussion in Chapter 20) is a tick-borne illness, prevalent in America, especially on the East and West Coasts. Anyone who contracts a viral-like disease during the summer, especially in north-eastern states, should visit their doctor. The symptoms are a red rash at the site of a tick bite, chills and fever, head and body aches, joint inflammation and arthritis. To be on the safe side, wear long trousers, long sleeves and a hat when walking in wooded or grassy areas. Stick to the paths, avoid contact with tall grass and use an insect repellent. After walking in the countryside, check your pet and yourself for ticks and carefully remove them.

The plant *poison ivy* is toxic to most people, causing an often intense itching sensation on exposed skin, which may lead to the formation of shiny dots or blisters. This may be accompanied by restlessness and a raised temperature. It is caused by coming into contact with the oil of the plant. The oil is released upon tearing or bruising of any part of the plant and is very easily spread – via pets (which do not react to the poison but may have the oil on their coats), clothing, especially boots, tools or picnic baskets. As soon as possible after exposure, wash your skin and the contaminating article repeatedly with soap and cold water, and apply calamine lotion to affected skin. The oil will persist indefinitely and give rise to a repeat of the dermatitis unless the articles are washed thoroughly.

One thing I had really been looking forward to on moving to America was more outdoor living; being able to sit outside on warm summer evenings, entertaining or just lazing with a book. However, hopes were soon dashed. Wherever it is warm and humid, *mosquitoes and other biting flies* can be a nuisance. Those tiny tormenters will send you running for the *Bug Off*, religiously burning scented candles and desperately wafting joss sticks about the place. So much for a relaxing summer's evening in the garden. Some people even go to the extreme of spraying their whole lawns in an effort to keep the little blood-suckers away. Having screens on your doors and windows is a necessary form of defence.

EPA (Environmental Protection Agency)-registered repellents may offer some protection. Choose a formula with 10% DEET or less, especially if you have children, but do not apply to the face or hands (to avoid possible ingestion or stinging eyes). Mosquitoes do not like botanical oils such as citronella, cedar, geranium, lavender and pine, or other strong-smelling herbs and spices like cinnamon, garlic and peppermint. A natural insect repellent comprises 20 drops of essential oil in 1 oz of olive oil or water. Wear light colours if you can out-of-doors as insects are attracted to dark, patterned and brightly coloured clothing. Bats are natural mosquito predators, and one bat can eat up to a thousand mosquitoes a night. So you might consider putting up a bat box.

Keep some hydrocortisone cream handy to relieve itching. This was a bathroom-cabinet necessity for us in America, used almost daily at particularly annoying times of the year (especially spring and autumn).

The American Way of Birth: An Example of Where America Has Got it Wrong

I make no apologies for including such an extensive discussion on obstetrics, because it is a good example of where the American health system differs from that in Britain, and indeed most other countries. Even if you feel this section of text does not apply to you, the picture presented is a useful analogy to other areas of health care in the United States. Some details were gleaned from talking to American friends about their hospital birthing experiences. Jessica Mitford's book, *The American Way of Birth*, is worth reading if you want more on the subject.

The American way of giving birth is highly organised, often very unnatural for the woman, and basically a money-making venture. One friend commented, ' It seems some doctors view their profession more in monetary terms than as providing a caring service. If you are pregnant or giving birth *and* very poor, uninsured, a teenage mother, drug addict or alcoholic, the life of your baby – even your life – can be at risk through bureaucratic and political neglect'.

Most Americans give birth in a hospital, though home births are not unusual in more liberal places, such as California (but note, state laws vary regarding whether you are allowed to home-birth or not). If you go to hospital, you will be attended by either a hospital midwife, doctor or both. In order to be a hospital midwife, the person must also be a certified nurse, i.e. she must have a degree in nursing. Even then, the nurse midwife is often very restricted in what she is allowed to do, and must follow the directions of the obstetrician. For instance, some hospitals do not permit the midwife to deliver the baby; this is considered the job of a doctor. However, in practice, the midwife *can* take charge if the doctor fails to show up for the birth. Additionally, for a couple of hundred dollars, you can hire a birthing coach or *doula.*

The concept of a nurse midwife is alien in Europe, where midwifery and nursing are two separate professions – there it is not considered necessary to have a degree in nursing in order to be a midwife.

Outside of hospital, lay (unlicenced) midwives may assist at home births or at 'free-standing birth centres', which are not associated with a hospital and offer a more natural birth with fewer or no drugs. However, in some states of America, practising without a licence is outlawed.

The role of midwives in American obstetrics is much less than in Britain. The valuable service provided by health visitors, who visit the new mother and baby at home for up to a week after the birth, is unheard of in the States. Moreover, especially in rural areas, there is a dearth of obstetrical services – from prenatal care to receiving proper treatment in delivery. Giving birth unattended in hospital corridors and emergency rooms is not uncommon, where doctors cannot be found or are unavailable at the time the woman arrives at the hospital.

A Policy of Intervention

America has a very medicalised view of birth and health care. During prenatal classes, information dwells on what drugs are available and how to behave in hospital; the emphasis is on how the *hospital* wants you to have your baby. You are expected to follow their routine procedures, and erring from this often results in a negative response from medical staff who do not appreciate disruptions to their set way of working. One friend complained of being interviewed during her first labour by numerous resident nurses as part of their learning process (not very considerate for the mother-to-be).

In many developed European countries, 7% caesarian births is the norm, whereas in America it is nearer 25%, and the rate is increasing. The reasons for this are:

- Convenience – for the woman, so she can decide exactly when the birth is going to happen; however, more particularly, for the doctor, who can schedule deliveries, perhaps to avoid weekends, night calls and interfering with holiday schedules. Before the holidays (especially Thanksgiving, Christmas and New Year's Eve) the caesarian rate soars; another prime time is just before the end of the working day.
- Liability – the doctor is in control of a fairly routine procedure. More affluent mothers-to-be are more likely to sue if their babies suffer problems during vaginal birth, which is why doctors may choose to operate.
- To avoid later complications for the woman from a vaginal delivery, e.g. urinary tract problems.
- Overreaction by tired, inattentive staff to fetal monitors (see discussion below). This is an example where advances in medical science are sometimes not in the best interests of women giving birth.

Of course, caesarian intervention is medically necessary in some cases. However, dystocia (difficulties in labour) is a catch-all reason given by many doctors to perform a caesarian; in particular, failure to progress in labour, which is a purely subjective judgement by the doctor in charge of the delivery. Some are simply not prepared to wait around for a baby to be born naturally. Slow progress is often seen as abnormal progress in this age of technology and efficiency. Even back in 1988, the American College of Obstetricians and Gynecologists was deploring the excess use of caesarians. The Cesarian Prevention Movement was founded in 1982, with three main goals:

(1) to educate women so that they can make informed choices regarding their birth experience;
(2) to act as a forum where women and men can vocalise their concerns about child birth;
(3) to provide a support network for mothers-to-be and for those in need of healing from past birth experiences.

Another example of excessive medical intervention in hospital births is induction. The administration of oxytocin to bring on contractions is very common. Artificial methods to speed up labour are routinely employed, often purely for the convenience of the delivering doctor so that he/she does not have to stay overnight or have vacation plans scuppered. One friend complained of being told to push too quickly by the doctor and not being allowed to take her time.

Gas and air and TENS machines are generally unheard of; an epidural is the most common form of pain relief. However, this can cause problems with the woman's ability to push. The intravenous drip restricts movement, and both external and internal monitors are further encumbrances. Electronic fetal monitoring (EFM) was first developed in the 1960s and thereafter used extensively, even for low-risk patients, with little proof of any benefit to the newborn. Fetal monitors strapped to the abdomen immobilise the mother, and this can lead to birthing difficulties and the requirement for more sedation in itself. Antibiotics are given as standard and episiotomies are frequently performed. Forceps and suction are routinely employed to 'help' the baby out.

As soon as the baby is born, it is customary to whisk him or her away, often to a separate nursery room, where the newborn is laid on a warming table and subjected to 'interrogation' – vital signs are checked, eyedrops may be administered, his or her weight is ascertained, and let's not forget those nasty vaccinations. All this can take an hour or more. Only then can the mother have her baby back for suckling. Babies are often born sleepy from all the drugs the mother has been given, and therefore do not suckle readily.

In Britain, Sheila Kitzinger pioneered the natural birth movement in the 1980s and is still active today. Her outlook and methods are well respected and followed. Polly Toynbee of *The Guardian* wrote, 'If Britain is now one of the most progressive countries in obstetrical practice, it is largely due to her'. Conversely, in America she is hardly known. This is perhaps indicative of the different viewpoints regarding obstetrics in the two countries. However, an underground movement is evolving in America to get back to more natural childbirth, as a backlash to the problems highlighted in the discussion above.

An Expensive Business

There is no such thing as 'free birth' in America; you have to pay for the experience. If you do not have adequate maternity insurance cover, your 'new bundle of joy' could cost a small fortune. Hospitals charge for every single thing the mother and newborn consume, from $8 for a pain relief pill to $15 for a plastic thermometer to take the baby's temperature; everything is itemised. An epidural costs *x*, the services of a caesarian doctor *y*. The only reason hospitals and other birthing centres can get away with charging such extortionate amounts is that insurance companies (usually) are footing the bill.

If you don't have maternity cover included in your health insurance plan, you should shop around for a best price for maternity care. Prices vary considerably. One friend was quoted between $500 and $1800 for prenatal care and delivery doctors' fees, plus between $2000 and $7500 for hospital fees, depending on the hospital. As a non-insured person, she was able to negotiate and ask for discounts. The $2000 for hospital costs contrasted with the norm for insured mothers-to-be of $5000 – for exactly the same care.

Most new mothers stay in hospital for two days after the birth, or longer if they have a caesarian. Even if you are insured, most policies only pay for a 48-hour hospital stay; anything longer is at your own cost. Therefore your length of stay could be a serious monetary consideration. Thus, in addition to the emotional and physical turmoil, you may be concerned about having as quick and painless a birth as possible for financial reasons. It is rather a gamble if you go into hospital without insurance cover. God bless the NHS.

Fear of Litigation

The fear of being sued has spurned the routine use of obstetrical devices and technology to diagnose, test and monitor procedures, which in the past would only have been used in serious cases. 'There is no question that physicians themselves firmly believe that the current medical liability climate has prompted them to change the way in which they practice obstetrics' (so said a report by the Institute of Medicine, 1989). Since the mid-1970s, malpractice insurance premiums have rocketed, particularly in obstetrics – one of the most highly litigious professions.

Family doctors often simply cannot afford to pay the high insurance premiums demanded for delivering babies, and consequently the task falls to specialised obstetricians. One criticism by many women is that, as a result, continuity of care is poor or lacking; they barely see the same doctor or midwife twice, and the doctor who attends the baby's delivery may be completely unknown to the mother. This only adds to the whole unnerving experience.

Dentistry

Americans really go in for good teeth, and like their dentists to fix everything. Their policy is, if there's a hole, then it needs drilling and filling (compared with the European attitude of, if it isn't broken, then don't fix it). Children commonly have braces and fillings and their teeth are even 'painted' with a white coating to fill in any gaps. Assuming you have insurance or are covered by an employer's dental plan, you might take the opportunity of getting as much work done to your teeth as possible while you are in America. Other people are wary of allowing American dentists carte blanche to their teeth and mouths, preferring not to let them treat their teeth, especially their children's, unnecessarily.

Following our first family visit to an American dentist for checkups, my teeth had never looked so clean and white. In Britain you might sit there for a couple of minutes with the hygienist scraping and polishing. In America, they conscientiously spend about 30 minutes cleaning and flossing your teeth; they really do a thorough job. You rarely see Americans with bad or discolored teeth.

Our local dentist was very welcoming and child-friendly, unhurriedly chatting with the children, pointing out the 'tooth wall' with the names of all the children who didn't have cavities. They were made to feel comfortable, given a choice of three flavours of toothpaste while in the chair, followed by stickers and the chance to add their name to the tooth wall at the end. (By the way, you cannot buy children's minty toothpaste in the States, only cherry or bubblegum flavoured paste. So you might want to think about bringing some minty supplies to America with you.)

A Preoccupation with Health

Personal well-being and happiness are at the forefront in most Americans' lives. Witness the plethora of chiropodists, dentists, dermatologists, physicians and surgeons in the *Yellow Book* (*Yellow Pages*). If your scalp is flaking or you have mild rosacea on your cheeks, you will be referred to a dermatologist. If your pet's coat isn't shiny, he needs special diet food and a visit to the grooming parlour. Americans like to feel safe, and ideally turn to professionals in the health industry for every cough, splutter, falling or greying hair. They depend on drugs to make them feel better, and seem to have a different pill to cure all ills.

The demand for health products is a little overwhelming. Sports nutrition, diet and energy, health and beauty are huge industries in the States. New products appear on the shelves daily. General Nutrition Centers (GNC) Inc., which was formed in

1935, is now the world's largest company of its kind. 'Devoted exclusively to helping its customers improve their quality of life through nutritional science', it has 4800 franchise stores, covering every state in America, and overseas, though for some reason there are no stores in Britain. Switch on the TV and yet another celebrity will be giving you his or her testimonial on the benefits of some wonder supplement that has improved his/her well-being and happiness. (However, it is mandatory that TV commercials and advertisements for health products come with a litany of serious side-effects and 'Do not take if…' warnings – enough, you would think, to put off the most ardent of would-be buyers.)

In a sample trawl through our local newspaper (and remember, we were not living in Beverly Hills), I noticed a number of recurring advertisements. Besides the usual ones for cars, furniture, home furnishings and financial products – which you would expect – there were a large number of ads for the following:

- weight loss and bariatric surgery;
- laser spine correction centres (to cure backache);
- breast enhancement surgery;
- home teeth bleaching.

A host of other medical and health-related advertisements suggest that the average American is rather preoccupied with his or her looks and health – from cosmetic surgery and liposuction, to brain support formulas and other anti-aging miracles of modern science. An advert for air sanitiser, which is supposed to kill bacteria in the air, is another case in point. Jackie Mason, a popular theatrical satirist, puts it like this:

> 'It's no longer a question of staying healthy. It's a question of finding a sickness you like'.

Jim agrees with this take on American health:

> 'So, just ask your Doctor/Pharmacist/Banker/Gardener/Letter carrier/Parole officer if Xinglezanglewheezycheesyramadangadingdong is right for you', blare out endless commercials cut from the same script. Individuals with all too perfect lives, apart from the one problem targeted, beam unfeasibly white smiles as their lives are transformed from purgatory to perfect with one easy product. The obstacle to complete perfection is cast aside by a wondrous concoction with projected results far too good to be believable; but believed they are. In the early days of the Wild West, a breed of con man found immortality by selling snake oil from riotously painted covered wagons. We see these swindlers outrageously portrayed on film and wonder how otherwise sensible people could be taken in; and yet the same trick is being used no less blatantly on TV today and the money still rolls in. In the medical version, any form of ailment can be cured, but there's always a cost in addition to the financial. 'ZXWCRD3 will

cure you after one course of 3,000 quarter-sized capsules taken over 6 days. The only side effects are uncontrollable flatulence, bad breath, profuse sweating, diarrhoea, nausea, feelings of despair, Tourette's, paranoia, hair loss and flat feet – but we have pills that can lessen the effects'. The commercials end with the same cheesy sentence, '…so ask your Doctor if ZXWCRD3 is right for you', and pictures of those most at risk enjoying a happy day with their perfect families that are somehow unaffected by the side effects. The worrying suggestion is that it's okay for people to call on their doctors merely to confirm whether the wonder drug is appropriate to them and their needs, and assumes that America is so awash with doctors that they welcome the invasion by TV-obsessed hypochondriacs to help them pass otherwise dull days.

A Doctor's Viewpoint

In order to get some first-hand information and experience from a medical professional, I talked to my American friend Julia, a long-time practising doctor. Here is what she had to say about her profession:

> 'Over the last 10–20 years, Americans have developed higher expectations, for example they come in with a headache and want a CAT scan. If I suggest this isn't necessary, they go elsewhere for one, go to the emergency room, or threaten to sue me. They expect blood work and tests, which pressurises doctors to perform too many tests. These tests are charged to the insurance company, thus generating revenue for the medical profession and insurers in the form of justified premium hikes. We [doctors] are under constant fear of litigation, so to cover ourselves, we perform more tests than are necessary. We could reduce the number of tests by up to half if we didn't have to worry about lawsuits. Every year I make it through without a lawsuit, I breathe a huge sigh of relief. Even threats make you practise differently. If the baby doesn't come out perfect, for instance it has a little nick on its face, you could be sued for malpractice. Malpractice insurance costs ten times more if you are engaged in obstetrics.
>
> Regarding insurance, in reality, hospitals will treat or take anyone who really needs it, whether insured or not. Doctors have the option to take on whatever number of Medicaid patients the practice decides, but often there are difficulties sending them on to specialists, which may not be available to these people. Moreover, unfortunately the majority of Medicaid patients are difficult – they don't follow instructions, often threaten to sue, aren't responsible, demand extra time from doctors and drain money from the practice.
>
> People today want a pill to cure everything – and the bigger the pill, the better. They want convenience. Some people don't take enough holidays from work, let

alone time off sick, and extra stresses and anxieties lead to sicker people. Hospital admissions are trying to reduce the length of hospital stays – get patients out sooner. Intensive care units have the technology to keep people alive longer, but what about their quality of life? These days, dying is not an option.'

Conclusion

The nation's health bill has rocketed over the last decades, and the litigious environment suggests a lack of self-control and responsibility. In order to cover themselves from malpractice suits, hospitals pay grossly high insurance premiums, and feel justified in passing the majority of these costs on to consumers, who may or may not (depending on whether they are insured) pass them back to the insurance company. It is a vicious circle, with the insurance companies at the hub, driving the wheel. They demand such huge premiums from both the hospital and the individual that the system appears to be spiralling out of control.

The stress of striving for the American Dream can have dire effects on health and longevity. In this fast-paced society, Americans don't have other options to missing work, e.g. the fall-back of grandparents living close by, or even the mother staying at home (so many women are out working these days). As one friend put it, 'I don't have time to be sick. I don't have time to exercise. Just give me a pill!' Lack of exercise is partly to blame for the nation's poor health. Walking is generally avoided. For one thing, there may be no pavements – a distinct disadvantage, especially when you have young children. For another, shops and amenities are so spread out that you need a car just to get between them. In modern-day America, you need wheels. Drive-throughs – from liquor stores, to pharmacies, food restaurants to banks – are everywhere. It is estimated that over half of all Americans get no form of daily exercise.

In America, there is no reliable government system of health care to fall back on, and ordinary families suffering health problems often go bankrupt. So while we complain about our National Health Service in Britain, spare a thought for those across the Atlantic who are paying huge amounts for their health care (if they can afford to), yet overall suffering from poorer health.

Useful Websites

www.cdc.gov – Centers for Disease Control and Prevention.
www.cms.hhs.gov – Centers for Medicare and Medicaid Services.
www.drpaul.com – information specifically about children's health and wellness.
www.eatingdisorderscoalition.org – look up 'Reports & Information', then 'Statistics', for statistics and study findings on eating disorders.
www.immunizationinfo.org – National Network for Immunization Information; search for vaccine requirements for school entry by state.

www.os.dhhs.gov – Department of Health and Human Services; for all sorts of health-related information.
www.poisonivy.com – facts about poison ivy.
www.vaccineinformation.org or **www.immunize.org** – Immunization Action Coalition; for vaccine information.

Wikipedia:
Clinton Health Care Plan – the 1993 health care reform plan.
List of smoking bans in the United States – by state.

Terminology

American term	Equivalent British term	Notes
Band-Aid	Plaster	
Co-payment/co-pay		A relatively small fixed fee you pay at each office visit, outpatient service or for a prescription
Cotton batting	Cotton wool	
Deductible	Excess	The amount you are liable for before your insurance company makes a payment
ER (emergency room) or Urgent Care	Casualty department or Emergency Care	
Office	Surgery	Doctor's or dentist's
Rubbing alcohol	Surgical spirit	
Shot	Injection	

19 · The Economy, Work and Retirement

The Economy

The United States is the most technologically advanced economy in the world, especially with regard to computers, and medical, aerospace and military equipment. The States is ranked third in the world (after Germany and China) with regard to exports. Table 19.1 shows her major exports and export partners. Other important products include wheat, skins and hides, cigarettes and movies. The country is also rich in minerals, has fertile farmland and extensive waterways and other transportation networks. Indeed, America has more roads, airports and railway tracks than any other country in the world.

Table 19.1 America's major exports and export partners (CIA *The World Fact Book*, 2006).

Export commodities (2003)	**Percentage**
Capital goods (transistors, aircraft, motor vehicle parts, computers, telecommunications equipment)	49
Industrial supplies (organic chemicals)	26.8
Consumer goods (automobiles, medicines)	15
Agricultural products (soybeans, fruit, corn)	9.2
Export partners (2005)	
Canada	23.4
Mexico	13.3
Japan	6.1
China	4.6
UK	4.3

International companies are attracted to America because of numerous advantages, among them:

- political stability;

- cheap land;
- room for expansion;
- a skilled, highly mobile and steadily growing labour force, with an estimated 151.4 million workers (including the unemployed);
- little labour union involvement;
- relatively low levels of taxation, regulation and government involvement;
- a legal system that generally protects property rights and enforces contracts.

America operates a free enterprise system, with a mixed economy of privately owned and government businesses. The market-orientated economy allows US businesses much more flexibility compared to those in most other Western European countries; they are free to expand, develop and lay off workers, as the market dictates, without government intervention. America's unemployment rate (4.4% in 2007) is roughly in line with other developed countries; rates are highest in Oregon, Alaska, Michigan, South Carolina and Ohio (in that order). However, job security is a big concern, as companies these days transfer work to other countries with low-paid employees.

Table 19.2 shows the basis of the US economy.

Table 19.2 The basis of the economy (CIA *The World Fact Book*, 2006).

GDP, composition by sector	**Percentage**
Services	78.6
Industry (petroleum, steel, motor vehicles, aerospace, telecommunications, chemicals, electronics, food processing, consumer goods, lumber, mining)	20.4
Agriculture (wheat, corn, other grains, fruits, vegetables, cotton, beef, pork, poultry, dairy products, fish, forestry products)	0.9
Labour force, by occupation	
Managerial, professional and technical	34.9
Sales and office	25.0
Manufacturing, extraction, transportation and crafts	22.9
Other services	16.5
Farming, forestry and fishing	0.7

Agriculture

Approximately two-fifths of the total US land area is devoted to farming. Agricultural belt regions tend to follow lines of latitude, frequently overlap and are not formerly defined; nonetheless they give some idea of the concentration of particular agricultural activity:

- Citrus Belt – southern California and Florida
- Corn Belt – northern prairie states in the Midwest
- Cotton Belt –southern states
- Dairy Belt – the North-East
- Fruit Belt – around the Great Lakes
- Grain/Wheat Belt – northern states in the Midwest
- Grazing Belt – prairie lands of central USA
- Peach Belt –south-eastern states
- Rice – the South
- Tobacco – south-eastern states.

California is the most agriculturally productive state, with a climate conducive to growing many crops, notably citrus, vines and garden produce. Texas is the next most productive with its beef herds, followed by Iowa, Nebraska and the Great Plains, with their large, heavily cultivated and very flat wheat and corn fields. Wisconsin is prime dairy country. The Southwest and Rocky Mountain states have large livestock farms. The Corn Belt produces a major part of the world's soybeans and grain, with Iowa, Indiana, Illinois, Missouri and Ohio supplying approximately 50% of all home-grown corn, and parts of Kansas, Nebraska, Wisconsin and Minnesota producing the rest. The Grain Belt produces about three-quarters of the continent's wheat and corn, and much of its pigs and cattle. Agriculture here is heavily capitalised, with limitless fields and monster tractors. Tobacco is an important crop in the south-east and Kentucky. Most forestry land is found in the West (including Alaska), but half the hardwood forests are in Appalachia.

Through the Department of Agriculture, the federal government takes an active role in agricultural affairs, setting policies, imposing legislation and devising subsides. Agricultural exports exceed imports, and one-third of the cropland grows crops destined for export. The average farm size in America is 436 acres (178 ha). Eighty five percent of farms are individual or family owned, but only 64% of the farmland. While the majority of farms are small, the 'big boys' account for 68% of production (according to the Agricultural Resource Management Survey, 2000). In 1870, half the US population was employed in farming; now it is less than 1% – not surprising when you consider that the median hourly wage for farm workers is between $7.70 and 8.31 (USDA Factbook). Recent immigrants and aliens with work permits undertake much of the seasonal and migrant agricultural work.

As a personal observation, when driving through the States, we saw very little free-range farm livestock. In Nevada we traversed miles of open country (rough grassland), interspersed occasionally by ranches and the odd cow or horse. The cattle there are grazed very extensively. Dairy cows are nowhere to be seen; I presume they must be hidden away in barns. In fact, according to the USDA Government Factbook on *American Farms*, very large numbers of cattle (up to 100,000) are kept inside in pens on feed rations, hence the dearth of cows out in the fields. Chickens and pigs (hogs) are similarly confined. Sheep, apart from the odd backyard animal, are pretty much absent (and lamb is not a feature on restaurant menus). I missed seeing the herds and flocks of animals grazing in fields along the roadside, as you see in Britain's countryside.

Industry

Jobs in technology and manufacturing have been hard hit over recent decades, especially in the Midwest, which 50 years ago was the powerhouse of the production industry. Pennsylvania, New York, West Virginia, Ohio, Indiana, Wisconsin and Michigan used to be known as the Manufacturing Belt. Nowadays, it's called the Rust Belt, because of its deteriorating infrastructure and machinery. Pittsburgh was very important for steel manufacturing, but the industry has lost out to third world countries. The region originally prospered owing to an immigration-driven population boom, its proximity to the coalfields of Kentucky, Tennessee and West Virginia, and good transportation links. It was one of the first areas of the States to develop a railroad service; furthermore, its canals and the Great Lakes acted as important shipping waterways.

After China, America is a foremost coal-producing nation. West Virginia, Kentucky, Pennsylvania, Illinois, Indiana, Ohio and Wyoming are the most important coal-producing states. Nine out of ten tons of coal mined is used to generate electricity, accounting for half the nation's output. America is the leading producer but also the world's largest consumer of energy (see Chapter 21).

New York City is the centre of the publishing, broadcasting, advertising, financial and fashion industries. Los Angeles has its film and television industries. Detroit's automotive production and Chicago's business and financial industries are second to none. In America, the food industry now employs more workers than construction, and the field of information technology has surpassed that of agriculture. The San Francisco Bay Area has the highest concentration of technology businesses.

Work

In America small business owners find it difficult to survive in the fiercely competitive free market, and there is a long-term trend away from self-employment towards working for a boss. According to the 2000 Census, only 3.3% of people work from home, though this rate is often higher in rural areas. Perhaps one reason for the reluctance to be self-employed is the high cost of health insurance (the self-employed have to pay double premiums – both employee and employer elements; see Chapter 18). Group-based schemes, such as those available through local chambers of commerce and professional organisations, are usually advantageous as they band together to create a large group in order to qualify for better rates.

Employees in America have very poor rights. You are not guaranteed any health or dental care benefits and there are no statutory rules regarding the granting of sick leave, bereavement leave or vacation time; instead you are subject to the whim of your employer. The Family Medical Leave Act granted some benefits, but you may not be paid for any time you take off for medical reasons. Regarding health insurance, about 61% of companies in America offer some cover to their employees (down 8% since 2000, according to the Kaiser Family Foundation). However, if a company gets into dire straits, it can often wriggle out of its responsibilities to its employees, e.g. by cutting back on manpower or eliminating pensions. If you belong to a union, you may have some additional powers as an employee, but only around 12% of jobs in the US are unionised, half of them government. The National Education Association (representing teachers) is the largest union. Employees may also be subject to a drugs test without warning at any time. Moreover, anti-discrimination laws in reality have no teeth. Very rarely do individuals win cases of sexual harassment, racial discrimination or age bias; the onus is on the employee to prove he/she was harassed or discriminated against, and the employee is liable for court fees.

The Working Day

Americans are working longer hours now than in 1969. One in four workers leaves home before 7 a.m. to commute to work, the average commuting time being just under 30 minutes. In cities such as New York, where approximately half the population uses public transport, commute times can be much longer. The average working day starts early at around 8 a.m. and many do not get home until gone 6 o'clock. Part of the reason for this extended day is that as people crave larger houses, better schools and greater safety, they move to the suburbs, often further away from their place of work.

Just because people are working long hours doesn't mean that productivity is that much greater as a result; in fact, per hour of work, Americans are less productive than Europeans. Time efficiency is not high priority in American business, which can lead to frustration, particularly where Britons and Americans work together.

> 'The average American worker has fifty interruptions a day, of which seventy percent have nothing to do with work.'

This quote is from W. Edwards Deming (1900–1993), statistician, management consultant and quality control expert, who did much for Japanese and American industry. Conversely, some Americans are working too fast and suffering from perpetual time urgency; they are on a vicious treadmill:

> Longer working hours → More stress → Greater tensions at home → Escape to work! → Longer working hours, etc.

Jim agrees with me on the subject of workload and hours worked:

Americans self-confess to being amongst the hardest workers in the world; admittedly, they do work long hours. There is no doubt that at the centre of the American powerhouse economy are some extremely talented and dedicated people (occasionally there are even talented dedicated people). In common with many modern economies, there is also a small underbelly of the population that exists by being carried by the rest. In between are the vast majority, who are seen to work long hours with few holidays, and on initial contact this appears inspirational. However, not all work hours are necessarily spent working. Heavily armed with coffee and doughnuts, some Americans arrive at their offices very early and proceed to slip gently into the work routine over a couple of placid hours reading the paper or discussing the previous night's ball game. Others arrive harassed from getting small disorganised offspring off to school, and launch straight into work, only to break off later to attend to some unquestionably important task such as shopping or visiting one of the many 'queuing clubs' of local government. Others feign working by researching trivia on the internet. So the hours are long, but for many the working day is stretched to match the hours rather than the other way around. This approach does make for a comfortable life and a lot still gets achieved, just not as much as the hours worked would suggest.

Taking Leave

According to the Organisation for Economic Cooperation and Development, full-time employees in America enjoyed just less than 4 weeks' vacation in 2005. Another study by the Families and Work Institute revealed that American workers have on average only 16.6 paid vacation days a year, but many fail to use even a third of their days off.

In the first year in a job, you may not be entitled to any more vacation than the statutory six or so public holidays, or (if you're lucky) you may be granted 1 week of paid vacation; then, usually each year an employee remains with a firm, another day of holiday is added. As most US public holidays do not fall on a Monday or Friday, you can't even look forward to a long weekend off work, as we do in Britain with our bank holidays.

Sick leave is also pretty mean, with long-serving employees often only entitled to 5 days or so a year.

Why Do They Do It?

Americans work their tails off, and for what? Europeans work far less and recognise that working isn't everything. Americans are very career driven and feel the need to be successful – which is usually measured materially. However, this doesn't necessarily convert into happiness. Love is often rated by the family vacation and gifts to the children, not in time spent with the family. Americans working long hours and vacationing less are generally stressed out.

They are brainwashed to work hard in order to secure a rosy future, with a corner office, big house and all the home comforts you could wish for. Compared with virtually every other developed nation, America's workforce is employed for longer hours and more days a year. One friend commented, 'There is a lot of pressure in the workplace to come in early and stay late. It is harder to get a job these days and people are scared of losing the one they have'.

A preoccupation with success as measured by wealth means that Americans are relatively rich compared to people in the rest of the world, but they lack tranquility:

> '...The accumulation of material goods is at an all time high, but so is the number of people who feel an emptiness in their lives.' (Al Gore)

As you work to buy more things, you have less time to enjoy them. You can acquire, accumulate and consume to excess, yet still feel discontented. Perhaps this is why many Americans feel a spiritual need and turn to some form of religion; their souls are empty.

Generally, the production gains from working hard convert into greater consumption of material items rather than increased leisure time. Almost two-thirds of the nation's total economic output is consumed by individuals for personal use, the rest being bought by government and business. Thus, it is apt to say that America has a 'consumer economy'. Moreover, delayed gratification is not normally one of her citizens' strong suits. In a 2000 poll, 34% of Americans cited shopping as their favourite pastime. Consider the following cycle:

> Working to satisfy expectation ⟶ Happy-go-spending shopping therapy ⟶ Instant gratification ⟶ Boredom and dissatisfaction ⟶ Working to satisfy expectation, etc.

Unfortunately, many people are slave to shopping and find it difficult to live within their income. In the late 1990s, PBS aired a documentary program entitled *Affluenza*; the spin-off was a book under the same title (published in 2001; see *Suggested Reading and Viewing*). It describes a 'disease' that is prevalent in America, and appears to be growing and spreading to other countries as they adopt the American way of life. It talks about superfluous possessions, personal fortresses, pathological consumption, material gratification, and buying more in the hope that happiness will come from consuming more things. The concept is nothing new; it has just been spreading faster than before, spurred on by modern commercial pressures (television and advertising, in particular) and technology. After all, greed was the Original Sin. Aristotle warned against those

'...who have managed to acquire more external goods than they can possibly use, and are lacking in the goods of the soul'.

Sitting Bull, Lakota Sioux chief, talking about the coming white man (in 1877), observed, 'The love of possession is a disease with them'. Americans have come a long way from those early Puritan colonists, who practised simple living. Henry David Thoreau, writing in 1845, advocated working half days to provide for material necessities *and* allow sufficient leisure time for self-chosen activities. Theodore Roosevelt in the late nineteenth century tried to stem the flow of consumerism. President Truman declared, 'Buy only what you really need and cannot do without'. He recognised that the American Dream of endless growth is not sustainable. However, by 1970, Americans were spending four times as much time shopping as Europeans. Jimmy Carter's speech on the 'national malaise' in 1979 included the statement:

'Too many of us now tend to worship self-indulgence and consumption'.

This was the last stand any American President ever made against the evils of affluence. Luxury or simplicity? Money or time? America has chosen the path of the former. Economic growth and capital development are simply ingrained in the American psyche.

Income and Expenditure

Median household income is on a par with the UK, but there are considerable variations across the States according to race (see Table 19.3). The highest paid professionals are physicians, CEOs, lawyers, physicists, air traffic controllers and nuclear engineers. Average household income is highest in the urbanised states of New Hampshire, New Jersey, Maryland and Connecticut (in that order), and lowest in West Virginia, Mississippi, Arkansas and Montana (lowest first), and generally throughout the rural South. Moreover, the gap between rich and poor is widening. A two-tier labour market is growing more evident, as those at the bottom lack education and professional and technical skills, while those at the top are enjoying increasing annual incomes. Those in the lower economic groups barely get by, with 12% existing below the poverty line. For them, wages are failing to keep up with inflation (estimated at 2.42% in 2007). A single elderly person with an annual income before tax (but not including benefits) of less than $8500 was defined as being below the poverty threshold, as was a single mother of three earning around $18,000 and a family of nine earning a combined $39,333. The poverty rate also varies according to race/ethnicity. In 2002, 12.4% of Americans overall were deemed poverty-stricken; but on the basis of race, 22.7% of black and 21.4% Hispanic people were impoverished (these figures are higher partly because of the greater number of black and Hispanic children, especially in the South and Midwest).

Table 19.3 Median household income in the United States according to race (Census Bureau 2006).

Race	Median household income ($)
Asian	57,518
White (non-Hispanic)	48,977
Hispanic	34,241
African-American	30,134
Average	46,326

Thus disposable incomes vary considerably according to where you live in the States and your racial background. According to the US Census Bureau (average figures), disposable income is spent in the following ways:

- 15% goes on food and tobacco (compare this with the 27% average spend on food and alcohol in the UK and you have some idea how much more expensive food in Britain is).
- Around 40% of this 15% is spent away from home, which indicates the extent of the great American passion for eating out. The average American spends more money on food out than on food cooked at home.
- 5% goes on clothing (about the same amount as in Britain).
- 20% goes on transportation.
- 27% goes on housing.

Americans spend considerably more (17 times more in fact) on medical insurance and care. Hooray for Britain's NHS. Some cannot afford to buy insurance and just have to cross their fingers they stay safe and healthy. On top of this, house insurance in some parts of the country (particularly those prone to natural disasters) can be prohibitively expensive. Hurricane Katrina revealed a major failing as people without money couldn't get help and the uninsured lost everything.

In California, house prices have outstripped incomes and the state has the highest median home price in the country. Conversely, West Virginia has the lowest (which is in keeping with its citizens earning the lowest median income). The ceiling of housing affordability is being pushed to the limits by many householders, whose total housing expenses (mortgage or rent payments, utility bills, insurance and taxes) are more than the 'safe' threshold of 30% of disposable income. It is estimated that 15% of homeowners and 31% of renters are shelling out more than 30% on housing. This is a dangerous position to be in.

On average, Americans save less then 4% of their incomes. According to economist Michael Mandel, the national savings rate fell below zero in 1998 for the first time since World War II (reference the article *What Bush v. Gore Means for Empty Piggy Banks, Business Week*, 11/09/00). Today, Americans are borrowing against their homes and selling stock market investments in order to finance their spending. Moreover, 4 out of 10 Americans admit to having some or much difficulty in paying their bills (*LA Times* poll, May 2000). Disposable income is not keeping up with increases in consumption, and higher incomes do not necessarily result in higher savings.

Jim remarks that it is perhaps not their fault:

> Americans are unquestionably ingenious. It is no accident that the majority of Nobel Prize winners come from the USA. One of the more successful applications of this brain power is the extraction of money from fellow Americans; and why do this just once if you can double your money for the same basic idea? On American TV many adverts entice people into buying something that can easily cause a problem so that they can then be sold the cure. Seldom will you see adverts for products that help people avoid the problem in the first place. The classic has to be food and, while the author has no supporting statistics, it's probably a safe bet that over half of all commercials sell food. You don't have to be weak to want this food as it has a drug-like attraction. Most is sold on taste or a value-for-money basis, not on its ability to provide a balanced diet. Alongside food adverts appear those for dietary supplements, exercise machines and magical obesity cures that involve no application of physical effort or willpower. Hence, those with a penchant for tasty food are charged at least twice– to put on fat and then remove it. A better use of money would be on selling education to learn how not to get fat in the first place, but there's no money in that. Other mismatched pairs include all manner of highly priced goodies versus house equity release products or debt management agencies; how to meet attractive members of the opposite sex (who never look like the photos shown) versus STD clinics; and golf clubs versus marriage guidance agencies.

Tax, Social Security and Other Drains on Income

Each state sets its own tax rates. Some tax social security payments and pension income, others don't; some have no sales tax (e.g. Delaware, Montana, New Hampshire, Portland, Oregon), others no inheritance tax, and/or no state income tax (Alaska, Florida, Nevada, South Dakota, Texas, Washington and Wyoming). However, they make it up in other ways, e.g. with higher property taxes and fees. Thus the total tax burden may amount to much the same. New Jersey and Indiana are high-tax states. The average base sales tax rate is 6%, with Mississippi and Rhode Island setting the highest rates. There may also be local sales tax on top of state sales tax, imposed by some cities and counties. The American Chamber of Commerce Researchers Association (ACCRA) calculates the cost of living in different states (see *Useful Websites*).

Cost of Government Day (COGD) or Tax Freedom Day is the mythical day on which Americans can technically stop working to pay for the cost of government (federal, state and local), and start earning for themselves. In both 2004 and 2005, beginning on 1 January, the average American had to work until 4 July before he or she could break even (according to the organisation Americans for Tax Reform), though the Tax Foundation claims mid-May is more realistic. Or looked at another way, 2 hours 47 minutes of every 8-hour working day is spent working for the government. How are these tax dollars spent? Americans are paying more now toward health care, defence and debt interest than a decade ago:

- social security, Medicare and Medicaid together use up around 45% of the budget;
- defence uses 19%;
- interest on the government's debt of $400 billion accounts for 15%;
- other departments, such as Agriculture, Education, Transportation and Housing, use up a mere 3.53, 3.10, 2.26 and 1.73%, respectively.

Every person who receives any income has to file an annual income tax return. There is a whole industry of accountants who handle this overcomplicated area, the bane of most Americans' lives. The system is that you estimate your allowances for the coming year, deduct these from your salary and pay tax on the remainder. At the end of the tax year, when you fill in your tax form, actual allowances are recorded, and any tax due or overpaid is calculated. You must keep records for 7 years. You have to pay both federal and state taxes (usually), which means filling in two sets of forms. You will fall into one of several income tax brackets, depending on your gross income less deductions, and status, e.g. whether you are

- single;
- married filing jointly (including widows and widowers);
- married filing separately; or
- the head of the household.

The tax rate varies from 10 to 35% and you can choose to file jointly as a couple or separately.

According to the Federal Insurance Contributions Act (FICA), everyone who earns has to make social security contributions (the equivalent of our national insurance), up to an income limit of $90,000. If you earn more than $90K, you do not pay any social security on the excess. Thus the rich are not taxed on their excess wealth. FICA takes 6.2% of gross earnings from an employee for the social security pot, and 1.45% for the Medicare portion. Employers pay similar rates. The self-employed have to cough up both employee and employer amounts combined – 15.3% of earnings in 2006, though these payments do attract some tax rebate. Just as in Britain, the social security payments of today's American workers are being spent on the aging baby boomers. Therefore the current working population is right to be cynical about what government payouts *they* can look forward to.

Stressing the 'Minimum' in Minimum Wages

The minimum wage in America is frighteningly low. In May 2007, President Bush graciously raised the bar a little by amending the Fair Labour Standards Act (FLSA) which specified an increase in the minimum federal rate as follows:

- from a paltry $5.15 (which hadn't changed for the last decade) to $5.85/hour, effective 24 July 2007;
- increasing to $6.55, effective 24 July 2008;
- culminating in $7.25 after 24 July 2009.

Compared with the UK's minimum wage of £5.52/hour (correct at the time of writing), the US federal rate is equivalent to £2.90 odd (at current exchange rates). However, as each state is allowed to set its own rate, this minimum varies considerably. Twenty-six states and the District of Columbia have set a minimum wage higher than the federal rate and some states have passed laws specifying a higher 'living wage' requirement within their boundaries; even individual cities have taken a stand. Sixteen states have set their minimum wage at the same level as the federal rate. Kansas operates a minimum wage lower than the national. Louisiana, Mississippi, Alabama, Tennessee and South Carolina have no minimum.

There are exceptions to the federal minimum wage. Employers with less than $500,000 revenue can generally pay what they like. Others employing farm workers, tipped employees, students and young workers under the age of 20, apprentices and workers with disabilities may also be let off the hook. Tipped employees can be paid as little as $2.13/hour, so long as with tips they earn the minimum wage; if not, their employer is supposed to make up the difference, though employers don't widely publicise this ruling to their staff.

Someone earning $5.85/hour and working 40 hours/week with only the statutory holidays may just manage to earn a little over $12,000/year, well below the federal poverty line of $15,735 for a family of three (such as a single parent with two children). Thus many people barely subsist on low-wage work. The unseen workforce that keeps the service industry running is notoriously badly paid. Housekeepers are hardly ever white, monolingual English speakers; instead the latter are earmarked as servers and front desk staff, though this is not much better paid. Restaurant staff often go without breaks for 6–8 hours at a time, with no sit-downs allowed unless they are rolling up cutlery. Often they are not allowed to eat on the job either (no free food, as you might have expected). Many service employers work their staff to the *n*th degree. There is not enough money left over to pay for health insurance, and when they get sick they often lose their jobs. Middle-class prosperity and complacency add to the problem. It is the served versus servers, homeowners versus homeless, in this divided society. Many people are struggling to survive in the current economic climate, with some working two jobs simultaneously in an effort to earn enough just to pay the bills.

Barbara Ehrenreich's experiment – living and working among America's poor – paints a vivid picture of the life of the low-wage earner. She describes it all in her book *Nickel and Dimed. On (Not) Getting By in America.* Read it to appreciate the extent of the problem.

Formalities for Foreigners

Every foreign national or 'alien' has to obtain a visa in order to legally work in America (see Chapter 1). These are not granted easily, and you will have to prove that you are not taking a job that an American could do. The company hiring you (if this is the case) should be able to act on your behalf in this matter. The H1B visa is the official and primary work visa/permit. You must work in a 'specialty occupation' such as teaching, health care, legal, computing and IT, marketing, sales, management or engineering. Usually the H1B is valid for up to 6 years and allows your spouse and children to also live with you in America.

The I-551, Permanent Resident Card or 'green card' grants you legal permanent residency. You can apply for it in one of four ways:

(1) by marriage to a US citizen;
(2) through a family member;
(3) through employer sponsorship; or
(4) through the annual green card lottery (available to people from countries that have sent less than 50,000 immigrants to the US in the last 5 years).

Once you are in America, the Employment Authorisation Document (EAD) (work permit) is your temporary passport to working in America. It can take up to 6 weeks to process an EAD, which is then valid for 2 years and you must renew it well in advance of the expiry date. The application can only be made once you have entered the States, because you need an I-94 Departure Record to process the application and this is only issued when you arrive in America. If you are a military dependant, you can generally obtain permission to work for the duration of your sponsor's (military husband or wife's) tour.

You cannot apply for a social security number (SSN) until you have an EAD. Among other things, your SSN allows the US government to track your earnings and benefits. To apply for an SSN, visit your local Social Security Administration office with your passport, visa, I-94 immigration form, letter from your American employer or the British Embassy, and EAD. At the time of applying you will have to submit evidence of your identity. Check with your local social security office for what documents are required; you will be asked for several, recent and original documents.

Make it a first priority to apply for these vital pieces of your American identity, because without an SSN, you will keep hitting a bureaucratic brick wall. An SSN is generally required when applying for loans, credit cards, telephone connection, cable TV and all manner of other practical elements of setting up life in the US.

You may need to obtain advice from a professional regarding your tax position as a foreigner. The general rule is that you are taxed in the country where you spend most of your time. The official term for this, according to the Internal Revenue Service (IRS), is 'substantial preference', and there is a rather complicated equation to work it out. If you reside in the UK for 183 days in any one tax year, the UK's HM Revenue & Customs deems that you are a UK tax payer. IRS Publication 519 (*US Tax Guide for Aliens*) might give some guidance. If you can, try to keep your residency status as the UK, and consistent from year to year; otherwise, switching between the UK and US system is going to cause you untold headaches. If you need to complete a federal income tax return, you should also apply for your children so that you can claim them as dependants.

For information on employment tax, visit your local library, call 1-800-TAX-FORM or go to the IRS website. Britain and America have an agreement regarding social security payments – see the Department for Work and Pensions website at the end of this chapter. If you are a NATO dependant, the Legal Affairs Office may also be helpful.

Unfortunately, many professional British qualifications are not recognised in America, despite reciprocal agreements between the UK and US. Therefore you may need to 'go back to school' to retrain or apply for US certification. In other instances, British qualifications may need to be verified.

Charity Giving and Volunteering

An American friend, when asked what she particularly associated her country (America) with, said, 'We bend over backwards to help each other, giving up time, donating money, sharing talents; no-one needs to deal with a problem alone unless they choose to'. I found this to be a true statement. Working in soup kitchens and homeless shelters, donating items to food donation centres and supporting the elderly are common examples of where Americans help those in society less fortunate than themselves.

Once a year there is a combined federal campaign (known as the United Way), inviting every employee of the federal government to give to charity. A list is circulated and you can choose to give to one or more charities throughout the coming tax year – either in the form of a one-off gift or by payroll allotment over the next 12 months. Like giving to your church, these donations are tax deductible. The Bible teaches that Christians should give a tithe (one-tenth) to their church, which is why many Americans give 10% of their salary. They feel this is only right, in order to pay the pastor's salary, church rents, etc. You have to admire their faith and devotion.

One hundred and ten million Americans volunteer around 20 billion hours of their time a year; and 62% of American women and 49% of American men volunteer 3.5 hours/week on average (according to Michael Leach, author of *I Like Being American*). However, memberships of organisations such as the Boy Scouts, Red Cross, Lions and Elks have declined, whereas the Sierra Club (conservation) and the American Association of Retired Persons have seen increases. People these days are much more time-conscious, and perhaps more readily volunteer if there is a fun factor; being committed to the cause and willing to put yourself out for others or the good of your community is less of a reason to help out or get involved. Still, the enthusiasm of many Americans for volunteering is admirable.

Retirement

There is no retirement age in America, and options for retirement living are second to none. Florida (the Sunshine State) is the number-one retirement state in the US, followed by California, Arizona and the coastal states. All have one thing in common – comfortable winters. Similarly, the states of Oregon and Washington are magnets, with their mild climate and scenic beauty. Balmy Florida receives 900 or so newcomers a day, and is the fourth most populated state. Central Florida is less densely populated than coastal parts. While the Gold Coast is especially popular, the Orlando area is a mecca for golfers. Some head to second homes in the mountains of Virginia, the Carolinas or Georgia to escape the summer heat. In Arizona approximately a quarter of residents are over 55.

Retirees commonly follow the sun, alternating between two homes: a winter residence in the warm south and a summer haven in the cooler north. If you like your four distinct seasons, head for the hills of the mid-south (the Smokies, Blue Ridge, Appalachian and Ozark Mountains). Here you'll find warm summers, spectacular autumns, short winters and gentle springs. No wonder Oklahoma, Arkansas, Missouri, Kentucky, Tennessee and West Virginia are attractive to retirees. John Howells' book *Where to Retire: America's Best and Most Affordable Places* (2006) is a good read, even if you aren't of retirement age, but just want an overview of the most popular places to live in the States.

Some people sell their homes as soon as they retire and buy a big, fancy, fully equipped motor home. These healthy, relatively young retirees travel all over the country, heading south in winter to enjoy the sun, sometimes spending years on the road in their home on wheels. They may join up with other roadies, happily part of 'the club'. How's that for making the most of your retirement, for getting out there and doing it while you still can?

Others eagerly buy into a retirement community in order to enjoy independence and freedom in their own home, with the benefit of nursing care on hand. Typical social and recreational facilities include tennis courts, a swimming pool, hiking trails, clubhouse, library, arts centre, billiards, golf course, fishing pond and/or health spa. Maintenance of the grounds and properties is all taken care of, as are housekeeping, meals and personal care, should you wish for these. You are buying into a lifestyle as much as real estate. Sun City in Arizona is a 7000-acre complex with more than 50,000 retirees, who enjoy eight golf courses, four multi-million-dollar recreation centres, a huge performing arts centre, and even their own hospital. A neighbouring development, Sun City Grand, will probably be even larger – just take a look at its website to see what lifestyle options there are for the 45 plus. America really seems to have retirement sewn up.

Conclusion

In most American families, both parents work (in 2002, 60% of women were working and 74% of men). As the service industry has expanded, so has the number of jobs, particularly employing women, whereas in traditional areas of work, men struggle to find employment. The class system is not as evident in America as it is in Britain, and most people are judged on their merits. Anyone who is willing to work hard can supposedly achieve the American Dream of owning a home and bettering their existence, at least that's the view of most Americans; it is possible to go from rags to riches if you are prepared to work at it. In a recent Gallup pole, 44% of Americans proudly describe themselves as workaholics. According to Jim Sollisch, writing in the *Wall Street Journal* (*The Joys of Workaholism*, 16 March 2007), they are high on 'a delicious mix of adrenaline, caffeine, self-importance and a heady rush of focus'.

However, at the other end of the spectrum, people who are working just as hard and similarly long hours are struggling to make ends meet. Poverty thresholds vary according to circumstance. In 2001, more than 13 million Americans were classed as severely poor, and 12 million as near-poor. Even so, the average poor American still owns a car or two, a washing machine and drier, at least one television, and air conditioning, and can enjoy the benefits of more living space than the average Londoner. It is obviously not a lack of material goods that makes them poor, but rather malnourishment, lack or absence of medical care and, in some cases, overcrowding. Most people are much better off than they ever were historically, yet they are not necessarily as a consequence any happier or more contented.

Useful Websites

www.cia.gov/cia/publications/factbook – the Central Intelligence Agency's World Factbook details specific country information.

www.coli.org – ACCRA Cost of Living Index; allows you to compare the cost of living in different parts of the States.
http://www.dol.gov/esa/minwage/america.htm – US Department of Labour; minimum wage laws in the States.
www.dwp.gov.uk – the UK Department for Work and Pensions; for instance, look up the Social Security Agreement between the UK and the USA.
www.h1base.com – for information on visas and working in the States.
www.irs.gov – US Internal Revenue Service; search for 'Alien taxation', among other topics.
www.taxfoundation.org – gives tax information on each state; just click on the map on the right.
www.uscis.gov – US Citizenship and Immigration Services.
www.volunteermatch.org – volunteering network. Type in your ZIP code and interests, and the site will show you what volunteering opportunities there are in your area.

Wikipedia:
Income tax in the United States – for information on income tax and tax bands.

Terminology

American term	Equivalent British term	Notes
Chief Executive Officer (CEO)		Managing director (MD)
Desk clerk	Receptionist	
IRA	Pension	Individual retirement account
IRS	US tax office	Internal Revenue Service
Résumé	CV	

20 · It's a Dog's Life

According to the most recent National Pet Owners Survey (2007–2008), conducted annually by the American Pet Products Manufacturers Association (APPMA), 63% of US households own a pet. Of these, 44.8 million households own a dog. The American Kennel Club (2005) found that the Labrador retriever is still by far the most popular purebred dog, followed by the golden retriever. However, the little Yorkshire terrier is gaining in appeal, weighing in third in the popularity stakes, having overtaken the German shepherd. Next down the list are beagles, dachshunds, boxers, poodles, Shih Tzus and, at number ten, the miniature schnauzer. The trend is towards a rise in popularity of small dogs. It is even possible to buy a specially bred designer puppy in some shopping malls.

More than 38 million US households have a cat, and usually more than one. Often cats are designated as indoor or outdoor, meaning that their owners decide from the outset whether to keep them inside the house permanently or allow them to roam outside. The former option is becoming increasingly common, as owners decide that the risks of their cat being hit by a passing car, bringing fleas into the house or causing neighbour problems outweigh Felix's right to roam. It is a low-maintenance, low-cost option – because the cat never goes out, it is not exposed to nasties in the environment and therefore does not need expensive jabs or veterinary attention. Indoor cats are also often declawed. The downside is that they can easily grow into fat, lazy moggies.

Licencing

In all but three states you are required by law to buy a licence for your dog annually (and sometimes also your cat). However, rules vary from one county to another so make sure you have the relevant information for where you live. Check with your local police or county government auditor exactly what is required and how to go about licencing your animal (look their phone number up under 'county government offices') or search the internet using 'dog laws, Ohio' (or whatever state is applicable to you).

The rules are basically as follows:

- Within 30 days of acquiring a dog or your dog arriving in the state, you must purchase a licence; you can apply for one before the dog arrives, in readiness.
- If you don't buy a licence you could end up paying a hefty fine, and if you are late buying one you will incur a penalty.
- Puppies 3 months old and younger are exempt.
- The annual licence costs anything between $8 and $16, depending on which county you live in. If you are applying for one after 1 July the cost may be half the full fee.
- You will be given a distinct number and certificate of registration, plus a metal tag (the colour of which changes each year). The tag must be worn by the dog at all times. (You may pay a little extra for bone-shaped or special heart-shaped tags, the extra cost going to support the county animal shelter or to pay for spay and neuter programmes.)
- Your local county building, animal shelter, humane society, veterinary clinic or pet shop may all offer a licencing facility.
- Between 1 December and 31 January, you should receive a renewal reminder in the post (think of it as a Christmas present for your dog). So remember to notify the auditor if you change your address or telephone number, so that this reminder gets to you.
- The licence acts as an insurance policy, so that if your dog goes missing, the local animal control agency or shelter can trace you. If the dog is wearing a tag they will try to locate you first by the phone number(s) you supplied on registering and then by certified mail. They may even drive out to your home.
- If after 14 days they have failed to locate you, then the dog will become legally theirs.
- If a dog is found without a tag, after 3 days if not claimed it legally becomes the property of the shelter. This doesn't necessarily mean that it will be put down, just that the shelter becomes the legal owner. They have the right to sell or destroy any dog that does not have a licence tag. Thus it is important that your dog is always wearing its tag.
- The benefits of licensing are also peace of mind; if you lose your dog you know that it will be given food, a warm bed and emergency care by the local animal shelter while they try to trace you. They may even give your pet a free ride home.
- Licence fees help support local pet shelters, where all lost or stray animals find a temporary home.

So, overall, it's a small price to pay for the safety and well-being of your dog and to support other lost animals and pets.

Health Care

Our local US pet store not only sold pet merchandise but also offered an on-site veterinary clinic, wellness insurance plan, grooming parlour, dog training sessions, and rescue and adoption centre. Prices for veterinary treatment vary considerably so do shop around your local veterinary clinics and compare prices before you sign up with one. Here is a basic list of costs to inquire about and compare:

- Routine check-ups – recommended as often as every 6 months.
- Vaccinations: annual parvovirus, coronavirus and distemper, the same as in Britain, and several additional vaccinations for nasties prevalent in America – parainfluenza, leptospirosis, bordetella, Lyme disease and giardia.
- Hepatitis vaccinations.
- Rabies test and booster jabs.
- Annual heartworm test.
- Heartworm prevention: either Hartgard or the cheaper Iverhart (which does the same thing). Ask for the price if buying in bulk, e.g. 6 months' supply, as this is usually cheaper than buying in single or smaller dosages.
- Flea and tick control: for instance, Frontline for ticks and fleas, Advantage for just fleas – again, ask about buying in bulk.
- Any initial registration charge.

We joined the veterinary clinic in our local large pet store (PetSmart) because it was competitively priced, convenient and friendly. Their policy was one of comprehensive, preventative care, a noble philosophy, but this meant that Jester was subject to much more veterinary attention than he had experienced in England. Back home you are lucky if your pet receives anything more than a cursory checkup; here in America they like to prod and probe, sample and test every 6 months or so. PetSmart's policy was to give Jester the same care you would give a family member.

Teeth are a case in point. Jester had never had his gnashers touched in all his 9 years; next minute, he was under anaesthetic, having them scraped and polished. We were advised to brush them regularly and to bring him in to have them scraped annually. The idea of daily brushing was totally foreign to me, but it was apparently advisable owing to his age and the possibility of further plaque buildup, necessitating another 'operation' under general anaesthetic. I had heard stories of dogs going in for what is considered routine operations in America, only to come out with further complications, and even dying in some cases. Therefore I was concerned to not put Jester through more than was absolutely necessary. However, the veterinarian was most persuasive concerning the plaque and gum swelling, intimating that this could be causing Jester pain on eating and acting as a reservoir for bacteria, which could lead to serious internal problems.

So, against my principles, I opted for PetSmart's Wellness Plan, paying a monthly fee that covered all his vaccinations, examinations, laboratory tests and the apparently necessary dental care. The Plan worked out cheaper in the long run, but was still scarily expensive; it made me realise the total cost of looking after an animal for a year – including both mandatory treatments and those strongly advised. Dogs can suffer more afflictions in America compared to Britain; thus there is an additional cost of bringing your pet with you to the US besides the repatriation costs.

Where you can save is in the purchase of medications and other veterinary products. 1-800-PetMeds, Care-a-Lot Pet Supply and other mail order/internet companies supply pet pharmacy at reduced prices, as well as a full range of other pet products. Ascertain the lowest price for a product and then ask your favourite supplier to price match; they are often willing to do this to keep your custom. If you order from one supplier regularly, they are also more likely to offer you coupon savings, and even send free doggie treats with your order – a nice touch to keep you loyal.

Nutritional counseling may be part of the preventative health care package you receive from your vet. Dog food in America is about half the price you pay in Britain, with the same brand names available as back home, though you may find the contents look (and are) different. Jester had been enjoying Pedigree Chum back in England, but our American vet dismissed this as a low-quality brand (at least in America), so don't assume your favourite dog chow has the same ingredients and goodness.

Rabies

Rabies is present across virtually all of America. Wild animals are the main carriers of the disease (especially raccoon, skunk, fox and bats). Check with your state veterinarian when your dog's next rabies vaccination is due; this initially depends on the type of rabies vaccination administered in the UK, and thereafter on the make of vaccine used by your American vet. The inoculation may last for 1, 2 or 3 years, depending on which preparation is used and what the ruling is in your state. You should ensure that each booster jab is given before the expiry date of the last one; otherwise you will have to vaccinate and blood test all over again.

If you intend to bring your dog back to Britain, you must wait 6 months from the date a successful blood sample is taken before your animal will be allowed back in under the PETS rules.

Worms, Fleas and Ticks

Heartworm is a worm transmitted by mosquitoes and is a fatal disease in dogs. In Britain, dogs do not require preventative treatment, but in America they do, as heartworm exists throughout the United States. Dogs 6 months and older need to be blood tested before heartworm preventative treatment can be purchased. Thereafter they must be given preventative medication monthly and tested for heartworm annually.

In Ohio, heartworm is the only worm that is routinely guarded against; *other intestinal worms* that simply cause loss of condition are treated only when detected. At any time, for a small charge, you can arrange for your pet to have a faecal examination. American vets advise doing this anyway twice a year.

Lyme disease was first discovered in the USA in the 1970s. It is caused by a bacterium that is transmitted to humans, cats, dogs and other animals by certain types of *ticks.* Therefore it is important to maintain preventative tick treatment for your dog during the tick season, particularly in the states of New York, Connecticut, New Jersey, Pennsylvania, Wisconsin and Minnesota, and if your dog regularly exercises in wooded, grassy areas. Once a month, douse your beast in chemicals to deter ticks. Frontline is the most common product used to keep both ticks and fleas at bay. In Ohio, from September to March, our vet suggested switching to Advantage to control just ticks, as fleas are not a problem during this colder time of the year.

It is a good idea to check your pet and yourself for ticks after a walk. Applying a repellant to clothes and skin, tucking trousers into socks, wearing long-sleeved shirts and avoiding contact with tall grass are all sensible measures to combat ticks.

Other Nasties

In America, vets give annual boosters comprising a cocktail of vaccines. The common abbreviation for the ingredients in most booster shots is DA_2PPC or DHPPC, which stands for

Distemper, Adenovirus or Hepatitis, Parainfluenza, Parvovirus, Coronavirus

Adenovirus or *infectious hepatitis* in dogs is not the same as hepatitis B in humans. Parainfluenza and bordetella are both possible causes of infectious tracheobronchitis (also known as kennel cough), a contagious respiratory disease of dogs.

Leptospirosis is a disease caused by a bacterium that attacks the liver and kidneys. Hunting dogs and those that like to swim in ponds are most at risk because the bacterium is transmitted by urine, which survives in the environment in stagnant water.

Giardia is a microscopic parasite that lives in the intestines of many domestic and wild animals and is shed in faeces. It can cause serious intestinal infection in both pets and people. One study revealed that as many as 12% of pets were carriers of the giardia parasite. It is advisable not to let your pet drink from streams or lakes owing to the risk of ingesting the parasite.

Exercise

Dogs do not enjoy as much freedom in America as in Britain. You do not see many people in residential areas out walking their dogs, perhaps simply because in places there are no pavements to walk on. Moreover, many Americans use their often-extensive back yards as dog exercise areas and do not feel the need to take Mutley out for a special walk. If you decide that walking is not your pet's thing, you could always buy a three-wheeled pet stroller. These come complete with mesh to protect your 'baby' from bugs and a 'parent tray' underneath for leash, treats and drinks.

If dogs do get the luxury of a walk, it tends to be in a wood, public park or 'bark park' (see below) – somewhere fairly safe and organised. America is young; the network of public footpaths, bridleways and rights of way that criss-cross the British countryside are missing, and the right to roam is unheard of in America. You may be disappointed trying to find areas of the countryside to walk in without trespassing. This stems from when the first settlers headed west with their official '1000 acre rights' (granting them free land ownership), which they avidly and jealously pursued.

In public areas your pet must be kept under close control at all times. Look for signs listing the rules and regulations of the park or area you are walking in; they often require dogs to be kept on leads, sometimes specifying the length of lead allowed. Look up the dog leash laws in your state (see *Useful Websites*).

Ask other people you see with dogs where they go to exercise. I hunted out numerous off-beat areas in an effort to find somewhere I could walk Jester off the lead without fear of upsetting anyone. Thankfully, despite initial impressions, there are some natural areas unfrequented by people, where I felt I could trust him to run free or enjoy a swim in the river. However, I was conscious of blowing his dog whistle too vociferously because in America blowing a whistle is usually a signal of distress and call for help.

The upside to all this is that dog fouling is virtually non-existent, so you don't have to look at your feet when out for a walk (unless you want to watch for snakes – see Chapter 3). People are much more responsible about dog mess and there is no need for signs, as in Britain, where it has become quite a problem and source of negative feeling between the general public and dog owners.

Bark parks are popular with dogs and owners alike. They comprise a fenced area where dogs can run freely off the lead and socialise. At the same time, so can their owners (socialise that is). In one local study, 52% of dog owners admitted coordinating play dates for their dogs once a week, while 45% claimed their pooch had a regular group of playmates. Some parks impose an annual charge for a pass; others are free to use. Our local park was pretty much looked after by the people who used it – there were dog bowls for water, toys for communal use, picnic tables to sit at, and plenty of plastic bags, a pooper scooper and bin to keep the park clean. Some dog parks hold special events. The swimming pool next to our local bark park held a 'dash and splash' at the end of the summer to mark its closure. Hundreds of dogs turned up to enjoy a last dip in the pool. There were contests (best costume, longest jump, best dive, ball roundup, best kisser, agility and tricks), pet-related stalls and entertainment. All good clean fun.

Grooming

It seems to be taken for granted that the average family pet needs frequent and professional grooming. Most grooming parlours offer a complete or partial coat trimming, wash and blow dry, nail cutting and ear cleaning.

I had never had Jester professionally groomed before. Back in England he had been enjoying regular dips in the river and the odd brushing – enough to keep him out of the parlour. Yet, after 2 months in Ohio, he had developed a strange unpleasant smell, despite being regularly encouraged to take dips where possible in the local rivers. However, it took me a while to realise that it was these rivers that were causing the smell. At one of our favourite haunts there were suspicious-looking pipes extending out of the riverbank and strange whiffs along the watercourse, suggesting that waste water was being piped into the river. So after that I endeavoured to keep him out of that particular watercourse, and became wary of others. I dutifully paid $25 to leave him for 3 hours in the beauty parlour to be 'decontaminated'. He came out looking and smelling incredible, his inner thigh hairs neatly trimmed, his fluffy coat sleek and shiny. Thereafter, I invested in a bottle of dog shampoo and an occasional home bath under the garden hose at a fraction of the cost of a parlour visit. He hated me for it and moped for several days afterwards, but at least he smelt better.

VIP Pets

> 'The greatness of a nation and its moral progress can be judged by the way its animals are treated.' (Mahatma Gandhi)

Apparently, the average American spends $350 a year on luxury dog treatments (according to the American Veterinary Medical Association). The APPMA 2007–2008 survey found that 8 out of 10 dog owners buy their dogs gifts at birthdays, Christmas, Easter, Halloween or Chanukah, or for no particular special reason, and on average spend $17 per gift. Around Valentine's Day, pet stores sell Valentine toys, clothing, heart-shaped treats and cushions, fluffy pink beds – everything for your canine or feline sweetheart. On Jester's birthday, he received a card from PetSmart addressed 'To the best dog ever' and a voucher for him to choose a free toy in store. Nine percent of dog and 5% of cat owners host birthday parties for their pets. Our local newspaper offered readers advertising space to celebrate their pet's birthdays, and at Christmas you could have your pet photographed with Santa; you could also place an ad wishing your pet a happy Christmas. Popular magazines such as *I Love Cats* contain essays, photo contests and other cat-loving paraphernalia. There are even cat and dog blogs on the internet these days, where owners pretending to be their furry friend exchange news about their day.

Your pet's spiritual needs are also well catered for in America, with special blessings at some churches and pet psychic readings. Book your pet in for a special Reiki massage at a dog spa. Learn how to bond more deeply with your canine and relieve stress in the process with the book *How to Meditate With Your Dog* (by author James Jacobson). Holistic veterinary care is also popular, offering acupuncture, herbal treatments and pet massage – including head-to-paw or senior massage for stiff joints. Another treat is VIP grooming involving, besides the usual cut and blow dry, tooth-brushing, remoisturising and cologne, and accessorising with bows or bandana. As one dog-lover put it, 'Dogs are just little people in fur coats'.

Shopping for Your Pet

Animals also appear to have a cushy life with regard to bedding. The only dog beds that are readily available in America are either soft or wicker-sided, with fleece or cushion linings; I could not find any basic hard plastic beds, such as you might use in the car for travelling – something practical for a wet, dirty, hairy beast. My advice is to buy a hard bed in the UK and bring it out with you. Moreover, 'So your little pal can get to his favourite spot', three-tiered, carpeted step systems are available to place against your bed or settee – apparently a must for small dogs and older dogs. Heaven forbid that they should have to run and leap to get up onto the bed or couch.

Electronic devices to discourage wandering off the home patch are popular; errant pets receive a mild electric shock if they try to cross the invisible fence line. Also sonic bark-control collars can stop annoying barking by emitting a high-frequency whistle that only your dog can hear, or you can buy a shocker. I have to say, the latter was very effective at stopping Jester barking at particular favourite things such as the lawn mower, garden strimmer, balloons, golf practice, kite flying and other exciting human activities.

If you fancy a fun half hour or so, walk round your local pet shop; they have become the animal equivalent of children's stores, with an amazing assortment of toys, clothing and accessories. You'll be astounded at what pet owners can buy for their animal loved-ones. Of course, it's not just Americans who go barmy over their pets – it happens wherever people have too much money to throw at frivolous things.

Apart from the usual merchandise, you may be surprised to find the following:

- training pads, disposable diapers, 'Tushie wipes' and scented pet wipes;
- a full range of oral care products, including breath spray, chewy mints and mouth rinse;
- inflatable dog houses;
- special canine brownie mix;
- electric water fountains;
- chic pet-carrying bags with coordinating accessories such as collars, leads, beds, bowls and placemats;
- pet pocket carriers;
- car booster seats for small dogs so they can look out the window;

- puppy's first yearbook;
- doglasses (sunglasses for dogs);
- hairpieces that can be dyed, highlighted and styled to order; as one wig-maker put it, they are a good choice for hairless dogs or dogs that have feelings. 'Sexy' dogs can get that glamorous 'Jessica Rabbit' look with a piece that falls down one side of the face. With tiaras and sunglasses, the look is complete movie star;
- a huge choice of fashion clothing – button-up coats, footwear, T-shirts, caps and hats, costumes (for those who feel the need to dress their animals up to look like frogs, reindeer, etc.), baseball jackets, pink fur wraps, bomber jackets, hair scrunchies, non-skid boots, Harley Davidson motorcycle jackets, snow bunny hats, bandanas to suit every occasion, football-fan outfits, pajamas, safari-inspired apparel for the adventurous dog, holiday dog wear – the list is endless.

Specifically for cats, there are:

- harnesses for walking out;
- a huge selection of snazzy collars, some with bells, bows and even jewelry.
- Barbie toys and accessories (but you know if you succumb to buying one of these, it could lead to wanting more);
- individual claw covers (if you haven't opted for declawing);
- kitty Prozac.

You can purchase videos, usually involving small creatures popping about the screen, to keep your moggie occupied and entertained at home. Some cats find them riveting, others couldn't care less. For dog owners there are music CDs, quote: 'based upon 200 canine participants' decisions as to what they would like to hear in songs'.

For small furry critters such as mice, ferrets and rabbits you can buy a range of clothing (such as Santa suits), tents, beds, and pretty coloured litter and cotton bedding to spice up their boudoirs. At least birds appear to have been saved the degradation of being dressed up so far, though you can indulge them with a vast array of toys and even buy fake sticks as perches (it just goes to show that some Americans don't ever think about walking in the woods).

Boarding

It may be kinder to leave your animal in the care of a good pet sitter or at a reputable boarding establishment, rather than taking it on a long, hot car journey. If you do decide to take your pet with you, car safety harnesses are now available. It is illegal in some states, not to mention extremely dangerous, to leave your animal loose in the back of a pick-up, even in the back of the car if it is roaming about. Amtrak and Greyhound buses do not allow pets other than service animals. Also be wary about leaving your pet unattended, as people often heartbreakingly steal animals.

Pet hotels and day camps for your special friend are growing in number and very reasonably priced. You will be asked for proof that your animal is up-to-date with its vaccinations before it can be boarded. Prices start at around $15/day. Some provide a separate, heated kennel and run for your pet, while others have outdoor and indoor play areas where dogs can run free, enjoy the company of friends, play with Little Tykes equipment, even go for a swim in the pool – a real holiday haven for pooches. It is not unusual for the dogs to also be given the run of a lounge, complete with comfy couches and TV, at some home-away-from-home boarding places.

If you send your pooch to an upmarket establishment, he may be treated to a manicure, movie, Evian water and special treats, and a bedtime story to round off the day. Exercise rooms with treadmills, personal activity programmes, or pool and spa time are other possibilities. In Philadelphia, Mazzu's luxury hotel and spa gives pets a private, decorated suite where they can enjoy their own TV and VCR. Some offer 'petiquette' school and obedience training classes as part of the boarding experience.

A growing number of pet day care and boarding centres across America now have live web cams. These facilities are used by owners who bring their dogs to daycare so they can socialise and the web cams allow the owners to watch what their animals are doing. Even 'grandparents' can watch their 'grandpets' on the web. The cameras give owners peace of mind that their pets are having fun and not missing mummy and daddy too much.

Conclusion

While out with Jester, we were always being stopped and asked, 'Can we stroke the beautiful puppy?' Despite being a veteran of 9 years, Jester would sit dutifully while little people squealed with delight and rubbed him up the wrong way. People in general were pleased to see him and make a fuss. This was in pleasant contrast to the often stand-offish reception back home in England.

Perhaps only in America can you visit an ice cream parlour and take your pooch. Our local one held regular 'dog days' specially for mutts, who could come for a free ice cream and socialise with other hairy ice cream lovers. How's that for involving the whole family? It also rather sums up how Americans view their animals. Perhaps it is taking it a little far, considering that almost half of American pets are overweight (according to one source). A veterinarian who had to deal with a 32-lb cat said that the cat's owner saw no problem with this. A recent study by Purina found that while 79% of veterinarians rated the dogs brought to them as overweight, 30% of dog owners disagreed and felt it was acceptable to give their furry friends table scraps or human food. Yet weight-control products represent the fastest growing products in the pet food industry, and obesity is not just in the eye of the beholder. It can reduce a dog's lifespan by 15%, on average approximately 2 years. Moreover, pudgy pets suffer the same health problems humans do: knee troubles, heart strain, diabetes, painful back and joints, and breathlessness. The answer may be not to love your pet less, but rather to reward him or her in different ways.

According to US Census Bureau data, in 2004 pet owners in America spent more money on their pets than on hardware, jewelry and candy combined. In 2007, over $40 billion was spent on pets, more than twice the amount spent in 1994. Pet care in America has become big business, and treating pets as humans seems to be the vogue.

Useful Websites

www.1800petmeds.com and **http://store.pets-life-rx.com/** – pet pharmacies, offering medications by mail at competitive prices.

www.animallaw.info – statutes/laws do do with animals; select by state and topic.

www.appma.org – American Pet Products Manufacturers Association, Inc.; industry statistics and trends.

www.carealotpets.com – as an example of the merchandise available, for all your pet's needs.

www.dogfriendly.com – lists dog-friendly accommodation, cities, RV parks and campgrounds, parks, beaches, restaurants, attractions and events throughout the US and Canada. Just click on a state.

www.onlinedoggy.com – to find a pet care provider in your area that uses web cam.

21 · American Issues and Problems

This chapter discusses some of the problems in society that I feel are peculiarly or more particularly American. I have tried to include facts and figures, media quotes and the opinions of other Americans, where possible, in order to present a balanced viewpoint. America is a culture of excess, with many of her citizens enjoying material abundance and lavish lifestyles, often in contrast to those living in segregated communities and/or suffering racial discrimination. American newspapers are full of articles on immigration reform, wealth inequality and the health of the nation, among other issues. Some of these are at the forefront of media attention in Britain, too.

Guns: An American Tradition

In April 2006, a deranged student shot 32 people at Virginia Tech, and another gun-homicide incident went down in history. However, every day, about the same number of people are shot to death in the US, on an individual basis.

Violent crime is ranked highest in the states of South Carolina, Florida, Maryland, Tennessee and New Mexico, in that order (according to the US Census Bureau); all have relatively permissive gun laws. However, imposing strict gun control laws in a state does not necessarily translate into a decrease in crime. Ten of the fifteen states with the highest homicide rates have restrictive or very restrictive gun laws. The cities of New York, Chicago and Detroit, with just 6% of the total population, account for 20% of all US homicides, despite the virtual prohibition on private hand guns in these three cities. Dallas, Phoenix, St. Louis, Atlanta, Detroit, Baltimore and Gary also come high in the crime league tables.

Michael Moore produced an Oscar-winning documentary in 2002 entitled *Bowling for Columbine.* It begins with him walking into a bank in Michigan and opening an account, which was offering free guns to new customers. The bank was a licenced firearms dealer and you could choose from over 500 guns. Michael quipped, 'Don't you think it's a little dangerous handing out free guns in a bank?' He next visited a barber's shop, which also sold bullets.

Interviewees for the documentary extolled the necessity for – and indeed responsibility of – American citizens to be armed in order to defend themselves and their families. Otherwise, apparently, 'you are in dereliction of your duty'. Armed citizenry is all part of what it is to be American. Many homes display a welcome sign at the front door, but downstairs don't be surprised to find a gun-locker, complete with semi-automatic weapons. The Second Amendment allows individuals the right to keep and bear arms, and, according to the National Institute of Justice (*Research in Brief*, May 1997), more than 50% of American households exercise this right.

As mentioned above, each state has its own gun laws, and there are even local laws, which are subject to frequent change. In the UK, you are subject to extensive background checks, have to obtain a firearm certificate and provide a legitimate reason why you need to own a gun (for sport or work, for example). Not so in America. Federal law states that, apart from certain ineligible individuals (e.g. those with convictions, fugitives, drug addicts, illegal aliens, etc.), anyone over 18 years old can purchase a rifle or shotgun in any state, and that over 21s can acquire a hand gun from a federally licenced dealer in the individual's state of residence.

After September 11th, sales of ammunition surged by 140% and gun sales by 70%, and the latter are now at an all-time high. Sales of burglar alarms also increased. Most Americans feel a real threat to personal safety, and their first reaction is to fight. Michael Moore remarks in his documentary that, 'A public that's this out of control with fear should not have a lot of ammo lying around'.

Television is as much to blame as anything. Some networks go from one tragedy to the next, highlighting crime, even though crime rates have decreased nationally. *Cops* first hit the airwaves in 1989 and is still one of the most popular reality TV shows on the air, proving that anger, hate and violence attract high ratings. This all fuels the fear of crime. Blacks and Hispanics in particular are demonised and portrayed as criminals, and this only intensifies the problem of segregation in the States.

America's neighbour, Canada, has a very different attitude. While Americans have three locks on their doors and guns down in the basement, Canadians are happy to leave their doors unlocked. They are not afraid, they are not being pumped with fear, their television isn't constantly talking about it. Canadians prefer negotiation to aggression, whereas Americans react first (e.g. by pulling a gun when they see someone trespassing on their property) and think second.

Table 21.1 shows the number of people killed each year by guns in various countries. America is way ahead in this respect. According to FBI and UK crime statistics, there were 5.5 murders per 100,000 population in the US in 2000, 70% of these involving firearms (of which 75% were obtained illegally). Compare this with 1.4 homicides per 100,000 population in the UK, 9.4% of which involved firearms. In 2004, New York City had 6.9 murders per 100,000 residents, compared with 2.4 in London. Europe has effectively banned handguns, whereas they are still legal in the States, which must explain why the US murder rate is so high comparatively.

Table 21.1 Number of people killed each year by guns, according to country. (Source: *Bowling for Columbine*, Michael Moore documentary, 2002.)

Country	Number killed
USA	11,127
Germany	381
France	255
Canada	165
UK	68
Australia	65
Japan	39

Americans live with an uneasy ambivalence towards guns, intent on protecting their right to bear arms but at the same time deploring gun violence. The National Rifle Association is a powerful lobby, making members of Congress reluctant to tinker with gun-control laws. Meanwhile gun-related crime is prevalent and growing. Gangs are popular, and young people have a tendency to pull a gun when they don't get the respect they feel is due to them, or in order to settle a dispute (rather than the old-fashioned way – with fists). Police give the main reason for the increase in gun crime as the easy availability of guns and weapons from out-of-state gun shops, which are then brought illegally into a state with tougher gun-control laws.

Other Criminal Activity

Apart from gun-related crime being a major concern, cases of child abduction tend to make Americans very vigilant towards their children. America has the third highest rate of major assaults of all the nations of the world, and only South Africa and Canada have higher rates of rape.

Drugs are a problem in today's Western cultures, and no more so than in the States. Americans illicitly produce cannabis, marijuana, depressants, stimulants, hallucinogens and methamphetamine (though some of these are used legally but prone to abuse). America is the world's largest consumer of cocaine, which enters the US through Mexico and the Caribbean from Colombia. Smugglers illegally import high-quality heroin from south-east Asia, and heroin, marijuana and methamphetamine from Mexico. The USA is also a prime money-laundering centre.

Of all the countries in the world, America has the highest rate of incarceration, at 702 per 100,000 population (compare this with 139 in England and Wales), and this number is continually rising. One in eight African-American males aged 25–29 years is currently locked up, and the Department of Justice estimates that a black male born today has a 29% likelihood of being incarcerated in his lifetime.

Native Americans, Hispanics and African-American women are also subject to higher than average rates of imprisonment. The following states do *not* operate the death penalty for murder: Alaska, Hawaii, Iowa, Maine, Massachusetts, Michigan, Minnesota, North Dakota, Vermont, West Virginia and Wisconsin.

Those engaged in criminal activity are likely to see their mug shots broadcast and advertised in local newspapers, on fliers and in the lobby of restrooms at service areas. The public is alerted to missing persons, 'most wanted' people, even those who have neglected to pay their court-ordered child support payments. We were fortunate to be living in an affluent, relatively safe provincial area of America (though 10 miles away, people in downtown Dayton were regularly being mugged and shot). An incident in our suburban neighbourhood shows how prompt local law enforcement can be. Youngsters throwing crab apples at the windows of a house had the police on to them 3 minutes after a phone call was made by the householder (3 minutes was apparently the average call-out time in our part of Ohio, even for such minor offences as this). How's that for prompt service? Also, in some American towns there is a curfew on teenagers being out alone after midnight.

In Britain, our lack of moral direction is causing serious social issues. Conversely (at least where we were living in America), it appeared that most Americans are respectful of others and their community. This is perhaps partly due to the churches' influence on people's lives (see Chapter 15 on religion). In provincial areas you do not see much graffiti or evidence of vandalism. Beside a main road near us, someone had set up a Christmas display of a large decorated tree with boxes covered in Christmas paper and bows. It appeared in mid-November and the site was used for a pre-Christmas community bash. The tree and 'presents' remained there intact until they were taken down just after Christmas. Every time I drove past I expected to find the tree denuded of its tinsel and baubles, the presents strewn all over the road or stuck on railings on the bridge. To my amazement, nothing was removed. I experienced the same surprise with regard to people's homes. The numerous decorations and homely touches adorning porches and front gardens did not appear to be sabotaged. Back in Britain, those inflatable Christmas snowmen, Thanksgiving straw-filled scarecrows and the ubiquitous rocking chair on the porch wouldn't stand a chance. Many houses have a stand-alone mailbox at the end of the drive. These boxes are not locked or triggered in any way to deter vandals or thieves. As an American, even as a child, you are preconditioned not to touch other people's mail, as doing so is a federal offence. I can't imagine the system working in Britain, and have visions of boxes being uprooted and carted off, post scattered, unwelcome packages left inside the box...I just don't think it would work. Yet in much of America, these open mailboxes are so commonplace that no-one bothers to interfere with them (although, in rural areas particularly, driving past and whacking mailboxes with a baseball bat is not unheard of).

Identity Theft

Identity theft is one of the fastest growing crimes in America today. In 2005, 8.9 million Americans (about 4 in every 100 adults) were victims of identity fraud. In 15% of cases, the thief was a relative, friend or acquaintance, or in-home worker. Thirty percent of cases occurred following theft of a wallet, purse or chequebook; others were due to internet scams and computer hacking.

To help prevent identity theft:

- Be careful about giving out your social security number and do not carry your social security card on your person.
- Never divulge personal information over the phone, internet or through the mail unless you initiated the contact.
- Even where you are asked for this information, question why it is necessary; if it is not mandatory, then don't disclose it.
- Do not leave mail sitting in your mailbox.
- Carry the minimum of personal information, credit and store cards with you.
- Annually review your credit history with the three credit bureaus (Equifax, Experian and TransUnion).
- If you have home help, do not leave your financial and personal information lying about or easily accessible.
- Shred documents that have your name, address and other details on; in particular you should destroy credit card receipts, credit applications, financial statements, bank cheques and insurance forms. Since June 2005, all employers and businesses are lawfully required to shred any documents with personal information on before disposing of them.
- Do not be offended when banks ask for personal identification before allowing you to cash a cheque or otherwise transact with them; this is for everyone's protection, in order to prevent fraud.
- If time is money and you can't face having to sort out the mess involved if you should lose your identity, then consider taking out identity theft insurance. Check your home insurance or renter's policy first, though, to see if you are already covered.

The Energy Crisis

> 'In the United States there is more space where nobody is than where anybody is. That is what makes America what it is.' (Gertrude Stein, *The Geographical History of America*, 1936)

It is also what makes Americans very reliant on their cars; and, as has always been the case, generally the bigger the better. They are used to owning large vehicles they can load up and head off in. Downsizing to more fuel-efficient, smaller vehicles and consuming less gasoline by making fewer trips would require a major change in their easy-going lifestyles, though some are trying it. Car manufacturers and dealers have concentrated on promoting the SUV market, and fuel-efficient cars have so far been in low demand, and hence supply. Added to this, the public transport system is hardly noticeable outside the cities. (New York is one of the most energy-efficient cities in the nation, with gasoline consumption on a par with the national average of the 1920s.) However, where people are less congregated – throughout the majority of the country – public transport simply doesn't work. Amtrak passenger trains are very expensive and it is often difficult to find a rail route to cover a proposed trip.

The nation consumes 25% of the world's annual supply of oil, importing more than half the petroleum it consumes. A further concern is that the country is in effect financing both sides of the war on terrorism: through funding the US military *and* purchasing oil from 'criminal' regimes such as Iran. The ongoing conflict in Iraq and problems in Nigeria (another oil supplier) have brought about a global reduction in petroleum production, while at the same time demand by China, India and the US has been increasing.

'America is addicted to oil', declared George W. Bush in February 2006. Acknowledging this is, perhaps, a first step to rectifying it. The President has pledged to replace 75% of America's Middle Eastern oil imports by 2025 by investing in alternative technologies. These include ethanol derived from wood chips, vegetable matter and grass. This is spurned not so much by the issue of global warming as by concerns over reliance on the Middle East. However, he is averse to increasing emissions regulations or raising gasoline taxes, which are currently a paltry 18.4 cents/gallon and have not increased since 1993; compare this with the 63.7 pence/litre tax we pay on petrol in Britain (www.petrolprices.com). Thus American consumers are still enjoying the benefits of cheap oil at the petrol pumps, with hardly any government taxes. The federal tax on gasoline is the same across the country, with each state imposing its own tax on top of that, thus creating price differentials between the states. We saw gas prices fluctuate daily by as much as 40 cents/gallon. If the US government fixed the price at the pump by taxing oil, consumers might change their behaviour and this would impact on car and truck manufacturers, and thus on the energy crisis. The President may think he is preserving the American way of life by holding out against such a tax, but if consumption continues at the rate of today, Americans will see a decline in their standard of living. Clearly, something needs to be done, as gas prices increase and public concerns become more vociferous.

Some trucks and buses are now powered by biodiesel fuel, a blend of soya beans or rapeseed or even old fryer oil. So if you get a whiff of French fries or doughnuts as a heavy vehicle passes by, say hooray for biodiesel. However, because biodiesel produces lower emissions than petroleum diesel, you may not even notice it. The disadvantages of biodiesel are that it can adversely affect rubber hoses and fittings in older engines and clog fuel filters; it also thickens in near-freezing temperatures, making the vehicle sluggish, though blending with petroleum diesel and kerosene can overcome this problem. This alternative fuel is not yet widely available.

Fossil fuels (in America's case, coal and petroleum) currently provide virtually 100% of the nation's transportation needs and most of its electricity requirement. America has invested very little in nuclear-generated electricity. France, for example, produces 80% of its electricity from nuclear power plants; compare this with America's 20.7% (though Britain is equally bad, with only 21% of its electricity produced by nuclear power stations). Green, energy-saving cars, homes, appliances and office buildings are making a little headway but require a major shift in public attitudes. Salt Lake City in Utah is the latest to offer free parking to people who drive vehicles that do over 50 miles/gallon, have low emissions or are powered by alternative fuel. Utah also gives an income tax credit of up to $3000 to residents who buy clean fuel vehicles and some electric hybrids. Some states offer similar schemes to encourage people to buy fuel-efficient vehicles. In other parts of America, you might find high-occupancy-vehicle lanes (HOVs), to encourage lift sharing and reduce the number of cars on the roads (see Chapter 11).

As billions of new consumers in India, China and the former Soviet Union are now vying for the American dream of a house, car and refrigerator, the world is fast using up non-renewable fossil fuels, and the law of supply and demand results in higher prices. These developing nations are growing at such an alarming rate that there is now a very real question of whether resources can keep up with spiralling demand. Many are worried about our energy future. Vijay Vaitheeswaran's book *Power to the People* is a very readable and thought-provoking account of the coming energy revolution and why it is inevitable.

Scientists agree that climate change is a reality and America's reliance on fossil fuels plays a big part in this. The United States as a whole is the single largest emitter of carbon dioxide from burning fossil fuels (China is the second largest). Continued dependence on these fuels will accelerate the problem of climate change and does nothing for international relations or the environmental standing of the US overseas. Efforts to tackle poverty in other parts of the world are being undermined by climate change. The NGOs Oxfam, Christian Aid, WWF, Greenpeace, Practical Action and others are campaigning for political action to cut gas emissions. Former Vice President Al Gore has made it his personal crusade to alert the public (in particular the American public) to the harm done to the environment by his country's short-sightedness. His book *An Inconvenient Truth* has become a best-seller, and the documentary film of the same name is just as hard-hitting. However, many Americans do not believe that global warming is scientifically proven and therefore choose to simply ignore it. It remains to be seen whether the world's greatest consumer will wake up and take action.

Waste, Pollution and Aesthetics

The Green Revolution has not really hit America yet and Americans are much less conscious or indeed concerned about their effects on the global environment, though some are becoming more environmentally conscious and looking at green options. People throw away far more than they use, and the average American is responsible for disposing of 4–7 lb of rubbish every day. Material goods are cheap and plentiful in the States, with shops promoting sales every other week, loosely based on seasonal events and 'special calendar days'. Americans are bombarded with marketing. This feeds the insatiable desire for more, newer, better, in order to keep up with the perceived expectations of others.

This obsession with consumer goods has been growing since the 1950s. It is a gripe of mine that applies the world over and is not specific to America, though the US is obviously a materialistic culture that prefers new things to old and is very much a throwaway society. I believe this has something to do with Americans' easy-going attitude to life; they feel free to live as they please, buying new things cheaply and not attaching any real value to them. Youngsters these days are brought up in this superficially materialistic world. Sadly, it is not much different in Britain; even my 12-year-old niece happily states that shopping is her favourite hobby. People need to pull themselves out of the norm, broaden their views and realise that amassing things does not necessarily make them better people or have much meaning. Prosperity brings with it a certain amount of craziness, and with each passing generation it is getting harder to go against the flow.

Wastefulness and a lack of care for the environment are evident everywhere in the Western world. Everything we buy comes in bags, boxes or cartons. However, as in many things, America excels in its wantonness. It is part of the convenience culture to use throwaway materials. Most foods are ubiquitously packaged in plastic – both a concern to human health and to the environment – and plastic jars in place of glass are becoming the norm. Recycling is not an economic option for polystyrene, though scientists are working on the problem. Nearly 80% of the 3 million tons of petrochemical plastic disposed of in the US each year – mostly in the form of foam coffee cups and take-away food containers – goes into landfill, where it takes aeons to break down. (That said, many fast-food places have now switched to paper packaging and wrapping in an effort to cut down on waste.) Schemes such as you see in British supermarkets encouraging you to reuse bags are not generally promoted in America and it is virtually non-existent to see someone with their own shopping bags. A single plastic supermarket bag can take up to 500 years to decay in landfill. Think of that when next you go shopping.

Another observation is that many Americans seem to be overconcerned with appearances. The onus on keeping your lawn green and clipped is not environmentally friendly. Leaf blowers and vacuums, strimmers, ride-on mowers and chemicals used in and around the home and garden are not without cost to the environment. Some people think nothing of spraying their whole yard with insect repellent. On the flip side, there are those living without any apparent concern for aesthetic appearances. While I am not a fan of overneatness and stylised homes, I was often amazed at the amount of stuff some people – particularly in more rural parts of the country – left outside their homes. Old rusting appliances and other turfed-out belongings, enough toys to fill a nursery and plastic bags containing who knows what lay strewn on or around some porches and front yards. I can only guess that the inhabitants of the home were too lazy to take it to the tip, or they just had too much stuff in a small house that it was literally overflowing.

Another form of sight pollution is unnecessary signage and other eyesores placed along roadsides. This is something we are addressing in Britain, with some towns actively involved in reducing such signage. Some cities in America are doing the same, though our locality obviously wasn't one of them. Sales notices and billboards on shops, bunting, flags and other decorations adorning homes, 'House for Sale by Owner' signs on road turns, all make for overstimulation of the senses. At local election time the roadsides were littered with candidate promotion boards and requests to vote for levies. It's a wonder there aren't more road accidents.

The Natural Versus Man-made Environment

At our local county show, it was proclaimed that Ohio ranks second in the United States with regard to the rate at which it is losing prime farmland to development. Our district (Greene County) alone was said to be losing 1000 acres of land each year to non-agricultural development. Many areas of America must be reaching saturation point in terms of the number of malls, restaurants and churches, yet new ones still appear, almost overnight. The first clue that another new building or complex is planned is when great swathes of countryside are suddenly razed by bulldozers and diggers. Wildlife is either exterminated or displaced to ever-decreasing areas of the countryside, pushed out of their habitat by human greed for yet another new amenity. It has been estimated that Ohio has lost 90% of its native wetlands since the days of the early settlers. America is far too commercial and materialistic in my mind, building more new shopping areas, food outlets and huge housing developments, when there seem to be more than enough to go round. As new malls pop up, old ones go into decline as people switch to using the next, more sophisticated commercial outlet. It just seems a lot of unnecessary expansion and choice.

According to the 2000 Census, only 1.6% of the population live on a farm and only 21% live in a rural area. Many Americans are concerned about the hazards of the countryside, such as Lyme disease and more recently the avian virus. They are afraid to venture out – one reason why you can enjoy a walk in America's wild places often without encountering a soul. The next generation to follow the baby-boomers appears to be either uninterested or too short of time (what with careers and children) to take much of an interest in agriculture, gardening and wildlife. Americans prefer instant gratification – a 'canned' product. Although outdoor living is becoming more popular and sophisticated, this does not necessarily spawn an increased interest in the great outdoors beyond the patio, deck and plant containers. Most Americans are not prepared to put in the time and effort involved in traditional gardening activities such as growing plants from seed, planting flower borders or cultivating a vegetable garden. Instead most gardens are decked and lawned, sparsely and carefully planted with shrubs, soil is obliterated with mulch, and compost heaps are an unusual sight. Wildlife-friendly gardening does not appear to cross the minds of most Americans, who prefer to remove garden 'rubbish' entirely, spray, green the lawn and generally destroy the small creatures that do so much good for our gardens. Many front yards in our suburban neighbourhood were neat, trimmed and apparently sterile of life apart from the ubiquitous grey squirrel. There are very few wildlife corridors between properties; instead one open lawned plot melds into the next, with barely a break between them. We felt quite rebellious leaving a pile of leaves and some logs in the garden as a place for wildlife to overwinter and not mowing the lawn to within an inch of its life. See Chapter 10 for more on this subject.

Moreover, America has so much land to play with that conservation issues are not high on the agenda. For example, in Colorado, Kansas, New Mexico, Oklahoma and Texas, during 1931–1942, farmers were encouraged to plough up the hardy native grasses that held the region's topsoil, and plant crops in their place. Two hundred and fifty million acres of prime soil was lost as whole fields simply blew away and black blizzards of soil enveloped towns. John Steinbeck's *The Grapes of Wrath* is a vivid portrayal of this era. This area of constant driving winds was never meant to be farmed, overgrazing and drought contributing to the problem. Dust storms resulted in part of rural America literally being blown away. 'There goes Oklahoma', Hugh Bennett (founding father of the Natural Resources Conservation Service) once famously said. Bennett was a soil surveyor and his ideas changed the face of America's landscape, serving as a basis for many other countries. Thanks to him, 3000 Soil Conservation Districts are now in operation, conserving the soil and water of the States and maintaining the ecological balance.

Tensions in Society

The United States has a very diverse population. Table 21.2 shows the number and percentage of the population according to race/origin. New Mexico has the highest percentage of Native Americans and Hispanics of any continental state. In 2000, 17.9% of Americans spoke a language other than English at home (see also Chapter 7); this number is doubtless higher now owing to the 13% annual immigration rate. In 1997 Tiger Woods claimed his race was 'Cablinasian' (a mixture of Caucasian, black, American Indian and Asian). Since 2000, people have the option of checking more than one race on their census forms. However, society puts pressure on multiracial people to choose one race, and they often identify themselves according to the neighbourhood they grew up in, e.g. black if they originated from a broadly black neighbourhood.

Table 21.2 Division of the population of America according to race/origin (US Census Bureau, 2004).

Race/origin of population	Thousand people	Percentage of population
White	236,058	75
Hispanic or Latino	41,322	12.5
Black or African-American	37,502	12.3
Asian	12,326	3.6
American Indian, Alaskan native	2,825	0.9

For a nation that prides itself on freedom for all, the treatment of Native Americans and the slavery of Africans 200 years or so ago are in sharp contrast. Even today, this legacy of racial tension and white supremacy is prevalent in many parts of America; witness the huge public debate concerning illegal immigrants and the discriminative treatment of many black Americans in southern states. Alexis de Tocqueville (a famous liberal thinker of the mid-1800s) said that Native Americans were faced with 'forced inclusion', while blacks faced 'forced exclusion' (the former did not want to be assimilated into the white man's society and culture, whereas the latter wanted to share it but were, and to some extent still are, excluded).

Despite America's historically renowned and recognised awful reputation for racism, it is still rife, especially in the South. Twenty years ago a white person would have been hounded for marrying a black; now it is accepted, though not always happily so. Blacks are still treated differently; where a white person is received positively, a black person in the same situation receives a different reception or attitude. Conversely, many institutions (companies, government and educational establishments) discriminate *in favour* of African-Americans and other minority groups, e.g. colleges must have a certain number of minority students these days. This is known as 'affirmative action', whereby employers have to employ a certain percentage of minorities.

There are also inner city versus suburban tensions. More affluent whites generally move out to the suburbs, leaving poorer members of the community (among them, a great many black, Asian and Hispanic people) in downtown areas. Once-thriving city downtowns are often abandoned as improvements in roads and the desire for more space take people further away from the city hubs.

Despite government's best efforts, America has its fair share of hate groups. The states of California, Texas, Georgia, Louisiana, Mississippi, Tennessee, Ohio, North and South Carolina, Florida and Virginia have the greatest concentrations. Hate groups active in the US in 2005 are described below:

- Black Separatists – they oppose racial intermarriage and integration, and are strongly anti-white and anti-Semitic. They want separate institutions and even a separate nation for blacks.
- Ku Klux Klan – see Chapter 6.
- Neo-Nazis – American groups are protected by the First Amendment and thus can publish material and host internet sites. European groups make use of this loophole in promoting their activities.
- Racist Skinheads – white supremacists. The movement originated in Britain and arrived in America in the early 1980s.
- Christian Identity – in the twentieth century, racist preachers in America took British Israelism and transformed it into a strongly anti-Jewish religion.
- Neo-Confederates – the League of the South (the core of the movement) had 9000 members in 2001. Neo-Confederates want Southern secession and to halt non-white immigration and interracial marriages.

Jim sums up Americans' attitudes towards diversity and toleration of other people very well:

> America is the Land of the Free, built on the premise that all men are born free and equal and have the right to voice their opinions (as enshrined in the Constitution). This strong foundation has proved the bedrock for a country that in many ways is great; and yet there are serious flaws that are carefully papered over to project a glossy image. There is supposed to be equal opportunism, but you might not necessarily want to be gay in the South, Southern in the North or, dare it be said, black in a lot of states. It's not that there is not serious effort to try to be fair, but individual biases run deep and are taking generations to eradicate. Certain issues have typified this struggle. The Anglican church in America is on the brink of separating from the English arm as it is considering the inauguration of openly gay clergy. Divorce amongst presidential candidates is an interesting paradox. Ronald Reagan was the first president who had been divorced, but as he was generally accepted as a great President, a single-divorcee President is now tolerated. However, there are candidates in the 2008 presidential election who are on their third marriage and the jury is out on how acceptable that is. Interestingly, few candidates are single or openly gay, suggesting that these attributes are considered more of a bar to presidential suitability than multiple divorces. Moreover, African Americans should be able to do as well as white colleagues, and there is a serious chance of a woman being president in the near future.

However, there is one issue over which there seems to be universal agreement: illegal Mexican immigrants. Americans, the majority of whom are derived from immigrants, find the audacity of Mexicans slipping into the country, and perhaps, more importantly, the economy, very irritating. There is an understandable view that the current population has generated this great country and its wealth, so why should it be shared with those who would enter with purely sycophantic aims. However, the country in its modern form was built on immigration, so it might appear a bit hypocritical to shut the door now. The USA does manage to accommodate great diversity. Toleration of this multiplicity of peoples with seemingly incompatible views is partly achieved by the Constitution, but is superbly aided by the sheer size of the country, allowing those who disagree to conveniently avoid each other.

Native Americans

Throughout the years, Native Americans have suffered at the hands of the white man. Originally disease brought by the colonists decimated huge numbers of these native people. Then came whisky, a new victual. Even today, American Indians are unused to hard liquor, which tends to have dire effects on them; there is also some evidence that genetics makes them more susceptible to alcohol. Years of white aggression and broken promises (as described in Chapter 6) resulted in the loss of around 8 million American Indians.

Approximately 562 federally recognised tribes are left in the US today; a third of Cherokee Indians still live in the Appalachian Mountains and have their own separate language. Indians living on reservations are deemed to be some of the poorest people in the nation, and they have still not been able to truly integrate into American society. Many homes on reservations lack indoor plumbing, unemployment is as high as 70%, and 57% of the Indian population is living below the poverty line. Families are scraping by on around $14,000 median annual income. Of the top-ten poorest counties in the US, six are in South Dakota – all home to Indian reservations.

Gaming and gambling (hereafter simply referred to as 'gaming') is an important part of Native American culture. Long before the white man came, gaming to the Native Americans was a spiritual pastime, representing birth, death or rebirth. It was used at ceremonies and certain times of the year to please the gods, in order to cure sickness, oust demons, prolong life, aid fertility or bring rain. Today, casinos, bingo and resorts provide much-needed income for tribes and jobs for the people. Of the 562 or so recognised tribes, 224 participate in gaming. Reservations are run by tribal governments, independent of the state in which they are located but still under federal law. Most of the revenue from gaming goes into community services and development, and to charities such as those offering substance abuse treatment programmes. Native Americans suffer from poor self-esteem, stress and cultural conflict; alcoholism and substance abuse are higher than average in this sector of society.

African-Americans

Despite efforts towards egalitarianism, statistics paint a worrying picture of African-American race inequality:

- An estimated 1 in 5 black families is disproportionately poor and 24.9% of blacks live below the poverty line (compared with 21.8% of Hispanics and 10.6% of whites).
- The annual median income for black families in 2005 was $31,101 (compared with $48,218 for white families).
- As few as 20% of black male teenagers are employed at any time, and only 6 in 10 black male adults.
- Fewer than half of black families have married parents (compared with 8 in 10 white families).
- An estimated 2–3 million African-Americans aged 16–24 are either not in school or not working and are without post-secondary education.
- The illegitimacy rate is extremely high (one reason why black Americans struggle at school).
- About a third of black male teenagers are involved in criminal activity.
- More than 1 in 8 black males in their late 20s are incarcerated.
- Black people suffer a higher rate of disease and infant mortality.
- Black males have a shorter life expectancy than white males, more so if they live in urban areas.

According to the US Census Bureau, African-Americans make up 12.3% of the population (2004 figures), yet only 42 (out of a total of 435) House Representatives are black and there is just one black senator. Figure 21.1 shows the spread of the non-white population across the US. Just over half of all black people live in the South, with the greatest number in Mississippi. In Detroit, they make up 83% of the resident population. Even today, black and white tend to live in their own residential areas, especially in the North-East and Midwest; other races, e.g. Asians and Hispanics, are less set apart. Black segregation goes back a long way, and it is a slow process in America to turn it around. In 1969, on average, black families had 63.3% of the income of white families; by 2005, this figure had only increased to 64.5%. So much for progress.

According to Dinesh D'Souza (a contemporary writer), African-Americans have fallen and continue to fall behind other non-white immigrants, even black immigrants. The latter groups have bettered themselves and achieved the American Dream, forging ahead through commitment to education, hard work and pooling

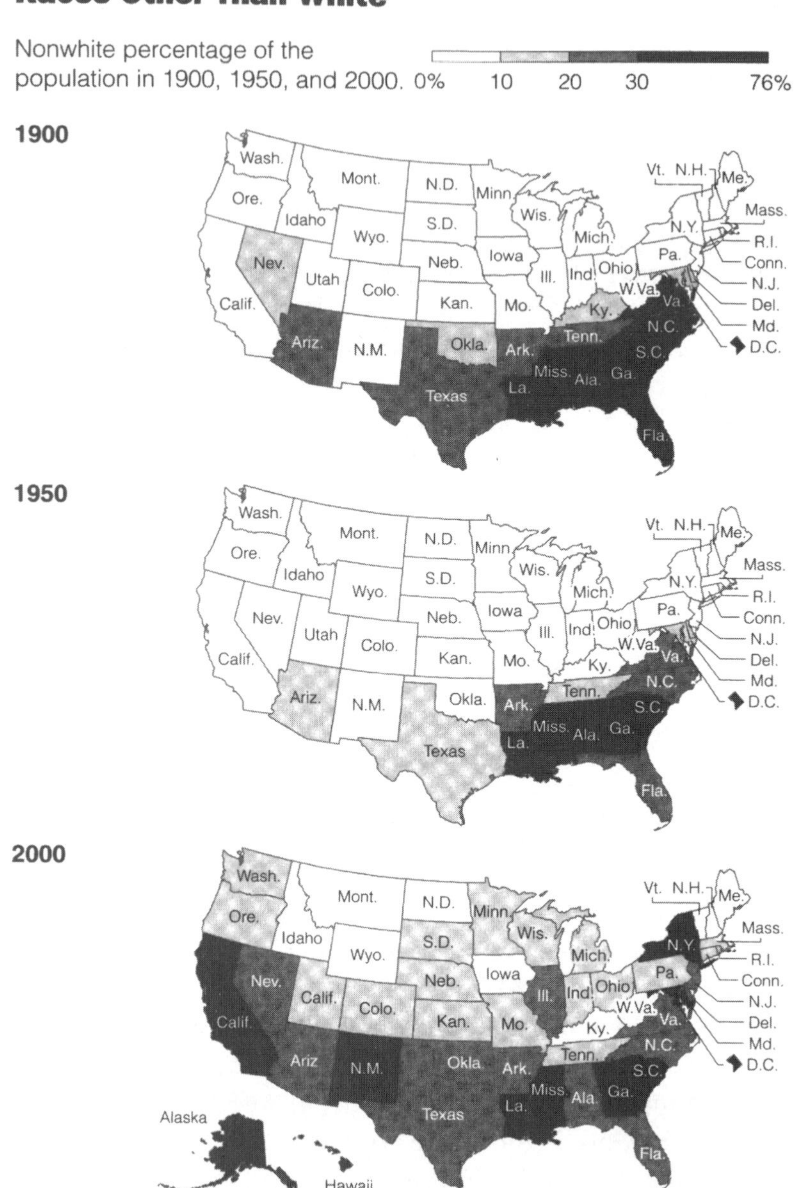

Fig. 21.1 The spread of races other than white across the United States (source: Matthew Ericson, taken from Sam Robert's book *Who We Are Now*).

resources. They are looking forward, not back, and making good progress. This reasoning for the inequalities African-Americans suffer may seem a little harsh, yet others support it. Once a year, Americans celebrate Black History Month. Morgan Freeman quoted it as 'ridiculous', saying that black history should not be relegated to one month, and the only way to get rid of racism is to stop talking about it. By constantly stirring up old issues instead of looking to the future, many black Americans appear to be stuck in a rut.

WASPs

WASP stands for White Anglo-Saxon Protestant and is a term often used in America in a derogatory way. Our version might be Preppy or 'Keeping Up With the Joneses'. These days, WASPs are not necessarily of Anglo-Saxon descent, but stereotypically hail from Western Europe as descendants of the founders of the nation, or are members of high society. The term has old money, elitist connotations, and is synonymous with the term Yankee (a native or inhabitant of the northern USA); hence, WASPs are heavily concentrated in the North-East. Nowadays, less than a quarter of Americans are WASP, yet they exert a disproportionate influence on society.

Animosity Towards America

The terrorist attacks on the World Trade Centre and Pentagon on 11 September 2001 killed around 3000 people. Before then, Americans had barely experienced terrorism on their own soil – apart from the first Trade Centre attack in 1992, which claimed only a few lives in comparison to 9/11. In defiance of 9/11, New Yorkers are building the new Freedom Tower on the site of the former WTC. It is intended to reach 1776 ft high (symbolic of the date the Declaration of Independence was signed) and to be the tallest building in the US. Planned completion date is 2011.

Unfortunately part of the problem lies in the fact that most Americans are ignorant of other cultures. America's leaders come across as lacking awareness of Islam and Middle Eastern culture, decrying Islamic terrorists as indiscriminate, cowardly lunatics. Carlos Fuentes (a Mexican writer) hit the nail on the head when he said, 'What the United States does best is to understand itself. What it does worst is understand others'. Moreover, US status in the world arena is not what it used to be. The United States has become less intimidating as other countries have become more powerful. Her enemies believe her soft – whether due to capitalist decadence or ethnic diversity.

Henry James (author and literary critic, 1843–1916) stated:

> 'It is, I think, an indisputable fact that Americans are, as Americans, the most self-conscious people in the world, and the most addicted to the belief that the other nations are in a conspiracy to under-value them'.

Perhaps the American populace is right. Anti-Americanism overseas is rife, as the country is viewed with resentment and scorn (where once there was resentment and respect). Europeans view Americans as cavalier, trigger-happy and blood-thirsty. Asians see America as economically and materially advanced at the expense of social and moral order. Many countries have strong religious and cultural beliefs and see the West as an atheist culture, with loose women, young people lacking respect for their elders, parents preferring to work than bring up their children themselves, materially obsessed – the list goes on. (Interestingly, this is similar to how some Americans view Europeans.) People in the Middle East in particular are ruled by their religion. They view the West as a society based on freedom rather than virtue, without divine authority or rule – overall, as a satanic atheist culture.

The American ideal is made up of a number of freedoms – economic, political and religious, and the freedom of speech. The Founders of America decided to separate religion and government in order to avoid conflict. They did not decree a national religion, but allowed America's inhabitants to freely practise any religion they chose. People were also encouraged to work, trade and amass property, instead of concentrating on their religious differences, and this capitalist society has endured and prospered. Other countries may decry this system of living, believing their religion to be all-important. New arrivals from other countries are often shocked by American society – its vulgarity and brazenness and apparent lack of sexual and moral ethics.

While there are strong feelings against America and the spread of westernisation in some parts of the world, America's influence on the rest of the developing world is considerable, as many people see and want 'the American life'. Immigrants flock to the US for a better life; comfort, money, leisure time, security, education – these all exert a powerful pull. It is an affluent, capitalist society, and not just for the upper classes. In America to a large degree you determine your own fate and can be the person you want to be. In other countries, your life is not necessarily your own; for instance, in Islamic society, your religion and the authorities direct your life. As a woman or child, you are dictated to by the man of the household and have very little say in matters that concern you.

Unfortunately, America lacks understanding of how the spread of its Western culture and democracy are being received and appreciated. However, one American friend admitted, 'I do think we have a better idea after 9/11'.

French Relations

In 1999, a Frenchman named Jos Bov ransacked a McDonald's restaurant in the name of anti-globalisation. In reality he was protesting against US trade restrictions on his local Roquefort cheese. The French nation cheered his personal fight against junk food, the obliteration of local cultures (excuse the cheesy pun) and homogenisation of their homeland. *Le Big Mac* became a big issue. The French are not alone in being protective of their culture and seeing America as unthinking and blinkered in its worldwide spread of its culture. China too is taking a strong stand in curbing Western excesses and negative impacts on its citizens (for instance, with regard to vandalism, graffiti and crime). While other countries may be accepting of modernisation, they may not necessarily want to be westernised.

French–American relations are an interesting case. Most Americans despise the French, and vice versa. Some common American jokes illustrate this:

Q. How do you say 'Give me liberty or give me death!' in French?
A. 'I give up.'
Q. How many Frenchmen does it take to defend Paris?
A. Nobody knows. It's never been tried.

Most Americans see the French as weak. France's contribution during World War II was considered negligible, and President de Gaulle was hardly consulted in deciding how the geography of the new Europe would be split up. It didn't help matters that de Gaulle openly expressed anti-American feelings. Even as long ago as 1781, relations with France – America's ally during the Revolutionary War – were difficult. General Washington, on being let down by General Rochambeau's refusal to send troops to recapture New York City from the British, was reported to have said, 'The French! The French! I wish to God they wouldn't keep raising our hopes, then letting us down'.

In an effort to understand the origins of these feelings and animosity, I asked several American friends for their views. Dave Shone, a fellow writer, gave me his thoughts:

> 'The French – aah, where to begin? As Americans, we love all democratic states – just some more than others. We love the city of Paris but hate its inhabitants. We are a weird lot, us Americans. We appreciate beauty, but not its creators. Funny! We see the French as many most likely see us – arrogant, extremely liberal, and weak. We don't see Napoleon and his Grand Army conquering Europe; we see a country that gave up fighting the enemy when they were on their home soil. In fairness, the French hosted a bloody war (the Great War) that stole a generation. By the Second World War, they were a little gun shy – understandably. We Americans enter wars when we see fit, thanks to our geographic location. I don't say this with pride, I say it with deep regret. Why didn't we fight in 1939, 1940 or 1941? We entered on December 7th, 1941 – two and a half years into battle. Crazy! We did the same thing during the Great War. Sat on the sidelines until the conclusion was obvious.'

Other American friends added:

> 'We have no concept of sacrifice; we think the world owes us because we are American.'

> 'Maybe the core of the rivalry is that the French refuse to acknowledge that we are superior!'

> 'More than anything, I think we like to have a country with a worse reputation than us'.

The French are typically rude to foreigners and those they bear a grudge towards, and recently French tourist offices have been working hard to discourage deliberate French rudeness in an effort to attract more American tourists. However, France's cultural condescension towards America and the view that America is a bullying hyperpower continue to cloud Franco–American relations. During the Great Depression, wealthy Americans were really the only American tourists visiting France. This led to the impression by the French that America is 'a nation of millionaires' – materialistic, puritan and racist. As black Americans fled to France, seeking a land where they would be treated as equals, this added to the idea that racism was rife in the great US of A (which was of course true in some states, but not all). During World War II, American troops did little to instill good relations, instead revelling in drunkenness, vandalism, assaulting and thieving from the local French. They returned to the States with stories of French rudeness and fleecing; and things haven't improved much since then. American feeling has been further soured in recent years by anger over France's policy on the war in Iraq. Americans are also suspicious of French food (for example, sauces that may be masking less-than appealing food); indeed, often they choose to visit France in spite of, not because of, her food.

These things go some way to explaining the poor relations between the two countries today. Of course, Anglo–French relations have often been rocky too, and perhaps Americans have 'inherited' some of this ideology from us. My husband Tim believes the problem stems from the fact that both America and France are deep down quite similar – both nationalistic and arrogant, believing their respective countries to be unique and best in the world – hence the frequent clashes.

Immigration

America has always been the land of freedom and opportunity. The lyrics to *Uncle Sam's Farm*, an early American social song, bear witness to this. (The words were written by Jesse Hutchinson Jr. in 1850. Reproduced with thanks to Amaranth Publishing, Fort Worth, Texas.)

> Of all the mighty nations in the East or in the West,
> O this glorious Yankee nation is the greatest and the best.
> We have room for all creation and our banner is unfurled,
> Here's a general invitation to the people of the world.
>
> (Chorus)
> Then come along, come along, make no delay;
> Come from every nation, come from every way.
> Our lands, they are broad enough – don't be alarmed,
> For Uncle Sam is rich enough to give us all a farm.

St. Lawrence marks our Northern line as fast her waters flow;
And the Rio Grande our Southern bound, way down to Mexico.
From the great Atlantic Ocean where the sun begins to dawn,
Leap across the Rocky Mountains far away to Oregon.

While the South shall raise the cotton, and the West, the corn and pork,
New England manufactories shall do up the finer work;
For the deep and flowing waterfalls that course along our hills
Are just the thing for washing sheep and driving cotton mills.

Our fathers gave us liberty, but little did they dream
The grand results that pour along this mighty age of steam;
For our mountains, lakes and rivers are all a blaze of fire,
And we send our news by lightning on the telegraphic wires.

The brave in every nation are joining heart and hand
And flocking to America, the real promised land;
And Uncle Sam stands ready with a child upon each arm
To give them all a welcome to a lot upon his farm.

A welcome, warm and hearty, do we give the sons of toil
To come to the West and settle and labor on free soil;
We've room enough and land enough, they needn't feel alarm
O! come to the land of freedom and vote yourself a farm.

Yes! we're bound to lead the nations for our motto's "Go ahead,"
And we'll tell the foreign paupers that our people are well fed;
For the nations must remember that Uncle Sam is not a fool,
For the people do the voting and the children go to school.

What a welcome to the nations of the world.

However, in the early twentieth century – particularly during the 1930s Depression era and following World War II – restrictive immigration laws attempted to stem the flood of immigrants by discriminating against certain immigrants according to race, colour, religion and/or national origins. In 1965, the Immigration and Naturalisation Act was passed, opening up America to people from the Third World. The Act was the result of the civil rights movement, which demanded an end to racial and ethnic discrimination. Following the end of the Vietnam War, there was a deluge of Asian refugees.

Recent booms in the economy (one in the mid-1980s, another in the early 1990s) have further boosted the rate of immigration. Political support for the USA's liberal immigration policy has allowed millions to repatriate to America, and the current influx of immigrants is nothing new. However, with the increasing volume of immigrants, the problem of illegal immigration has come to the fore. As socio-economic disparities increase and media focus intensifies, America's citizens are becoming less tolerant of newcomers. This sensitivity towards new immigrants has also been fueled

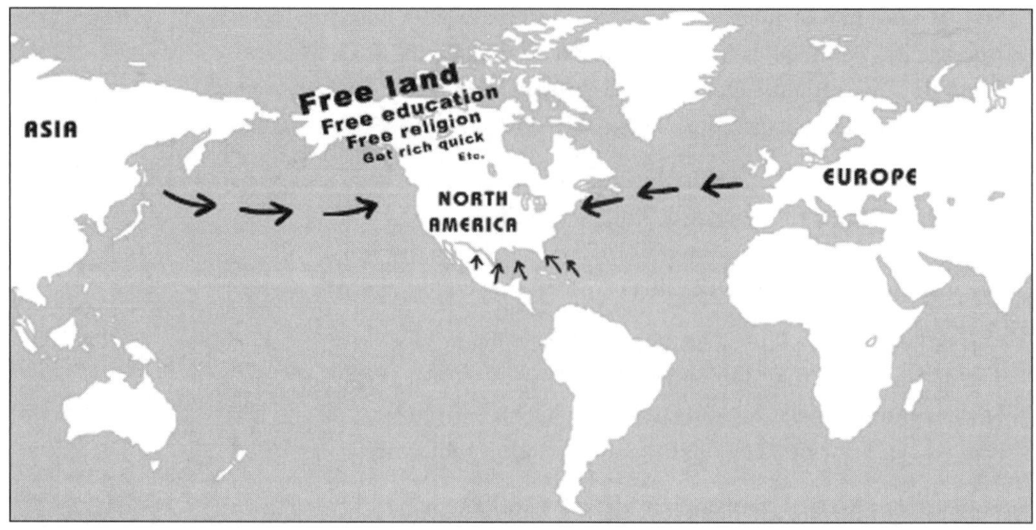

by 9/11. America's loose immigration laws were seen as part of the trouble, allowing illegal people to enter the country and train for terrorist activities on America's own soil. Locally and nationally, opinions are divided over whether the US should remain open to all, and this topic is increasingly debated.

The statistics are a little worrying:

- In 2006, more than 1 million immigrants entered the USA lawfully and were granted permanent residence.
- Approximately 700,000 new unauthorised migrants arrive annually.
- Nearly half fly in as tourists and overstay their visas.
- Since 2001, the number of fugitive aliens (foreigners who have ignored orders to leave the US) has nearly doubled, to 636,000.

Native-born and legal migrant families earn on average $47,750 p.a. (US Census Bureau, 2003), while illegal migrant families arriving within the last decade earn around half that ($25,700, rising to almost $30,000 for those who have lived in America longer than a decade). Many earn their living in construction, agriculture (especially meat and poultry processing), dishwashing and cleaning jobs – taking the bulk of the low-paid manual jobs and those jobs most Americans wouldn't want to do anyway. Such people often work 7 days a week and all the overtime they can get, in an effort to earn enough money to send to their families in their home country. Indeed, some American businesses rely heavily on these low-paid workers and would not be as profitable if they did not have ready access to this cheap workforce.

New York, Florida, California, Texas and Illinois are the states most saturated with immigrants, both legal and illegal. Latinos account for the vast majority of these foreign incomers, and targeting this huge group of new Americans has become a prime focus for many businesses. In the Southwest, there is a debate over whether to make

English and Spanish the joint official languages of these states, and indeed many signs are bilingual.

Five thousand miles of border country between the USA, Canada and Mexico is a lot of border to control. Immigration statistics show that by far the greatest number of illegal immigrants originate from Mexico, followed by the Caribbean, Soviet Union, China and Africa. The four southern border states are California, Texas, Arizona and New Mexico, and the harsh Sonora Desert in Arizona is one of the most common crossing points. In 2005, 69% of illegal immigrants now living in America crossed the southern border, and between 400 and 500 people die each year trying.

The border is recognised as being underguarded. President Bush has authorised doubling the number of border patrol agents from 11,000 to 21,000 agents by 2010. If the current border patrol recruitment drive works, it will make it the largest federal law enforcement agency (even larger than the FBI). Agents will be taught Spanish, including phrases such as, 'How much did you pay the smuggler?' and 'Where are the rest of you?' Around 3000 unauthorised migrants are apprehended each day, so the police have their work cut out. The 2000-mile-long Mexican border is only 3.8% fenced. Erecting additional fencing would cost billions of dollars and some people are convinced this would still not do the job of keeping unauthorised immigrants out. However, Congress recently authorised the construction of a two-tiered fence virtually the entire length of Arizona, with other stretches between border towns in California and Arizona, New Mexico and Texas.

Wealth Inequality

Besides other pressures on American society, wealth inequality and debt are serious problems. It is estimated that 37 million people live below the poverty line, representing about 12.7% of the population (US Census Bureau, 2004). With a decline in average household income between 2003 and 2004, and the cost of every-day basics rising sharply, 2004 became the fifth straight year that millions of American families suffered food insecurity (i.e. they lacked adequate nutrition to lead a healthy life). This is particularly so in parts of the Midwest such as Appalachia, an area that decades ago was dubbed 'Invisible America'. Here, unemployment averages 6% and 1 in 5 families live on less than $22,000/year (the average annual family income across the US is around twice that). The main reason is that manufacturing and other labour-intensive jobs have moved to countries with lower costs and pay, and new jobs are not yet available.

As discussed in Chapter 19, the federal minimum wage is $5.85/hour (at the time of writing), and a state's minimum wage may be even lower. Restaurant servers, dishwashers, cooks, retail cashiers and clerks, cleaning maids, hotel workers and child-minders are some of the worst paid. Some do not even earn the minimum wage, owing to the Fair Labor Standards Act of 1938, which allows employers of workers who receive more than $30/month in tips to consider such tips as part of their wages. This means that some employers can pay a direct wage that is less than the minimum wage if they claim tip credit. With a hike in consumer prices and home heating costs, many workers on these or minimum wages have to rely on food pantries to help out in lean periods, such as over the holidays. Food banks deliver millions of dollars of food a year to children's centres, food pantries and soup kitchens.

In 2001, according to the US Census Bureau, blacks earned 62% less median income than whites and it is therefore no surprise to find that most people below the poverty line live in Louisiana, Mississippi, New Mexico, West Virginia and Kentucky, in that order. The least affluent states are, again, Mississippi, West Virginia and Arkansas, followed by many other Southern and Mountain states. In contrast, most of New England and the Mid-Atlantic states (in particular the District of Columbia, Connecticut, Massachusetts and New Jersey) are the richest. Table 21.3 shows how the population is split ethnically, and reiterates the disparity in incomes according to region.

Table 21.3 Greatest head of population ranked according to state (US Census Bureau, 2004).

Rank	White population alone	Black	Asian	Hispanic, Latin American, Indian*
1	Maine	Mississippi	Hawaii	Alaska
2	Vermont	Louisiana	California	New Mexico
3	New Hampshire	Georgia	New Jersey	South Dakota
4	Idaho	South Carolina	New York	Oklahoma
5	West Virginia	Maryland	Washington	Montana

*American Indians and Alaskan natives.

The region known as the Black Belt comprises 11 states (Alabama, Arkansas, Florida, Georgia, Louisiana, Mississippi, North and South Carolina, Tennessee, Texas and Virginia); it is an area characterised by poverty, rural decline, and poor education and health. It used to be an important cotton-growing area based on the plantation system. Following the Civil War, sharecropping by freed slaves who remained there was prevalent; nowadays peanuts and soya beans are the major crops grown. The Black Belt has a higher than average percentage of black residents, but the socio-economic problems also affect whites living in the region.

Conclusion

E.E. Cummings (American poet, 1894–1962) stated that:

'America makes prodigious mistakes, America has colossal faults, but one thing cannot be denied: America is always on the move. She may be going to Hell, of course, but at least she isn't standing still'.

Henry Ford (American industrialist, 1863–1947) also obviously felt positive when he commented:

'What's right about America is that although we have a mess of problems, we have great capacity – intellect and resources – to do something about them'.

America has her fair share of issues and problems. Because she is a leading country of the world, from which many contemporary aspects of society originate, she is heavily scrutinised and chastised as the instigator of a decline in moral standards and other twenty-first-century standards. Britain follows suit to America in many ways, and often problems in British society mirror those in America. There are many examples of where the two countries cross-fertilise; we exported our skinheads, America her sex, drugs, and rock and roll. Perhaps learning from each other is the way forward?

Useful Websites

www.climatecrisis.net – all about Al Gore's film *An Inconvenient Truth* and how you can take action.
www.history.com/minisites/blackhistory – Black History Month.
www.nyc-tower.com – the new Freedom Tower in New York City.
http://tolerance.org/maps/hate/index.html – map of the US, showing number and breakdown of hate groups across the States.
www.uscitizenship.info – US Immigration and Naturalization Service.

Wikipedia:
Gun law in the United States.
Gun laws in the United States (by state).

22 · Preparing for the Move Back and Final Thoughts

After spending almost 2 years in America, our time was up and we had to prepare for the move back to England. We took the news with mixed feelings. Tim would have been happy to stay on and experience more that the States had to offer. I, on the other hand, was missing life in rural Dorset. I felt drawn home by the family – my father's dementia had become more worrying and my mother was sorely missing seeing the grandchildren growing up. Living in America had been a temporary existence – it wasn't 'true' life and it wasn't the life for us. Many Britons revel in the new lifestyle and determine to stay on, some permanently. Being rather an old-fashioned girl, who missed dear old England, I was happy to return.

So we embarked on the rather involved process of winding down, clearing out and packing up, all over again. Once you know the date of your repatriation, you can devise a schedule for action. Moving back involves almost as much time and effort as the original move out, though you will be an old hand at it this time. Work back from your moving date when planning a timetable of activities.

Table 22.1 is a list we devised to help us organise this huge task. Of course, everyone's situation is different, but the list may give you a basis to work from.

Selling the House

If you are selling your house in America, you can either market through a licensed real-estate agent or discount broker or do it yourself. Ninety eight percent of homes are sold through marketing on the Multiple Listing Service (MLS); this is a local listing, usually owned and operated by your local association of professional realtors and brokers. If you want to try selling your home yourself (For Sale By Owner or FSBO), you can gain access to the list (and post your home on it) by going through a discount broker, who will usually charge a flat fee of between $300 and $500 for the privilege.

If you decide to use the FSBO method, there are numerous online real estate service operators you can market your property through (see some suggestions on the Roving Press website). Some give access to the same kinds of information and tools

Table 22.1 Preparing for the move back.

Timing	Task	Action taken and needed
Ideally 7 months before	Make final US purchases, especially big items	Keep receipts in case of Customs queries
As early as possible	Start going through paperwork, and make a list of what needs to be done	Close superfluous accounts, memberships, mailings, etc.
	Devise a schedule of dates for things to happen	
	Plan last trips and holidays	Use up airmiles and hotel reward points
	Arrange removals shipment	Obtain necessary forms
	Ascertain method and timing of any pets to be shipped back	Obtain necessary forms and ensure you understand the procedure
	Decide last day of work and school (as appropriate)	Inform work/school of finishing date
Two months to go	Arrange for medical and dental check-ups	Have any necessary work done
	Cancel subscriptions to magazine, etc.	
	Cancel superfluous credit and shopping cards	
	Get your name and address taken off mailing lists	
	Sell extraneous belongings	Advertise in paper; have a garage sale
	Give notice to your landlord	Check lease for amount of statutory notice required, and any other tenant responsibilities
One month or less to go	Notify authorities and other official bodies that you are repatriating	
	Arrange for mail redirection to a UK address, to start on or around your move date	Decide on date to stop mail
	Cancel telephone and internet services	Return adapters

Timing	Task	Action taken and needed
One month or less to go (cont'd)	Cancel television viewing subscription	
	Cancel refuse account	Decide last day you need rubbish collection
	Cancel water and sewage	Decide last day of service
	Cancel electricity account	Decide last day of service
	Sell vehicles	Arrange for a hire car if necessary
	Cancel auto insurance and obtain proof of no claims	Or retain insurance to cover the hire car
	Cancel AAA membership	Check what cover comes with the hire car
	Children finish school	Arrange day care if necessary
	If claiming Social Security benefits, inform the authorities you are leaving the country. If you aren't claiming, there's no need to inform them (once issued, that SSN is yours for life and the authorities cannot cancel, delete or otherwise take you off the system)	
	Cancel library membership and other memberships	Return cards
	Hand back rental house to owner	Confirm process Clean carpets and upholstery Make good any damages
	Cancel house contents insurance with your American provider	
	Arrange for transit insurance for possessions being both shipped and carried back by you	
	Decide what to do with bank account	Discuss with bank manager Arrange for excess funds to be withdrawn/forwarded to UK account

traditional agents use. Get your home inspected before advertising and make any repairs recommended by the report. Property disclosure laws (which vary by state) make it mandatory that sellers list any flaws in their homes.

Whole books are written on the subject of selling a house, so I'm not going into too much detail here, but below are a few marketing tips:

- Contact a mortgage broker and offer to pass would-be buyers on to them; in return they may already have clients on their books that are looking for a home.
- Ask nearby schools if they have any families new to the area who are presently renting.
- Use an online database to find out what your property is worth (just enter your ZIP code and city to look up the information).
- Be savvy regarding mortgage financing deals, so you can help would-be buyers work out whether and how they might afford to buy your home; for instance, what grants or community loans are available? Are zero down or 2–1 buy-down options available and at what cost?
- Before you list your home, design a plan of how you are going to advertise and when to hold viewing days.
- Keep the home inspection report available for potential buyers to look at, and attach receipts for work undertaken.

Giving Up a Rented Home

If you are renting, check the wording of the lease and ensure that you give the landlord the mandatory notice to vacate. Then confirm the date of handover. Other practical things to consider are as follows:

- Check who is responsible for cleaning the carpets and/or soft furnishings (the landlord or renter), and organise this if necessary. Carpet cleaning is best done when the house is empty (perhaps on the last day), though cleaning companies are usually used to lugging furniture out of the way.
- If the house has an inventory, ensure you are leaving everything that was originally listed, and any breakages are repaired or items replaced.
- Ask whether the landlord wants the electricity supply disconnected (as there is usually a reconnect fee) – when the meter reader comes to do the final reading, you will probably be asked this question.
- As long as there aren't any issues with the house, don't forget to ask for your deposit back.

Planning the Removals Operation

Decide when you want the removals operation to take place. Then choose a removals company and fix a date with them. Goods can take up to 8 weeks to ship across the Atlantic, so decide whether you can do without your worldly possessions for a period at the end of your American tour or when you first get back to the UK. Either way, it is likely that you will be in limbo and living out of suitcases for quite a long time. If your company is responsible for the removals, it is likely you will have a space allowance limit. Make sure you know what this is, as going over could cost dearly.

During our move, we elected to send our possessions back in two consignments. The first was an owner-pack job; the second was packed by the removals company, and we were allowed a percentage amount over our allowance for this consignment, to allow for the extra space used by the packers in filling the boxes (on international moves they tend to use a lot of paper padding to protect box contents). I had left out several piles of non-essential items that we could do without if the packers calculated we had gone over our limit. Our packer decided we were within the limit so went ahead and packed everything. However, we were later informed that we had gone over our allowance because the packers had been working to the wrong allowance, and that we could be charged. I had been so careful in filling boxes to the full on our first consignment, and doubling things up (for instance not leaving any space inside boxed items such as games, jigsaws, kitchenware, etc.). So learn from our experience and ensure the removals company is working to the same figures as your employer.

Don't forget to insure your belongings in transit. Your home contents insurance probably won't cover this, and you will have to take out a policy elsewhere. We used JBI International (see *Useful Websites*).

Winding Up the House

As soon as you know you are going back, start thinking about scaling down. It can take months to eat through the contents of the freezer and pantry or drink all those bottles of spirits (believe me, we've tried), or use up those extra toiletries and cleaning products you have mysteriously acquired. Don't underestimate your hoarding capabilities. Removals companies are not supposed to pack and move any liquids, so plan to use or dispose of these items (though in the event you may be able to sweet-talk the packer into slipping some things in, or you could transport them in your checked luggage). I ingeniously used up what I could, amazing the family with my recipe concoctions (we hardly ate out in the last few months as I emptied the house of food), while the kids had never had so many bubble baths or lotions slapped on them.

You may decide to have a garage sale at the end. You can buy special signs (black with fluorescent lettering) to put up around the neighbourhood, directing people to your house (for instance, Wal-Mart sells them for a few cents). However, don't expect to make much money. I opted instead to donate all extraneous possessions to our local Catholic Social Services, who were collecting household and personal items for the constant flow of refugees coming to America (some arriving with little more than one suitcase of personal possessions). It felt good to know that our excess belongings would benefit directly people who were in need.

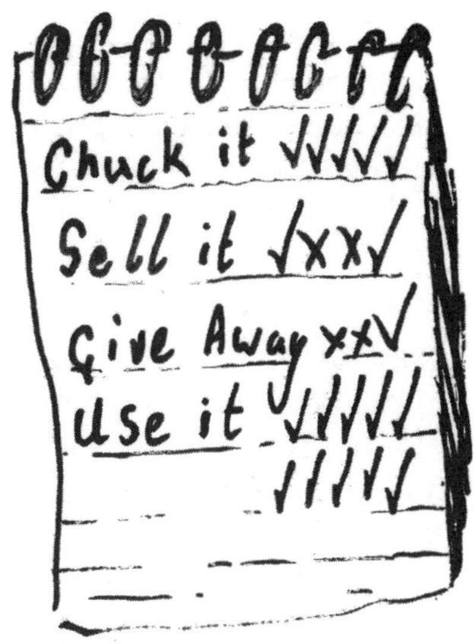

When you move out, you will have to cancel all utility accounts, or switch them over to the new tenant/owner as appropriate. Organise meter readers to come out and take final readings. Check with each utility company when they plan to post the final bill, so you can decide what address they should use. Ask how you can make the final payment – ideally over the phone for instant clearing, rather than waiting for the paperwork to arrive and then having to organise payment and clearing as you yourself are in the throes of repatriating.

Financial Matters

If you are likely to return to America, it may be useful to keep your bank account open and at least one credit card running. Even if you aren't coming back, keeping these open until you've returned to England and then closing them from there makes sense, as you are likely to need them all through your move and even a little while afterwards, to allow things to clear, transfers to go through, etc. Ask your bank how best to handle this. You will obviously need to update your profile information. This is not always as easy as you might think. When I tried inputting a UK address online, the system didn't recognise the details and I had to get an online representative to make the changes. I had to phone several times more before the change was eventually accepted, because our address was stored in two places and only one had been updated. The banking system in America is not as advanced and efficient as in Britain, and bank managers do not always give you the same advice as other banking colleagues. It was a hassle trying to get everything working right. My advice is to visit your local branch to arrange things well in advance of the move, as it can take some time for changes to take effect and your requests to be fully actioned.

Below is a list of questions or matters you might consider relating to bank and/or credit card accounts:

- Clarify whether there are any charges involved; for instance, if you do not use the account or credit card for a while, will they impose a monthly charge?
- Switch to paperless billing so that you can view your statements online.

- Ensure you can access and operate your account fully over the internet. Give it a test try before you leave America, in case there are any glitches.
- Ask your bank manager about the procedure for depositing cheques into your account. It is possible that after you leave the country, refund cheques (for instance, on overpaid utility bills) will be issued. Can the issuers mail cheques direct to the bank, for payment into your account? If so, how will the bank tie up the cheque with your account number without a bank deposit slip? My bank manager kindly agreed to me giving out his name and the bank's address, so that mail would come direct to him for processing.
- Ensure you have all the necessary contact details (names, addresses, telephone numbers, email addresses) in case you have questions or need to contact the bank from the UK.
- Does the bank have an online bill payments system? (I had to switch to a different bank account in order to access this facility, at no charge.) This allows you to organise payments electronically, without having to post cheques to payees in the US. The bank may be able to do this on your behalf (that is, issue a cheque and mail it to the payee) and you can track the payment online. No need for the cheque book any more. I wish I had known this before.
- Opt for personalised email alerts (for example, if your balance falls below a certain figure, there is any particular activity on the account, the account goes overdrawn, a bill payment exceeds a certain amount, etc.) – useful to keep track of your account's activities, and watch for anything suspicious.
- Ask for a bundle of stationery (e.g. deposit slips and envelopes) so you have plenty of paperwork to operate your account long distance.

Try to obtain last-minute credit refunds by visiting offices rather than waiting for electronic transfers or cheques in the post to arrive and then clear. Otherwise you may have the long-distance hassle of chasing for missing credits.

On entering the UK, you should declare any sums of cash in excess of 10,000 Euros (or the equivalent amount in dollars) by filling in form C9011 (see *Useful Websites*). Duty and VAT are charged (if applicable) on any item not owned by you or bought and used by you for less than 6 months prior to return to the UK. In other words, you can bring back into the UK, duty paid, anything you have possessed and used for more than 6 months. Second-hand items do not count; it is only new things the authorities are interested in, especially if it looks like you might be intending to sell on. You may be asked to show receipts for newly bought articles. So buy new items ahead of time to ensure you don't fall foul of this Customs rule and end up having to pay duty.

Redirecting the Mail

Start notifying everyone of your change of address as early as practicable, as it is quite an onerous task sifting through all the paperwork, deciding on what to retain, and updating the rest with your new information.

You can organise mail redirection with USPS free of charge (yes – even if you are moving overseas, for instance back to the UK). Before you move, fill out and post the Change of Address Form (available at post offices or online). Then all regular mail, Priority Mail and Express Mail should be forwarded for 12 months, newspapers and magazines for 2 months. Any packages weighing 16 oz or more will incur a forwarding charge. Circulars, books, catalogues and advertising circulars (thankfully) will not be forwarded unless you ask for this.

If you haven't done so already, or are still receiving annoying unsolicited mailings (for example, for credit and insurance), put a stop on these by visiting the Consumer Credit Reporting Industry's website (see *Useful Websites*). This is a good safety precaution in any case, to ensure that these offers of free credit are not indulged in by the next owners or tenants of your house in your name. However, don't make the mistake I did of writing 'Gone Away' or 'No Longer At This Address' on unwanted mail and putting it back in your mailbox for the postman to take away. He took this as meaning that we had already left the house and so initiated the mail redirection service before the date I had specified on the card. I wondered why all our post suddenly stopped arriving.

Selling the Car

For most people, selling their vehicle(s) is one of the major hassles and concerns when repatriating (few opt to ship such an expensive and bulky item home). The problem is whether to sell early and hopefully get a good market price or pitch it low at the last minute to ensure you get a sale. If you sell too soon before you leave America, you will have to cost in the amount of a hire car. If you hold on to your vehicle and sell last minute, you will be under pressure to sell and therefore not in a good position. Either way, it's a dilemma.

When selling a vehicle, the usual avenues are open to you:

- auction sites;
- over the internet;
- classified newspaper ads;
- through a dealer;
- 'For Sale' sign in car window;
- bulletin boards at supermarkets, college campuses, etc.

We had luck selling our cars online through Auto Trader. We also had a good response from local callers who had seen the 'For Sale' signs in the windows of the cars. It should go without saying that in order to secure a fast positive sale, your car should be in the best possible condition – perhaps recently serviced so you can show potential buyers up-to-date paperwork, and of course empty, valeted and perfumed (see Chapter 11, *The Car Wash*).

Selling laws vary from state to state, so check with your local Department of Motor Vehicles (DMV). To determine a realistic asking price, look in the *National Automotive Dealers Association (NADA) Gold Book* or *Official Used Car Guide, Kelley Blue Book* and/or the *Black Book*, which catalogue wholesale prices on used cars and motorcycles. There is no shortage of demand for family sedans, SUVs and pickups.

To safeguard against dodgy buyers and scams, ask the buyer to pay in cash. If this is not possible, the next best thing is a cashier's (certified or official bank) cheque. However, even with a certified cheque, our bank could not guarantee the funds would still be in the payee's bank account the next day, and we ended up having to accept the cheque in good faith. Also, for what it's worth, write out a receipt and get the buyer to sign and print his or her name and address on it.

Once the money side has been dealt with, record the vehicle's mileage, sign the Certificate of Title over to the new owner in the presence of a notary, make out a bill of sale, and complete any other forms required by your state. Finally remove the plates and registration tags, and hand over the keys.

Selling your vehicle should not be difficult, but if all else fails, you can always donate it to the Goodwill organisation and receive a tax deduction.

Hiring a Rental

Your existing auto insurance may or may not cover you driving a hire car. Ours unfortunately didn't, and we had to cancel our old car insurance once we sold the cars and buy new insurance for the rental. However, we got a good deal through our credit card (American Express), which was cheaper than most. When you cancel your car insurance, ask the insurer to send proof of no claims, so that you can use this when you apply for UK insurance.

If you have AAA membership you might want to keep this going to cover the rental car. Ask the rental company what breakdown service they offer; if there are gaps in cover then it might be worth retaining your AAA membership a while longer. The AAA should give you a pro-rata refund on cancellation.

If You Have Children

If you have children in school, you will need to work out the their last day and inform the school authorities. Get all bills paid up to date and/or ask for a refund of fees paid (earlier than the leave date if possible, to allow banking time). If your child takes the yellow bus to school, and you will be moving out of the house and into temporary accommodation for the last week or so (as we did), ask whether the bus can pick up/drop off at another location, at or close to your hotel for instance. Make the enquiry ahead of time so you can make other arrangements if necessary.

Ask your child's teacher to provide a written report of the standards your child has attained, so that you can show this to the new school. This is particularly important when switching from an American school to a British one, as standards and levels of education are different.

Check what the procedure is regarding applying for a school place back home in Britain. What is the earliest date you can start the ball rolling? It may be that you cannot formally apply for a school place until you are resident in the area. Again, if possible, allow plenty of time to make enquiries and submit the necessary paperwork, or you may be disappointed with the options available to you.

Flying an Animal Home

When it comes to flying your pet back to the UK, you have to go through a similar process to when you arrived, only this time, you have already taken care of some of the requirements:

- Your animal's EU Pet Passport will need to be shown on re-entering Britain.
- You should have kept your pet's rabies vaccinations up-to-date (administering booster jabs on time) in order to continue to qualify for the Pet Travel Scheme and avoid having to repeat the blood test or 6-month wait.
- Ten days before the intended travel date, obtain a health certificate from the vet stating that your animal is fit to travel.
- Between 24 and 48 hours before check in, obtain a note from the vet stating that your animal has been treated for ticks, fleas and tapeworms.
- Ensure you use an approved route and carrier.
- Contact APHIS (the Animal and Plant Health Inspection Service) regarding international animal export regulations.
- Contact the UK Embassy to obtain their rules.
- Contact a shipping agent regarding Customs procedures on arrival in the UK.
- Contact DEFRA to coordinate with the quarantine facility for re-entry.

Ask the airline or shipper exactly what paperwork is required at both US and UK airports, and how you should present your animal. Ask plenty of questions to ensure you haven't forgotten anything, for instance:

- Is an acclimation certificate necessary?
- Do I require a tick and tapeworm certificate?
- What vaccination records will I need to present?
- What size crate do I need? (according to the size and/or weight of your animal)
- How should I provide food and water?
- What bedding is allowed?

'Operation Jester' All Over Again

Everyone's experience of shipping a pet across the Atlantic will be slightly different. What follows is a description of our experience of flying Jester back home.

Our return date was going to be May, so we planned to repatriate Jester ahead of time, so that we didn't fall into the summer embargo period (which was between 15 May and 15 September, when summer temperatures can affect animals flying). Our family was tasked with looking after Jester for the month or so before we were all due back. We also picked a time when I could fly to the UK as an escort, so that I could handle the 'Operation' directly and ensure Jester was happily settled back home.

Initial enquiries were made online. We consulted the APHIS and DEFRA websites to determine which local airport we could use. We had flown Jester into Cincinnati on a Delta flight, but for some reason this was not an option for the return leg. Instead, the nearest approved route was Cleveland to London Gatwick, using Continental Airlines' Cargo Quick Pack Service or Pet Safe scheme. We duly contacted Continental and ascertained the details. They told us that no escort was required and there were no weather restrictions. They could offer us a flight via Newark (with a 2-hour layover), or a non-stop flight after 5 May until the end of the summer. Unlike normal passenger tickets, the price of Jester's ride home was not affected by the date or day of travel. However, we opted for a weekday in March to keep my ticket cost in the low-season bracket.

Continental Airlines charge according to the combined weight of the crate and animal. It did not matter what size crate was used, so long as Jester had the statutory minimum 4 inches of room to stand up, turn around and be comfortable in. The following prices for the flight were correct at the time of travel:

- Weight 71–100 lb: $1039
- More than 100 lb: $1539

Your local veterinarian should have a

weighing machine you can use to check your animal plus crate combined weight, which is easier than trying to persuade a big hairy beast to balance on the bathroom scales or trying it yourself. Jester was unfortunately just tipping the scales at 55 lb body weight, plus 47 lb for the crate, which probably meant he would go into the 'heavy-weight' price bracket. However, in case we could swing it the other way, we started a diet and exercise regime, to see if we could bring his weight down the extra 5 lb and squeak him into the lower price range.

On top of the cargo charge, there was a fuel and security surcharge of 60 cents/kg and the shipping customs charge of $125, which is unavoidable.

Having ascertained all the information to 'do-it-yourself', we then contacted some animal shippers, so see what price they were charging. We were shocked to be quoted $4950 for airport to airport service, and an incredible $6695 for door to door delivery. That option was definitely out. We went back to our contact at Continental and asked her to verify the airline's prices again, because we couldn't believe the difference. Nor could she. Suffice to say, we went the DIY route. We checked the procedure for scanning Jester's microchip, as some UK chips cannot be read by US scanners, but he had a bona fide chip. We scheduled an appointment with our local vet to obtain a health certificate. This had to be dated no later than 10 days from the date of arrival at our destination (so if you are arranging this yourself, work the date out carefully). The morning of the day before we were due to fly, I took Jester along for his tick, flea and tapeworm treatment and the vet issued a document detailing the treatment.

The next day, we duly arrived 2 hours before the scheduled departure time at Continental's Cargo area. We unloaded the crate and Jester demurely walked in and immediately sat down on his blanket. We gave him some water. He is not an enthusiastic eater, so I decided he could go without food, to avoid any tummy upsets and hassle feeding him at the appropriate time. We had a 2-hour layover at Newark – allowing enough time for him to be deboarded, given a leg stretch and chance to pee, then to be transported and loaded onto the next aircraft for the trans-Atlantic leg. It was going to be a long journey, poor thing.

On arrival at Gatwick, I disembarked and proceeded to the air cargo depot. Although the agent's office did not officially open until 8.30 a.m., I paid $50 extra to get someone in early to process Jester, so that we were not waiting around longer than necessary. You have to allow a couple of hours to clear an animal through Customs in any case. After a little paper processing and a 3-hour wait, Jester was pronounced fit to go and he was wheeled out to us in his crate. Operation Jester had gone without a hitch, though the time involved going through all the procedures and worrying that we had done everything right, not to mention the expense, had been quite draining.

At the risk of scare-mongering, I must add that we had heard from various sources that shipping an animal is very expensive and fraught with potential difficulties. Some customs officials are unduly strict and can refuse to accept an animal if they consider anything to be wrong or out of place. They have the ultimate power to put a spanner in the works, and can be a law unto themselves. Repatriating an animal is not for the faint-hearted.

Useful Contacts for Pet Transportation

British Airways World Cargo
PETS Passport Desk (telephone 1-888-578 4806)
PBS (telephone +44 1293 551140)
Continental Airlines (telephone 1-800-523 3273)
Animal Land Pet Movers (telephone 1-877-379 8635)
World Wide Pet Transport (telephone 1-516-625 2683)

Initial Thoughts on Being Back

We arrived home in glorious May. I had been particularly missing the English countryside, the freedom of walking miles on rough footpaths and cycling the country lanes, discovering little gems of culture and history. In our experience of living in Ohio, these elements had been all but missing. During our first week back we ate fish and chips three times (what a treat). However, the first restaurant meal was disappointing. I ordered steak and was presented with something barely edible, it was so tough, tasteless and overcooked (I'd asked for it rare). We couldn't help harking back to those wonderful succulent American steaks. We were also surprised to be declined a doggy bag/box, on the grounds that the restaurant could not take the risk of being sued for food poisoning. I guess litigation-fever is affecting Britain too.

Everyone commented on the children's American accents, and months afterwards they were still using Americanisms. We really appreciated how easy communicating was – on the phone, for instance, when checking financial details or organising updates to correspondence details (no need to spell everything out or laboriously have to explain yourself).

But what we noticed most on arriving home was how small and congested Britain is compared to America:

- how busy the roads are and how fast everyone drives;
- some people walk and cycle out of necessity, rather than solely for recreation;
- shops are crammed with items;
- there is standing room only in some public places, e.g. pubs;
- parking spaces are tight;
- homes and gardens are small, enclosed and private, and often scruffy-looking in comparison to American homes;

(I could go on).

We looked with new-found amazement at our towns and roads. On a practical level, getting used to driving a car with a clutch while at the same time negotiating faster roads and close traffic caused some initial problems, for me at least.

Final Thoughts

When asked for our five lasting impressions of America, we didn't have much difficulty in responding:

(1) *Space* – working, living and recreational space; there is just so much of it.
(2) *Scale* – everything is on the big scale. In America it is hard to find small, locally owned businesses (for instance, hardware shops, pharmacies, booksellers, restaurants, etc.). They have been usurped by the chains and franchises, driven out by economies of scale.
(3) *Modern development* – America is very much into the ideal of 'new is better', and the consumer culture dictates that you use it once then throw it away. Old buildings are demolished to make way for new, and countryside is alarmingly being lost to yet more new building and infrastructure. Take restaurants, for instance. Slightly dated premises are torn down at the drop of a hat and new ones put up almost overnight in their place. According to Bill Bryson, in his book *A Walk in the* Woods, 'Half of all the offices and malls standing in America today have been built since 1980. Half of them'.
(4) *Marvellous eating and shopping opportunities* – I don't think anywhere else in the world has such quantity and variety of eating and shopping opportunities than the States.
(5) *Friendly, enthusiastic people* – they tend to view things optimistically, rather than negatively. Some every-day phrases that sum this up and will endure in our memories are:

> 'Hi, how y'a doing?' – for instance, when passing a stranger (instead of the cursory nod you might receive in Britain).
> 'I just love your accent!' – from about every American we initially met.
> 'Thanks, and have a nice day' – said with a smile.
> 'You're welcome' – the response whenever you thank someone.
> 'Hey, guys' – often in place of hello.
> 'Good job!' – used especially with respect to children.

Moreover young Americans are often refreshingly respectful of their seniors. In my experience they are more sociable – happily talking to adults, rather than simply grunting a response. They dress better than their British counterparts too, wear neat hairstyles and clean-cut clothing, and look healthy; their image is not intimidating or deliberately slovenly. Although tattooing and body piercing are now commonplace on both sides of the Atlantic, American youths do not come across quite so aggressively. Compared to Britain, there seems to be less of a yob culture.

Americans are more laid-back and on the face of it appear to have a better quality of life than most people in Britain. Newspapers do not dwell on stress as an issue in daily life and people do not refer to it. They seem happier and less grumpy; although they may bemoan their government and certain things about their country, they do not talk much about their own trials and tribulations. I found this a very refreshing character trait, one that would be good to bring back and spread around a little in dour old Britain.

According to Michael Leach, author of *I Like Being American*, ten great American values are:

- honesty and hard work
- generosity
- fair play
- respect for differences
- family
- self-reliance and responsibility
- faith
- ingenuity
- gratitude
- optimism

In fact, the following 12 words appeared variously on the months of my American calendar – Motivation, Optimism, Power, Vision, Courage, Teamwork, Strength, Soar, Creativity, Determination, Energy, Inspiration and Perseverance. Americans love to display words like this on workplace posters and calendars, to remind themselves of the values they hold most dear. This is part of their great 'can-do' attitude; anything is possible if you are prepared to work at it. Dinesh D'Souza (an Indian-born immigrant) commented in his book *What's So Great About America?*:

> 'This notion of you being the architect of your own destiny is the incredibly powerful idea that is behind the worldwide appeal of America'.

In February 2007, the five top-selling non-fiction books (according to the *Washington Post*) were:

- *The Best Life Diet.*
- *You: On a Diet: The Owner's Manual for Waist Management.*
- *The Audacity of Hope: Thoughts on Reclaiming the American Dream.*
- *The Secret* (relating to money, health, relationships and happiness).
- *What Got You Here Won't Get You There: How Successful People Become Even More Successful.*

It's clear from the first two that Americans are rather preoccupied with health (and they should be); the other three books demonstrate the abiding popularity of striving for happiness and success – for what is commonly known as the American Dream. Moreover, Americans are very proud of their country and independence: 'Ours is the only country deliberately founded on a good idea', declared John Gunther (American journalist).

Conclusion

> 'There is nothing like returning to a place that remains unchanged to find the ways in which you yourself have altered.' (Nelson Mandela, A Long Walk to Freedom)

Like any travelling experience, living in America will change you and the way you look at things. Among other things, we came home with a strong desire to travel and explore our own country more, especially appreciating the countryside and our rich past. Britain's long history is remarkable (especially appreciated when you look at it from an American perspective) and we are so lucky to have that part of our identity. We also determined to make an effort to schedule more play time with the children (making use of the equipment and 'toys' we had acquired in America). We also had a break from shopping – me, in particular, suffering from commercial overload and just wanting to get back to a simpler life.

Everyone's experiences of travelling and living in the USA will be unique, and you will return with different thoughts and feelings. Some aspects of American life I've described aren't peculiar to America; it's just that the scale and/or extent is always bigger in the States. This book has endeavoured to lift the lid on America and Americans, by using observations, research, surveys, interviews and the personal experiences of fellow Brits and American friends to get as broad a view of the nation as possible. However, the United States is an incredibly complex country – with regions and states at opposite ends of the spectrum, and her inhabitants so different from each other that it is virtually impossible to define what America is. Claus Christian Malzahn, writing in the German magazine *Der Spiegel*, noted how easy it is to demonise Americans as 'too fat or too obsessed with exercise, too prudish or too pornographic, too religious or too nihilistic…too isolationist or too imperialistic'; that is the paradox. Not only is America a melting pot of people and cultures, but also the environment – the geography and climate – vary so much that no two places are the same. I have come to the conclusion that my own slice of apple pie is limited and quite frankly biased – being based on a middle-income, white family living in the Midwest. Despite having travelled quite extensively throughout America, it would entail a lifetime of studying and pondering to get even somewhere close to identifying the many faces of America. I can only hope that this book has given you a taste of the pie and instilled a desire to delve deeper, to gain your own appreciation of what it means to live in the land of opportunity and 'be American'.

Useful Websites

www.aphis.usda.gov/vs/ncie – National Center for Import and Export (NCIE); veterinary services for exporting animals.

www.baworldcargo.com/products/pets – British Airways World Cargo; information on unaccompanied pets.

www.customs.hmrc – HM Revenue and Customs; search for 'C9011' for information about declaring cash when entering or leaving the UK, and 'C110' for bringing your belongings and private motor vehicle to the UK.

www.defra.gov.uk/animalh/quarantine – DEFRA information on bringing pets to the UK.

www.jbionline.com – JBI International Insurance Brokers.

www.optoutprescreen.com – Consumer Credit Reporting Industry to opt-out of offers of credit or insurance and to stop unsolicited mailings.

www.usps.com – United States Postal Service; or call 1-800-275-8777 for all change of address queries.

Suggested Reading and Viewing

The books, films, documentaries and websites listed below are but a small selection of the thousands available on the subject of America. They are personal favourites that should give you some insight into the country and her inhabitants – both historically and today; some proved to be very helpful in writing this book. They are listed in no particular order.

Non-Fiction Books

I'm a Stranger Here Myself, *Made in America* and *A Walk in the Woods*, in particular. Bill Bryson
Bryson is probably the best known contemporary writer about America, yet to many Americans he is unknown. *A Walk in the Woods* is the story of his reaquaintance with the motherland while walking the Appalachian Trail after 20 years living in Britain. At the same time, it gives you a real taste of one of America's last true wilderness areas and the commitment and danger involved in walking the trail.

Nickel and Dimed. On (Not) Getting By in America. Barbara Ehrenreich
Highlights the plight of America's working poor, through first-hand experience. Working in hotels, restaurants, shops and nursing homes on the minimum wage, while living in temporary accommodation, Ehrenreich shows the profound difficulties such people have just getting by, let alone advancing themselves.

Affluenza: The All-Consuming Epidemic. John de Graaf, David Wann and Thomas H. Naylor
Based on PBS documentaries, this book describes the obsessive quest for material gain, problems arising and ways you might be able to reverse the trend (at least as an individual). *Affluenza* is portrayed as a modern-day disease, especially prevalent in the consumer culture of America.

Letter from America and *American Journey.* Alistair Cooke
Alistair Cooke was born British but became an American citizen in 1941. In 1942 he undertook an immense journey across the American continent to discover how the war was affecting the country and ordinary Americans; his book *American Journey* gives his perspective. Cooke's weekly radio show *Letter from America* is the world's longest-running radio programme and his most famous achievement.

Democracy in America. Alexis de Tocqueville
Published in two volumes, 1835 and 1840, a classic text on why the republican representative democracy of the United States prevailed and succeeded where other democracies of the time failed; a discerning analysis of America in the 1830s. It is required reading for all Americans who wish to consider themselves educated about their own country.

What's So Great About America. Dinesh D'Souza
A great contemporary read discussing anti-Americanism, how/why the West prevails, why the American idea is unique, African-Americans, and freedom – basically, what the United States is all about.

Who We Are Now. Sam Roberts
A look at demographic trends based on data from the 2000 census. Full of interesting statistics and a good discussion of how America is changing.

Where to Retire: America's Best and Most Affordable Places. John Howells
It's an interesting read even if you aren't in the retirement-age bracket.

Let's Go USA
Extremely easy to use, entertaining and informative.

The Story of America. Allen Weinstein and David Rubel
A very readable story of America's history, with thousands of illustrations to boot.

Living and Working in America. David Hampshire (published by Survival Books).

Living and Working in America. Steve Mills (published by How To Books).

Fiction Books

Uncle Tom's Cabin. Harriet Beecher Stowe (1852)
An Ohio author, Harriet Beecher Stowe became famous with this story of the brutal treatment of African slaves and their bid for freedom. Although fictional, it was based on true accounts of slave life. President Lincoln half-jestingly said that she was the little woman who wrote the book that galvanised anti-slavery feelings and instigated the Civil War. It certainly moved and inflamed Americans at the time and is today a classic text.

Narrative of the Life of Frederick Douglass. An American Slave. Written by Himself (1845)
Frederick Douglass was a famous black abolitionist, having himself escaped from slavery at the age of 21. His autobiography is a first-hand account of the savagery and inhumanity endured on the pre-Civil War plantations of the South.

Adventures of Tom Sawyer, Life on the Mississippi and *Adventures of Huckleberry Finn.* Mark Twain
Twain was a humourist and critic, writing about life in America in the late 1800s.

The Last of the Mohicans and *The Deerslayer.* James Fenimore Cooper
Brings to life the American wilderness.

Of Mice and Men and *The Grapes of Wrath.* John Steinbeck
The latter describes the Dust Bowl era and the social injustice of the eviction of the 'Oakies' from their land by big corporations. The film of the same name starred James Fonda.

The Sun Also Rises and *A Farewell to Arms*, among others. Ernest Hemingway
American novelist, short-story writer and journalist (1899–1961), a canon of American literature. Many of his stories were adapted to film.

Sister Carrie. Theodore Dreiser
Author (1871–1945) who dealt with the gritty reality of life, especially social inequality.

The Great Gatsby. F. Scott Fitzgerald
A depiction of America in the 1920s.

Death of a Salesman. Arthur Miller
The study of the disintegration of an American family.

Bonfires of the Vanities. Tom Wolfe
Explores the inner workings of corporate America during the 1980s. Great fun; don't be put off by its length.

Leaves of Grass, and other works, by Walt Whitman
Nineteenth-century American writer; especially read his Civil War elegies.

The Jungle. Upton Sinclair

The House of Mirth. Edith Wharton.

The Catcher in the Rye. J.D. Salinger.

The Scarlet Letter. Nathaniel Hawthorne.

Films and Documentaries

Super Size Me. Morgan Spurlock
Morgan goes on a 30-day McDonald's-only diet and reveals all. It makes for both entertaining and shocking viewing, and suggests why America is the fattest nation in the world.

The Straight Story. David Lynch
An emotional and funny true story, demonstrating gritty American determination. An old man travels 320 miles on a ride-on lawnmower, from Iowa to Wisconsin, to visit his dying brother. Filmed along the real route travelled by Alvin Straight in 1994.

Fahrenheit 9/11, Bowling for Columbine, The Awful Truth, etc. Michael Moore
Despite (perhaps because of) being an oversized, underdressed, opinionated American, M.M. has become a cult figure, who gives an exposé of American life, psychology and politics; he is not afraid to go where others fear to tread. Loathe him or love him.

Borat: Cultural Learnings of America for Make Benefit Glorious Nation of Kazakhstan. Sacha Baron Cohen
S.B.C., star of the *Da Ali G Show*, won Best Actor in the Golden Globe 2006 awards with his hilarious look at real American people in real situations. The American Film Institute voted it a Top 10 film of the year.

An Inconvenient Truth: A Global Warning (2006)
This eye-opening and compelling documentary on global warming could change your view of things. Don't be put off by Al Gore's critics – watch it and make up your own mind.

Stepford Wives
A scary view of the suburbs.

RV
Comedy starring Robin Williams, who takes his family on a road trip in a recreational vehicle – that classical American holiday experience.

The Horse Whisperer
Great Montana scenery. Directed by and starring Robert Redford.

L.A. Story
Crazy Los Angeles living in the early 1990s, with Steve Martin.

Midnight in the Garden of Good and Evil
An evocative portrayal of southern living.

American Beauty
A dark comedy about a suburbanite family.

Films Featuring American Sports

Baseball

Field of Dreams

Eight Men Out
Major League
The Natural
Bull Durham
For the Love of the Game

American football

Rudy
The Longest Yard
Brian's Song
Remember the Titans

Golf

The Story of Bobby Jones
Caddy Shack
Tin Cup

Basketball

Hoosiers

Motor Sports

Days of Thunder

Cheerleading

Bring It On

 Useful Websites

The 'Life in the USA' website (www.lifeintheusa.com) provides much further information and reading, plus its sister site – 'Life in the USA Magazine' – has feature articles.

Other useful websites are listed on the Roving Press website (www.rovingpress.co.uk).

About the Author

Though this is the first book published under her own name, Julie Musk is a seasoned writer who has worked in publishing all her life. After studying agriculture and business at Shuttleworth Agricultural College, she joined the editorial team at Farming Press Books. Since then she has edited, proofread and project-managed hundreds of books and journals, working in-house at Farming Press and Blackwell Science, and then freelance for such well-known publishers as Elsevier, Springer and Blackwell Publishing. As a writer, for years she has contributed monthly articles to local newspapers on wildlife and countryside topics, has produced video scripts and written guides to nature reserves for the Dorset Wildlife Trust. *A Slice of Apple Pie* is the culmination of more than three years spent researching, experiencing and writing about life in the United States, including two years living there. She now lives in Dorset, writing and publishing other travel and local interest books, and working as a freelance editor and project manager.

About Roving Press

The Company – Roving Press is a small publisher producing unusual, distinctive and practical books which give you that little bit extra – more than just a good read. Our titles explore areas and subjects in a down-to-earth way, giving you a real feel for the subjects and places described.

The Website – our website (www.rovingpress.co.uk) has lots more useful information. View photo snapshots of life in America – a great supplement to the text (sometimes a picture says it all). Further useful websites are also listed and change over time, so please keep checking back. The website also gives information about our other books, and has special offers from time to time if you would like to place an order for additional copies of this book.

Email – feel free to email us at enquiries@rovingpress.com with any comments, queries or suggestions.

Larger orders – this is an ideal book for companies and organisations to give or sell to their staff or customers, and we can offer discounts for large orders. Please see the website for details or phone 01300 321531.

Sales commission (££) – assuming you enjoyed this book, we would like to make you an offer of earning some sales commission. All you have to do is recommend the book to others. We can give you a unique agent code and leaflets incorporating an order form. Simply pass these on to friends, family, colleagues and/or any businesses or organisations you think might be interested, and for the first order placed by each individual/business we will give you £2 per book ordered, up to a maximum of £30. Alternatively, you may wish to nominate a charity or organisation that we could donate the commission to. Just contact us for details and help spread the word. Thanks.

Index